MISSION STATEMENTS

GARLAND REFERENCE LIBRARY
OF SOCIAL SCIENCE
(VOL. 900)

MISSION STATEMENTS

*A Guide to the Corporate
and Nonprofit Sectors*

John W. Graham
and
Wendy C. Havlick

With a Foreword by
Prof. John A. Pearce II
Eakin Endowed Chair
in Strategic Management,
George Mason University

GARLAND PUBLISHING, INC.
NEW YORK & LONDON / 1994

Library of Congress Cataloging-in-Publication Data

Graham, John W.
   Mission statements : a guide to the corporate and nonprofit
sectors / John W. Graham and Wendy C. Havlick
      p.   cm. — (Garland reference library of social science ; vol.
900)
   Includes bibliographical references and indexes.
   ISBN 0-8153-1297-0
   1. Mission statements. I. Havlick, Wendy C. II. Title.
III. Series: Garland reference library of social science ; v. 900.
HD30.28.G697   1994
658.4'012—dc20   94-540
                                                                        CIP

Printed on acid-free, 250-year-life paper
Manufactured in the United States of America

TO OUR PARENTS

Contents

Foreword

Why Read This Book?

Mission Statements: A Guide to the Corporate and Nonprofit Sectors offers the most exciting opportunities for advancing the study of organization direction in the four decades that it has been actively pursued. The study of missions of organizations has remained on the "back burner" of scholarly pursuits because of the great difficulty that researchers have faced in gathering appropriate formal statements from corporations and nonprofit organizations. As a result, the importance of missions to distinguish among organizations and to guide the development and execution of implementing strategies has become a nearly universally endorsed but unenthusiastically practiced element in organizational planning activities.

This information laden new book by John Graham and Wendy Havlick invites managers and academic researchers to undertake the study of missions with greater expectations that much can be learned about the organizations, their leaders, and their strategies through a comprehensive assessment of their written statements of values and priorities. While little can be learned about the processes by which the mission statements were produced, much can be learned about the reportable intentions that leaders hold for their organizations.

What Is a Mission Statement?

To develop a new organization or to reformulate the direction of an ongoing organization, strategic decision makers determine the basic goals, characteristics, and philosophies that will shape the strategic posture of the organization. The outcome of this task, known as the organization's mission, provides the basis for a culture that will guide future executive decision making.

The organization's mission is a broadly defined but enduring statement of purpose that distinguishes it from other organizations of its type and identifies the scope of its operations in product and market terms. Not only does the organization mission embody the strategic decision makers' philosophy, it also reveals the image of the organization that they seek to project, reflects the organization's self-concept, and indicates the principal product or service areas and the primary customer or client needs that the organization will attempt to satisfy. In short, the mission describes the organization's product, service, market, and technology in a way that reflects the values and priorities of the strategic decision makers.

An organization's systematically and comprehensively developed mission statement can serve as an invaluable tool in directing the formulation and implementation of strategy. An organization achieves a heightened sense of purpose when its managers address the issues of: "Why does this organization exist?" "What needs do we fulfill?" "What customers do we serve?" Through its mission statement, or vision statement as it is sometimes known, managers and leaders attempt to clearly articulate its long-term intentions so that its goals can serve as a basis for shared expectations, planning, and performance evaluation.

The critical role of the organization mission as the basis of orchestrating managerial action is repeatedly demonstrated by failing organizations whose short-run actions are ultimately found to be counterproductive to their long-run purpose.

The principal value of a mission statement as a tool of strategic managers is derived from its specification to the ultimate aims of the organization. It thus provides managers with a unity of direction that transcends individual, parochial, and transitory needs. It promotes a sense of shared expectations among all levels and generations of employees. It consolidates values over time and across individuals and interest groups. It projects a sense of worth and intent that can be identified and assimilated by organization outsiders, i.e., customers, clients, suppliers, competitors, local committees, and the general public. Finally, it affirms the organization's commitment to responsible action, which is symbiotic with its needs to preserve and protect the essential claims of insiders for sustained survival, growth, and financial viability of the organization.

Owing to *Mission Statements: A Guide to the Corporate and Nonprofit Sectors*, the issues, components, and priorities raised in mission statements can now be enumerated, compared, and contrasted with greater ease and comprehensiveness than has ever been done before.

Formulating the Mission Statement

The process of defining the mission for a specific organization is usually based on several fundamental beliefs:

- Belief that the organization's product and service can provide benefits commensurate with its cost or price;
- Belief that the product or service can satisfy a customer need not currently met adequately for specific market segments;
- Belief that the technology to be used in the production process will provide a product or service that is cost and quality competitive;
- Belief that with hard work and with the support of others, the organization can do better than just survive; it can grow and meet financial objectives;
- Belief that the managers' and leaders' philosophy will result in a favorable public image and will provide financial and psychological rewards for those willing to invest their labor and money;
- Belief that the self-concept that the managers and leaders have of the organization can be communicated to and adopted by employees, investors, and other stakeholders;
- Belief that the organization can provide a quality product or service which satisfies a customer need.

The following sections look at the logic behind including each of these components in a mission statement.

Product or Service, Market, and Technology

Three indispensable components of a mission statement are the organization's basic product or service, the primary market, and the principal technology to be used in producing or delivering the product or service. In combination, these three components define the organization's present and potential involvements.

Often an organization's most referenced public statement of products or services and markets is presented in "silver bullet" form in the mission statement. For example: "Dayton-Hudson Corporation is a diversified retailing organization whose business is to serve the American consumer through the retailing of fashion-oriented quality merchandise." Such a statement serves as an abstract of organization direction and is particularly helpful to outsiders who value condensed overviews.

Organization Goals: Survival, Growth, and Profitability

Three long-term goals guide the strategic direction of almost every organization. Although not always explicitly stated, an organization mission reflects the organization's intention to secure its survival through sustained growth and financial viability. Unless an organization is able to survive, it will be incapable of satisfying any of its stakeholders' aims.

Profitability is the main goal of a business organization. No matter how it is measured or defined, profit over the long term is accepted as the clearest indication of the organization's ability to satisfy the principal claims and desires of employees and stockholders. Clearly, the key phrase here is "over the long term," since the use of short-term profitability measures as a basis for strategic decision-making would lead to a focus on terminal aims. For example, an organization might be misguided into overlooking the enduring concerns of customers, suppliers, creditors, ecologists, and regulatory agents. Such a strategy could be profitable in the short run, but over time its financial consequences are likely to be seriously detrimental.

In the case of nonprofit organizations, profit objectives exist for the purpose of financial viability. Without financial support adequate to cover the cost incurred in providing its service or product, a nonprofit organization will see its objectives underachieved, its effectiveness questioned, and its survival jeopardized.

An organization's growth is inextricably tied to its survival and financial viability. In this context, the meaning of growth is broadly defined. While market share growth has been shown to be strongly correlated with organization profitability, there are other important forms of growth. For example, growth in the number of markets served, in the variety of products or services offered, and in the technologies used to provide goods or services frequently leads to improvements in the organization's competitive ability. Growth means change, and proactive change is a necessity in the dynamic organizational environment.

Organization Philosophy

The statement of an organization's philosophy, or creed as it is sometimes known, usually accompanies or appears as part of the mission. It reflects or explicitly states the basic beliefs, values, aspirations, and philosophical priorities that the strategic decision makers and leaders are committed to emphasize in their management of the organization.

Organization Self-Concept

A major determinant of any organization's continued success is the extent to which it can relate functionally to its external environment.

Finding its "place" in a competitive situation requires that the organization be able to evaluate realistically its own strengths and weaknesses as a competitor. This idea—that the leaders of the organization must be realistically introspective—is the essence of the organization's self-concept. The organization's ability to survive in a dynamic and highly competitive environment would be severely limited if it did not understand the impact that it has or could have on the environment, and vice versa.

Public Image

The issue of public image is an important one, particularly for a growing organization that is involved in redefining its mission. Both present and potential customers or clients attribute certain qualities to a particular organization. Thus, mission statements often reflect the expectations of the public, since this makes the support of the goals more likely.

Sensitivity to Consumer Needs

Customers. "The customer is our top priority" is a slogan that would be claimed by the majority of organizations in the U.S. and abroad. For companies including Caterpillar Tractor, General Electric, and Johnson & Johnson this means analyzing consumer needs before but also after a sale. For these firms, RCA, Sears, 3M, Calgon, Amoco, Mobil Oil, Whirlpool, Zenith, JCPenney, and many others, an overriding concern for the company, as espoused in corporate statements, has been identified as consumer satisfaction. [Professor Pearce uses examples from his own research which may or may not be included in this book.]

Concern for Quality

"Quality is job one!" is a rallying point not only for Ford Motor Corporation but for many resurging U.S. businesses as well. First embraced by Japanese managers whose quality consciousness led to global dominance in automobile, TV, audio equipment, and electronic components manufacturing, the "quality" component is becoming a mainstay of mission statements worldwide.

The Contribution of Graham and Havlick

As those of us who have been involved in the study of mission statements can testify, one of our greatest challenges is to collect large numbers of statements that satisfy our needs for currency, completeness, and representativeness. Finding recent and complete mission statements on several organizations that compete in the same industry or for the same consumer or client group can be prohibitively difficult. The systematic research by Graham and Havlick has greatly simplified the search process for us. In this book, we can find the documents that we need to conduct a meaningful assessment of mission statements that are appropriate to the questions that we wish to ask.

Whether we are leaders attempting to articulate our sense of organization purpose, values, strategies, and practices in either companies or nonprofit organizations; consultants on executive activities assisting in the development of a mission statement and a strategic management plan; research scholars endeavoring to understand organization intent; or job seekers trying to identify organizations with compatible philosophies and interests to our own, Graham and Havlick have facilitated our search and made rewarding results more likely. *Mission Statements: A Guide to the Corporate and Nonprofit Sectors* will be an indispensable aid to all of us who seek to understand organization leaders and managers as they understand themselves.

John A. Pearce II, Ph.D.
Eakin Endowed Chair in Strategic Management
George Mason University

Preface

Introduction

This book is the first and largest published compilation of mission statements. It contains 622 mission statements from the United States and Canada, from the corporate and nonprofit sectors, from dozens of industries, and from just one sentence long to several pages in length. Including indexes by type of industry and by geographic area, *Mission Statements: A Guide to the Corporate and Nonprofit Sectors* is a unique book that will fill a void for many types of readers. The mission statements contained here represent the aspirations, goals, and dreams of some of North America's largest and best known companies, government agencies, nonprofit organizations, and charitable foundations.

Why produce a compilation of mission statements? The answer to that question is larger and more complex than the authors first envisioned. As librarians, the authors have both encountered people who visit libraries and ask for copies of corporate mission statements. Whether for job search, school papers, or as a model for a yet-to-be-drafted statement, these people all invariably found the answer to be the same: mission statements are generally nonpublished items and are not available in most libraries. While academic and larger public libraries will be an important audience for this book, it does have others. Consultants, public relations executives, corporate communications officials, and others who help draft mission statements also will be interested in this book.

The goal of this book is to include mission statements from a large sample of businesses and nonprofit organizations in the United States and Canada, with a wide mix of large and small organizations involved in all possible areas of economic activity. The objective is neither to critique the statements or point out shortcomings between corporate words and corporate deeds, nor is it to promote or endorse any particular corporation, nonprofit organization, or set of values or beliefs. Furthermore, our intent is to provide verbatim mission statements as a complement to the vast published literature on this topic.

xv

Methodology and Scope

To accomplish our goal, we relied on several well-known published lists of larger organizations. We also contacted organizations we knew had mission statements from our prior research. These lists included *Black Enterprise 100*, 1992; *Business Week 1000*, 1992; *Canadian Business 500* June 1992; *Forbes 500*, April 27, 1992; *Forbes 400* Top Private Companies, December 9, 1991; *Forbes Non-Profit 500*, November 26, 1990; *Fortune 500* (Industrial, April 20, 1992; Service, June 1, 1992); and the *Inc. 500* list of fastest-growing private companies, December 1991. We also found a list of top labor unions in the 1993 *World Almanac* and a ranking of top foundations in the 1992 edition of the *Foundation Directory*. After eliminating duplicate entries and those for which a current address and contact name could not be verified, we had a list of approximately 3,000 organizations from whom we wanted a mission statement.

The method used for soliciting a mission statement was a one-page letter, typed on specially prepared Garland Publishing stationery, mailed to the chief executive of each organization in late 1992 and early 1993. The letter stated the purpose of our book, asked for a copy of the mission statement, and sought permission to reproduce that statement in the book. Statements were not solicited by phone, and those who provided statements received no form of remuneration from either the authors or the publisher. Conversely, neither the authors nor the publisher received any payment or fee to include any mission statement.

Mission statements were currently in effect at the time they were provided. Organizations may change, revise, revoke, or reword their mission statements at any time, however. The reader is cautioned to consult with any organization to make sure that the statement included here is still the current one for that organization. An older mission statement usually remains in effect until a newer one takes its place. In at least two cases, an organization had provided a mission statement to us for inclusion in the book but then refused to let us print it because it was being revised.

A total of 2,905 letters was sent to target organizations in the initial mailing. We received a total of 593 usable mission statements, a response rate of 20 percent. We then mailed 135 follow-up letters to organizations that did not respond to the first letter. These organizations were chosen either because they were well known or because we had seen a reference to the fact that they did indeed have mission statements. We received 29 additional mission statements from these follow-up letters, bringing our total to 622. With follow-up letters, we sent a total of 3,040 letters, a response rate for usable mission statements of 20 percent. In addition to the 622 mission statements received, we received 156 other responses, bringing our total number of responses to 778. The 156 other responses included either general corporate information or a response to confirm the fact that the organization did not have a formal mission statement. This book as published contains 622 mission statements, although the entry numbers end at 624. At press time, two organizations whose mission statements were represented by entry numbers 143 and 384 requested their listings be withdrawn due to the recent task of revising their statements. As published, the book includes mission statements from forty-two states, nine Canadian provinces, and the District of Columbia.

The method of organization and solicitation guaranteed a good geographic and industry cross section. Yet some readers will review the entries and wonder, for example: why Wendy's is here but not McDonald's, or why include Ford and General Motors but exclude Chrysler? Several reasons exist. First, participation was strictly voluntary. No company or organization was required to allow us to use its mission statement. Secondly, other studies have shown that many organizations do not have formal mission statements.[1] Still, other companies responded that they had a mission statement either under construction or in the process of revision due to a merger or takeover. Furthermore, some organizations did indeed have mission statements but do not release them to the public. Hershey Foods was a prominent example of this corporate attitude. In short, we did not exclude any organization that sent us a usable mission statement. The only exceptions were if the statements were too long or if the organization placed restrictions on our using them.

Organization and Arrangement

Once the mission statements were received, two tasks still remained. The first was deciding, for the purpose of this book, what exactly is a mission statement? The second was re-keying the text of individual mission statements into a format that may not look like the original. No standard definition of what a mission statement is exists. Two schools of thought, however, do exist. One version sees the mission statement as a straightforward recitation of a firm's line-of-business. Another view holds that the mission statement should be a list of goals or aspirations for the organization. We received many of each. Mission statements included here go under many names, such as creeds, goals, inspirations, visions, values, beliefs, charters, or purposes. In general, we included only those statements specifically identified to us as the organization's mission. If we were unsure as to what the organization's mission actually was, then it was not included in this book. For example, if an organization marked a sentence or section from an annual report or other corporate document signifying it was the mission statement, then it was excluded. To be included, the statement had to be either a separately labeled, freestanding item or a clearly marked, identifiable mission statement in a larger document. Some other exclusions were necessary, however. Among the entries excluded were short descriptions of the line-of-business, environmental policies, quality policies, corporate funds giving guidelines, or any lengthy verbiage introducing or expounding on the mission statement. Even so, many mission statements may contain some of these elements if excluding them would alter their meaning or make them incomplete.

The second challenge was to take mission statements received in many different forms, including single sheets, wallet cards, posters, booklets, pamphlets, or annual reports, and fix them in a standardized format. Our goal was to get the text correct, with a secondary concern for the layout and style of the original. The text of the mission statements is exactly how it was provided to us. We attempted to re-key to match the layout of the originals in terms of capitalization, italics, section headings and the like. Although graphics, colors, typefaces, and photos are not included, we have kept the text correct, even if the visual appearance of the mission statement may not be the same as it was provided.

The compiled entries are arranged alphabetically by company or organizational name. All entries are included in one overall sequence, with for-profit corporations and nonprofit organizations interfiled. We chose to keep all entries in one order, rather than separating out profits and nonprofits. The alphabetical arrangement eliminates the need to offer any organization preferential treatment and have its statement listed first. The book also includes an alphabetically arranged table of contents. In addition, many internal cross references are included to direct the reader to the desired entry. Entries are alphabetized by first letters or names of companies. For example, Geo. Hormel Company may be found in the "G's," while E.W. Scripps Company will be found at the end of the "E" listings filed as by letters "E.W." Cross references in both cases will refer the reader from "Hormel" or "Scripps" respectively. Numerous cross references are used, and they direct the reader to entry numbers, not to page numbers. Therefore, a cross-reference to (123) directs the reader to entry 123, not to page number 123. Sample filing sequence:

Eastman Kodak
E.W. Scripps Company
General Mills
Geo. Hormel Company
Hermann Hospital

Servistar Corp.

SPX Corporation

Two indexes are included: one by industry and one by geographic location. These indexes are included to meet the needs of different types of readers. An index by industry is included for those who wish to use those statements as models for drafting their own statement for their organization. A geographic index is included, with job hunters in mind, as an easy way to locate companies in a specific geographic area. The industry index relies upon the most recent 1987 Standard Industrial Classification (S.I.C.) system, as published in the U.S. Government's *Standard Industrial Classification Manual*.[2] S.I.C. codes give the reader an easy and uniform way to identify companies in broad industry categories. S.I.C. codes are applied to organizations at the broad, two-digit level. Codes assigned to entries are derived from entries in standard business directories, such as the Dun & Bradstreet *Million Dollar Directory,* Standard & Poor's *Register of Corporations, Dun's Business Locator,* or the Dun & Bradstreet *Key Canadian Business Directory.* The goal was to assign one or two primary S.I.C. codes to entries, rather than attempt to represent every line of business. The geographic index arranges entries by city within the appropriate state or Canadian province. United States entries come first, followed by Canadian entries.

Entries are presented in a uniform format. Each entry is assigned an entry number, 1–624. Organization name, headquarters address, and phone number are included. One or two S.I.C. industry codes are assigned. Following the mission statement itself, the appropriate credit, acknowledgment, or copyright notice is given. Credit is given only to those organizations that expressly asked for it, since all mission statements are included with the permission of the issuing company or nonprofit organization. Also included is the source for the mission statement itself, only if the statement was found in some larger document, such as a brochure, pamphlet, booklet, or annual report. If supplied, the date drafted is included. Unless we could verify when the statement was drafted, we did not list a date. The date of the annual report from which some mission statements are derived is included. This date may not necessarily be when the statement was written, but it does give readers an idea of when the mission statement was in effect.

Sample Entry

Entry Number   Company Name

Address, City, State or Province Zip
Telephone Number
S.I.C. Codes and Brief Industry Description
Mission Statement, Purpose, Creed, or Values
Text of mission statement
Source and date, if known
Trademark or copyright acknowledgment as required

Acknowledgments

Many people had a role in this book, and we are pleased to acknowledge their contributions. First, thanks go to the 622 organizations that provided us with their mission statements and gave us permission to use them. Without them, the book could not have been possible. Secondly, thanks go to Professor John A. Pearce II, Eakin Endowed Chair in Strategic Management at George Mason University in Fairfax, Virginia, for writing the book's Foreword. Professor Pearce has published several excellent and widely known articles on mission statements. At Garland Publishing, we would especially like to acknowledge the help of our editor, Marie Ellen Larcada, and Director of Computer Resources, Chuck Bartelt. Thanks also go to Lana and Warren Brown, of Tulsa, Oklahoma, for their invaluable computer assistance. And thanks, finally, to our parents, who have given us support and encouragement throughout this entire project.

NOTES

1. John A. Pearce II and Fred David, "Corporate Mission Statements," *Academy of Management Executives* 1 (May, 1987): 110. Pearce and David found in their survey a 40.4 percent figure for firms without a mission statement.
2. United States, *Standard Industrial Classification Manual* (Washington, DC: Government Printing Office, 1987).

PART I

Introduction

Writing a mission statement means stating the purpose of a corporation or nonprofit organization. This statement may be a brief line-of-business description or it may even be expanded to include the goals, aspirations, and beliefs of a particular organization. Defining a mission in writing is one element in the larger context of strategic management. Proper strategic management includes defining long-range objectives, motivating employees to work toward these objectives, organizing work to reach these goals, and evaluating performance along the way. This introductory section to *Mission Statements: A Guide to the Corporate and Nonprofit Sectors* is a concise look at the mission statement document. Defining what a mission statement is, exploring the history of this document, drafting one for a particular organization, and looking at the future of this important document is the mission of this introductory section.

Definition and History

What exactly is a mission statement? No clear and easily stated answer exists to this question. Exactly 622 mission statements are included in this book, and no two follow the same exact format, formula, or pattern. Length and language vary, as well. Numerous articles and several books have been written about mission statements, and few of them state a rigorous or precise definition of what this document is. Thomas Falsey's *Corporate Philosophies and Mission Statements* does not offer a concise definition of a mission statement; instead it illustrates commonly included elements in separate chapters.[1] *A Sense of Mission* by Andrew Campbell and Laura L. Nash devotes its entire first chapter to answering the question, What is a mission?[2]

Nevertheless, experts in the field and examples from this book reveal many common elements for any mission statement. A mission statement should include many or most of these elements: a statement of purpose for the organization, indication of line of business or specialty, geographic parameters, and mention of important groups in the organization's life, such as employees and shareholders. Perhaps the best concise definition comes

3

from a landmark 1982 article by John A. Pearce II in the *Sloan Management Review*.[3] He writes:

> The company mission is a broadly defined but enduring statement of purpose that distinguishes a business from other firms of its type but identifies the scope of its operations in product and market terms. Not only does the company mission embody strategic decision makers' business philosophy, but it also reveals the image the company seeks to project, reflects the firm's self-concept, and indicates the principal product or service areas and the primary customer needs the company will attempt to satisfy. In short, the company mission describes the firm's product, market, and technology in a way that reflects the values and priorities of the strategic decision makers.

Company mission statements come with a variety of names, as the entries in this book reveal. Organizations may label their mission statement a "creed," "values," "purpose," "vision," "beliefs," or "objectives." Regardless of the names, most fit our basic definition of a mission statement. For the purpose of inclusion in this book, we included a statement, regardless of its name, if it contained the elements listed above. It was also included if the organization that provided it said it was indeed their mission statement.

In the broadest sense, there probably can never be an overall, concise definition or format for all mission statements. The goals of a wheat cooperative in Alberta and a software company in the Silicon Valley are quite different, and these differences will be reflected not only in the language but also in the layout of their missions. Ideally, the mission statement should spring from values and beliefs already at work in an organization. A company should not have to invent its basic values at the same time it sets out to create its mission statement document.

Mission statements, at first glance, may appear to be yet another management fad. Most of the statements included in this book were drafted in the last few years; some were written just weeks or even days before we solicited a statement. An accompanying explosion of mission statement literature is also underway, with books, studies, and popular articles appearing almost weekly. Consultant Dan Thomas, in his new book *Business Sense,* proclaims "mission statements have become a management rage in the late 1980s and early 1990s."[4] While writing a corporate document labeled a mission statement may be new, recording the purpose and objectives of an organization certainly is not.

Company and nonprofit mission statements in one form or another have been around for most of the twentieth century. In fact, if a broad enough definition of a mission statement is included, this document is a centuries-old idea. James K. Brown, in his article "Corporate Soul-Searching," cites the 1636 mission of Harvard College and the phrase "E Pluribus Unum" as early examples.[5] Most early corporate mission statements usually express thoughts from the company's founder, and these documents remain surprisingly fresh and modern today. Some of this language is even included in some companies' current statements. Early examples include Cooper Tire, 1916 (Entry number 161); Kellogg Company (326); Medtronic, Inc., 1960 (369) or the well-known and widely reproduced Johnson & Johnson Creed (319).

An excellent and quite typical example is the mission statement from Leo Burnett Company, Inc. (338). Leo Burnett is a major advertising agency based in Chicago. Its mission statement dates from 1955 and is composed mostly of words from Leo Burnett himself. In part it reads, "our primary function in life is to produce the best advertising in the world, bar none." When reproduced on the company's stationery with the firm's famous "reach for the stars" logo, it provides a powerful and direct message to employees almost forty years after those words were written.

Creation of the Mission Statement

How does one go about writing a mission statement for a company or nonprofit organization? Just as when one tries to define what a mission statement is, there is probably no one "right" way to do it. Some mission statements in this book are the words of the company's founder, often written in a direct if untutored style. Others are the work of internal committees, and they often contain drab and uninspiring prose. Some organizations solicit employee input before writing or rewriting their statements; Michigan Consolidated Gas Company (376) went to the rather extraordinary step of obtaining comments from over 2,600 employees—75 percent of its work force—before its last mission statement revision.

A mission statement contains the strategic intent and business direction for an organization. As such, it conveys the ideas and plans of top management. Neither janitors nor public relations executives set policy for any organization; that is the job of top executives and boards of directors. Therefore, the first step in writing or revising any mission statement document is getting the full support of top management. This support could mean either specific language or concepts and ideas the mission statement should include.

Other steps follow. Based on an extensive review of the literature and discussion with several people who have developed mission statements, we believe writing a mission statement involves five steps after securing management approval for this task. The first step is to gather as much information about the organization and its goals as possible. Ideally this includes not only reviewing company documents and plans but also seeking real and meaningful input from employees. The second step is to produce a rough outline of the proposed mission statement. The next step is to get feedback on this draft. Feedback should come both from top management and lower level employees. Seeking employee input is important. While management sets strategy, employees must understand what this strategy is if they are to implement it. Involving employees in the process of shaping the identity and direction of the organization provides the employees with a sense of ownership as well. After receiving feedback, the fourth step is to revise the mission statement. This includes not only tinkering with the language but considering layout and format. Getting management approval and support is the final step in the process.

Yet writing a mission statement is more than simply following a set pattern or formula. This book is written to help those drafting mission statements to have a pattern to follow, but no one pattern will fit all companies or nonprofit organizations. Managers and employees will need to make up their own minds as to what their own organization's mission statement will look like. Some organizations take the phrase mission "statement" literally, producing a one-sentence statement. Other organizations decide on a longer document, with sections to encompass all those touched by corporate activities. The final length and format of the statement should be determined not by examples in this book but by what the organization wants to say and how it wants to say it.

Three additional factors need to be considered in writing a mission statement. They should be considered in each step of the five-part process outlined above. The first step is to avoid jargon and buzzwords in the mission statement. Some of the mission statements in this book seemed to be drafted to contain the latest business jargon, such as "continuous improvement," "competitive advantage," or "quality." Other terms are so ill-defined as to be meaningless. What exactly does "world class" mean? What are the "highest ethical standards?" Other organizations use very dense or complex language in their mission statements, and one finds inscrutable references to terms such as "six sigma quality" or "dialectic problem analysis" in the pages that follow. Mission statement writers should avoid terms such as these for two reasons.

First, jargon words have no meaning to most people in that organization. Secondly, the mission statement should be for all employees. By employing the latest MBA-speak, the mission statement then applies only to selected groups of employees such as engineers or marketing staff.

The language of a mission statement should be sufficiently general to apply and have personal meaning to all employees in an organization.

As a second observation, jargon can be avoided and at the same time, mission statements can be written to convey complex thoughts in understandable language. Some organizations define what they mean by different jargon words. Northrop (422), for example, defines what it means by the concept of "quality." Pennsylvania Power & Light (446) goes to the trouble of defining what they mean—in additional materials supplied to us—by the business terms "mission," "vision," "values," and "business philosophy." Borg-Warner Corporation (90) manages to find a straightforward way to convey the concept of "continuous improvement" without the need to resort to this overworked term. In short, creative writing can make popular business concepts understandable in the mission statement.

Finally, companies must put their mission statements into action. Deeds must back up the rhetoric. Organizations must "walk the talk." This concept shows how important top management support is for drafting a mission statement. Management must live by the mission statement it creates; it will be judged both by employees and outsiders on how the words are put into action. Thomas Falsey, in his important book on corporate mission statements and beliefs, argues " . . . the true test of any company is not what it says but rather what it does. The true test is not how a company views itself, it is in how it is viewed by its many publics."[6] Some organizations acknowledge realistically that deeds and words are not synonymous. For example, Goulds Pumps (253) states "our commitment is to continually close any gaps between existing practices and these values."

After the mission statement is completed, the work is not finished. Getting the word out to employees, stockholders, vendors, regulators, and other "stakeholders" is vital. In the responses we received, it was obvious some organizations had given considerable thought to disseminating their mission statements, while others had not. How will the statements be distributed and how will new employees learn of the statement? As noted in the Preface, mission statements came to us in at least a dozen formats, including posters, wallet cards, annual reports, booklets, brochures, and signs of different kinds. Ideally, the organization should invest in reproducing its mission statement in various formats. Posters may be ideal for a staff cafeteria, meeting room, or public area, while wallet cards are suited to employees who travel away from headquarters. AMAX Gold Inc. (15), a mining company, for example, reproduces its mission statement on wallet cards, presumably so employees in remote mining sites can keep their eyes on company strategy.

Indoctrinating new employees to the mission statement is important as well. Do new employees learn about the mission statement in orientation sessions? This would seem to be a matter of course, but it is worth mentioning. We received over 770 responses, and these came to us from many different corporate offices and departments. More than a few were sent back (dusted off?) from the company's archives. Very few of these, however, came from human resources departments. One wonders if employees received a copy of the organization's mission statement when they started work, along with tax information and other company employee manuals.

Directions for Further Inquiry

Reading hundreds of mission statements from all types of organizations in the United States and Canada raises many unanswered questions. One of the purposes of this book was to produce a big enough selection, or "database," of mission statements to support and to spur further research into the mission statement, its function, and its effects. Three broad areas of study invite further research.

The first area may be labeled "intra-organizational." Research here would try to answer questions on the mission statement as written and applied in one given company or nonprofit organization. Here are some sample questions for study. In a given company, how do employees learn about the mission statement? How is input solicited for writing or rewriting a mission statement? If staff at an organization were surveyed, how many would know what their mission statement was or where to find it? Is the mission statement perceived as another management fad or as a document by which to live? When and why do organizations decide to write a mission statement? Who is involved?

A second category of inquiry may be termed "inter-organizational." These questions try to determine mission statement differences or similarities among more than one organization. Here are some sample areas for inquiry. How do mission statements vary in the same industry? In the same state or province? How do mission statements change over time in different industries? In one industry? How do mission statements compare for the same industry in different nations? How do concerns for the environment or other new issues manifest themselves in mission statements? What is the process by which new business jargon and buzzwords find their way into mission statements?

A final category for inquiry will address other issues. Many of these will focus on the mission statement as a written document itself. Research here may attempt to answer some of these questions. Is there an ideal length for a mission statement? An ideal format? What is the best way to communicate the mission statement to employees? What is the role of top management in implementing a mission statement? What is the role of one's fellow employees in implementing a mission statement? The mission statements in this book represent those in effect during the window of time of early 1993. How will these statements read in five years? Were they different five years ago?

Perhaps the ultimate area for future research is this: Does having a mission statement in an organization make any difference? This may prove to be an unanswerable question because it may be impossible to design a controlled experiment to measure such a question. Yet some research has been attempted in this area. Vardi, Wiener, and Popper surveyed workers in Israeli defense industries and concluded that "organizational mission can affect the level of normative commitment of members."[7] John A. Pearce II and Fred David, in a 1987 article, studied mission statements from both "high performing" and "low performing" groups of Fortune 500 companies. They found support for a thorough mission statement and argued that ". . . this study may understate the importance of a carefully and comprehensively developed mission statement."[8] This area is ripe for future research, and many organizations who returned mission statements to us were eager to see a study to support the value of developing a mission statement.

Based on the authors' examination of the pace and form of mission statement developments, it may be possible to project, or to "handicap," the future of the mission statement document. Some trends appear to be sure bets. More organizations will develop mission statements. Mission statements may indeed be a "fad," but putting organizational strategy in writing is also a timelessly good business idea. Organizations will also feel the urge to develop more types of documents to accompany and supplement the mission statement. Many organizations not only have mission statements but also have prepared vision statements, environmental guidelines, corporate giving policies, and quality objectives. Organizations will realize that mission statements and these related documents not only inspire employees but also entice investors, pacify regulators, and advertise the organization's products or services. Companies may be pressured to state publicly their views on many contentious social issues. As this book was being prepared, a Cincinnati-based company made news by requiring its suppliers to state their views on abortion. While preparing a corporate view on a fiery issue such as abortion may be impossible, especially in a large organization, that does not mean critics and reformers won't ask companies to try.

In conclusion, the authors hope this book will help to make the mission statement a needed and respected document. The process of writing or revising a mission statement does not simply offer a chance to send another memo to employees. It offers the chance for management and employees to re-define, re-create, or "re-engineer"—to use the latest business jargon— their organizations. Writing a mission statement ultimately challenges organizations to measure their performance.

NOTES

1. Thomas Falsey, *Corporate Philosophies and Mission Statements: A Survey and Guide for Corporate Communicators and Management* (New York: Quorum Books, 1989), 1–14.

2. Andrew Campbell and Laura L. Nash, *A Sense of Mission: Defining Direction for the Large Corporation* (Reading, Mass.: Addison-Wesley Publishing Company, 1992), 11–35.

3. John A. Pearce II, "The Company Mission as a Strategic Tool," *Sloan Management Review* 23 (Spring, 1982): 15.

4. Dan Thomas, *Business Sense: Exercising Management's Five Freedoms* (New York: The Free Press, 1993): 206.

5. James K. Brown, "Corporate Soul-Searching: The Power of Mission Statements," *Across the Board* 21 (March, 1984): 50.

6. Falsey, *Corporate Philosophies and Mission Statements*, 31.

7. Yoav Vardi, Yoash Wiener, and Micha Popper, "The Value Content of Organizational Mission as a Factor in the Commitment of Members," *Psychological Reports* 65 (1989): 31.

8. John A. Pearce II and Fred David, "Corporate Mission Statements: The Bottom Line," *Academy of Management Executives* 1 (May, 1987): 113.

Bibliography

Ackoff, Russel L. "Mission Statements." *Planning Review*, 15, no. 4 (July/August 1987), 30–31.

Ainsworth, T.H., Jr., and M.D. Thomas. "Statement of Mission: Essential Ingredient in Planning." *Trustee*, 29, no. 9 (1976), 34–36.

Anderson, Joyce S. "Mission Statements Bond Corporate Culture." *Personnel Journal*, 66 (October 1987), 120–22.

Bertodo, R. "Implementing a Strategic Vision." *Long Range Planning*, 23, no. 5 (October 1990), 22–30.

Bettinger, Cass. "Behind the Mission Statement." *ABA Banking Journal*, 77, no. 10 (October 1985), 154–160.

————. "Community Bank Strategies: Marketing-Driven Banks Thrive on Mission Statements." *Bank Marketing*, 19 (August 1987), 4–5.

Brown, James K. "Corporate Soul-Searching: The Power of Mission Statements." *Across the Board*, 21 (March 1984), 44–52.

Byars, Lloyd L., and Thomas C. Neil. "Organizational Philosophy and Mission Statements." *Planning Review*, 15, no. 4 (July/August 1987), 32–35.

Calfee, David L. "Get Your Mission Statement Working!" *Management Review* (January 1993), 54–58.

Campbell, Andrew, and Kiran Tawadey. *Mission and Business Philosophy: Winning Employee Commitment*. Stoneham, Mass.: Butterworth-Heinemann, 1990.

Campbell, Andrew, and Laura L. Nash. *A Sense of Mission: Defining Direction for the Large Corporation*. Reading, Mass.: Addison-Wesley, 1992.

Campbell, Andrew, and Sally Yeung. "Creating A Sense Of Mission." *Long Range Planning*, 24, no. 4 (August 1991), 10–20.

————. *Do You Need a Mission Statement?* London: Economist Publications, 1990.

Cochran, Daniel S., and Fred R. David. "The Communication Effectiveness of Organizational Mission Statements." *Journal of Applied Communication Research*, 14, no. 2 (Fall 1986), 108–118.

Cochran, Daniel S., Fred R. David, and C. Kendrick Gibson. "A Framework for Developing an Effective Mission Statement." *Journal of Business Strategies*, 2, no. 2 (Fall 1985), 4–17.

Collins, James C., and Jerry I. Porras. "Organizational Vision and Visionary Organizations." *California Management Review*, 34, no. 1 (Fall 1991), 30–52.

David, Fred R. "How Companies Define Their Mission." *Long Range Planning*, 22, no. 1 (February 1989), 90–97.

De Haan, Jacqueline A. "Blessed Be the Ties That Bind: A Critical Analysis of the Changing Language in the Organizational Mission Statement as a Form of Downward Communication." Master's Thesis, Western Michigan University, 1990.

Dubberly, Ronald A. "Why You Must Know Your Library's Mission." *Public Libraries* (Fall 1983), 89–90.

Falsey, Thomas A. *Corporate Philosophies and Mission Statements: A Survey and Guide for Corporate Communicators and Management*. New York: Quorum Books, 1989.

Farnham, Alan. "State Your Values, Hold the Hot Air." *Forbes*, 127 (April 19, 1993), 118–124.

Frohman, Mark, and Perry Pascarella. "Creating the Purposeful Organization." *Industry Week*, 229 (June 9, 1986), 44–50.

———. "How to Write a Purpose Statement." *Industry Week*, 232 (March 23, 1987), 31–34.

Fuchsberg, Gilbert. "'Visioning' Missions Becomes Its Own Mission." *Wall Street Journal* (January 7, 1994), B1, B4.

Germain, Richard, and M. Bixby Cooper. "How a Customer Mission Statement Affects Company Performance." *Industrial Marketing Management*, 19 (1990), 47–54.

Gibson, C. Kendrick, et al. "An Empirical Investigation of the Nature of Hospital Mission Statements." *Health Care Management Review*, 15, no. 3 (Summer 1990), 35–45.

Gordon-Hall, Amanda. "Does Your Company Really Need A Mission Statement?" *Industrial Marketing Digest (UK)*, 15, no. 1 (First Quarter 1990), 105–112.

Griffith, J.R. "The Mission of the Well-Managed Community Hospital." *Michigan Hospitals*, 24, no. 7 (July 1988), 43–46.

Herbert, Elliott. "Corporate Culture: Add 99 Years of Seasoning." *IEEE Transactions on Professional Communication*, 32, no. 2 (June 1989), 69–75.

Hunter, Jairy C. "Managers Must Know the Mission: If it Ain't Broke Don't Fix it." *Managerial Planning*, 33, no. 4 (January/February 1985), 18–22.

Ireland, R. Duane, and Michael A. Hitt. "Mission Statements: Importance, Challenge, and Recommendations for Development." *Business Horizons*, 35 (May/June 1992), 34–42.

Keller, Maryann. "Corporate Vision." *Automotive Industries*, 172, no. 2 (February 1992), 11.

Landen, Delmar, and Gayle A. Landen. "Corporate Constitutions Help Define Companies' Character, Culture, and Quality." *Employment Relations Today,* 18, no. 2 (Summer 1991), 203–211.

Langeler, Gerard H. "The Vision Trap." *Harvard Business Review,* 70, no. 2 (March/April 1992), 46–55.

Lee, Chris. "The Vision Thing." *Training,* 30 (February 1993), 25–34.

Lloyd, Bruce. "Riding the Whirlwind into the Twenty-First Century." *Leadership & Organization Development Journal,* 13, no. 2 (1992), 22–26.

Lundberg, Craig C. "Zero-in: A Technique for Formulating Better Mission Statements." *Business Horizons,* 27, no. 5 (September/October 1984), 30–33.

McGinnis, Vern J. "The Mission Statement: A Key Step in Strategic Planning." *Business* (November/December 1981), 39–43.

McMillan, Norman H. "The Mission Statement: Where It All Begins." In *Planning for Survival: A Handbook for Hospital Trustees.* 2nd ed. Chicago, Ill.: American Hospital Association, 1985, pp. 95–99.

Medley, G.J. "WWF UK Creates a New Mission." *Long Range Planning,* 25, no. 2 (April 1992), 63–68.

Morrisey, George L. "Who Needs a Mission Statement? You Do: How to Go About Devising Your Reason for Being." *Training and Development Journal,* 42 (March 1988), 50–52.

Nelton, Sharon. "The Mission of Finding a Mission." *Nation's Business,* 78, no. 11 (November 1990), 58.

Nicholas, Ted. *Secrets of Entrepreneurial Leadership.* Chicago: Dearborn Financial Publishing, Inc., 1993.

Nolan, Timothy M., Leonard D. Goodstein, and J. William Pfeiffer. *Plan or Die! 10 Keys to Organizational Success.* San Diego, CA: Pfeiffer & Company, 1993.

Panchak, Patricia L. "How to Implement a Quality Management Initiative." *Modern Office Technology,* 37, no. 2 (February 1992), 27–31.

Pascarella, Perry. "Creating the Future." *Industry Week,* 231 (October 13, 1986), 65–72.

Pearce, John A., II, "The Company Mission as a Strategic Tool." *Sloan Management Review,* 23, no. 3 (Spring 1982), 15–24.

Pearce, John A., II, and Fred David. "Corporate Mission Statements: The Bottom Line." *Academy of Management Executives,* 1, no. 2 (May 1987), 109–116.

Pearce, John A., II, and Kendall Roth. "Multinationalization of the Mission Statement." *SAM Advanced Management Journal,* 53, no. 3 (Summer 1988), 39–44.

Placenti, Frank M. "Firm Must First Know Its Mission." *The National Law Journal,* 14, no. 19 (January 13, 1992), 23.

Posner, Barry Z., James M. Kouzes, and Warren H. Schmidt. "Shared Values Make A Difference: An Empirical Test of Corporate Culture." *Human Resource Management*, 24, no. 3 (Fall 1985), 293–309.

Public Library Association. *The Public Library Mission Statement and Its Imperatives for Service.* Chicago: American Library Association, 1979.

Reyes, James R., and Brian H. Kleiner. "How to Establish an Organizational Purpose." *Management Decision*, 28 (December 1990), 51–54.

Roman, Mark B. "The Mission: Setting Your Vision in Words is the Crucial Executive Act." *Success*, 34 (June 1987), 54–55.

Ruddell, Tom, and Loyd Pettegrew. "The Best Companies Have and Heed Codes-Creeds." *Communication World*, 5 (September 1988), 30–31.

Scott, Cynthia D., Dennis T. Jaffe, and Glenn R. Tobe. *Organizational Vision, Values and Mission.* Menlo Park, Calif.: Crisp Publications, Inc., 1993.

Staples, William A. and Ken U. Black. "Defining Your Business Mission: A Strategic Perspective." *Journal of Business Strategies*, 1, no. 1 (1984), 33–39.

Thomas, Dan. *Business Sense: Exercising Management's Five Freedoms.* New York: Free Press, 1993.

Vardi, Yoav, Yoash Wiener, and Micha Popper. "The Value Content of Organizational Mission as a Factor in the Commitment of Members." *Psychological Reports*, 65 (1989), 27–34.

Wall, Bob. *The Visionary Leader: From Mission Statement to a Thriving Organization, Here's Your Blueprint for Building an Inspired, Cohesive Customer-Oriented Team.* Rocklin, Calif.: Prima Publishing, 1992.

Want, Jerome H. "Corporate Mission: The Intangible Contributor to Performance." *Management Review*, 75 (August 1986), 46–50.

Webley, Simon. *Company Philosophies and Codes of Business Ethics: A Guide to Their Drafting and Use.* London: Institute of Business Ethics, 1988.

Whiteley, Richard C. "Creating a Customer Focus." *Executive Excellence.* 7, no. 9 (September 1990), 9–10.

Yauger, Charles Clay. "A Study of Organizational Culture, Marketing, and Mission Statements in Hospitals." Ph.D. Dissertation, University of Mississippi, 1990.

List of Organizations

This is an alphabetical arrangement of organizations included. Numbers in parentheses are entry numbers, not page numbers. Entries are arranged alphabetically by the first word in the organization's name. Therefore, James Irvine Foundation is filed in the "j's," and Chas. Levy Company may be found in the "c's." Acronyms are interfiled with other entries beginning with the same letter and not placed at the beginning of that letter's entries. Numerous cross references may be found within the text of the book, rather than in this listing. Therefore, cross references under "Irvine" and "Levy," from the examples above, will direct the reader to the proper entry number. The organization's name is printed exactly as it appeared in materials sent to the authors.

Abbott Northwestern Hospital (1)
Ace Hardware Corporation (2)
Advanced Micro Devices, Inc. (3)
A.G. Edwards & Sons, Inc. (4)
AGRA Industries Limited (5)
Alabama Electric Cooperative, Inc. (6)
Alberta Wheat Pool (7)
Albertson's, Inc. (8)
Alcan Aluminium Limited (9)
Alex Lee, Inc. (10)
Algoma Central Corporation (11)
Allied-Signal, Inc. (12)
ALZA Corporation (13)
Amax Gold Inc. (14)
Ambulatory Medical Care, Inc. (15)
Amcast Industrial Corporation (16)
Amdahl Corporation (17)
American Association of Museums (18)
American Association of Retired
  Persons (19)
American Bar Association (20)
American Bureau of Shipping &
  Affiliated Companies (21)

American Cancer Society (22)
American Family Life Assurance
  Company of Columbus (AFLAC
  Inc.) (23)
American Federation of Labor and
  Congress of Industrial Organizations
  (AFL-CIO) (24)
American Federation of Teachers (25)
American Heart Association (26)
American Hotel & Motel Association
  (27)
American Library Association (28)
American Lung Association (29)
American Management Association
  (30)
American Medical Association (31)
American Oil Chemists' Society (32)
American Petroleum Institute (33)
American Power Conversion (34)
American President Companies, Ltd.
  (35)
American Red Cross (36)

American Telephone & Telegraph
  Company (AT&T) (37)
American Turnkey Corp. (38)
AMETEK, Inc. (39)
AM International, Inc. (40)
AMSCO International, Inc. (41)
Anacomp, Inc. (42)
Analog Devices, Inc. (43)
Andersons Management Corporation
  (44)
Anheuser-Busch Companies, Inc. (45)
A. O. Smith Corporation (46)
Apache Corporation (47)
APCOA, Inc. (48)
Apple Computer, Inc. (49)
ARCO Chemical Company (50)
Armstrong World Industries, Inc. (51)
Arthur Andersen & Co., SC (52)
Art Institute of Chicago (53)
Associated Wholesale Grocers, Inc.
  (54)
AST Research Inc. (55)
Austin Industries, Inc. (56)
Avis Rent A Car System, Inc. (57)
Avon Products, Inc. (58)

Ball Corporation (59)
Baltimore Gas and Electric (60)
Banc One Corporation (61)
BankAmerica Corporation (Bank of
  America) (62)
Bankers Trust New York Corporation
  (63)
Baptist Memorial Hospital (64)
Barnes Group Inc. (65)
Barnett Banks, Inc. (66)
Bashas' Markets Inc. (67)
BASIS International Limited (68)
Battle Mountain Gold Company (69)
Baxter Healthcare Corporation (70)
Bay Health Systems (71)
BE&K, Inc. (72)
BeautiControl ® Cosmetics (73)
Beckman Instruments, Inc. (74)
Belcan Corporation (75)

Ben & Jerry's Homemade, Inc. (76)
Bendco/Bending & Coiling Co., Inc.
  (77)
Best Products Co., Inc. (78)
Bethlehem Steel Corporation (79)
BFGoodrich Company (80)
Biomet, Inc. (81)
Black River Manufacturing, Inc. (82)
Blockbuster Entertainment Corporation
  (83)
Blue Diamond Growers (84)
Boatmen's Bancshares, Inc. (85)
Bob Evans Farms, Inc. (86)
The Boeing Company (87)
Boise Cascade Corporation (88)
Borgess Medical Center (89)
Borg-Warner Corporation (90)
Boston Bank of Commerce (91)
Branch Banking and Trust Company
  (BB&T) (92)
Brinker International, Inc. (93)
Bristol-Myers Squibb Company (94)
British Columbia Ferry Corporation
  (95)
British Columbia Hydro and Power
  Authority (96)
British Columbia Systems Corporation
  (97)
British Columbia Telephone (98)
Broadway Federal Savings and Loan
  Association (99)
Brooklyn Union Gas Company (100)
Browning-Ferris Industries (101)
Burlington Northern Railroad (102)

CAE Industries Limited (103)
Calgary Co-operative Association
  Limited (104)
Calgon Carbon Corporation (105)
California Farm Bureau Federation
  (106)
Cambior, Inc. (107)
Canadian Airlines International Limited
  (108)

Canadian Broadcasting Corporation (109)
Canadian Commercial Corporation (110)
Canadian National Railway Company (111)
Canbra Foods (112)
Cardinal Distribution Inc. (113)
CARE (114)
Cargill, Inc. (115)
Carnegie Corporation of New York (116)
Carolina Freight Corporation (117)
Caterair International (118)
Catholic Medical Center of Brooklyn and Queens, Inc. (119)
Catholic Relief Services (120)
Cedars-Sinai Medical Center (121)
Celestial Seasonings, Inc. (122)
CENEX (Farmers Union Central Exchange, Inc.) (123)
Central Louisiana Electric Company, Inc. (124)
Champion International Corporation (125)
Champlin Foundations (126)
Charles Schwab Corporation (127)
Charles Stark Draper Laboratory, Inc. (128)
Charter One Bank, F.S.B. (129)
Chase Manhattan Bank, N.A. (130)
Chas. Levy Company (131)
Chemical Leaman Tank Lines, Inc. (132)
Chesapeake Corporation (133)
Chevron Corporation (134)
Children's Defense Fund (135)
Children's Hospital Medical Center (136)
Children's Hospital of Philadelphia (137)
Chiquita Brands International (138)
Christian Broadcasting Network Inc. (139)
Christian Children's Fund (140)

Chugach Electric Association, Inc. (141)
CITGO Petroleum Corporation (142)
Clay Electric Cooperative, Inc. (144)
The Cleveland Foundation (145)
CN North America (146)
Cobb Electric Membership Corporation (147)
Colonial Williamsburg Foundation (148)
Colorado National Bankshares, Inc. (149)
Columbia Gas System, Inc. (Columbia Gas System Service Corporation) (150)
Commerce Bancshares, Inc. (151)
Commonwealth Edison Company (152)
Cone Mills Corporation (153)
Conseco, Inc. (154)
Consolidated Rail Corporation (155)
Consumers Gas Co. Ltd. (156)
Consumers Union (157)
Continental Airlines, Inc. (158)
Continental Medical Systems, Inc. (159)
Cooper Industries (160)
Cooper Tire & Rubber Company (161)
Corning Inc. (162)
Costco ® Wholesale Corp. (163)
Countrymark Cooperative, Inc. (164)
Covenant House (165)
Cox Enterprises, Inc. (166)
Cray Research, Inc. (167)
C.R. Bard, Inc. (168)
Crestar Financial Corporation (169)
CSX Corp. (170)
CUC International (171)
Cullen/Frost Bankers, Inc. (172)

Dahlin Smith White, Inc. (173)
Dakota Electric Association (174)
Dana Corporation (175)
Daughters of Charity National Health System (176)

David Mitchell & Associates, Inc. (177)
Davis Distributing Limited (178)
Deere & Company (179)
Delmarva Power & Light Company (180)
Destec Energy, Inc. (181)
Devtek Corporation (182)
DeWitt Wallace-Reader's Digest Fund (183)
Dexter Corporation (184)
Dial Corporation (185)
Diebold, Incorporated (186)
Dime Savings Bank of New York, FSB (187)
Dofasco Inc. (188)
Dollar General Corporation (189)
Dominion Bankshares Corporation (190)
Dominion Resources, Inc. (191)
Dominion Textile Inc. (192)
Domino's Pizza, Inc. (193)
Dover Corporation (194)
Downey Savings and Loan Association (195)
Dresser Industries, Inc. (196)
Dr Pepper/Seven-Up Companies, Inc. (197)
DUAL Incorporated (198)
Ducks Unlimited Inc. (199)
Duke Power Company (200)

Earth Care Paper (201)
East Coast Computer Systems, Inc. (202)
Eastern Enterprises (203)
Eastman Kodak Company (204)
Eaton Corporation (205)
Ecolab Inc. (206)
Edison Electric Institute (207)
Edna McConnell Clark Foundation (208)
Educational Broadcasting Corporation (Thirteen/WNET) (209)

E.I. Du Pont De Nemours & Company Incorporated (210)
Electric Power Research Institute (211)
Electrohome Limited (212)
Empire Company Limited (213)
Englehard Corporation (214)
Equifax Inc. (215)
Ethix Corporation (216)
Ethyl Corporation (217)
Evangelical Health Systems (218)
E.W. Scripps Company (219)

F&C International, Inc. (220)
Farm & Home Savings Association (221)
Father Flanagan's Boys' Home (222)
Federal Express Corp. (223)
Federal-Mogul Corporation (224)
Federated Department Stores, Inc. (225)
Fiesta Mart Inc. (226)
Firstar Corporation (227)
FirsTier Financial, Inc. (228)
First Tennessee Bank National Association (229)
First Union Corporation (230)
Fiserv Inc. (231)
Fishery Products International Limited (232)
Fluor Daniel (233)
Food Lion Inc. (234)
Ford Motor Company (235)
Frisch's Restaurants, Inc. (236)

Gale Group Inc. (237)
Gandalf Technologies, Inc. (238)
Gannett Co. Inc. (239)
Gates Rubber Company (240)
Gaz Métropolitan, Inc. (241)
GEICO Corporation (242)
GenCorp (243)
General Mills, Inc. (244)
General Motors Corporation (245)
Geo. A. Hormel & Company (246)
Gerber Plumbing Fixtures Corp. (247)

Gerber Products Company (248)
Gibson Greetings, Inc. (249)
Gillette Company (250)
Golub Corporation (251)
Gordon Food Service (252)
Goulds Pumps, Inc. (253)
Granite Broadcasting Corporation (254)
Graphic Communications International
  Union (255)
Great Western Bank (256)
Groupe Laperrière & Verreault Inc.
  (257)
Group Health Cooperative of Puget
  Sound (258)
Grumman Corporation (259)
GTE Mobile Communications (260)
Guilford Mills, Inc. (261)
Gulf States Utilities Company (262)

Halliburton Company (263)
Hallmark Cards, Inc. (264)
Handleman Company (265)
H&R Block, Inc. (266)
Harley-Davidson, Inc. (267)
Harris Bankcorp, Inc. (268)
Harsco Corporation (269)
Hartford Steam Boiler Inspection and
  Insurance Co. (270)
Harvard Community Health Plan (271)
Haworth, Inc. (272)
H R Fuller Company (273)
Health Net (274)
HealthTrust, Inc. (275)
Henry Ford Health System (276)
Hercules Incorporated (277)
Hermann Hospital (278)
Hernandez Engineering Inc. (279)
Hillcrest Medical Center (280)
Hillenbrand Industries (281)
Hilton Hotels Corporation (282)
H.J. Heinz (283)
H.J. Russell & Company (284)
Hoechst Celanese Corporation (285)
Holland Mark Martin (286)
Holnam Inc. (287)

Home Oil Company Limited (288)
Honeywell Inc. (289)
Hospital Corporation of America (290)
Household International (291)
Houston Lighting & Power (292)
Howard Hughes Medical Institute (293)
Humana Inc. (294)
Humiston-Keeling, Inc. (295)
Husky Oil (296)
Hydro-Québec (297)

Illinois Power Company (298)
IMC Fertilizer Group, Inc. (299)
Immunex Corporation (300)
Information Resources, Inc. (301)
Inova Health Systems (302)
Insilco Corporation (303)
Institute for Defense Analyses (304)
Institute of International Education
  (305)
Intermountain Health Care, Inc. (306)
International Dairy Queen, Inc. (307)
International Game Technology (308)
IPSCO Inc. (309)
ISO Commercial Risk Services, Inc.
  (310)

James Irvine Foundation (311)
JCPenney Company, Inc. (312)
Jewish Hospitals, Inc. (313)
John Hancock Financial Services (314)
John H. Harland Company (315)
John S. and James L. Knight
  Foundation (316)
Johns Hopkins Health System (317)
Johnson & Higgins (318)
Johnson & Johnson (319)
Johnson Controls, Inc. (320)
Jordan Motors (321)
Jostens, Inc. (322)

Kaiser Foundation Health Plan, Inc.
  (323)
Kash n' Karry Food Stores (324)

Kaufman and Broad Home Corporation (325)
Kellogg Company (326)
Kemper Corporation (327)
Keystone International, Inc. (328)
Kmart Corporation (329)
Knight-Ridder, Inc. (330)
Knights of Columbus (331)
Kohl's Department Stores (332)
The Kroger Company (333)
KZF Incorporated (334)

Lands' End, Inc. (335)
Lee County Electric Cooperative, Inc. (336)
Lee Enterprises, Incorporated (337)
Leo Burnett Company, Inc. (338)
Levi Strauss & Co. (339)
Levitz Furniture (340)
Liberty National Bank and Trust Company (341)
Lila Wallace-Reader's Digest Fund, Inc. (342)
Lillian Vernon Corporation (343)
Lilly Endowment Inc. (344)
Long Island Lighting Company (345)
Long John Silver's Inc. (346)
LSI Industries Inc. (347)
Lukens Inc. (348)

Maclean Hunter Limited (349)
Magma Copper Company (350)
Manitoba Hydro (351)
Manitoba Telephone System (352)
March of Dimes (353)
Marin Community Foundation (354)
Marion Merrell Dow, Inc. (355)
Maritz, Inc. (356)
Marriott Corporation (357)
Mary Kay Cosmetics, Inc. (358)
Maxtor Corp. (359)
Mayo Foundation (360)
McCormick & Company, Inc. (361)
McKesson Corporation (362)
The McKnight Foundation (363)

McSwain Carpets, Inc. (364)
MDS Health Group Limited (365)
MDU Resources Group, Inc. (366)
Mead Corporation (367)
Medica (Physicians Health Plan of Minnesota) (368)
Medtronic, Inc. (369)
Merck & Co., Inc. (370)
Merrill Lynch & Co., Inc. (371)
Methodist Hospital of Indiana, Inc. (372)
Methodist Hospital System (373)
Metropolitan Financial Corporation (374)
Metters Industries, Inc. (375)
Michigan Consolidated Gas Company (MichCon Gas Company) (376)
Mid-American Waste Systems, Inc. (377)
Minnkota Power Cooperative, Inc. (378)
Modern Technologies Corp. (379)
Modular Casework Systems Inc. (380)
Mohawk Oil Canada Limited (381)
Molson Companies Limited (382)
Monenco AGRA Inc. (383)
Moon Lake Electric Association, Inc. (385)
Mosler Inc. (386)
Moto Photo, Inc. (387)
Motorola Inc. (388)
Multimedia, Inc. (389)
Municipal Bond Investors Assurance Corporation (390)

Nalco Chemical Company (391)
Nash Finch Company (392)
National Association of Manufacturers (393)
National Association of Postal Supervisors (394)
National Association of Realtors ® (395)
National Association of Securities Dealers, Inc. (396)

National Audubon Society (397)
National Collegiate Athletic
    Association (398)
National Education Association (399)
National Gallery of Art (400)
National Geographic Society (401)
National Rifle Association (402)
National Westminster Bancorp (403)
National Wildlife Federation (404)
Nationwide Mutual Insurance
    Company (405)
The Nature Conservancy (406)
Nebraska Municipal Power Pool (407)
Nevada Power Company (408)
New Brunswick Power Corporation
    (409)
New England Electric System (410)
New England Medical Center Hospitals
    (411)
New England Mutual Life Insurance
    Company (412)
New Science Associates, Inc. (413)
New York Blood Center, Inc. (414)
New York Public Library (415)
New York State Electric & Gas
    Corporation (416)
Niagara Mohawk Power Corporation
    (417)
Noranda Inc. (418)
Nordson Corporation (419)
Norfolk Southern Corporation (420)
Northrop Corporation (421)
Northwest Airlines, Inc. (422)
Northwest Area Foundation (423)
The North West Company, Inc. (424)
Northwestern Memorial Hospital (425)
Northwestern Mutual Life Insurance
    Company (426)
Norwest Corporation (427)
NovaCare Inc. (428)
Nowsco Well Service Limited (429)
NWNL Companies (430)
NYNEX Corporation (431)

Ocean Spray Cranberries, Inc. (432)
Office Depot, Inc. (433)
Ohio Casualty Insurance Company
    (434)
Oklahoma Natural Gas Company (435)
Orlando Regional Healthcare System
    (436)
Outboard Marine Corporation (437)
Owens-Corning Fiberglas Corporation
    (438)

PacifiCare ® Health Systems, Inc.
    (439)
Pacific Mutual Life (440)
Parker Drilling Company (441)
Parker Hannifin Corporation (442)
Parkland Industries Ltd. (443)
The Partnership Group, Inc. (444)
Paychex ®, Inc. (445)
Pennsylvania Power & Light Company
    (446)
Pepsico, Inc. (447)
Perkin-Elmer Corporation (448)
Phelps Dodge Corporation (449)
Philip Morris Companies, Inc. (450)
Phillips Petroleum Company (451)
Pioneer Hi-Bred International, Inc.
    (452)
Pitney Bowes Inc. (453)
Plourde Computer Systems, Inc. (454)
Potlatch Corporation (455)
PPG Industries, Inc. (456)
Premier Bank, N.A. (457)
Preston Trucking Company, Inc. (458)
Price Waterhouse (459)
Prima Communications, Inc. (460)
Procter & Gamble Company (461)
Progressive Corp. (462)
Promus Companies Incorporated (463)
PSI Energy, Inc. (464)
Public Broadcasting Service (465)
Public Service Company of Colorado
    (466)
Public Service Company of New
    Mexico (467)

Public Service Company of Oklahoma (468)
Puget Sound Power & Light Company (469)

Quaker Oats Company (470)
Quaker State Corporation (471)
QuikTrip Corporation (472)
Quintiles Transnational Corp. (473)

Raley's Inc. (474)
RAND (475)
Raychem Corporation (476)
Redken Laboratories, Inc. (477)
Rhode Island Hospital (478)
Rhône-Poulenc Rorer, Inc. (479)
Rich Products Corporation (480)
Ritz-Carlton ® Hotel Company (481)
RJR Nabisco Inc. (482)
Roadway Services, Inc. (483)
Robbins & Myers, Inc. (484)
The Robert R. McCormick Tribune Foundation (485)
Robert Wood Johnson Foundation (486)
Rochester Gas and Electric Corporation (487)
Rochester Telephone Corp. (488)
Rockwell International Corporation (489)
Rohm and Haas Company (490)
Rollins, Inc. (491)
Royal LePage Limited (492)
RR Donnelley & Sons Company (493)
Rubbermaid Incorporated (494)
Rush-Presbyterian-St. Luke's Medical Center (495)
Ryder System, Inc. (496)
Ryland Group, Inc. (497)

Safety-Kleen Corp. (498)
Safeway Inc. (499)
St. John Medical Center (500)
St. Jude Children's Research Hospital (501)

St. Paul Companies, Inc. (502)
Salvation Army (503)
San Francisco Foundation (504)
Sara Lee Corporation (505)
Saskatchewan Oil and Gas Corporation (506)
Saskatchewan Wheat Pool (507)
Save the Children (508)
SCEcorp (Southern California Edison) (509)
Schneider National, Inc. (510)
Seagram Company Limited (511)
Sematech (512)
Sentara Health System (513)
ServiceMaster Company Limited Partnership (514)
SERVISTAR Corporation (515)
Shaw Industries, Inc. (516)
Shell Oil Company (517)
Shoney's Inc. (518)
Sierra Club (519)
Sisters of Providence (520)
Skillman Foundation (521)
Smith International, Inc. (522)
Smithsonian Institution (523)
Snap-on Tools Corporation (524)
Software Spectrum Inc. (525)
Sonoco Products Company (526)
Southern Company (527)
Southern Indiana Gas and Electric Company (528)
Southern National Corp. (529)
The Southland Corporation (530)
Southwest Airlines Co. (531)
Southwest Gas Corporation (532)
Special Libraries Association (533)
The Spencer Foundation (534)
Sprint Corp. (535)
SPX Corporation (536)
SRI International (537)
Standard Federal Bank (538)
Stanford University Hospital (539)
The Stanley Works (540)
Staples, Inc. (541)

State Street Bank and Trust Company (542)
Steelcase Inc. (543)
Stelco Inc. (544)
Storage Technology Corporation (545)
Stride Rite Corporation (546)
Student Loan Marketing Association (547)
Sun Company, Inc. (548)
Sundstrand Corporation (549)
Supervalu Inc. (550)
Sutter Health Inc. (551)
Symmetrix Inc. (552)
Synergen, Inc. (553)
Syntex Corporation (554)

Tambrands ® Inc. (555)
Team Bankshares, Inc. (556)
Tektronix Inc. (557)
Telesat Canada (558)
TELUS Corp. (559)
Tembec Inc. (560)
Texaco Inc. (561)
Texas Industries, Inc. (562)
Texas Instruments (563)
Thiokol Corporation (564)
Tiffany & Co. (565)
Times Mirror Company (566)
Timken Company (567)
Toro Company (568)
Toromont Industries Ltd. (569)
Toronto Hydro-Electric System (570)
Tracor, Inc. (571)
TransAlta Utilities Corporation (572)
TransCanada Pipelines (573)
Tribune Company (574)
TRW Inc. (575)

Unifax Inc. (576)
Unilever United States, Inc. (577)
Union Carbide Corp. (578)
United Airlines Inc. (579)
United Farm Workers of America AFL-CIO (580)

United Food and Commercial Workers International Union, AFL-CIO (581)
United Grain Growers Limited (582)
United Parcel Service (583)
United States Air Force (584)
United States Central Intelligence Agency (585)
United States Junior Chamber of Commerce (586)
United Van Lines, Inc. (587)
Universal Foods Corporation (588)
Upjohn Company (589)
USAir Group, Inc. (590)
U.S. Bancorp (591)
U.S. Bioscience (592)
U.S. Chamber of Commerce (593)
U.S. Shoe Corp. (594)
U S West, Inc. (595)
UtiliCorp United Inc. (596)

Vanguard Cellular Systems, Inc. ® (597)
Varian Associates (598)
VIA Rail Canada, Inc. (599)
The Vons Companies, Inc. (600)

Wachovia Corporation (601)
Wallace Computer Services, Inc. (602)
Wang Laboratories, Inc. (603)
Waste Management, Inc. (604)
Waverly, Inc. (605)
Weirton Steel Corporation (606)
Wendy's International, Inc. (607)
Western Publishing Group, Inc. (608)
Western Resources, Inc. (609)
Weyerhaeuser Co. (610)
WGBH Educational Foundation (611)
Wheeling-Pittsburgh Steel Corporation (612)
Whirlpool Corporation (613)
William and Flora Hewlett Foundation (614)
William Penn Foundation (615)
Wisconsin Electric Power Company (616)

W.K. Kellogg Foundation (617)
W.L. Gore & Associates, Inc. (618)
Woods Hole Oceanographic Institution (619)
Woolworth Corporation (620)

World Vision International (621)
WPL Holdings, Inc. (622)
W.W. Grainger, Inc. (623)

XCAN Grain Pool Limited (624)

PART II

Mission Statements

Headnote

Entries are arranged alphabetically letter by letter. Company names consisting of more than one word are alphabetized as if they are one word (spaces are ignored). For example, AM International follows Amax Gold.

Acronyms are interfiled with other entries beginning with the same letter and not placed at the beginning of that letter's entries.

A

AARP
see American Association of Retired Persons (19)

1. **Abbott Northwestern Hospital**
   800 East 28th Street at Chicago Avenue; Minneapolis, MN
   55407-3799
   (612) 863-4000
   Industry: 80—Hospital

   Mission Statement

   Abbott Northwestern Hospital is a private, not for profit health care provider committed to meeting the health care needs of the communities we serve.

   Our primary purpose is care and service to our patients, supported by clinical research and education.

   Abbott Northwestern Hospital with its medical staff strives to be the best provider of cost effective, comprehensive health care through dedication to quality, service and value.

   Revised 1989

2. **Ace Hardware Corporation**
   2200 Kensington Court; Oak Brook, IL 60521
   (708) 990-6600
   Industry: 50, 52—Hardware wholesale and retail

   Mission Statement

   The Ace corporate mission is to be a retail support company . . . providing independent Ace dealers with quality products, programs and services. The philosophies of low up-front pricing and highly efficient, productive management will always guide our basic operating decisions.

   We are committed to offering the best overall program to our dealers. To do so, we must maintain our market share and expand it where possible by supporting our existing dealers, as well as broadening our dealer base, where necessary.

We are also committed to understanding the dynamics of retailing, the effects of competition and the importance of communication with Ace dealers. We are here to serve the Ace dealer, and we know our success is based on that independent dealer's success.

April, 1988

3. **Advanced Micro Devices, Inc.**
    901 Thompson Place; P.O. Box 3453; Sunnyvale, CA 94088-3453
    (408) 749-3938
    Industry: 36—Semiconductors and integrated circuits

    Mission Statement

    The company's primary mission today is to supply the manufacturers of equipment for personal and networked computation and communication with solutions executed in submicron CMOS silicon. These solutions include hardware and software development and support tools.

1992

AFLAC Inc.
   see American Family Life Assurance Company of Columbus (23)

AFL-CIO
   see American Federation of Labor and Congress of Industrial Organizations (24)

4. **A.G. Edwards & Sons, Inc.**
    One North Jefferson; St. Louis, MO 63103
    (314) 289-3070
    Industry: 62—Securities dealers

    MISSION STATEMENT

    Our purpose is to furnish financial services of value to our clients. We should act as their agents, putting their interests before our own.

    We are confident that if we do our jobs well and give value for what we charge, not only will mutual trust and respect develop, but satisfaction and a fair reward will result.

    ETHICS STATEMENT

    The highest standard of ethical conduct is expected of all A.G. Edwards personnel. When faced with possible conflicts of interests, we should give preference to the client and the firm over personal interests. We should not, without management approval, use the firm or our positions in it for personal gain other than our direct compensation.

OPERATING PHILOSOPHIES

During 1968 and '69, our top management team spent two days a month for 24 months developing a model of the firm we wanted to be and to which we were determined to commit our careers and our capital. We agreed that building this firm would take precedence over our concerns for our personal estates or positions.

We committed ourselves to delivering financial services of value to a market we called the "mass, class market" through a network of retail branches acting as agent for the customer. We wanted to be customer-driven, and the agency relationship meant that our first allegiance had to be to the client. We should eliminate any profit centers or incentives that conflicted with the welfare or interest of the client. We realized that this plan would not allow us to manufacture our own financial products.

We recognize that the most important relationship in our business is a bond of trust between the client and the investment broker, and we should build and strengthen this relationship. If we are to be customer-driven, we must listen to our customers and be conscious of their interests in all our decisions.

Our growth should come naturally and involve only people of high character who share our philosophy of putting the customer first. Only after we have found better-than-average quality and a philosophical fit should we then look toward viability.

Profit is not the purpose of our business and should not be sought for its own sake. Rather, it is a necessity if we are to be able to continue to deliver value to our clients, so we must be careful to do what we have chosen to do in a manner that is efficient and cost-effective. We should be more concerned with the client than with the competitor.

It is one of our corporate objectives to have fun. To enjoy what we are doing, we must like those with whom we work. In order to do this, we must respect each other and work together in mutual trust. To encourage trust, we must strive for completely open communication: management must not keep secrets and must not be defensive when criticized. We must foster an atmosphere that encourages fellow employees to speak candidly and without fear of reprisal. How else can we learn?

It is important for all of us to remember why we are here and to be careful to deliver value to our customers for what we charge them. We should try to do our jobs better each week and to have fun doing them.

Ben Edwards
December, 1991

5. **AGRA Industries Limited**
   2233 Argentia Road, Suite 400; Mississauga, Ontario; Canada
   L5N 2X7
   (416) 858-8000
   Industry: 20, 87—Food and engineering services

AGRA's Mission

AGRA Industries Limited is a diversified international company dedicated to growth and enhancement of shareholders' value through professional management of services in Engineering, Environment, Construction and Technology, and Resource Recovery and Recycling.

We are committed to our Customers, to our Employees, to our Shareholders, to Society and to our Environment. We will encourage Innovation, Professional Excellence and the Highest Standards of Business Practice in all our endeavours.

See also Monenco AGRA Inc. (383)

AGT
   see TELUS Corp. (559)

Air Force
   see United States Air Force (584)

6. **Alabama Electric Cooperative, Inc.**
   P.O. Box 550; Andalusia, AL 36420
   (205) 222-2571
   Industry: 49—Electric cooperative

MISSION STATEMENT:

The long-range strategy of Alabama Electric Cooperative, Inc., shall be primarily directed to providing an economical and reliable power supply for our members through purchase, generation and transmission of electric energy. However, increasing emphasis shall be placed on protecting our environment and developing and providing energy-related services for the wise use of electricity. These efforts will support achievement of long-range system unification strategies and improve the quality of member services.

7. **Alberta Wheat Pool**
   P.O. Box 2700; 505 Second Street, SW; Calgary, Alberta;
     Canada T2P 2P5
   (403) 290-4736
   Industry: 51—Grain wholesale

Alberta Pool® Mission Statement

Together, our Mission is to competitively produce, process and aggressively market diverse, world class agricultural products, and to respond to the changing demands of our customers and our environment with integrity so we share in an enhanced social and economic future.

Our Vision Is:

To build on the values, principles and uniqueness of our co-operative enterprise.

To give all people in our organization the opportunity to build and use their skills and knowledge in work that has meaning in a climate where trust and co-operation prevail.

To be the leading agribusiness, consistently knowing what farmers value, meeting their expectations, and by contacting and keeping new farmer customers.

To link farmers to world customers, thus creating opportunity for farmers and their business.

To combine the excellence of our farmer members and all Alberta Pool® staff to deliver together as a team what no one person and no one group could deliver alone—food for the world.

8. **Albertson's, Inc.**
   250 Parkcenter Boulevard; P.O. Box 20; Boise, ID 83726
   208-385-6200
   Industry: 54—Supermarkets

Corporate Operating Philosophy

Albertson's is engaged in the business of operating retail food and drug stores with integrated distribution and manufacturing facilities to support the retail effort for the purpose of satisfying consumer needs. To fulfill this service, we must provide the customer:

(1) Distinctive quality and personalized service in all perimeter departments;

(2) Helpful friendly service throughout the store;

(3) Fast, clean, one-stop convenience;

(4) Attractive, competitive prices;

(5) Conveniently laid out, well stocked grocery and drug departments with good selection of regular and seasonal merchandise.

Albertson's is, in effect, a big store with a specialty store approach. We must be "big" in terms of low prices, convenience and wide selection of brands. We must be a "specialty" store in terms of quality, personal service, and specialized selection. All programs, plans and actions initiated and implemented by all personnel should have the objective of satisfying the above criteria.

Albertson's Corporate Creed

Customers—Albertson's Corporate Philosophy is to give our Customers the merchandise they want at affordable prices, with friendly, efficient service in clean, attractive stores.

Employees—In support of this philosophy, we are committed to our employees' success and well-being and endeavor to provide the business climate and resources to maintain a productive, satisfied, work force that is dedicated to taking care of our Customers' needs.

Community—We endeavor to be good corporate citizens in the communities in which we operate through practicing good business ethics and through Corporate and Employee participation in civic and charitable responsibilities.

Shareholders—Our business decisions and strategic plans are predicated upon providing our shareholders with a long term and sustained return on their capital investment.

Suppliers—We recognize the extreme importance of our loyal suppliers who provide the products, goods and services that permit our continued growth and service to our Customers and work to insure a fair and mutually satisfactory business relationship.

Management—We place great importance on continuing to attract, develop and maintain the high caliber of Management required to fulfill the needs of all our above constituents.

9. **Alcan Aluminium Limited**
   1188 Sherbrooke Street West; Montreal, Quebec; Canada H3A 3G2
   (514) 848-8000
   Industry: 33—Aluminum

Alcan will be the most innovative aluminum company in the world. Through its people, Alcan will be a global, customer-oriented and environmentally responsible enterprise committed to excellence and lowest cost in its chosen aluminum and related businesses. In the 1990s, Alcan's return-on-equity target is to outperform the Standard & Poor's Industrials.

Revised 1990

10. **Alex Lee, Inc.**
    P.O. Box 800; Hickory, NC 28603
    (704) 323-4475
    Industry: 51, 54—Food wholesale and supermarkets

Alex Lee, Inc.

PURPOSE

We feed people. We are a vital link in the food chain. We provide a plentiful, continuous & affordable variety of food and related products.

MISSION

Alex Lee will be acknowledged by our customers, employees, suppliers and shareholders as the dominant food company in each of the markets in which we compete. This will be accomplished by continually striving for excellence in all we do, by being proactive, and by delivering what our customers want in products and services 100% of the time.

OUR VALUES

Customers are the focus of everything we do. Our commitment is to redefine our service quality to exceed customer requirements, the first time and every time. We pledge to listen constantly to our customers and to be flexible in meeting their needs and concerns.

Employees are the strength of our company. We encourage and expect all employees to grow personally and professionally on a daily basis. We will work together as a team and treat each other with integrity, honesty, trust, and respect.

Continuous quality improvement and the elimination of unnecessary costs are our way of life. Our work environment will promote open communication, participation and innovation.

Profits are key to our survival and growth. We will achieve a satisfactory return on investment and a competitive edge by being a low cost provider.

August 29, 1992

MDI MISSION (Merchants Distributors, Inc.)
[Subsidiary of Alex Lee, Inc.]

MDI will double our market share within a 200 mile radius of Hickory by the year 2000.

The primary focus of MDI is growing successful supermarket retailers by:

1. Providing the best procurement and distribution of goods—in our trade area
2. The best retailer support and services in our industry
3. Developing the finest perishable programs in our trade area
4. Helping our retailers to be on the leading edge of our industry in automation and technology
5. Being pro-active in:

    a. Developing viable formats for our customers
    b. Helping our customers to meet the needs of the consumers in their trade area while constantly searching and responding to new consumer trends and needs
    c. Develop the best locations in our markets
    d. Dominate our home market (Hickory)
  6. Continuing to second supply chain stores where it makes sense and provide economies of scale

September 28, 1992

LOWES VISION
[Subsidiary of Alex Lee, Inc.]

To run our stores so well that customers make Lowes foods their primary place to shop.

1990

IFH STRATEGIC VISION
[Subsidiary of Alex Lee, Inc.]

To consistently and profitably provide products (and services) to foodservice customers in such a fashion that the majority of their purchases are from IFH.

May 21, 1991

11. **Algoma Central Corporation**
    P.O. Box 7000; 289 Bay Street; Sault Ste. Marie, Ontario;
      Canada P6A 5P6
    (705) 949-2113
    Industry: 40—Railroad

ALGOMA CENTRAL RAILWAY
[Subsidiary of Algoma Central Corporation]

OUR VISION

A team of quality railroaders achieving excellence in customer service and dedicated to growth and prosperity.

OUR VALUES

- Customer satisfaction through excellence in friendly, reliable, competitive service.
- Human Resources:
  - treating co-workers with respect, dignity and fairness
  - a healthy and productive working environment
  - fostering teamwork, co-operation and participative communication
  - fair compensation to all employees

- providing opportunities for personal development, growth and advancement
- encouraging, recognizing and rewarding innovative ideas, leadership and outstanding performance
- recognizing that each individual, through the responsible performance of his or her duties makes a valuable contribution to the success of the Rail Division
- A safe work place for the protection of all employees and the public.
- Conducting all activities honestly and ethically.
- Innovation and improved productivity toward retention and expansion of business opportunities.
- Striving for profits and reinvestment to maintain a modern operation and to provide reasonable investor return.

OUR COMMITMENT

We at the Rail Division of the ACR are committed to the consistent application of the principles contained in our Values and the realization of our Vision.

12. **Allied-Signal, Inc.**
P.O. Box 2245; Morristown, NJ 07962-2245
(201) 455-4674
Industry: 28, 30, 37—Chemicals, rubber, and aerospace

Our Vision

We will be one of the world's premier companies, distinctive and successful in everything we do.

Our Commitment

We will become a Total Quality Company by continuously improving all our work processes to satisfy our internal and external customers.

Our Values

Customers—Our first priority is to satisfy customers.

Integrity—We are committed to the highest level of ethical conduct wherever we operate. We obey all laws, produce safe products, protect the environment, practice equal employment, and are socially responsible.

People—We help our fellow employees improve their skills, encourage them to take risks, treat them fairly, and recognize their accomplishments, stimulating them to approach their jobs with passion and commitment.

Teamwork—We build trust and worldwide teamwork with open, candid communications up and down and across our organization. We share technologies and best practices, and team with our suppliers and customers.

Speed—We focus on speed for competitive advantage. We simplify processes and compress cycle times.

Innovation—We accept change as the rule, not the exception, and drive it by encouraging creativity and striving for technical leadership.

Performance—We encourage high expectations, set ambitious goals, and meet our financial and other commitments. We strive to be the best in the world.

Drafted September, 1991

13. **ALZA Corporation**
     950 Page Mill Road; P.O. Box 10950; Palo Alto, CA 94303-0802
     (415) 494-5000
     Industry: 28—Pharmaceuticals

ALZA'S MISSION

ALZA's mission is to be the world leader in the development, manufacture and sale of therapeutic systems, thereby providing high quality therapy for important human and veterinary applications. ALZA shall provide: significant therapeutic contributions to society, high quality products to its customers, a challenging and rewarding environment for its employees, and substantial rewards to its investors.

VALUES

In carrying out our mission, ALZA is guided by respect for people, quality in our products, and sustained profitability, as essential values. Every employee has the responsibility to ensure our collective commitment to this value system, and to the Company's Guiding Principles.

GUIDING PRINCIPLES

-    Maintain quality as an essential component of all our efforts—intellectually, interpersonally, and in the products and services we provide to our colleagues and customers.

-    Extend ALZA's leadership in all areas of therapeutic systems through both internal R&D and acquisition of innovative ideas, or organizations.

-    Provide leadership regarding the manner in which pharmaceutical products are defined, developed, registered, and presented to their users.

-    Maximize ALZA's royalty stream by the systematic support of our clients at all stages in the product selection, development, and marketing processes.

-    Maintain a safe and professional environment that provides stimulation, excitement, respect, and enjoyment for every member of the organization.

- Eliminate or minimize any and all waste generated by, and waste emissions or discharges resulting from, our Corporate activities.
- Achieve sustained growth in corporate profitability via creativity, innovation, productivity, and hard work.

14. **Amax Gold Inc.**
    350 Indiana Street; Golden, CO 80401-5081
    (303) 273-0600
    Industry: 10—Gold mining

AGI'S MISSION IS QUALITY

Quality at Amax Gold is a team of professionals dedicated to dynamic growth by increasing low cost production and reserves, for the maximum benefit of our shareholders, in harmony with the world around us.

Quality. . . . the Driving Force!

CORE VALUES

- Excellence
- Integrity
- Cooperation, respect and caring
- Profit motivation
- Environmental responsibility
- Safety consciousness

MANAGEMENT PHILOSOPHY

- Provide vision, direction and motivation
- Assure a safe work environment
- Adhere to the Amax Gold Core Values and set an example for others
- Listen to other employees and promote two-way communication
- Attack problems, not people
- Create an environment that encourages innovation and improvement
- Delegate to the lowest effective level
- Recognize performance
- Require accountability and be accountable
- Act professionally and expect it of others
- Be a team player who encourages teamwork
- Inspire enthusiasm
- Cultivate trustworthiness
- Demonstrate accessibility and involvement
- Support the organization and your colleagues
- Acknowledge mistakes, correct them and learn from the experience

- Foster employee development
- Ensure a balance of life and work

Drafted June, 1990

15. **Ambulatory Medical Care, Inc.**
     935 State Route 28; Milford, OH 45150
     (513) 831-5955
     Industry: 80—Outpatient clinics

VALUE STATEMENT

AmCare believes in the dignity of every person and appreciates the unique qualities that distinguish one from another. As such we will treat everyone fairly, ethically and with respect. This fosters an environment of accountability, creativity and excellence.

MISSION STATEMENT

AmCare's focus is to provide high quality, cost-effective and efficiently managed healthcare services in the areas of ambulatory care, occupational medicine and other non hospital-based services. As a team of highly motivated individuals, we are committed to excellent care and service.

The ability to respond to the rapidly changing healthcare needs of society is the key to AmCare's growth. We will manage this growth through the expansion of existing services, prudent acquisitions and development of new products and services. Our success will be measured by the degree to which our actions enhance profitability and foster mutually beneficial stakeholder relationships.

Revised 1991

STAKEHOLDER RELATIONSHIPS

AmCare's mission demands a common belief in excellence, accountability, and mutually beneficial relationships with all stakeholders:

PATIENTS AND CLIENTS

We will strive to exceed our patients' and clients' expectations. We will provide care that affirms:
- the dignity and self worth of the individual.
- empathy and compassion.
- sound and ethical medical practice.
- confidentiality of treatment.
- promptness.
- a high value/price relationship.

EMPLOYEES

Employees are our most valued assets. We will:
- respect each employee as an individual, and a team member.
- provide a stimulating work environment.
- provide fair compensation.
- encourage personal and professional development.
- demand accountability for individual action.

STOCKHOLDERS

We recognize our responsibility to the stockholders. We will:
- strive to increase the value of their investment.
- keep them informed about matters of strategic importance.
- focus our efforts on the long-term prosperity of the company.

VENDORS/SUPPLIERS/andTHIRD PARTY PAYORS

These relationships must be founded on:
- honesty.
- mutual respect.
- sound business practices.

COMMUNITY

We recognize our responsibility to the community and the environment.
We will:
- operate in an environmentally sound manner.
- be active participants in the community.

AmCare
see Ambulatory Medical Care, Inc. (15)

16. **Amcast Industrial Corporation**
3931 South Dixie Avenue; Kettering, OH 45439
(513) 298-5251
Industry: 34—Valves

Mission Statement

The primary mission of Amcast Industrial Corporation is to fulfill market needs more effectively than competitors in order to provide a competitive return to shareholders through increases in the value of their shares and a consistent dividend policy.

AMD
see Advanced Micro Devices, Inc. (3)

17. **Amdahl Corporation**
    1250 East Arques Avenue; P.O. Box 3470; Sunnyvale, CA
    94088-3470
    (408) 746-3100
    Industry: 35—Computers

MISSION STATEMENT

To respond to the central business issues of our large-systems customers by giving them choices through the delivery of an innovative, leading-edge product set.

VALUES

Customer Problems Are Our Problems

Because we strive to establish long-term relationships with our customers, we take their needs and requirements seriously. We have an obligation to maintain the highest standards of product performance, value, and service. To do this we must:
- Listen closely to our customers to understand their needs.
- Make the satisfaction of our customers' needs our primary mission.

We Do It Better

We seek innovative ways to apply advanced technologies to products that are recognized for their quality, performance, and value. Our success derives from products and services that earn us the respect and loyalty of our customers. To earn this we must:
- Accept the risks of long-term research and development.
- Be a leader in providing innovative technological advances.
- Deliver products and services that are competitively priced, conform to requirements, and provide more value.

People Are the Company

The ability, commitment, and enthusiasm of our people are central to the success of our company. We continuously strive to develop and encourage these qualities. Therefore, we must:
- Attract exceptional people who will work together to produce superior products and services.
- Treat our people with honesty, fairness, and consideration.
- Provide a challenging environment that encourages growth and personal satisfaction.
- Encourage our people to be productive, take initiative, and be innovative.
- Expect every individual to take responsibility for quality products and services.

Everybody's Contribution Is Valued

Our performance as an organization is dependent on the maximum individual and collective efforts of our people. Therefore, our managers must:

- Treat our employees, customers, vendors, and stockholders with honesty and integrity.
- Practice a management style that is participative, disciplined, and systematic.
- Support responsible risk taking by our employees.
- Reward outstanding accomplishments and innovations.

We Are Financially Responsible

Profit and growth are essential Amdahl objectives because they allow our continued business success. These are achieved through responsible actions. Therefore, our managers must:

- Ensure that the risks and costs of an endeavor arc commensurate with the potential rewards.
- Seek to maximize the return on our investments.
- Provide an attractive return to our shareholders.

Amdahl Is a Good Citizen

It is vital to our success that the communities in which we operate grant us the ability to prosper, an environment in which to attract outstanding people, and give fair consideration to our plans. In return we strive to be good citizens and to contribute to every community where we do business. This means that we must:

- Conduct our business with the highest ethics and integrity.
- Contribute our resources, time, and talent to community improvement.
- Offer equal employment and advancement opportunities.

Quality, innovation, and caring are the hallmarks of the Amdahl philosophy. These characterize our dealings with our employees, customers, stockholders, and the communities where we work and live.

18. **American Association of Museums**
     1225 Eye Street, NW; Washington, DC 20005
     (202) 289-1818
     Industry: 86—Museum association

The American Association of Museums (AAM) is the national organization that represents the museum community and addresses its needs, thereby enhancing the ability of museums to serve the public. Established in 1906, the AAM has four major goals:

To lead the effort to promote **professional standards** by improving the quality of museum programs, services, and operations;

To be a **representative and advocate** for museums by promoting understanding of the responsibilities, functions, and needs of museums before government, corporate, foundation, and community leaders throughout the nation;

To provide **professional development** opportunities for museum professionals, trustees, and volunteers through publications, meetings, and other activities; and

To provide **member services** that give members access to selected goods and services which are more economically priced or which might otherwise be unavailable to them.

19.   **American Association of Retired Persons**
      601 E Street, NW; Washington, DC 20049
      (202) 434-2277
      Industry: 86—Membership organization

OUR VISION

Bringing lifetimes of experience and leadership to serve all generations.

OUR MISSION

AARP is a nonprofit membership organization of persons 50 and older dedicated to addressing their needs and interests. We seek through education, advocacy and service to enhance the quality of life for all by promoting independence, dignity and purpose.

OUR VALUES AND BELIEFS

LIFELONG DEVELOPMENT

Aging is a lifelong process of development.

DIGNITY AND INDEPENDENCE

A person's right to make decisions affecting his or her life does not diminish with age.

MEMBER EMPOWERMENT

Our members and volunteers contribute to each other and to all of society from an abundance of talent, leadership, experience and wisdom. They are empowered through education and service opportunities.

RESPONSIBILITY

AARP responds to its members' needs with a balanced consideration of our entire society's interests, with sensitivity to those most in need.

EXCELLENCE

Excellence must characterize all of our activities in serving our members, our volunteer colleagues, our staff and our society.

INTEGRITY

All our activities and dealings will be based on a foundation of honesty and truthfulness.

OUR GOALS

QUALITY SERVICE

Provide quality service to our members, communities, volunteers and staff.

HEALTH AND LONG-TERM CARE FOR ALL

Lead in achieving universal access to comprehensive, affordable health and long-term care.

WORK OPPORTUNITIES

Enhance dignity and equality in the work place through positive attitudes, practices and policies toward work and retirement.

ECONOMIC SECURITY

Reduce poverty and promote economic security for individuals as they age.

QUALITY RESEARCH

Conduct and support research to understand how best to meet the needs of an aging population.

EFFECTIVE OPERATIONS

Employ tools, methods, applications, processes and systems that enable AARP to maximize the effectiveness of its volunteers, staff, technological and fiscal resources.

MOTTO

"To serve, not to be served"

May, 1991

20. **American Bar Association**
    541 North Fairbanks Court; Chicago, IL 60611-3314
    (312) 988-5000
    Industry: 86—Membership organization

ABA MISSION AND GOALS

The mission of the American Bar Association is to be the national representative of the legal profession, serving the public and the profession by promoting justice, professional excellence and respect for the law.

Drafted 1990

GOAL I To promote improvements in the American system of justice.

GOAL II To promote meaningful access to legal representation and the American system of justice for all persons regardless of their economic or social condition.

GOAL III To provide ongoing leadership in improving the law to serve the changing needs of society.

GOAL IV To increase public understanding of and respect for the law, the legal process, and the role of the legal profession.

GOAL V To achieve the highest standards of professionalism, competence, and ethical conduct.

GOAL VI To serve as the national representative of the legal profession.

GOAL VII To provide benefits, programs and services which promote professional growth and enhance the quality of life of the members.

GOAL VIII To advance the rule of law in the world.

GOAL IX To promote full and equal participation in the legal profession by minorities and women.

GOAL X To preserve and enhance the ideals of the legal profession as a common calling and its dedication to public service.

GOAL XI To preserve the independence of the legal profession and the judiciary as fundamental to a free society.

21. **American Bureau of Shipping & Affiliated Companies**
Two World Trade Center, 106th Floor; New York, NY 10048
(212) 839-5000
Industry: 86—Membership organization

MISSION

The mission of the American Bureau of Shipping is to serve the public interest as well as the needs of our clients by promoting the security of life, property and the natural environment primarily through the development and verification of standards for the design, construction and operational maintenance of marine-related facilities.

Drafted Spring 1992

22. **American Cancer Society**
1599 Clifton Road, NE; Atlanta, GA 30329-4251
(404) 329-7909

Industry: 86—Membership organization

Mission Statement

The American Cancer Society is the nationwide community-based voluntary health organization dedicated to eliminating cancer as a major health problem by preventing cancer, saving lives from cancer, and diminishing suffering from cancer through research, education, and service.

Annual Report 1991

Copyright © 1992, American Cancer Society, Inc.

23. **American Family Life Assurance Company of Columbus AFLAC Incorporated**
1932 Wynnton Road; Columbus, GA 31999
(706) 323-3431
Industry: 63—Life and health insurance

MISSION

The principal business of AFLAC U.S. is the provision of innovatively designed and competitively priced supplemental health insurance products to consumers using distribution systems that assure usage of the most effective and appropriate means of product delivery. AFLAC U.S. customers are current and potential policyholders, as well as field management and representatives responsible for delivery of products to those policyholders. The mission of AFLAC U.S. is to combine aggressive strategic marketing with effective and efficient operational management to achieve a position of dominance in the supplemental health insurance industry in respect to quality service to our customers, market share, revenue growth, operational expense containment and profit.

24. **American Federation of Labor and Congress of Industrial Organizations (AFL-CIO)**
815 Sixteenth Street, NW; Washington, DC 20006
(202) 637-5000
Industry: 86—Labor Union

ARTICLE II: OBJECTIVES AND PRINCIPLES

The objectives and principles of this Federation are:

1. To aid workers in securing improved wages, hours and working conditions with due regard for the autonomy, integrity and jurisdiction of affiliated unions.

2. To aid and assist affiliated unions in extending the benefits of mutual assistance and collective bargaining to workers and to promote the organization of the unorganized into unions of their own choosing for their mutual aid, protection and advancement, giving recognition to the principle

that both craft and industrial unions are appropriate, equal and necessary as methods of union organization.

3. To affiliate national and international unions with this Federation and to establish such unions; to form organizing committees and directly affiliated local unions and to secure their affiliation to appropriate national and international unions affiliated with or chartered by the Federation; to establish, assist and promote state and local central bodies composed of local unions of all affiliated organizations and directly affiliated local unions; to establish and assist trade departments composed of affiliated national and international unions and organizing committees.

4. To encourage all workers without regard to race, creed, color, sex, national origin or ancestry to share equally in the full benefits of union organization.

5. To secure legislation which will safeguard and promote the principle of free collective bargaining, the rights of workers, farmers and consumers, and the security and welfare of all the people and to oppose legislation inimical to these objectives.

6. To protect and strengthen our democratic institutions, to secure full recognition and enjoyment of the rights and liberties to which we are justly entitled, and to preserve and perpetuate the cherished traditions of our democracy.

7. To give constructive aid in promoting the cause of peace and freedom in the world and to aid, assist and cooperate with free and democratic labor movements throughout the world.

8. To preserve and maintain the integrity of each affiliated union in the organization to the end that each affiliate shall respect the established bargaining relationships of any other affiliate and that each affiliate shall refrain from raiding the established bargaining relationship of any other affiliate and, at the same time, to encourage the elimination of conflicting and duplicating organizations and jurisdictions through the process of voluntary agreement or voluntary merger in consultation with the appropriate officials of the Federation, to preserve, subject to the foregoing, the organizing jurisdiction of each affiliate.

9. To aid and encourage the sale and use of union made goods and union services through the use of the union label and other symbols; to promote the labor press and other means of furthering the education of the labor movement.

10. To protect the labor movement from any and all corrupt influences and from the undermining efforts of communist agencies and all others who are opposed to the basic principles of our democracy and free and democratic unionism.

11. To safeguard the democratic character of the labor movement and to protect the autonomy of each affiliated national and international union.

12. While preserving the independence of the labor movement from political control, to encourage workers to register and vote, to exercise their full rights and responsibilities of citizenship, and to perform their rightful part in the political life of the local, state and national communities.

Amended 1991

Extracted from *Constitution of the American Federation of Labor and Congress of Industrial Organizations*

25. **American Federation of Teachers**
    555 New Jersey Avenue, NW; Washington, DC 20001
    (202) 879-4400
    Industry: 86—Labor union

AFT'S VISION FOR THE FUTURE

The future we set out to create is an AFT that will expand our leadership role in organizing, collective bargaining, educational programs, and political action to create opportunities for our members to enjoy continual professional development, together with justice, dignity and empowerment at work.

Further, we envision an AFT that is recognized by members and the public at large as a union dedicated both to the well-being of its members and to the people they serve. We envision a membership empowered to improve the quality of their own working lives as well as effectiveness of their service to the public. If public institutions are effective, the public will support them, with the result that members' jobs will be more secure and the union strengthened.

We must win collective bargaining rights for all our members so that there is an opportunity to gain for all the same rights and benefits now enjoyed by the strongest among us. Establishing employment security and fairness at work is the platform for professional development and the basis for cooperative efforts to improve organizational effectiveness. By driving out fear, providing the means for resolving labor-management conflict, and contributing to the knowledge members apply to their work, the AFT will meet the evolving needs of its members and their clients.

To guarantee our future, we must improve not only the working conditions of our members but also the effectiveness of the institutions in which they work. America demands a workforce better prepared to meet the challenge of global competition. At the same time, many people bear the handicaps of poverty, poor nutrition, lack of decent housing and unequal access to quality health care. America will not succeed unless we attend to basic human needs. Children are America's future, and it is they who suffer most when these needs are not met. For ourselves and for the people we serve, we must be concerned with issues such as school reform, better health care for all Americans, child care for working parents, affordable housing, public safety, good transportation and decent employment. The AFT must be able to influence public policy that determines both investment and the administration of public service at the local, state and national levels.

The AFT will gain strength from unity and common goals determined democratically. We shall also gain strength from our diversity.

Each of AFT's constituencies—teachers, higher education faculty and professionals, paraprofessionals and school-related personnel, nurses and health professionals, state and local government employees—shares common goals of professional development, empowerment at work and building more effective institutions. Each must develop its own vision of a better workplace, its own agenda of how to realize this vision.

Likewise, each level of the AFT—local, state and national—must interpret this vision as it relates to its special needs and circumstances. Each level must also recognize its interdependence with, and responsibilities to, the others and work interactively with them.

To help advance this vision, the AFT Futures Committee proposes recommendations based on two interrelated strategic goals:

1. Strengthening the Union:
- Structure and systems that integrate the union across constituencies and at all levels
- Management that effectively implements policy
- Mutually supportive relationships among the national union, state federations and locals
- Effective organizing
- Opportunities for participation by all members in the union in many different ways

2. Serving Locals Effectively:
- Leadership training
- Improved communication of policy, goals and priorities
- Facilitation of organizational learning
- Assistance in workplace transformation

The recommendations are intended to be evolutionary so as to allow opportunities for experimentation and mid-course correction. The AFT must be a union willing to try new approaches and learn from mistakes. This requires the integration and involvement of all levels of the union and all sectors of membership in addressing issues of common concern. The AFT must design policies, programs and services that match the changing values, needs and work environments of members. These policies, programs and services also must be developed and implemented with a high degree of participation by the members they affect. The AFT must ensure that each sector of the membership has a role in decision making at the highest levels of the union. In so doing, the entire AFT will benefit from the contributions of all sectors of its membership, and all members will take pride in the AFT as a democratic union in which they have a real voice.

26. **American Heart Association**
    7272 Greenville Avenue; Dallas, TX 75231-4596
    (214) 373-6300
    Industry: 86—Membership organization

The mission of the American Heart Association is to reduce disability and death from cardiovascular diseases and stroke.

27. **American Hotel & Motel Association**
    1201 New York Avenue, NW; Washington, DC 20005-3931
    (202) 289-3131
    Industry: 86—Membership organization

AH&MA Mission Statement

To provide to state associations and their member properties, representation and cost effective services at the national level in governmental affairs, education, and communications which stimulate and encourage a free market lodging industry.

Adopted April 8, 1990

In Governmental Affairs

A. To identify proposed legislation and regulation that will be unfair and/or harmful to the lodging industry and take actions to defeat the proposal or modify the terms so as to mitigate the effects of that legislation or regulation on the lodging industry.

B. To promote legislation or regulation that will be favorable to the lodging industry.

C. To communicate to members the enactment or proposal of legislation that affect their operations and to educate the members as to actions they should be taking in response to such governmental actions.

In Education

A. It is the responsibility of the AH&MA leadership to establish and ensure that the Educational Institute of AH&MA is the Federation's principal provider of education, training, and certification programs for the lodging industry.

In Communications (Internal & External)

A. To act as the principal national spokesperson for the lodging industry.

B. To collect and disseminate information regarding significant lodging industry developments.

C. To enhance the lodging industry and its impact on the economy by promoting the development of a national travel and tourism policy.

D. To assist the member state associations to increase their membership.

American Lebanese Syrian Associated Charities, Inc.
   see St. Jude Children's Research Hospital (501)

28.   **American Library Association**
      50 East Huron Street; Chicago, IL 60611
      (312) 944-6780
      Industry: 86—Membership organization

1. MISSION, PRIORITY AREAS, GOALS

1.1 INTRODUCTION

Any organization as large, diverse, and dynamic as ALA must periodically reassess priorities in order to make progress in selected areas determined to be of prime concern to its members. The diversity of the membership dictates a wide range of interests that frequently overlap or complement one another. Nonetheless, we can identify overriding priorities that ALA should pursue vigorously within the United States and coordinate with groups abroad. Only such focusing of efforts and the subsequent allocation of Association funds and evaluation of its activities can ensure needed progress within the profession.

ALA recognizes its broad social responsibilities. The broad social responsibilities of the American Library Association are defined in terms of the contribution that librarianship can make in ameliorating or solving the critical problems of society; support for efforts to help inform and educate the people of the United States on these problems and to encourage them to examine the many views on and the facts regarding each problem; and the willingness of ALA to take a position on current critical issues with the relationship to libraries and library service set forth in the position statement.

ALA promotes the creation, maintenance, and enhancement of a learning society, encouraging its members to work with educators, government officials, and organizations in coalitions to initiate and support comprehensive efforts to ensure that school, public, academic, and special libraries in every community cooperate to provide lifelong learning services to all.

1.2 MISSION

The mission of the American Library Association is to provide leadership for the development, promotion, and improvement of library and information services and the profession of librarianship in order to enhance learning and ensure access to information for all.

Approved 1986

29. **American Lung Association**
    1740 Broadway; New York, NY 10019-4374
    (212) 315-8700
    Industry: 86—Membership organization

    The American Lung Association (ALA) is dedicated to fighting lung disease, the third leading cause of death in the U.S., and seeks the eradication and control of tuberculosis and chronic obstructive pulmonary diseases, including chronic bronchitis, asthma, and emphysema. It develops materials and programs for professional publication, research, and advocacy in four major areas: (1) occupational health, (2) clean air conservation, (3) smoking and health, and (4) pulmonary disease.

30. **American Management Association**
    135 West 50th Street; New York, NY 10020
    (212) 903-7915
    Industry: 86—Membership organization

    MISSION STATEMENT:

    American Management Association provides educational forums worldwide where members and their colleagues learn superior, practical business skills and explore best practices of world-class organizations through interaction with each other and expert faculty practitioners. AMA's publishing program provides tools individuals use to extend learning beyond the classroom in a process of life-long professional growth and development through education.

    Effective as of August 3, 1992

31. **American Medical Association**
    515 North State Street; Chicago, IL 60610
    312-464-5629
    Industry: 86—Membership organization

    Constitutional Purpose and Key Objective

    Within the framework of the American Medical Association's constitutional purpose "to promote the science and art of medicine and the betterment of the public health," the Key Objective of the AMA is to foster an environment that supports member physicians' efforts to provide patients with high quality, affordable health care by:

> advocating on behalf of patients and physicians in health policy forums;
>
> promoting self-regulation of the medical profession;
>
> advancing medical science, education, and accreditation; and
>
> disseminating information on the art and science of medicine to the public and the medical community.

Revised April, 1992

32. **American Oil Chemists' Society**
    P.O. Box 3489; Champaign, IL 61826-3489
    (217) 359-2344
    Industry: 86—Membership organization

Mission Statement

To be a forum for the exchange of ideas, information and experience among those with a professional interest in the science and technology of fats, oils and related substances in ways that promote personal excellence and provide a high standard of quality.

33. **American Petroleum Institute**
    1220 L Street, NW; Washington, DC 20005
    (202) 682-8280
    Industry: 86—Membership organization

MISSION

The American Petroleum Institute (API) is the U.S. petroleum industry's primary trade association. API provides public policy development and advocacy, research and technical services to enhance the ability of the petroleum industry to meet its mission which includes:

- meeting the nation's energy needs, developing energy sources, and supplying high-quality products and services;
- enhancing the environmental, health, and safety performance of the petroleum industry; and
- conducting research to advance petroleum technology and develop industry equipment and performance standards.

In performing our mission, API advocates government decision-making that encourages efficient and economic oil and natural gas development, refining, transportation, and use; API promotes an improved public understanding of the industry's value to society; and API serves as a forum for the exchange of views on issues affecting the petroleum industry.

VALUES

We hold these core values:

- **Performance.** Our effectiveness depends upon the performance of the men and women who make up API. They are the key to our success.
- **Excellence.** We are committed to excellence in serving the petroleum industry. We will do everything possible to meet or, wherever possible, exceed the industry's needs.
- **Highest Standards.** We will adhere to the highest ethical and professional standards. We must do so in order to achieve the public credibility that is key to our success.

OBJECTIVES

We are committed to achieving these objectives:

- **Continuously improve the quality and the value of the services we provide.** We are committed to being an industry asset widely respected for providing services that meet high standards of excellence. We will anticipate and respond quickly to the changing needs of both our members and our staff.
- **Strive for excellence and efficiency in our operations.** We will maintain the respect of our members through employee initiative, improved productivity, and cost effectiveness.
- **Foster team spirit among employees.** We will provide a work environment built on open communication, teamwork, trust, and personal development and recognition.

October, 1992

34. **American Power Conversion**
P.O. Box 278; 132 Fairgrounds Road; West Kingston, RI 02892
(401) 789-5735
Industry: 36—Uninterruptable power supply

OUR MISSION

To provide our customers with high-quality, cost-effective solutions to problems which hinder productivity. We serve markets which represent opportunities for long-term success.

OUR PHILOSOPHY

To listen to our customers. Their wants, needs and wishes are our strategic blueprint.

To justify our expenditures as they relate to our goals.

To quantify all aspects of our business in order to create benchmarks for success.

To avoid bureaucracy. Employees must make direct contributions to our goals.

To emphasize quality. We believe that good enough never is.

To respond quickly and decisively to opportunity.

To create an environment where ideas are encouraged, recognized and rewarded.

To help employees grow personally and professionally.

To work together towards our goals and be rewarded together when they are achieved.

To commit to leadership in every aspect of our business.

OUR GOALS

To achieve dominant share in world-wide markets which represent long-term opportunity to the Company.

To provide shareholders with exceptional return on their commitment to the Company.

To extend our reputation for high-value products, and high-quality people.

35. **American President Companies, Ltd.**
    1111 Broadway; Oakland, CA 94607
    (510) 272-8000
    Industry: 42, 44—Trucking and shipping

Values

Three primary values determine how we work together. Each of us must practice these values to contribute to an environment that is characterized by teamwork and participation.

Integrity—We will meet our commitments, we will be consistent in our actions and standards and we will be truthful.

Trust—We will rely on the competence and commitment of others, we will share information actively and we will maintain individual and company confidences.

Respect for Individuals—We will be fair and support diversity, we will treat each individual with dignity, we will encourage individuality and differences of opinion, we will respect each person's contribution and we will be sensitive to each other's needs.

Mission

We are committed to being the customers' choice for container transportation in North America, Asia and the Middle East by:
- Providing superior service reliability and customer responsiveness.
- Continuously improving our network of services and systems.

- Developing long-term relationships with customers who value service.
- Creating a Total Quality environment to benefit our customers, employees, shareholders and partners.

General Strategies

Quality—Apply Quality Principles and Practices to all aspects of our business.

Employees—Develop the potential of our people to contribute to the mutual success of the company and the employee.

Customers—Continuously measure and improve customer satisfaction.

Service—Deliver superior service reliability.

Shareholders—Manage our resources and costs consistent with the value customers place on our services.

Industry Environment—Anticipate and proactively manage major industry issues consistent with our mission.

1991

36. **American Red Cross**
   17th and D Streets, NW; Washington, DC 20006
   (202) 737-8300
   Industry: 83—Social service organization

MISSION

The American Red Cross is a humanitarian organization, led by volunteers, that provides relief to victims of disasters and helps people prevent, prepare for, and respond to emergencies. It does this through services that are consistent with its congressional charter and the fundamental principles of the International Red Cross Movement.

GOALS

July 1, 1991–June 30, 1997

1. The American people can expect the American Red Cross to deliver quality mission-related products and services in a consistent and responsive manner.

2. The American people can expect the American Red Cross to provide nationwide—

- Disaster planning, preparedness, and education;
- Prompt relief to victims of major disasters;
- Emergency communication between members of the United States Armed Forces and their families and supporting casework management services; and
- International tracing services.

3. The American people can expect the American Red Cross to be a leading provider of—
- Prompt relief to victims of single-family disasters;
- Information, referral, and financial assistance to members of the United States Armed Forces and their families;
- First aid training;
- Cardiopulmonary resuscitation (CPR) training;
- Swimming and lifeguard training; and
- HIV/AIDS education.

4. The American people can expect the American Red Cross to provide a reliable and adequate supply of blood, blood products, tissue services, and related biomedical products and services to meet the needs of those it serves, as well as to support corporate and regional biomedical research and development.

5. As a member of the International Red Cross and Red Crescent Movement, the American Red Cross will mobilize the support of the American people for international disaster relief and international humanitarian law.

6. American Red Cross products and services, governance and management, and paid and volunteer staff will reflect the diversity of the communities served.

7. The American Red Cross will adapt its volunteer development and management practices to reflect the changing needs of volunteers.

8. The American Red Cross will develop sufficient financial support by the American people to provide quality products and services consistent with its mission, and will continue to demonstrate fiscal responsibility and stewardship to the American people.

9. The American Red Cross will be a unified organization for its customers, clients, and contributors.

37.   **American Telephone & Telegraph Company**
      32 Avenue of the Americas; New York, NY 10013-2412
      (212) 605-5500
      Industry: 48—Telecommunications

AT&T's Mission

We are dedicated to being the world's best at bringing people together—giving them easy access to each other and to the information and services they want—anytime, anywhere.

Drafted First Quarter, 1992
Annual Report 1991
Copyright © AT&T 1992

38. **American Turnkey Corp.**
   3601 Harbor Boulevard, Suite 200; Santa Ana, CA 92704
   (714) 557-9050
   Industry: 73—Computer software

AMERICAN TURNKEY'S MISSION:

To be widely recognized as the best operations management and control software and services company in the world.

Copyright © 1992

39. **AMETEK, Inc.**
   Station Square; Paoli, PA 19301
   (215) 647-2121
   Industry: 38—Measuring equipment

CORPORATE STATEMENT

VISION: AMETEK will be an internationally recognized and respected company that produces the highest value products and services for the markets it serves while:
- Investors actively seek the Company for investment.
- Customers and suppliers are eager to do business with the Company.
- The Company's employees actively participate and flourish in their work.
- Communities welcome the Company openly.

MISSION: AMETEK's primary mission is to enhance shareholder value by giving consistent and superior returns on its equity and by increasing cash flow.

VALUES: AMETEK is committed to:
- Providing our investors with consistent and superior returns on their investment.
- Providing customers with world-class quality products and services at competitive prices.
- Treating our employees fairly and giving them an opportunity to contribute and develop to the fullest, while sharing the responsibilities of success and the rewards of achievement.
- Forming mutually beneficial business partner relationships with our customers and suppliers, based on fairness and integrity.
- Being responsible citizens in the communities where we live, maintaining high ethical standards of business and environmental responsibility.

STRATEGIES: To achieve our mission, AMETEK will:
- Recognize TQM as the process AMETEK is committed to utilize to achieve our Vision and Mission.

- Develop a strategic plan for each business.
- Focus on continuous improvements in customer satisfaction (both internal and external); all business processes and procedures; growth; asset utilization and profitability.
- Actively encourage and foster an environment for employee growth and development through proper communications, training, employee participation, and recognition.
- Have a pro-active environmental management, committed to providing a safe and healthy environment for our employees, neighbors, and customers.
- Develop and implement the means to measure and be accountable for the various steps required to achieve the Mission.

40. **AM International, Inc.**
     333 West Wacker Drive, Suite 900; Chicago, IL 60606-1265
     (312) 558-1966
     Industry: 50—Wholesale

OUR VISION

We are the leading supplier of products and services in our global markets.

We respond aggressively to our customers' needs and are recognized by them for our excellent quality.

We encourage and reward results, hard work, individual initiative, and insist on ethical behavior.

We are committed to profitability and growth and we foster employee ownership.

We enjoy and are proud of what we do!

41. **AMSCO International, Inc.**
     One Mellon Bank Center; 500 Grant Street, Suite 5000; Pittsburgh,
       PA 15219
     (412) 338-6500
     Industry: 38—Analytical equipment

The mission of AMSCO International, Inc. is to create value for all our stakeholders by achieving global leadership through the development, production and marketing of the highest quality products and services to our healthcare, laboratory, scientific and industrial customers.

Annual Report 1991

42. **Anacomp, Inc.**
     P.O. Box 40888; Indianapolis, IN 46240-0888
     (317) 844-9666
     Industry: 73—Micrographics

Vision

We are the world's leading full-service micrographics company.

Our commitment is to continue to provide innovative, cost-saving products, services and solutions to meet our clients' information storage and retrieval needs today, tomorrow and into the 21st century.

43. **Analog Devices, Inc.**
One Technology Way; P.O. Box 9106; Norwood, MA 02062-9106
(617) 329-4700
Industry: 36—Integrated circuits

Corporate Purpose and Scope of Business

Our purpose is to search continuously for opportunities where we can make unique or valuable contributions to the development and application of analog and digital signal processing technology. In so doing, we strive to offer our customers products that improve the performance, quality and reliability of their products, and thereby increase the productivity of human and capital resources, and contribute generally to upgrading the quality of life and the advancement of society.

Our primary product focus is on monolithic integrated circuits manufactured on semiconductor processes developed by and proprietary to Analog Devices. We also manufacture hybrid circuits and assembled products, including components and board-level subsystems and systems.

Our customers consist primarily of original equipment manufacturers (OEMs) who incorporate Analog's products into a wide variety of instruments and systems. The Company's served markets include laboratory and industrial automation, military/aerospace, telecommunications, transportation, computer peripherals and selected high-end consumer products. We pursue business in these markets worldwide.

Our Employees

Our employees' personal motivation and interests are primarily related to ascending needs for security, safety, purpose, recognition, identity and the realization of one's full potential. Our corporate goals are thus best achieved in an environment that encourages and assists employees in the achievement of their personal goals while helping Analog Devices achieve its goals. We therefore seek to offer our employees a challenging and stable work environment where they can earn above average compensation for above average performance and contribution to the Company. It is our policy to offer unrestricted opportunity for personal advancement irrespective of race, creed, color, sex, national origin, age or disability.

Our objective is to build mutual respect, confidence and trust in our personal relationships based upon commitments to integrity, honesty, openness and competence. Our policy is to share Analog Devices' success with the people who make it possible.

Our Customers

Satisfying our customers' needs is fundamental to our survival and our prosperity. These needs can best be understood in terms of the support we lend our customers in helping them meet their objectives with the minimum use of their resources. Thus, our goal must be to provide superior, easy to use, reliable products that conform to specifications and offer innovative solutions to our customers' problems. We must back up these products with excellent product literature and strong customer service that includes highly effective applications assistance, quick response to inquiries and dependable delivery. We must work hard at understanding our customers' businesses so that we may anticipate *their* needs and enhance *their* effectiveness. We wish to be major suppliers to our key customers and to establish long lasting business relationships based on quality, performance and integrity.

Our Stockholders

Our responsibility to our stockholders is to satisfy their desire for a secure and liquid investment that provides an attractive rate of return. Our objective is to consistently earn a return on invested capital that is well above average for all manufacturing companies and comparable to the most successful companies in our industry. By achieving consistent growth with a high return on capital we can offer our stockholders an attractive opportunity for capital appreciation.

Our Suppliers

Our suppliers are partners in our efforts to develop market share by fulfilling our customers' needs. This requires that we be open and frank about our plans and requirements as they would affect our suppliers. It also requires that we seek to understand the constraints placed upon our suppliers by their technology, cost structure and financial resources. We place strong emphasis on associating with suppliers who are financially stable, competent and honest, and who are consistent in meeting their delivery and quality commitments to us.

Our Community

Our goal is to be an asset to every community in which we operate by offering stable employment and by lending effort and support to worthy causes. We encourage our employees to take an active interest in their communities and contribute their efforts toward making their communities better places to live and work. We make a special effort to aid and support those universities and colleges that are an important source of scarce resources.

Growth

Growth is an important means by which we satisfy the interests of our employees, our stockholders and our customers. High caliber people look for opportunities for personal development and advancement which can be best achieved in a growth environment. Our stockholders look for an above average return, which is much more likely to be achieved by a growth company.

To achieve growth we continuously search out and focus on applications for our products and technology that have above average long-term potential. We also continuously broaden the range of our products and technology, mostly through internal development.

Profit

Profit generated by our business is the primary source of the funds required to finance our growth. Without growth and profits we cannot achieve our corporate objectives. Our financial goals are to generate profit after tax and return on capital comparable to the best-performing companies in our industry and—without taking unreasonable risks—self-fund our growth.

Market Leadership

Our goal is to obtain the largest share of each market segment we serve. We believe the key to achieving market share is to enter growth markets early with superior, innovative products, and to provide a high level of quality and customer service. Our markets are worldwide in scope, and our objective is to achieve comparable penetration in every major geographical market.

Quality

Customer satisfaction, and thus our success, is critically dependent on dependable delivery of high quality products and services. A high quality product or service is one that is delivered when promised and performs as specified under all intended operating conditions throughout its intended life.

The achievement of high quality begins with product planning, but it must also be an integral part of product design and the design and implementation of manufacturing processes. High quality depends upon the commitment of all employees to the on-time production of defect free products and services.

High quality is not a static condition. It is susceptible to continuous improvement through systematic identification and elimination of causes of errors and variances, through development of improved designs and processes and through education and training. Continuous improvement of quality leads not only to greater customer satisfaction, but also to higher productivity and lower costs.

The concept of quality improvement is applicable to every area of the Company, including marketing, customer service, finance and human resources, as well as manufacturing and engineering. Every employee should be committed to quality improvement and should be determined to "do it right the first time and do it better the next time."

Summary

Achieving our goals for growth, profits, market share and quality creates the environment and economic means to satisfy the interests and needs of our employees, stockholders, customers and others associated with the firm. Our success depends on people who understand the interdependence and congruence of their personal goals with those of the Company, and who are thus motivated to contribute toward the achievement of these goals.

Extracted from *The Corporate Objective*

44.   Andersons Management Corporation
    The Andersons
    P.O. Box 119; Maumee, OH 43537
    (419) 893-5050
    Industry: 51—Wholesale and retail lawn and garden supplies

Our statement of principles expresses beliefs and philosophy, held by the founding partners of The Andersons, forming the basis for the development of operating principles and the Company's Mission, which follow. What is written here represents a commitment of the Board of Directors and a guide for all members of the organization.

This document has been developed with the input of many people at various levels of the Company. It is not intended that everyone fit the same mold by acceptance of identical basic beliefs or personal philosophy. Knowledge of and compliance with established operating principles, policies and guidelines by all, however, is expected.

The Company is founded on the belief that all of us are subject to a higher and divine authority, and that we should aspire to goodness, integrity and those virtues which we discern to be consistent with divine will. We believe that possession of these qualities develops self-esteem, merits the approval of others and enhances both private and public welfare.

We believe in the traditions of freedom and liberty that exist in the United States. We believe in the free enterprise system, fair competition, the incentives of profit and personal gain and the importance of capital accumulation. We also believe that profit or personal gain must never come at the expense of personal integrity or the public welfare, and that a balance must be struck between the inequalities which come with freedom on the one hand and aspirations for equality on the other.

We recognize that our competitive economic system makes it essential that we place constant and primary focus on satisfying the needs of our customers. We also understand that our business will not survive if it does not meet the legitimate needs and aspirations of its employees and owners.

Our challenge is to provide the leadership which will inspire all who work with the Company to exert the uncommon effort that is essential to achieving excellence and success. We all should recognize that in these efforts we should not lose sight of our fundamental responsibilities to our families, to our communities and to our society as a whole.

Our task is to manage our Company in such a way that a thoughtful balance is maintained among the long-term interests of our customers and those with whom we have other business relationships, our employees, our owners and our communities.

All of us should conduct ourselves so the following objectives are met:
- Business affairs reflect complete integrity.
- Products and services serve useful, constructive purposes.
- Opportunities are provided for employees to progress toward personal goals and to receive an equitable share of the income.
- Owners of the Company receive a return on investment which is fair and sufficient to provide for growth and security.
- We contribute to the welfare of our communities, our nation and our world.
- Business activities reflect a proper concern for the health and safety of our customers, employees and owners and for the quality of our environment.
- Employment in the Company enhances, rather than jeopardizes, the proper functioning of the family, which we believe to be the foundation of society.
- The enjoyment of life and happiness of those with whom we are involved is enhanced.

In both our underlying philosophy and our Mission, we recognize our concurrent responsibilities to four stakeholder groups:
- Our customers
- Our employees
- Our owners

- Our communities

One of our primary challenges and responsibilities is to achieve profit and growth objectives while fulfilling obligations to all stakeholders in a balanced and thoughtful way. Profit is essential, but should not be an end in itself. Affecting all stakeholder groups in a positive way, it:

- Enables us to remain a reliable source of products and services for customers and a dependable market for suppliers.
- Permits us to continue to offer meaningful work, competitive compensation, profit sharing and advancement opportunity to employees.
- Provides a return for those who have risked investment in the Company as owners.
- Generates resources which can be shared with our communities.
- Provides for expansion and new opportunities.

Our objective is to be a company which creates value for and builds beneficial, enduring and mutually reinforcing relationships with all of our stakeholders.

Mission

We firmly believe that our Company is a vehicle through which we channel our time, talent and energy in pursuit of the fundamental goal of serving God by serving others. Through our collective action we greatly magnify the impact of our individual efforts to:

- Provide extraordinary service to our customers.
- Help each other develop.
- Contribute to the improvement of the community.
- Grow our Company profitably.

We are a multi-business company with historical roots in agriculture and with a keen interest in new horizons of service. We seek to satisfy our customers' needs by offering a combination of products and services of extraordinary value, in a convenient manner, with pride, enthusiasm and integrity.

Each of our businesses and support units operates within a specific plan that is focused on the achievement of this mission.

January, 1991
Extracted from "Statement of Principles"

45. **Anheuser-Busch Companies, Inc.**
   One Busch Place; St. Louis, MO 63118-1852
   (314) 577-2000
   Industry: 20—Beer and food

A MISSION STATEMENT FOR ANHEUSER-BUSCH COMPANIES, INC.

This mission statement clarifies the direction and general goals of Anheuser-Busch Companies, enabling employees at all levels to better understand their company and the role they play in its success. Additionally, by looking beyond any one product or operating company, this statement provides a reference point from which specific business strategies can be assessed and progress can be measured.

In the broadest sense, our field of competition is the leisure industry. Our place in that industry is clear . . .
- Beer is our core business and always will be.
- Other businesses complementary to beer will be needed over the long-term to maintain our status as a growth company.

BEER

Our goals are to:
- Maintain our reputation for the highest quality products and services in the brewing industry.
- Market our products aggressively, successfully and responsibly. At no time will we encourage the abusive consumption of our products, or their consumption by minors.
- Sustain and enhance our competitive position within the United States through continued market share growth.
- Increase our share of global brewing industry sales through our historic emphasis on quality products, and by adapting our marketing and distribution expertise to meet the cultural demands of the local marketplace.

DIVERSIFICATION EFFORTS

Our goals are to:
- Broaden the business base of our company and maintain its strong growth trends by successfully developing opportunities in the entertainment, packaging and food products industries.
- Focus on businesses that permit us to earn a premium on our investment by providing superior products and services; that have substantial room for financial and market share growth; that complement our beer business, and that are compatible with our existing corporate culture.
- Rely on technical expertise, investment spending and careful management to achieve and maintain the position of low-cost-producer in commodity businesses which we have entered to support our brewing operations.

- Provide approximately one-third of our company's earnings from diversified businesses and international brewing by the end of this century.

STAKEHOLDERS

In discharging our responsibility to the various stakeholders we serve, Anheuser-Busch must translate its business strategies to more specific objectives. Our goals are to provide:

- Our **employees** at all levels with satisfying and financially rewarding work, and with continuing opportunities for personal development and advancement.
- Our **shareholders** with a superior return on their investment in our company.
- Our **consumers** with premium quality products and services that have the highest value-to-cost ratio in their category.
- Our **wholesalers** with a commitment to our ongoing and mutually beneficial relationship, including opportunities for profitable growth, supporting services and financing.
- Our **suppliers** with the opportunity for a long-term relationship built on open negotiations to provide state-of-the-art products and services capable of meeting our quality standards at the lowest possible price.
- Our **society** with an exemplary demonstration of corporate social responsibility and good citizenship in all areas, but with particular attention to the reduction of alcohol abuse through research and education, the protection of our environment, and the full integration of all peoples into the life of our nation.

GUIDING BELIEFS OF THE ANHEUSER-BUSCH COMPANIES

In working together to achieve our mission, the men and women of Anheuser-Busch are guided by a set of shared beliefs that make progress possible. Our task is to strive for constant improvement in making these beliefs a reality.

OUR PRODUCTS AND PEOPLE

We believe in:

- A commitment to quality as the cornerstone of our success.
- Maintaining the highest standards of personal and business integrity.
- Earned pride in our company at all levels . . . in its products and services, its marketing activities, its community responsibility, and in its progressive approach to social and environmental issues.

OUR WORK METHODS

We believe in:
- A sense of urgency and commitment that aggressively seeks to develop every opportunity open to our company.
- Teamwork . . . involving people with a diversity of disciplines to reach decisions that are right, and benefit the entire company.
- Long-range planning that is based on conclusive analysis of problems at all levels, including sensitivity and dialectic problem analysis.
- Innovation and creativity in all aspects of our business.
- Learning from today's mistakes to build tomorrow's successes.
- Full debate; then all close ranks behind decisions.

OUR WORKING CONDITIONS

We believe in:
- Encouraging all employees to work at their maximum potential.
- Motivating our employees through meaningful work that involves them in appropriate problem-solving and decision-making activities.
- Caring for and standing behind our employees.
- Honesty and the forthright expression of opinions at all levels.

46. **A. O. Smith Corporation**
One Park Plaza; 11270 West Park Place; Milwaukee, WI 53224-3690
(414) 359-4000
Industry: 34, 36, 37—Transportation equipment

OBJECTIVES

Our success is dependent upon the collective performance of individuals who comprise our most important asset. These objectives are interdependent and, therefore, of equal priority.

A. O. SMITH WILL ACHIEVE PROFIT GROWTH

Planned profit growth is essential if A. O. Smith is to provide the general benefits that justify the existence of our business. These benefits include:
- Improved products for customers and an increased standard of living for the general public through the continual development of new products and markets.
- Greater opportunity for advancement and improved job security for employees.
- Growing investment value for stockholders.

In order to deliver these benefits we seek profitable growth. Not only will we seek an above average return on the stockholders' investment, but we will grow in a planned way so that:

- Various business units will have differing growth rates which together produce a company growing faster than the national economy.
- The capital requirements of growth can be supported by funds generated by our above average earnings.
- The growth is steady enough to produce stability in employment and profits.

A. O. SMITH WILL SEEK STABILITY

Recognizing that high cyclicality can reduce the benefits of good profit growth, we seek to avoid large swings in sales and profit. In pursuit of this objective, we will:

- Be a diversified company that is balanced with respect to the youth and maturity of products and with a business mix in countercyclical markets.
- Be predominantly a manufacturing firm while actively pursuing opportunities in service businesses.
- Seek opportunities in replacement and consumable goods markets.

A. O. SMITH WILL PRESERVE ITS GOOD NAME

In all dealings with people and organizations we will have uncompromising integrity. We will:

- Be fair and truthful in all claims and advertising.
- Strictly adhere to all laws and seek only honorable goals while rejecting unethical procedures.
- Strive for high standards of quality in all aspects of the business.

A. O. SMITH WILL EMPHASIZE INNOVATION

Innovation is a primary cause of profit growth. Therefore, we will:

- Seek market leadership in all major product lines through innovation that improves the value of our products and services to our customers.
- Seek innovative ways of working together to improve our effectiveness as an organization and the productivity of our facilities.
- Foster the development of attitudes and skills in our people that encourage innovation and an orientation toward the future.

A. O. SMITH WILL BE A GOOD PLACE TO WORK

In operating our company, we will attract imaginative and competent people. We will emphasize teamwork in seeking our objectives. We will:

- Create a climate where respect for the individual is fundamental.
- Encourage the freedom and personal growth that comes with self-discipline and enthusiasm for work.
- Treat each other fairly and without discrimination.
- Pay individuals equitably according to their contributions.
- Provide safe equipment, proper materials and training and always insist on safe practices.

A. O. SMITH WILL BE A GOOD CITIZEN

To serve the public and our own best interests, we will:
- Strive for growth that contributes to the economic well-being of the communities in which we are located.
- Insist that our plant settings and operations meet accepted environmental standards.
- Encourage our people to involve themselves in worthwhile civic activities.
- Provide financial support for worthwhile community programs.
- Encourage in every appropriate way the protection and preservation of our free American system so necessary for the attainment of these objectives.

47. **Apache Corporation**
    One United Bank Center; 1700 Lincoln Street, Suite 1900; Denver, CO 80203-4519
    (303) 837-5000
    Industry: 13—Oil and gas

Apache Corporation's mission is to increase shareholder value by growing a dynamic and profitable oil and natural gas exploration, production and marketing company, international in scope, while serving our constituencies with integrity.

Annual Report 1988

48. **APCOA, Inc.**
    25550 Chagrin Boulevard; Cleveland, OH 44122-5637
    (216) 765-8800
    Industry: 75—Airport parking

MISSION STATEMENT

APCOA's mission is to be the leading parking property management company in customer satisfaction. That means each APCOA associate in every area of the company puts the customer first in all we do through total quality management.

OBJECTIVE

Over the next three years, our objective is to add value to the existing business by improving upon and standardizing the core skills of APCOA and that of each company associate and nearly doubling in size by accelerating its efforts to improve customer-defined quality and being an aggressive investor.

49. **Apple Computer, Inc.**
    20525 Mariani Avenue; Cupertino, CA 95014
    (408) 996-1010
    Industry: 35—Computers

Apple Computer, Inc. mission statement:

It is Apple's mission to help people transform the way they work, learn and communicate by providing exceptional personal computing products and innovative customer services.

- We will pioneer new directions and approaches, finding innovative ways to use computing technology to extend the bounds of human potential.

- Apple will make a difference: our products, services and insights will help people around the world shape the ways business and education will be done in the 21st century.

1991

50. **ARCO Chemical Company**
    3801 West Chester Pike; P.O. Box 708; Newtown Square, PA
    19073-2387
    (215) 359-3117
    Industry: 28—Chemicals

OUR MISSION

ARCO Chemical Company will produce chemicals, related products, and services in a manner that enhances value for our stockholders, customers, employees, and the public. To achieve this mission, we will:
- manage our assets to produce a superior return on our stockholders' investment;
- sell high-quality, competitive products and provide superior service to customers;
- create an environment for employees that fosters personal growth and allows individuals to achieve their full potential; and
- operate our facilities in an environmentally responsible manner, provide a safe work place for our employees, and produce only those products we believe to be safe for customer use.

OUR PRINCIPLES

High ethical standards and integrity

As a company, we will operate in an ethical manner; as individuals, we will conduct ourselves with honesty, integrity, fairness, and respect for one another.

Safe and environmentally sound operations

Taking precedence over all other operational matters is providing a safe work place and operating in an environmentally sound manner. Each employee is charged with reporting any potentially dangerous or harmful situation.

Superior profit performance

Our goal is to produce a superior return on our stockholders' investment, which means improving both short- and long-term profitability. Every employee contributes to this goal by working to his or her maximum potential.

Efficient and cost-effective manufacturing

We will operate the most efficient, cost-effective plants in the industry. Manufacturing performance should focus on doing things right the first time, which reduces the number of accidents, production problems, and customer complaints.

Complete customer satisfaction

We strive for long-term business relationships with customers because our growth depends on keeping customers satisfied. We must be sensitive to customer needs and produce high-quality products to meet those needs.

Innovation and creativity

We must continually find new ways to combine our marketing, technical, and manufacturing skills to enhance stockholder value. The key to our continued growth lies in creating new products, processes, and business opportunities.

Personal initiative and team effort

Individuals make a difference at ARCO Chemical and we encourage participation at all levels in the decision-making process. Qualified, motivated employees are our best guarantee of a successful business; we must encourage and reward both individual contributions and team effort.

Career development and individual growth

We value our employees and encourage their development by providing training opportunities and a work environment that fosters individual growth. Our open management style promotes a free flow of information throughout the organization, giving employees access to the knowledge they need to do their jobs and placing their work in the context of overall corporate goals and strategies.

Compliance with laws and regulations

We will comply with all laws and regulations, including local, state, and national legislation; securities and environmental regulations; and laws regarding our operations in foreign countries. Any question about legal interpretations or improper activities should be discussed openly and immediately with supervisors or higher management levels.

Equal treatment of vendors

We will treat fairly and equally all suppliers of goods and services. Vendors will have an equal opportunity to submit price and specification quotations to our company.

51. **Armstrong World Industries, Inc.**
    P.O. Box 3001; Lancaster, PA 17604
    (717) 397-0611
    Industry: 22, 26, 32—Carpet, tile, and building supplies

Armstrong's four Operating Principles go back to the company's very beginnings in 1860. We believe that our adherence to these principles is a central reason for the success we have attained. They have stood through successions of management and with tens of thousands of employees working in numerous core businesses during periods of stability as well as those of dramatic change. The principles are as meaningful to Armstrong people today as when they were first set down in writing.

OPERATING PRINCIPLES

1. To respect the dignity and inherent rights of the individual human being in all dealings with people.

2. To maintain high moral and ethical standards and to reflect honesty, integrity, reliability and forthrightness in all relationships.

3. To reflect the tenets of good taste and common courtesy in all attitudes, words and deeds.

4. To serve fairly and in proper balance the interests of all groups associated with the business—customers, stockholders, employees, suppliers, community neighbors, government and the general public.

These Operating Principles overlay the workday experiences of all Armstrong employees as they strive to increase the value of the company and in this way to enhance the market price of its stock.

1960

CORPORATE STRATEGY

1. To build on the existing strengths in our core businesses.

2. To continue searching for ways to expand into related businesses through technology that is either developed in-house or acquired.

3. To attempt to acquire companies in related businesses.

4. To look outward to our markets and customers using the Quality Management process to continuously improve the value of our products and services.

The last part of the Corporate Strategy affirms Armstrong's dedication to its customers—and to satisfying the requirements of those customers. It also refers to the company's commitment to the Quality Management process. Armstrong men and women around the globe are dedicated to this process and to the demanding criteria that underlie the Malcolm Baldrige Award. Their determination to achieve continuous improvement through the Quality Management process is reflected in the following policy.

1983

CORPORATE QUALITY POLICY

1. We are committed to quality performance.

2. As an organization—and as individuals—we will continually seek out the specific needs of those who depend upon us.

3. We will then consistently satisfy those needs by doing everything *right the first time*.

Above all, Quality Management teaches that quality improvement must always be seen as a process, not a program. That means it is a never-ending quest, with new challenges and rewards for each generation.

In our journey as a world-class company, we cannot be satisfied with simply being as good as or better than our current competitors. We must be able to identify our customers and clearly understand their needs. We must create products and services that clearly meet those needs. We must continually define the characteristics of our processes and the corporate culture necessary to achieve those goals. And we must know the order in which we need to improve things.

In simple terms, we must do the right things right. And we must be the best at doing it.

Together, the Operating Principles, Corporate Strategy and Quality Management process give Armstrong employees a compass to steer by.

1985

52. **Arthur Andersen & Co., SC**
    69 West Washington Street; Chicago, IL 60602-3002
    (312) 580-0069

Industry: 87—Accounting firm

Our Vision

To be the world's Premier Professional Services Organization

Our Mission

To provide quality professional services that meet the information needs of the global marketplace

Our Values

Quality Service

We focus on the client in order to deliver quality service that exceeds expectations.

Quality People

We recruit the best people and train them to be the best professionals in the world.

Meritocracy

We provide our people with challenging opportunities for career advancement based on their effectiveness in serving the client.

One-Firm Approach

We employ the same methodologies and share resources on a global basis to ensure that we deliver high-quality service consistently throughout the world.

Integrity

We adhere to personal and professional standards that exceed those required by legal and professional codes.

Innovation

We deliver unique solutions to each client's needs, providing a groundbreaking example for others to follow.

Stewardship

We are committed to investing heavily in the future in order to bequeath a stronger worldwide organization to future generations of our people.

1991

53. **Art Institute of Chicago**
    Michigan Avenue at Adams Street; Chicago, IL   60603-9947
    (312) 443-3600
    Industry: 84—Art museum

As amended, the Articles of Incorporation provide:

"The purposes for which The Art Institute of Chicago is formed are: to found, build, maintain, and operate museums, schools, libraries of art, and theatres; to provide support facilities in connection therewith; to conduct appropriate activities conducive to the artistic development of the region; and to conduct and participate in appropriate activities of national and international significance;

To form, conserve, research, publish, and exhibit a permanent collection of objects of art of all kinds, to present temporary exhibitions including loaned objects of art of all kinds, and to cultivate and extend the arts by appropriate means;

To establish and conduct comprehensive programs of education, including preparation of visual artists, teachers of art, and designers; to provide education services in written, spoken and media formats;

To provide lectures, instruction and entertainment, including dramatic, film and musical performances of all kinds, which complement and further the general purposes of the Institute;

To receive in trust property of all kinds and to exercise all necessary powers as trustee for such trust estates whose objects are related to the furtherance of the general purposes of the Institute or for the establishment or maintenance of works of art."

54. **Associated Wholesale Grocers, Inc.**
    5000 Kansas Avenue; Kansas City, KS 66106-1192
    (913) 321-1313
    Industry: 51—Food wholesale

GUIDELINES FOR PROGRESS

The following is a statement of purpose and philosophy for our Company. It has been developed by many people over the years. We believe in it; and we believe that if we adhere to it faithfully, it will guide us safely into the future.

OUR MISSION

Our mission is to satisfy our retail members' needs for quality supermarket merchandise and superior support services. We will do this at the lowest possible cost in order to keep our retail members profitable, competitive, and to give them the advantage required for growth and expansion of their market shares. In order to fulfill this purpose, our Company must maintain its financial strength and provide for a continuity of membership and management that will assure our future existence.

OUR RETAIL MEMBERS

Our customers' satisfaction is the most important factor in *all* our decisions and programs. Our retail members have invested their money in our Company with the clear expectations of a fair return on their investment. They expect us to adhere to the above-stated mission and display sound judgement and moral and financial responsibility in exercising our stewardship.

OUR EMPLOYEES

Dignity, concern, respect and responsibility will apply to all policies and practices concerning our employees.

Each employee must make a meaningful contribution to the accomplishment of the Company's mission. Therefore, all employees will be provided with the proper tools, training and supervision necessary to achieve superior levels of performance.

We will listen to our employees and will accept suggestions from our employees in a positive manner.

We will give our employees full recognition of merit and achievement.

We will require superior performance every day and refuse to accept mediocrity.

We will expect honesty, character and integrity from our employees.

We will encourage individual initiative, innovation, creativity, participation, and contribution. We are, however, a "team-effort company" where every player is important, and the emphasis in on team performance.

We will, when possible, promote from within the Company.

All employees should share in the responsibility for the Company's success and in the fruits of that success.

OUR PRODUCTS AND SERVICES

We will seek to provide products and support services which are needed by our customers to ensure that they have a competitive edge.

OUR SUPPLIERS

Our suppliers are our partners in progress. We will work together with them in pursuing the common goal of service to our retail members and collectively solve mutual problems for our common goal.

We will treat our suppliers fairly, honestly, openly, impartially and with dignity and respect. We expect the same treatment in return.

OUR COMMUNITY AND INDUSTRY

Our Company will accept the responsibility for being a good corporate citizen, strive for good public relations and assume responsibility in the communities in which we have facilities. We encourage our employees to do likewise.

We accept the responsibility for being a contributor to the improvement of our industry and will assume our fair share of involvement and input into the process of solving problems in our industry.

OUR MANAGEMENT

We will stress growth and profitability, develop long and short-term goals and objectives, and measure our performance against them.

We will keep our staff lean and will discourage bureaucracy and politics within the Company. We will manage our employees in a manner that is fair, impartial and consistent. We will display understanding yet be demanding of superior performance.

We will encourage individual growth and initiative, but will emphasize team work and pride in team accomplishments.

Our executive personnel will possess requisite skill, talent, experience, ability, common sense and understanding. They will be hard-driving, highly motivated and will be subscribers to the highest standards of conduct, business ethics, fairness and principles for themselves and the Company.

DEDICATION TO EXCELLENCE

We are dedicated to being better than our competitors at all times, and we will strive to make excellence in everything we do a reality. We are dedicated to being the best there is in our industry!

55. **AST Research Inc.**
    16215 Alton Parkway; Irvine, CA 92713-9658
    (714) 727-7962
    Industry: 35, 73—Computer hardware and software

NEW OPERATING PHILOSOPHIES

- We will respect and build working relationships with our:
  Employees
  Customers
  Vendors
- AST employees exist to serve customers (both internal and external) and will expend extra efforts to do so
- Process improvement must become a valued goal
- We will delegate responsibility, measure performance, and hold ourselves accountable
- We will make decisions by "WHAT IS BEST FOR AST"

July, 1992

AT&T

see American Telephone and Telegraph Company (37)

56. **Austin Industries, Inc.**
    P.O. Box 1590; Dallas, TX 75221
    (214) 443-5501
    Industry: 16—Construction

The Austin Advantage—People and Performance

An intense concern for the development, success and well-being of all Austin people . . . And an unrelenting emphasis on performance.

We're committed to bringing out the best in ourselves and in each other. Shared values like open communication, a "can-do" spirit, personal accountability, participation and ownership create in our organization a climate of remarkably high standards for how well we do what we do.

What we do is create value, for ourselves and for others, through exemplary performance.

Exemplary performance means being the very best that we can be in terms of lower cost, faster project completion, quality work, quick response to customer needs, safe operations and uncompromising integrity in everything we do. That's the basis upon which we compete in the marketplace and is, therefore, the means by which we serve our customers and our employee-owners as well as the communities where we work and live.

Building on the base of our proud past, we're now creating our own future. We're determined to build a truly great company on the foundation of our commitment to people and performance. That's our mission. That's the Austin Advantage.

57. **Avis Rent A Car System, Inc.**
    900 Old Country Road; Garden City, NY 11530
    (516) 222-3000
    Industry: 75—Car rental

The Avis Quest For Excellence

At Avis Rent A Car, our business is renting cars; our mission is total customer satisfaction.

Our goal is to provide the best quality customer service: to treat each customer the way we ourselves want to be treated. To exceed our customer's expectations.

We believe that only by maximizing our service and our productivity can we maximize our employee equity and our profits.

We are dedicated to a vigorous program of self-evaluation and improvement.

We continually strive to provide better and innovative services to enhance the travel experience for our customers. We work to strengthen our bonds with all active participants in the delivery of our service: our customers, our suppliers, and our co-workers in all areas.

We know that total customer service and satisfaction require the team effort of all employees, at all times.

"We try harder."

58. **Avon Products, Inc.**
   9 West 57th Street; New York, NY 10019-2683
   (212) 546-8472
   Industry: 28, 39—Cosmetics and jewelry

Our Vision

To be the Company that best understands and satisfies the product, service and self-fulfillment needs of women—globally.

Our Commitment to Women

Our relationship with women and our commitment to them is the cornerstone of our future.

We are committed to reaching women more directly and serving them better than any other company in the world. In everything we do, we will endeavor to help women lead more satisfying and fulfilling lives.

Avon recognizes the need women consumers have to better control their lives. Therefore, we will strive to build a reputation as the Company most sensitive and responsive to the complex challenges and ever-changing demands women face.

Our understanding of and respect for women will take many forms—from the quality products we develop, to the personalized shopping experiences we offer, to the flexible and rewarding earnings opportunities we provide. We will continually seek ways to assist women in enhancing self-esteem and self-fulfillment in areas where Avon can make a difference.

As Avon assists women in enhancing the quality of their lives, we will fulfill our vision for the future.

Our Customers

By better understanding our Customers, we will strengthen our leading positions in beauty and direct selling worldwide.

Satisfied customers are the best measure of Avon's success. Our future growth will depend on our ability to address the diverse needs of targeted consumer segments worldwide.

We are committed to providing the most convenient ways to buy quality products, with service and value that are unmatched, and with a guarantee that delivers on its promise every time. This means multiple access opportunities, differentiated service and a focus on value. Most of all, it means caring and building long-lasting relationships.

Therefore, we are dedicated to being creative, responsive, innovative and continually focused on understanding the needs of our Customers.

We know our Customers' needs and aspirations will continue to change. As their needs change, so will Avon.

Our Representatives

When our Representatives succeed, we all succeed.

This is the partnership and competitive advantage that is uniquely Avon.

We want to be known by Representatives as the Company that provides them with the very best ways to work, earn, grow and enhance their self-esteem.

We are committed to providing a broad range of business opportunities to attract Representatives who seek and value the flexibility we offer them in serving their Customers.

We will strive to create partnerships with our Representatives by providing multiple business approaches to satisfy their diverse needs and the specific demands of their markets.

Together, we will build a reputation worldwide for providing, as no one else can, the products and service women seek—when, where, and how they want them.

Our Associates

We will provide Associates worldwide the opportunities that allow them to live up to their highest potential.

People are our greatest asset.

Avon recognizes that only when a company truly values people can it expect, in turn, to be valued as an employer.

Thus, we will strive to create an environment of opportunity that attracts and rewards talented, ambitious people.

Avon is committed to the training and development of its Associates worldwide. As they grow, the Company grows.

We will recognize, reward and compensate teamwork, excellence and innovation, and provide opportunities consistent with these contributions. We will foster diversity among our Associates and value the broad spectrum of thought and skills they bring to Avon.

We are committed to helping Associates achieve rewarding careers. Therefore, we will strive to help Associates find employment with Avon an enriching experience that enables them to fulfill their highest potential.

A company doesn't choose the best people—the best people choose the company.

Our Principles

We will provide individuals an opportunity to develop and earn in support of their betterment and happiness.

We will serve families throughout the world with products of the highest quality, backed by a guarantee of satisfaction.

We will provide service to Representatives and Customers that is outstanding in its helpfulness and courtesy.

We will rely with full confidence on Associates and Representatives, recognizing that our corporate success depends on their individual contributions and achievements.

We will share with others the rewards of growth and success.

We will honor the responsibilities of corporate citizenship by contributing to the well-being of the society in which we function.

We will cherish and maintain the friendly spirit of Avon.

David H. McConnell, Avon's Founder
Published 1992

B

59. **Ball Corporation**
   345 South High Street; Muncie, IN 47305-2326
   (317) 747-6100
   Industry: 26, 30, 34, 37, 39—Packaging

Mission Statement

Ball Corporation's mission, as a manufacturing and services company, is to provide consistent customer value through competitive levels of technology, quality and service, while maintaining high standards of integrity, ethical conduct and social responsibility.

60. **Baltimore Gas and Electric**
   Charles Center; P.O. Box 1475; Baltimore, MD 21203-1475
   (410) 234-5000
   Industry: 49—Electric utility

Mission:

To achieve complete customer satisfaction by providing superior energy products and services.

Vision:

To perform as a world class energy company.

Approved February, 1992

61. **Banc One Corporation**
   100 East Broad Street; Columbus, OH 43271
   (614) 248-5944
   Industry: 60—Banking

Banc One stands for the best of American values. We believe that good ideas and a lot of hard work will take you a long way. We'll deal with you straight, no fluff and no excuses. We're partial to new ideas and we're proud of the ones we've brought to American banking. We also know that was then and this is now. We're humbled that we're regarded as one of the best in the business, and we're confident enough to believe we can keep living up to that reputation.

Annual Report 1991

62. BankAmerica Corporation
Bank of America

Bank of America Center; San Francisco, CA 94137
(415) 622-3456
Industry: 60—Banking

STRATEGIC OUTLOOK

BankAmerica's strategic goals are twofold: to continue to be the premier provider of retail and wholesale banking services in the western United States, and to be a top-tier international wholesale bank supplying specialized financial products and services to corporations, government agencies, and financial institutions through its existing and highly competitive global network.

To these ends, the corporation continues to grow in a controlled manner, increasing its levels of equity capital and earning assets, and expanding its products and delivery systems where opportunities exist to produce attractive returns. At the same time, the corporation exercises strict control over operating expenses and seeks to streamline and simplify its operations, wherever it is possible to do so and still meet the needs and expectations of customers.

The strategy is highly focused, with the objective of making BankAmerica the best performing financial institution in the markets in which it chooses to participate. BankAmerica is placing strong emphasis on increasing consumer deposits and loans, particularly residential mortgages, auto loans, and credit card balances; increasing the base of middle market and small business accounts and increasing the size and depth of relationships with these business clients; providing trade finance services globally, particularly in the Pacific Rim; and increasing investment banking and treasury management services to large national and international companies and financial institutions, as well as mid-sized West Coast corporate clients.

To meet the challenges of an increasingly competitive financial services environment, the corporation focuses on the creation and delivery of financial products and services that are competitively priced and specifically tailored to meet customers' needs. BankAmerica brings to this effort an outstanding professional and technical workforce, a seasoned management team, a unique global presence, and a strong franchise in major domestic and international markets.

Annual Report 1989

63.   **Bankers Trust New York Corporation**
      280 Park Avenue; New York, NY 10017
      (212) 250-2500
      Industry: 60—Banking

Mission for the 90's

Our mission in the 90's is to become the leader in global finance.

We will achieve this by evolving into the world's premier manager of risk for our own account and those of our clients. This generic definition of our business accurately describes Bankers Trust as a firm devoted to adding value through intermediation/arbitrage of financial, information, and processing flows.

We will become the leader because our singularity of business purpose will be matched by an equally singular commitment to attract and retain the best people.

Execution

Execution will accomplish 80 percent of the task of becoming the leader. To accomplish our objective, we must do the following:

Become the Preeminent Manager of Risk for Our Clients

Over the past ten years we have built a formidable risk transfer capability which will be expanded as the winning basic skill of our firm in the 90's. By perfecting our intermediary/arbitrage skills, Bankers Trust can address risks at the client or market level. We can take risks off the client's hands and hedge or retain them for our own account. We can act for clients to acquire risks they find attractive.

Our competencies today are significant, and we are committed to maintaining a climate in the firm that fosters continued innovation.

We can accomplish our goal by continuing to harness our mental technology (brain power) and also utilizing our balance sheet to advantage. We will continue to act as a risk transfer manager in a principal capacity and also envision a core of more stable agency businesses that will produce a competitive return on equity for the firm, before taking into account a contribution from our activities as principal.

Build Marketing and Origination

Bankers Trust evolved as a strong, product driven organization in the 80's and continues to build that strength. In the 90's it will be essential to create enduring client relationships built on the roles our firm can play as a highly valued advisor and purveyor of essential products dealing with client risk management priorities of the highest order.

Our organization will become more balanced; there will be product units "looking out" at the world and marketing/sales units with responsibility for clients "looking in" at the bank's total capabilities. As we build origination, in this sense, our approach will consistently be to position ourselves as a trusted advisor that can draw on the strength of the bank for execution.

We will broaden our client base throughout the network by reentering the middle and retail markets as a wholesaler of products to primary distributors. Bankers Trust will become a universal institution as a result.

Achieving the seamlessness and common purpose suggested by a product/client balance in our organization, and doing so while retaining creativity, responsiveness, and opportunistic skills, is the challenge. It is a level of sophistication that must be mastered to succeed in the 90's.

Extend Globalization

We are committed to truly multinationalizing the professional staff at all levels. We will further elaborate the global positioning of our client function and product lines to increase our opportunity for profit and to prolong the period of profitability for our product lines.

We will build more leadership firms in selected local markets; our focused "local" international network, linked to Bankers Trust's cross-border and domestic U.S. capabilities, will give us a competitive advantage.

Achieve Critical Mass in Technology and Information

We are committed to building a fully automated operating and information infrastructure in this decade. We want to be the most productive financial institution and support our professional staff with technology in a manner which the competition will find hard to duplicate. Attaining these goals will create critical mass advantages for Bankers Trust.

Liquify Assets and Carry at Marked-to-Market Value

We are committed to fully liquifying the assets on our balance sheet, except for the portfolio of private equity investments we wish to maintain. All assets will be carried at marked-to-market values.

Attract and Retain the Best People

Most importantly, we are committed to building a distinctive human environment in the firm. Senior management will be leaders of businesses; manager-leaders and specialists will be equally honored. All professionals will be doers. Bankers Trust people will be known as people with a state of mind that makes things happen, who earn psychic income from playing on a championship team, whose values are consistent with those of the firm.

We will be a partnership of professionals. Senior partners will be compensated by a greater percentage of equity than cash. The partners will become the largest ownership block in the company. They will behave like owners and insist on excellence in everything we do. Pay for performance will continue to be the standard. The partnership will participate in governing the firm and will consist of a broad mix of people in terms of sex, age, ethnicity, and race. This environment will permit us to attract and retain the best people in the industry.

Values

First, and without argument, Bankers Trust is different.

Essentially, we are not guardians of the status quo. We're restless, innovative change agents who have a vision of the future and keep expanding parameters to meet it.

Our vitality is supported by an unusual capacity for accommodating opposites as we create a culture uniquely matched to our merchant banking strategy.

The popular wisdom is that you cannot build an organization based on extraordinary, creative, entrepreneurial, driven people and still have teamwork. But we do and keep looking for exceptional individuals who can excel as team players.

People, exceptional people, are the creators of our future. Consequently, our commitment to recruiting, developing, and motivating the best person for every job in the firm will be never-ending.

In a competitive world the ability to "make it happen" separates the leader from the pack.

We seek the most productive risk and demand its skillful management.

Global at Bankers Trust is not part of a slogan. It is an imperative that infiltrates and penetrates everything we think about and aspire to do.

You are not supposed to be able to run a large, publicly-owned company in a relatively informal, non-bureaucratic, flexible, entrepreneurial, "small company" style. But we do.

Bankers Trust is a place where we respect the idea that somebody else can help you—and there is somebody you can help, too.

Mistakes can happen. We try to learn from our mistakes—and don't tolerate the same one twice. The one unacceptable mistake is unethical behavior. Absolutely unacceptable.

We encourage dissent. But it has got to be right on top of the table. Active participation by everyone is essential.

A Bankers Trust person is provided with opportunity and faced with the constant challenge to improve. Most meet the challenge.

Outstanding individual performance, coupled with a common purpose state of mind, leads to the greatest rewards.

We need people who are committed, lead satisfying lives, and thoroughly enjoy what they do.

We are not without tension here but we think it's creative tension. Since we were once newcomers to parts of our overall business, we have had to run faster, and to keep running. But now the urge to "keep running" is a basic part of our personality. Even when we're out front.

Yes, Bankers Trust is different.

> Extracted from "Bankers Trust New York Corporation—
> Vision and Values"

64. **Baptist Memorial Hospital**
     899 Madison Avenue; Memphis, TN 38146
     (901) 522-5252
     Industry: 80—Hospital

Mission

The mission of Baptist Memorial Hospital is to be a healing institution in accordance with the threefold ministry of Christ: preaching, teaching, and healing. In this role, Baptist Memorial Hospital shall be the flagship hospital within the Baptist Memorial Health Care System, and shall provide a comprehensive range of health care and health promotion services. Baptist Memorial Hospital shall also provide and support education and training programs for a wide spectrum of health care professionals and associated personnel, and shall conduct all its activities in an atmosphere of Christian influence and compassion.

Values

- Friendly and responsive care
- Teamwork, respect, and trust
- Continuous improvement
- Efficient resource management

Vision

Baptist Memorial Hospital will be *THE* leader in health care quality, value, and service in this region, and one of the leading health care providers in the world.

Commitment

We will work together to meet the emotional, physical, and spiritual needs and exceed expectations of our patients, other guests, and fellow teammates with skill, love, and care.

> "A Leader in World Medicine . . . Caring People Who Serve."
>
> Revised August, 1992

Bard

> *see* C.R. Bard, Inc. (168)

65. **Barnes Group Inc.**
     123 Main Street; Bristol, CT 06010
     (203) 583-7070
     Industry: 34—Metal parts

Guiding Philosophy

Barnes Group is a diversified public company consisting of three separate businesses dedicated to providing superior quality products and services to selected industrial markets. We believe that:

We exist to serve our customers.

We must focus on those customers who recognize and reward superior quality and service.

We must focus on manufacturing and distributing products and services where we have or can gain a competitive advantage.

People are our most important resource. We will foster a decentralized, entrepreneurial environment where each person is respected as an individual who can make significant contributions to the success of the company. We will provide an atmosphere of participation and partnership which encourages open communication, individual creativity, and a continuing search for better ways to conduct our business. We expect superior performance and will pay for it.

Our vendors are business partners. We intend to develop long-term relationships at fair prices with vendors who help us attain competitive advantage through quality, innovation and on-time delivery.

We are a responsible corporate citizen. We will conduct our business in accord with the highest ethical standards, and be responsive to the concerns of the countries and communities in which we operate.

Superior financial results will follow as a natural outcome of our efforts.

Our actions as a corporation will be fully consistent with these beliefs enabling Barnes Group and its stockholders to continue to prosper in an ever changing world.

> Adopted February 20, 1987

66. **Barnett Banks, Inc.**
50 North Laura Street; Jacksonville, FL 32202-3638
(904) 791-7720
Industry: 60—Banking

Mission Statement

Barnett will create value for its owners, customers and employees by creating and capitalizing on market leadership positions to sell and service a broad range of high quality, profitable, financial services. Our sales emphasis will be full service to consumers and businesses in our communities and advisory and processing services to others. We will operate at the lowest possible cost consistent with maintaining high service quality and market leadership.

67. **Bashas' Markets Inc.**
P.O. Box 488; Chandler, AZ 85244
(602) 834-4542
Industry: 54—Supermarkets

Mission Statement

We will hold our customers' wants and needs to be paramount, and through warm, quality customer service and efficient operations we will do all we can to meet those needs.

Our method of achieving this mission encompasses four goals. Our goals are to continue to offer friendly, helpful customer service; to provide quality products at a genuine value; to offer a combination of variety of choice, quality merchandise, competitive pricing and availability; and to operate at a reasonable profit. This profit will provide the resources for us to expand and fortify our position against continuing competitive infiltration and to increase our ability to serve our customers.

Philosophy of the Family of Companies

Of first importance is the Bashas' family heritage, the loyalty to the family and to the foundations of the past. The commitment, hard work and honesty, which characterize the Family of Companies today, have existed since its beginning. These ideals have permeated Bashas' and are a mainstay of our identity.

Secondly, the appreciation for the people associated with Bashas' reflects back to the family notion that was so instrumental in the Companies' early days. As people were brought into the Companies, they were accorded a status similar to that of a family member. This philosophy underscores the Bashas' policy regarding member relations. We truly care about all the people associated with the Bashas' Family of Companies.

Respect for differences in creed and color is another milestone in the Bashas' vision: that we are all one people, irrespective of race or religion. We extend to one another respect for those differences yet we believe that the bonds of mutual understanding and friendship are far greater than whatever our perceived differences might be.

Fourth, with respect to economic well-being, we strive diligently to develop the financial strength to ensure the well-being of members. The success of this goal is visible in one of the most solvent pension plans in the state of Arizona.

Pride in our country emanated from the humble beginnings of Lebanese immigrants who recognized the value of political, religious and economic freedom. Patriotism is a cornerstone for Bashas'. There is continuous public evidence of the endeavors of our Companies showing the importance of economic, religious and political freedom.

Bashas' Report 1988

68. **BASIS International Limited**
     5901 Jefferson Street, NE; Albuquerque, NM 87109
     (505) 345-5232
     Industry: 73—Software

The Mission

The mission of BASIS International is to provide professional software vendors with the most efficient and effective suite of integrated development tools available for the creation of sophisticated horizontal and vertical business application systems. BASIS will offer a complete array of fully integrated application development tools including languages, screen generators, report writers, data dictionaries, development libraries, and relational data management tools. BASIS will fully support open computer systems architectures and the most popular operating systems standards. BASIS will provide the BB^X PROGRESSION application software development community with marketing, technical support, and training services. BASIS will always strive to provide the highest possible quality in its products and services and to fully and satisfactorily meet the needs of its customers.

69. **Battle Mountain Gold Company**
     333 Clay Street, 42nd Floor; Houston, TX 77002
     (713) 653-7248
     Industry: 10—Gold mining

MISSION STATEMENT

Battle Mountain Gold Company is an international gold mining company. Using our core skills and technologies, we will seek to enhance shareholder value through growth and industry leadership. We will succeed by exploring for or acquiring reserves, constructing and operating profitable mines, and providing challenging opportunities for our employees.

We will apply our resources to the fundamental obligations that we have to our shareholders, employees, communities and the environment, while capitalizing upon opportunities in the Western Hemisphere and the Western Pacific.

CORE VALUES

Respect: Show concern for your fellow employees, community, environment and shareholders.

Excellence: Strive to achieve world-class status.

Safety: Promote the well-being of employees and the public.

Profit motivation: Encourage low costs through innovation and entrepreneurship.

Environmental stewardship: Commit to responsible environmental activity.

Cooperation: Talk with people, not about people; teamwork is the basis for achievement.

Truth: Act honestly and openly with the highest ethics.

70. **Baxter Healthcare Corporation**
One Baxter Parkway; Deerfield, IL 60015-4633
(708) 948-2000
Industry: 28, 38—Medical supplies

Mission: Our Primary Objective

We will be the leading health-care company by providing the best products and services for our customers around the world, consistently emphasizing innovation, operational excellence and the highest quality in everything we do.

Principles: What We Stand For

We are committed to:
- Customers: Aggressively meeting customer needs.
- Employees: Respecting employees as individuals and providing opportunities for their personal development.
- Stockholders: Achieving long-term growth and the best return for our investors.

Through:
- Teamwork: Working strongly as a Baxter team.
- Quality: Reaching an objective understanding of customer requirements and using all our resources to satisfy those requirements.
- Business Excellence: Acting ethically and continually striving for excellence in our performance.

Strategy: The Course We're Taking

We are unique in our product and service breadth and our technological depth. We will use these strengths to:
- Grow our businesses by providing the best quality in products and services to customers and to suppliers.
- Provide products and services to deliver effective therapy to patients in lower-cost settings, inside and outside the hospital.
- Creatively apply technology to develop and maintain high-return leadership positions in selected markets worldwide.
- Be the best-cost producer by emphasizing innovative technology, cost and quality.
- Manage a balanced portfolio of businesses that increases the long-term value of shareholders' investments.

Drafted 1990
Annual Report 1991

71. **Bay Health Systems**
     1900 Columbus Avenue; Bay City, MI 48708
     (517) 894-3800
     Industry: 80—Hospital

OUR MISSION OF SERVICE

The mission of Bay Health Systems is to provide comprehensive services which maintain and improve the physical and mental health of all people who come to us in need. To this end, we will deliver compassionate, high quality, cost effective health care to those we serve; and we will provide our employees and physicians with the most advanced technology and education within our resources.

PHILOSOPHY

The principles that govern all who are associated with Bay Health Systems in carrying out its Mission of Service

- We are dedicated to the philosophy that each human being is unique, is to be valued, and will be treated with dignity and respect;

- We are committed to excellence in patient care and our relationships with physicians, employees, purchasers, vendors, and the public we serve;
- We will strive for innovation and continuous improvement in our services and facilities, and will promote ongoing training and education for achieving the full potential of all our employees and physicians.

Revised 1987

BB&T
see Branch Banking & Trust Company (92)

BC Hydro
see British Columbia Hydro and Power Authority (96)

BC Tel
see British Columbia Telephone (98)

72. **BE&K, Inc.**
P.O. Box 2332; Birmingham, AL 35201-2332
(205) 969-3600
Industry: 16—Construction

MISSION

To be the premier provider of engineering and construction services and a leader in capital intensive ventures worldwide.

To offer innovative and creative technology and management systems to provide customers with quality, cost effective projects from concept through full life cycle.

To provide a work environment that recognizes and rewards outstanding employee contribution, provides the stockholder with appropriate compensation, and contributes to the long term well being of the communities in which we live and work.

73. **BeautiControl® Cosmetics**
2121 Midway; Carrollton, TX 75006
(214) 458-0601
Industry: 59—Direct sales of cosmetics

MISSION STATEMENT

To offer women a lifetime of self-confidence through products and services designed to enhance their personal appearance . . . and within a nurturing environment, provide women with a rewarding full-time or part-time earnings opportunity limited only by their own initiative.

74. **Beckman Instruments, Inc.**
2500 Harbor Boulevard; P.O. Box 3100; Fullerton, CA 92634-3100
(714) 871-4848

Industry: 38—Medical equipment

Vision—What we aspire to be

Our business is the chemistry of life, and we seek to be the world's acknowledged leader in providing laboratory systems that advance scientific discovery and speed the diagnosis of disease. In so doing, we will help science improve the quality of life.

Mission—What we must do

Our mission is to profitably gain and retain customers by providing quality products and services that simplify and automate chemical analysis across the continuum from academic bioresearch to applications in the bioindustrial and diagnostic laboratory.

Our affairs will be conducted at the highest level of excellence, so as to create lasting customer partnerships, provide growth and opportunity for employees, and return superior value to our investors.

Values—Our shared beliefs & behavior

We at Beckman believe . . .

-      **"There is no satisfactory substitute for excellence."** These are the words of our founder, Dr. Arnold O. Beckman, and we are committed to living up to his standards. We also set high standards for ourselves, and strive through quality commitment programs to continually make the best even better. We know that out of excellence comes uncompromised value and quality in our products and services, and a consistent improvement in shareholder value. Excellence lies in the skilled hands and minds of we the people of Beckman.

-      **Integrity is the virtue that guides Beckman business.** In business and personal relationships, we operate with fairness and honesty. Our enterprise is based on ethical behavior, trust and promises kept. We strive to do what's right for the customer so the customer continues to do business with us. We strive to do what's right for our fellow employees so they feel a part of the Beckman family. And we strive to do what's right for the world and the environment so that it is a better place to live for all.

-      **We have a dedication to customers.** For the customer, we diligently strive to deliver the finest products and the most responsive total customer service in the life sciences and diagnostic markets. Our first responsibility is to our customers, and by serving them well we will be able to profitably serve our shareholders. Within the company, we are committed to treating each other as customers, providing services that are complete, reliable and on time, every time. Striving to exceed customer expectations is what makes Beckman service superior.

- **Our outlook is global.** We take a world view in all aspects of our business, because scientific and medical discoveries transcend national boundaries. With business throughout the world, and more analytical chemistry systems in use than anyone else, we are truly a global company. Our purpose is to help laboratory professionals advance scientific discovery and speed the diagnosis and treatment of disease, ultimately improving the quality of life for all of the world's people.

- **Innovation is essential to our progress.** Innovation, creativity and entrepreneurship are the cornerstones to Beckman's business. These qualities are encouraged, nurtured and rewarded throughout the company. We view innovation not only as breakthrough technology but also steady steps, taken every day, to achieve a competitive edge. We continually search for new ideas and work with the research communities to bring their ideas to fruition. Our challenge is to retain the pioneer spirit as part of the day-to-day work ethic.

- **Individuals make Beckman's success possible.** We place a high importance upon the individual and each person's contribution to our team. We strive to maintain a safe, congenial environment that allows us to pursue personal career satisfaction. It is the consideration of individual views and the mobilization of individual energies through teamwork that lead to company success.

Drafted January, 1992

75. **Belcan Corporation**
   Belcan Engineering Group, Inc.
   10200 Anderson Way; Cincinnati, OH 45242
   (513) 891-0972
   Industry: 73, 87—Temporary help and engineering services

   The Strategic Direction of Belcan Engineering Services, Inc.

   MISSION

   We will provide engineered solutions to firms who value:
   - continuous improvement in the quality of their products, industrial processes, manufacturing systems and facilities;
   - and the establishment of long-term alliances with their engineering suppliers.

   VISION

   - We will set the standard for quality in the engineering field.

   VALUES

   Continuous Customer Focus

   - To set customer sensitivity as the cornerstone of our culture

- To recognize that we all have customers—external and/or internal
- To identify all individual customers' requirements

Relentless Drive for Improvement

- To continuously identify improvement areas in our work
- To make change an ongoing process—a race without a finish line
- To value the flexibility to accept change and respond accordingly

Management by Fact

- To support individual and team recommendations with factual data
- To recognize that systems, not people, generally constrain performance
- To define and improve all business processes based on data

Respect for People

- To expect constructive interpersonal relationship qualities from each of us
- To value constructive feedback
- To trust in our fellow workers and respect their opinions

Teamwork

- To recognize teamwork as fundamental to our business success
- To value positive team play as a key individual characteristic

Safety, Health, and Environmental Responsibility

- To ensure that neither our actions nor our products negatively impact our fellow employees, our customers, or the community
- To consciously protect our environment

Consistent Ethical Behavior

- To live by our word
- To never compromise our personal or professional ethics

Sharing our Success

- To recognize and reward winning as a team
- To share our collective success in a fair and equitable manner

Positive Attitude Toward Work

- To meet our objectives with a positive attitude
- To have fun in our day-to-day tasks
- To be gratified by the attainment of long-term milestones

Community and Industry Contribution

- To value participation in local community activities
- To encourage active participation in technical and industrial organizations

Standards of Performance

Fundamental Objectives	Improvement Guidelines
Total Quality Management	- Involve All Employees
	- Apply CIP Philosophy, Processes, and Tools in Day-to-Day Activities
	- Monitor Performance Against Quantifiable Measurements
Customer Satisfaction	- Identify All Internal and External Customers
	- Establish Customer Feedback Mechanisms
	- Assess Performance Against Customer Requirements
Human Resources	- Attract and Retain Quality Personnel
	- Improve Individual Performance and Teamwork
	- Foster a Culture for Growth and Involvement
Technology Integration	- Seek and Integrate the Most Effective Technology to Meet Client Needs
	- Innovate in the Absence of Available Technology
Business Development	- Maintain Flexibility to Meet Market Needs
	- Identify New Needs Within the Existing Client Base
	- Identify New Client/Partners Based on our Mission Statement
Financial Strength	- Make Decisions and Measure Success with a Long-Term Corporate Perspective
	- Maintain Positive Profits/Cash Flow with Steady Revenue Growth

Adapted from poster

76. **Ben & Jerry's Homemade, Inc.**
Route 100; P.O. Box 240; Waterbury, VT 05676
(802) 244-6957
Industry: 20—Ice cream

Ben & Jerry's Statement of Mission

Ben & Jerry's is dedicated to the creation and demonstration of a new corporate concept of linked prosperity. Our mission consists of three interrelated parts:

PRODUCT MISSION:

To make, distribute and sell the finest quality all-natural ice cream and related products in a wide variety of innovative flavors made from Vermont dairy products.

SOCIAL MISSION:

To operate the company in a way that actively recognizes the central role that business plays in the structure of society by initiating innovative ways to improve the quality of life of a broad community: local, national and international.

ECONOMIC MISSION:

To operate the company on a sound financial basis of profitable growth, increasing value for our shareholders and creating career opportunities and financial rewards for our employees.

Underlying the mission of Ben & Jerry's is the determination to seek new and creative ways of addressing all three parts, while holding a deep respect for individuals, inside and outside the company, and for the communities of which they are a part.

Drafted 1988
Annual Report Copyright © 1991

77. **Bendco/Bending & Coiling Co., Inc.**
P.O. Box 3384; Pasadena, TX 77501-3384
(713) 473-1557
Industry: 33—Pipe bending and coiling

Mission Statement

1. Quality safety thru attitudes and team effort.
2. Quality products and service. A fundamental principle of quality theory is that the workers closest to a process understands it best.
3. Quality production and 0-defects thru excellent workmanship.

Drafted March 29, 1991

78. **Best Products Co., Inc.**
P.O. Box 26303; Richmond, VA 23260-6303
(804) 261-2000
Industry: 59—Discount stores

OUR MISSION IS TO BE A CUSTOMER-DRIVEN RETAILER.

We will exceed our customers' expectations every day in every way.

We will provide friendly, knowledgeable, courteous and prompt service in all areas of our business.

We will provide an environment in which our associates are offered opportunities for growth and recognized for their accomplishments.

We will provide destination assortments of quality brand name merchandise at exceptional value.

We will provide an attractive return on investment.

79. **Bethlehem Steel Corporation**
    Martin Tower; Bethlehem, PA 18016-7699
    (215) 694-2424
    Industry: 33—Steel

BETHLEHEM'S GUIDING PRINCIPLES

CUSTOMERS

We know that our ability to meet our objectives depends on anticipating and satisfying our customers' needs. To be a premier supplier, we will continually focus our efforts on improving product quality and customer service and reducing costs.

We will invest in new technologies and facilities that are required to maintain our competitiveness and support our objectives.

EMPLOYEES

We recognize that our employees are our most valuable asset. Therefore, we will:
- Promote an environment for our employees that is both challenging and rewarding and that fosters individual initiative and teamwork,
- Provide ongoing communication of Bethlehem's affairs to our employees in order to enhance awareness of our strategies and progress toward our objectives, and
- Support labor/management partnership programs and encourage employee participation in improving Bethlehem's performance.

We will strive for excellence in management and focus appropriate responsibility and authority at all levels of supervision. Our managers are expected to demonstrate leadership, exercise sound business judgement, promote innovation, and be sensitive to the needs of all of our constituents.

We will require strict adherence to the letter and the spirit of all laws applicable to the conduct of our business and to high standards of integrity and sound ethical judgement by all employees.

PUBLIC

We will be a responsible corporate citizen. We will take appropriate actions directed at government and public issues and events which we feel are important to our constituents or affect our ability to attain our objectives. Our employees will be encouraged to participate in community and charitable affairs.

SUPPLIERS

We consider our suppliers as key partners in serving our customers' needs, and we will work with them to improve our mutual competitiveness. We expect to receive quality products and services that are cost competitive, and those suppliers who meet these requirements will have ongoing business opportunities with Bethlehem.

STOCKHOLDERS

We intend to enhance our long-term value for our stockholders through the accomplishment of our Objectives by following our Strategy and Guiding Principles.

BETHLEHEM'S OBJECTIVES

- To be a customer-driven, premier producer and supplier of quality products.
- To generate sustained profitability and enhance long-term value for our stockholders.
- To have a sound financial base for meeting the challenges and opportunities of the future.

BETHLEHEM'S STRATEGY

- We will manage our resources to make our businesses competitive and profitable on a long-term basis and to improve our financial base.
- We will continually restructure our businesses, as appropriate, to support our Corporate objectives.
- We will pursue business opportunities that provide increased value to Bethlehem and our constituents.

80. **BFGoodrich Company**
     3925 Embassy Parkway; Akron, OH 44333-1799
     (216) 374-2999
     Industry: 28, 30—Chemicals and rubber

Mission

The basic purpose of The BFGoodrich Company is to provide customers with quality products, systems and services that represent the best use of our technological, financial and human resources. We achieve leadership positions in specialty markets by helping our customers improve the performance of their products and reduce their costs. By creating economic advantages for our customers, we generate wealth for our shareholders, provide rewarding careers for our employees, and build our worldwide businesses in a profitable and responsible manner.

Vision

The BFGoodrich Company today is the product of a dramatic transformation initiated during the 1980s. We are building what, in effect, is an entirely new Company—stronger and more-balanced—on the firm foundation of technological excellence and superior service. We are renewing our commitment to customer satisfaction through quality products and superior service. We are refocusing our resources on specialty businesses where our efforts—and our shareholders' investments—can achieve higher returns.

Our transformation is not complete, and still more change lies ahead. That change will be more evolutionary in nature, however, because the basic framework for The BFGoodrich Company of the mid-1990s already is in place. We have the necessary resources and the strategic plans to make optimum use of those resources. The refinements we will make in the years ahead will nevertheless be important to our ultimate success.

Our businesses will continue to be diverse and our operations decentralized, but they will share several strategic characteristics. They also will reflect certain values fundamental to our organization and shared by all our employees.

These strategic characteristics and fundamental values are increasingly evident throughout BFGoodrich. In the future they will play an even more important role in helping us produce the financial and operating synergies that will make our Company more valuable than the sum of its parts.

The financial results generated by our businesses will be consistent, sustainable and above average. Return on shareholder equity will average at least 15 percent (within a range of 12–18 percent), and return on net capital employed in each division will be in excess of 20 percent. Our balance sheet will remain investment grade, with a debt-to-capital ratio not exceeding 35 percent. We will have ready access to both debt and equity capital markets, so that we can take full advantage of growth opportunities. Continuing increases in sales and income will be ensured by research and development programs and by intensified product commercialization efforts.

Our financial performance and commitment to continued improvement in all facets of our operations will create added wealth for our shareholders, offer economic advantages for our customers, provide rewarding careers for our employees and foster a healthful and productive environment for the communities where our facilities are located.

Values

Our business strategies and tactics can be adjusted to capitalize on changing market and economic conditions. However, our fundamental values—our philosophy and the way we do business—endure. The manner in which we achieve business objectives is just as important as the objectives themselves, and we will not deviate from the principles of ethical conduct embodied in our fundamental values. These values reflect our commitment to satisfied customers and empowered employees. They also reflect our respect and concern for the environment, for the communities in which we operate and for one another.

- Our dealings with others—inside and outside the Company—are based on mutual respect, open communications and unquestioned integrity.
- We accept responsibility for providing a safe and healthful environment for our employees, suppliers, customers and neighbors.
- Empowered employees are the ultimate source of our success.
- A leadership role in public affairs benefits our Company, our communities and our employees.
- Results are the ultimate measurement of our success in creating economic advantage for our customers, wealth for our shareholders and career opportunities for our employees.
- Satisfying the customer is a basic responsibility shared by each and every employee.
- Progress requires a bias to action that encourages calculated risk-taking.

Employee Annual Report 1991
Copyright © The BFGoodrich Company 1992

81.   **Biomet, Inc.**
      P.O. Box 587; Warsaw, IN 46581-0587
      (219) 267-6639
      Industry: 38—Medical supplies

Biomet Corporate Mission

To continue our growth as an orthopedic company, while expanding our presence in other compatible market segments through cost-effective product introductions.

To contribute the quality of products necessary to aid individuals in need and to continuously improve our products through research and developmental efforts.

To always recognize the importance of our customers by providing high service levels and continued dedication to meet their needs.

To recognize the value of our team members and offer the resources and opportunities necessary to achieve personal satisfaction and professional growth opportunities.

To preserve the confidence of our shareholders by maintaining superior communications and continued dedication to manage Biomet to the best of our abilities.

82.   **Black River Manufacturing, Inc.**
      2625 Twentieth Street; Port Huron, MI 48060

(313) 982-9812
Industry: 37—Automobile parts

Mission Statement

Black River Manufacturing is committed to securing our future in the market place, by supplying a world class quality product, and meeting or exceeding the customers expectations as a full service supplier.

Block, H&R, Inc.
see H&R Block, Inc. (263)

83. **Blockbuster Entertainment Corporation**
P.O. Box 407060; Fort Lauderdale, FL 33340-7060
(305) 832-3250
Industry: 78—Video stores

Mission Statement

We are in the entertainment business to be profitable. We are committed to providing our customers with good value, our employees with a rewarding and enjoyable job experience, and our shareholders with exceptional return on investment. We will be entreprencurial in response to tactical or strategic opportunities and create the greatest value possible for customers, ourselves, and our shareholders.

Six Operating Philosophies

Provide the best customer experience through:
Selection—Service—Convenience—Value
Keep it simple and direct.
Constantly strive to create the greatest value.
Set and demand standards of Excellence. Lead by example.
Work together to create opportunities.
Aggressively accomplish goals and have fun.

Key Result Areas

Customer Experience—Excitement followed by satisfaction.
Employee Experience—Feeling valued, successful and involved.
Financial Results—Growth consistency and integrity.
Quality of Operations—*How* we do *what* we do.

84. **Blue Diamond Growers**
P.O. Box 1768; Sacramento, CA 95812
(916) 442-0771
Industry: 51—Wholesale almonds

MISSION STATEMENT

We at Blue Diamond Growers are in the business of processing and marketing almonds and complementary products.

Consumers and customers make our existence possible. We will provide them quality products and superior service.

Our owners are California almond growers. Employees at Blue Diamond Growers will return to them superior and secure returns relative to the competition.

Blue Diamond owners will provide their employees competitive pay and benefits in return for high productivity, focus on continuous improvement, and participation in achieving the company's stated goals.

We believe our people are our most valuable resource. The Almond People® are expected to treat others with respect, dignity, and fairness. Our reputation has been built on the cornerstones of integrity and honest dealings.

We recognize an equitable balance of interests must be maintained for the good of our members, employees, customers, suppliers, and the communities in which we operate.

The Almond People® shall strive to maintain a climate which nurtures these values.

85. **Boatmen's Bancshares, Inc.**
    800 Market Street; P.O. Box 236; St. Louis, MO 63166-0236
    (314) 466-7720
    Industry: 60—Banking

    Mission Statement

    Build the leading financial institution in the central United States, in terms of size, consistent financial performance, quality of service and work environment.

                                                                              1992

86. **Bob Evans Farms, Inc.**
    3776 South High Street; P.O. Box 07863; Columbus, OH
       43207-0863
    (614) 491-2225
    Industry: 20, 58—Food and restaurants

    MISSION STATEMENT

    Bob Evans Farms, Inc. is dedicated to being the best company in the food industry and related businesses. Our mission is to provide quality products and services to meet our customers' needs, which allows us to prosper as a business and to provide a reasonable return for our stockholders.

Principles:

Employees—Our people are the source of our strength. They provide our corporate intelligence and determine our reputation and vitality. We are committed to their growth, development and job satisfaction.

Quality, Service and the Customer—We pledge to be responsive to customer needs and provide quality products and services that are measurably and consistently superior to our competitors.

Profit—We are committed to providing a profit sufficient to ensure the growth, improvement and continuity of the business.

Integrity—We are honest and straightforward because we believe these qualities are the foundation of our success.

Tradition—Our tradition is built on the values of pride, honesty and a strong work ethic.

87.   **The Boeing Company**
      P.O. Box 3707; Seattle, WA 98124-2207
      (206) 655-2121
      Industry: 37—Aircraft

CORPORATE DIRECTION

Long-Range Mission

To be the number one aerospace company in the world and among the premier industrial concerns in terms of quality, profitability, and growth.

Fundamental Goals

Quality as measured by: Customer, employee, and community satisfaction

Profitability as measured against our ability to achieve and then maintain: 20 percent average annual return on stockholders' equity

Growth over the long term as measured against a goal to achieve: Greater than 5 percent annual real sales growth from 1988 base

Objectives

To achieve the above goals and fulfill Boeing's mission, the following objectives will guide company actions:

Continuous improvement in quality of products and processes

Our commitment to steady, long-term improvement in our products and processes is the cornerstone of our business strategy. To achieve this objective, we must work to continuously improve the overall quality of our design, manufacturing, administrative, and support organizations.

A highly skilled and motivated workforce

Our most important resource is our human resource: the people who design and build our products and service our customers. Given the right combination of skills, training, communications, environment, and leadership, we believe our employees will achieve the needed gains in productivity and quality to meet our goals.

Capable and focused management

To employ our technical and human resources with optimum efficiency, we must ensure that managers are carefully selected, appropriately trained, and work together to achieve our long-range goals.

Technical excellence

In a world of fast-changing technology, we can only remain competitive by continuously refining and expanding our technical capability.

Financial strength

The high-risk, cyclical nature of our business demands a strong financial base. We must retain the capital resources to meet our current commitments and make substantial investments to develop new products and new technology for the future. This objective also requires contingency planning and control to ensure the company is not overextended should a severe economic downturn occur during the plan period.

Commitment to integrity

Integrity, in the broadest sense, must pervade our actions in all relationships, including those with our customers, suppliers, and each other. This is a commitment to uncompromising values and conduct. It includes compliance with all laws and regulations.

Statement announced September, 1989

88. **Boise Cascade Corporation**
    P.O. Box 50; Boise, ID 83728-0001
    (208) 384-6161
    Industry: 24, 26—Paper and lumber

OUR MISSION

To continuously improve the company's long-term value to customers, employees, shareholders, and society.

OUR TOTAL QUALITY COMMITMENT

To continuously make improvements that will enable us to anticipate, understand, and fulfill both internal and external customer expectations so that the company becomes the preferred supplier of each of our customers.

WHAT WE VALUE

Safety	Trust
Health	Integrity
Caring	Respect
Innovation	Responsibility
Teamwork	Citizenship

OUR STRATEGY

We will pursue efficiency, distinctive competence, and focused growth in the paper and paper products, office products, and building products businesses, while applying the principles of Total Quality.

1991

89. Borgess Medical Center
1521 Gull Road; Kalamazoo, MI 49001
(616) 383-7000
Industry: 80—Hospital

MISSION

In harmony with the healing mission of the Catholic Church, the mission of Borgess Medical Center is to operate as a major referral center that provides holistic health care for its regional service area. In fulfilling its mission, the fourfold purpose of Borgess Medical Center is:
- to provide compassionate, comprehensive quality patient care to its regional service area;
- to provide an environment which is supportive of education for health care providers, patients and families;
- to be a leading institution in developing new concepts in health care;
- and to fulfill community social responsibilities.

SHARED VALUES AND BELIEFS

Touchstones

Competence

We pursue excellence in our healing efforts.

Compassion

We enhance the dignity of all people by demonstrating care and respect.

Collaboration

We work together in a spirit of teamwork to serve others.

Creativity

We seek the best way to serve and to use the resources entrusted to us.

Contribution

We empower each person to fully use gifts and talents, and hold each other accountable to the fullest extent.

Choices

We pursue the highest ethical standards in our decisions and in our actions.

Developed Fall 1989

90. **Borg-Warner Corporation**
     200 South Michigan Avenue; Chicago, IL 60604
     (312) 322-8511
     Industry: 37—Automobile parts

". . . to reach beyond the minimal"

The Beliefs of Borg-Warner

Any business is a member of a social system, entitled to the rights and bound by the responsibilities of that membership. Its freedom to pursue economic goals is constrained by law and channeled by the forces of a free market. But these demands are minimal, requiring only that a business provide wanted goods and services, compete fairly, and cause no obvious harm. For some companies that is enough. It is not enough for Borg-Warner. We impose upon ourselves an obligation to reach beyond the minimal. We do so convinced that by making a larger contribution to the society that sustains us, we best assure not only its future vitality, but our own.

This is what we believe . . .

We believe in the dignity of the individual.

However large and complex a business may be, its work is still done by people dealing with people. Each person involved is a unique human being, with pride, needs, values, and innate personal worth. For Borg-Warner to succeed we must operate in a climate of openness and trust, in which each of us freely grants others the same respect, cooperation, and decency we seek for ourselves.

We believe in our responsibility to the common good.

Because Borg-Warner is both an economic and social force, our responsibilities to the public are large. The spur of competition and the sanctions of the law give strong guidance to our behavior, but alone do not inspire our best. For that we must heed the voice of our natural concern for others. Our challenge is to supply goods and services that are of superior value to those who use them; to create jobs that provide meaning for those who do them; to honor and enhance human life; and to offer our talents and our wealth to help improve the world we share.

We believe in the endless quest for excellence.

Though we may be better today than we were yesterday, we are not as good as we must become. Borg-Warner chooses to be a leader—in serving our customers, advancing our technologies, and rewarding all who invest in us their time, money and trust. None of us can settle for doing less than our best, and we can never stop trying to surpass what already has been achieved.

We believe in continuous renewal.

A corporation endures and prospers only by moving forward. The past has given us the present to build on. But to follow our visions to the future, we must see the difference between traditions that give us continuity and strength, and conventions that no longer serve us—and have the courage to act on that knowledge. Most can adapt after change has occurred; we must be among the few who anticipate change, shape it to our purpose, and act as its agents.

We believe in the commonwealth of Borg-Warner and its people.

Borg-Warner is both a federation of businesses and a community of people. Our goal is to preserve the freedom each of us needs to find personal satisfaction while building the strength that comes from unity. True unity is more than a melding of self-interests; it results when values and ideals also are shared. Some of ours are spelled out in these statements of belief. Others include faith in our political, economic, and spiritual heritage; pride in our work and our company; the knowledge that loyalty must flow in many directions; and a conviction that power is strongest when shared. We look to the unifying force of these beliefs as a source of energy to brighten the future of our company and all who depend on it.

Copyright © 1982 Borg-Warner Corporation

91. **Boston Bank of Commerce**
    133 Federal Street; Boston, MA 02110
    (617) 457-4400
    Industry: 60—Bank

THE BANK'S MISSION

- to provide professional, high quality banking services for all of our customers
- to assure that all customers receive pleasant, consistent, and ethical attention in every transaction

- to use its expertise and resources to foster economic growth for our customers and their communities

In order to achieve the mission, we have created banking services that are valuable to our customers. We serve as a link in joining the economic interests of the minority community with those of the broader community.

Boston Bank of Commerce serves as a model for financial institutions throughout the country who seek to encourage broad-based economic development in the demographically, ethnically and economically diverse urban areas of our major cities.

Boys Town
   see Father Flanagan's Boys' Home (222)

92. **Branch Banking and Trust Company**
    BB&T
    P.O. Box 1847; Wilson, NC 27894-1847
    (919) 399-4317
    Industry: 60—Banking

BB&T MISSION

To make the world a better place to live by:
- Helping our **customers** achieve economic success and financial security;
- Creating a place where our **employees** can learn, grow, and be fulfilled in their work;
- Making the **communities** we serve a better place to be;
- Optimizing the long term return on our **shareholders**, while providing a safe and sound investment.

                                                        Revised January 1, 1992

93. **Brinker International, Inc.**
    6820 LBJ Freeway; Dallas, TX 75240
    (214) 980-9917
    Industry: 58—Restaurants

MISSION STATEMENT

-      To be a premier and progressive growth company, with a balanced approach towards people, quality and profitability.

-      To empower our team to exceed customers' expectations . . . to become customer obsessed.

-      To enhance a high level of excellence, innovation, integrity and ethics.

-      To attract, retain and develop a team of superior people.

- To be focused, sensitive and responsive to our employees and our environment.
- To enhance long-term shareholder wealth.

94. **Bristol-Myers Squibb Company**
345 Park Avenue; New York, NY 10154-0037
(212) 546-4000
Industry: 28—Toiletries and pharmaceuticals

The Bristol-Myers Squibb Pledge

To those who use our products . . .

We affirm Bristol-Myers Squibb's commitment to the highest standards of excellence, safety and reliability in everything we make. We pledge to offer products of the highest quality and to work diligently to keep improving them.

To our employees and those who may join us . . .

We pledge personal respect, fair compensation and equal treatment. We acknowledge our obligation to provide able and humane leadership throughout the organization, within a clean and safe working environment. To all who qualify for advancement, we will make every effort to provide opportunity.

To our suppliers and customers . . .

We pledge an open door, courteous, efficient and ethical dealing, and appreciation of their right to a fair profit.

To our shareholders . . .

We pledge a companywide dedication to continued profitable growth, sustained by strong finances, a high level of research and development, and facilities second to none.

To the communities where we have plants and offices . . .

We pledge conscientious citizenship, a helping hand for worthwhile causes, and constructive action in support of civic and environmental progress.

To the countries where we do business . . .

We pledge ourselves to be a good citizen and to show full consideration for the rights of others while reserving the right to stand up for our own.

Above all, to the world we live in . . .

We pledge Bristol-Myers Squibb to policies and practices which fully embody the responsibility, integrity and decency required of free enterprise if it is to merit and maintain the confidence of our society.

95. **British Columbia Ferry Corporation**
1112 Fort Street; Victoria, British Columbia; Canada V8V 4V2
(604) 381-1401
Industry: 44—Water transportation

MISSION STATEMENT

The mission of the British Columbia Ferry Corporation is to provide effective, dependable and safe coastal ferry transportation services in the most efficient manner possible.

CORPORATE OBJECTIVES

A. Service

(i) To provide effective, dependable and safe ferry transportation services in the most efficient manner possible;

(ii) To be aware of the Corporation's responsibilities to travellers and of their transportation needs.

B. Planning

To anticipate and plan for future coastal ferry requirements of the Province with due regard for the social, economic and environmental considerations and to integrate such planning with the overall transportation policies of the Province.

C. Ethics

To conduct the business and affairs of the Corporation to a standard commensurate with that of responsible public corporations and in accordance with the code of business conduct adopted by the Corporation.

D. People

To maintain a well balanced, efficient work force through sound recruitment, training, development, promotion of employees, the establishment of progressive personnel policies, and effective communication at all levels of the organization.

E. Financial

To provide transportation services within the subsidy and tariff structure authorized by the shareholder.

F. Communications

To inform and keep informed the Government of the Province of British Columbia and the people of the Province of events occurring or planned in connection with the Corporation's operations.

Approved 1985

96. British Columbia Hydro and Power Authority
333 Dunsmuir Street; Vancouver, British Columbia; Canada
V6B 5R3
(604) 663-2212
Industry: 49—Hydroelectric power

Vision for 1990s and beyond

In the year 2000, BC Hydro will continue to provide safe and reliable electric service to British Columbians at fair and reasonable prices. In addition, as the province's largest Crown corporation, BC Hydro will use its financial, technical, and human resources to provide leadership in the economic and social development of the province.

Mission

BC Hydro's corporate mission is to support the development of British Columbia through the efficient supply of electricity.

Objectives

Five objectives have been established to support BC Hydro's corporate mission:
> To be a leader in the economic and social development of British Columbia
> To be a leader in stewardship of the natural environment
> To be the most efficient utility in North America
> To be a superior customer service company
> To be the most progressive employer in British Columbia

Corporate Values

Employees of BC Hydro share these common values:
> Integrity: Our actions match our words
> Commitment: Our enthusiasm is contagious
> Innovation: We try new ideas and learn from our mistakes
> Teamwork: We work together towards shared goals
> Empowerment: We have the responsibility to act, and we do

Business Principles

As employees of BC Hydro we are committed to being:
> Open, Courteous, and Responsive–Safety Conscious
> Customer Focused–Environmentally Responsible
> Community Sensitive–Excellence Driven
> Results Oriented–Market Competitive

Corporate Motto

Together, BC Hydro employees share a common understanding of the company's purpose, and reflect this in the motto "Proud of our Service."

Extracted from "BC Hydro Corporate Strategic Plan"

97. **British Columbia Systems Corporation**
    4000 Seymour Place; Victoria, British Columbia; Canada V8X 4S8
    (604) 389-3101
    Industry: 73—Software

BUSINESS MISSION

BC Systems' mission is to provide information technology solutions that assist public sector organizations in B.C. to maintain and fundamentally improve the quality of service to the public.

The corporation does this by developing an understanding and appreciation of its customers' business needs; then responding to these needs by providing services that build on and integrate the expertise of the corporation's people, and its information processing, telecommunications and data storage capabilities.

Annual Report 1991/92

98. **British Columbia Telephone**
    3777 Kingsway; Burnaby, British Columbia; Canada V5H 3Z7
    (604) 432-2151
    Industry: 48—Telephone

MISSION STATEMENTS FOR BC TEL AND DIVISIONS

BC TEL CORPORATE

We make it easy for people to exchange information-anywhere, anytime-by devising imaginative telecommunication solutions that are economic and exceed customer expectations.

SMALL BUSINESS AND CONSUMER DIVISION

Our mission is to improve the productivity and profitability of small business and the quality of life of consumers by making it easy for them to exchange information anytime, anywhere with innovative, economic telecommunications solutions and extraordinary customer service.

BUSINESS DIVISION

Our mission is to improve the productivity, competitiveness and financial performance of business and government through making it easy to exchange information anywhere, anytime by providing imaginative solutions directly or in partnership with others.

EMERGING BUSINESS DIVISION

We improve people's competitiveness and quality of life by making it easy to exchange information anywhere, anytime through commercializing emerging personal and enhanced communications solutions and by providing support services that make it easy for people to do business with BC TEL.

TELECOMMUNICATIONS OPERATIONS DIVISION

Our mission is to improve the profitability and exceed the expectations of the front-end business units by providing them with a responsive, economic telecommunications infrastructure which makes it easy for their customers to exchange information anywhere, anytime.

BUSINESS PLANNING DIVISION

We make it easy for teams in BC TEL to have clear strategies that focus and mobilize their distinctive excellence to exceed their customer's expectations and to make BC TEL's mission a reality.

FINANCE AND ADMINISTRATION DIVISION

Building partnerships with the Business Units and breathing life into financial information, we provide innovative solutions and services which foster sound business decisions and action!

HUMAN RESOURCES DEVELOPMENT DIVISION

Our mission is to equip people to manage their own change and effect corporate transformation.

LEGAL AND CORPORATE AFFAIRS DIVISION

We help BC TEL to achieve its mission by making it easy for people to do well what they know they have to do.

SCIENCE AND TECHNOLOGY DIVISION

The mission of the Science and Technology Division is to deliver world class, integrated telecommunications and information technology solutions that provide competitive advantage to the BC TEL Divisions, as well as national and international customers.

99. **Broadway Federal Savings and Loan Association**
   4835 Venice Boulevard; Los Angeles, CA 90019
   (213) 931-1886
   Industry: 60—Savings and loan

STRATEGIC PLANNING MISSION STATEMENT

Broadway Federal is a minority owned and operated financial institution serving real estate financial and depository needs primarily for the communities in which our branches are located, with a commitment to quality service, efficiency, profitability and planned growth.

100. **Brooklyn Union Gas Company**
    One Metrotech Center; Brooklyn, NY 11201-3851
    (718) 403-2000
    Industry: 49—Natural gas utility

VISION

Brooklyn Union's vision is to become the premier energy company in the Northeast.

MISSION

Brooklyn Union's mission is to achieve growth by providing high-quality products and services which will result in enhanced customer satisfaction and shareholder value. Growth will result from existing and new markets and by our becoming a diversified energy company.

101. **Browning-Ferris Industries**
    P.O. Box 3151; Houston, TX 77253
    (713) 870-8100
    Industry: 49—Waste collection

The Challenge

We in the waste industry are facing the most challenging times in our history. The environment, every aspect of it, is on the minds of people everywhere; it is an issue confronting political leaders daily. At BFI we are at the center of those environmental concerns that deal with the disposal of wastes and their potential impact on the earth, water and air.

Guided by the sound business principles that have led to our success to-date, we will meet the challenge of waste collection and disposal with respect for our environment and sensitivity to social desires.

The Mission

Our mission is to provide the highest quality waste collection, transportation, processing, disposal and related services to both public and private customers worldwide. We will carry out our mission efficiently, safely and in an environmentally responsible manner with respect for the role of government in protecting the public interest.

Our financial goal is to achieve consistently superior results that maintain BFI as a premier growth organization and maximize shareholder value.

The Foundation

BFI is built upon a solid foundation of sound operations, financial strength, and management depth and experience, but we must integrate our company further into the framework of our social, political and regulatory surroundings.

Values and Beliefs

We are dedicated to:
Our customers,
Our people,
The highest quality,
Continuous improvement,
Flexibility in the face of change,
Superior ethical conduct.

These are our values; these are what BFI stands for and what we believe to be the tools to accomplish the mission to which we are committed.

Our Goals

In our strategic planning for the decade ahead, we have reduced our goals to five specific areas. Each is supported by several strategies to attain the goal and by priority tactics to act upon in concert with those strategies.

Goal I: **Quality**

Provide the highest quality service to our customers so as to guarantee their satisfaction.

Goal II: **Growth**

Assure long-term growth and increase market share.

Goal III: **People**

Ensure that BFI has the people necessary to carry out our mission.

Goal IV: **Ethical Conduct**

Manage our business in a manner consistent with the public interest.

Goal V: **Financial**

Achieve consistently superior results that maintain BFI as a premier growth organization and maximize shareholder value.

With this Corporate Vision of the future, BFI is committed to these five goals.

The Future

The strategic plan, some elements of which are summarized here, is intended as a living document . . . and a document to live by. The core strategic planning group arrived at the elements of the plan after consolidating the deliberations of task forces that included 60 managers.

The plan is not just words on paper. We will exert all of our energies to live up to the goals for the future that we have set for ourselves and BFI.

We are moving very quickly toward the next century. While coping with day-to-day demands, we must always keep part of our attention fixed on the future. If all of us at BFI commit to our strategic plan, our company will be well-positioned to grow and prosper in the next decade and beyond.

Extracted from "PLANNING FOR THE FUTURE—
Our Mission for the 1990's" brochure

102. Burlington Northern Railroad
2900 Continental Plaza; 777 Main Street; Fort Worth, TX 76102
(817) 878-3045
Industry: 40—Railroad

Mission Statement

Our goal is to design and consistently deliver transportation and information services that exceed our customers' expectations. A successful railroad will be at the heart of this effort. We will achieve this goal by developing an atmosphere that stimulates the productivity and innovativeness of our people and leads to profitability and growth for our owners and employees.

Drafted 1988

Burnett, Leo Company, Inc.
see Leo Burnett Company, Inc. (338)

C

103. **CAE Industries Limited**
Royal Bank Plaza, Suite 3060; P.O. Box 30; Toronto, Ontario;
Canada M5J 2J1
(416) 865-0070
Industry: 36, 38—Electronic equipment and flight simulators

MISSION STATEMENT

CAE Industries is committed to enhancing its position as a world leader in the production of real-time, data-based computer systems and engineered products for selected markets, and the provision of flight training and aircraft maintenance services. The Company will continue to build on its core business of design and development of simulation and training systems and services for commercial, military and manned space flight operations.

An integral part of CAE's success is its emphasis on research and development to ensure products and services embrace the latest technology.

The Company will continue to pursue opportunities in its current businesses through internal development or by selective acquisition to ensure long term growth in earnings and cash flow.

To accomplish its mission CAE will continue to operate with the integrity which has always characterized its business relationships. The Company will meet its customers' needs with products and services which are competitive and of the highest quality and value. CAE will maintain high standards of ethics and corporate responsibility in all its dealings. The Company will seek to ensure its employees are challenged to perform at their highest level and to live up to the trust its customers place in them.

Annual Report March 31, 1992

104. **Calgary Co-operative Association Limited**
8818 Macleod Tr. SE; Calgary, Alberta; Canada T2H 0M5
(403) 299-4000
Industry: 54—Supermarkets

Mission Statement

To be the leading retailer of food and of selected products and services in Calgary by consistently exceeding the expectations of our customer-owners.

Approved September 3, 1992

105. **Calgon Carbon Corporation**
       P.O. Box 717; Pittsburgh, PA 15230-0717
       (412) 787-6700
       Industry: 28, 49—Chemicals and wastewater treatment

MISSION

The Mission of Calgon Carbon Corporation is to meet customer needs by developing, making and selling products and services with significant technical content for purification, separation and concentration in liquid and gas processing, principally through employing activated carbon adsorption.

BUSINESS CHARTER

Calgon Carbon Corporation is a worldwide organization whose business is to meet customers' needs by providing high quality, cost-effective products and services for purification, separation, and concentration in the processing of liquids and gases.

In order to do this, the company will:

1. Maintain worldwide marketing, manufacturing, and technology leadership in the production, use, and recycling of activated carbon.
2. Develop or acquire products or services which are complementary to its existing business and organization.
3. Continue to develop the technology of its products and services to meet ever-changing customer needs.
4. Stress quality and professionalism in all areas of its business—its people, its products and services, and its business conduct.
5. Earn income which will support growth of its business and provide an above-average return to its shareholders.
6. Expand the applicability of its technology to all appropriate markets, including commercial and consumer markets.

QUALITY POLICY

Calgon Carbon Corporation is committed to providing products, equipment, and services which meet or exceed our customers' requirements—on time—the first time—every time. Specifically, we will focus on:

Understanding our customers' needs and our own capabilities.

Preventing defects before they ever occur.

Continuously improving everything we do.

We believe the only way to achieve this is through Total Quality Management.

CORPORATE QUALITY GOALS

Improve customer service

Improve first time conformance of all work outputs

Improve data accuracy and utility

Improve company safety performance

Improve performance and service of equipment

Improve product development process and cycle

Improve capital appropriation system

Extracted from 1992 "Quality Plan"

California Almond Growers
see Blue Diamond Growers (84)

106. **California Farm Bureau Federation**
1601 Exposition Boulevard; Sacramento, CA 95815
(916) 924-4075
Industry: 86—Membership organization

MISSION STATEMENT

Farm Bureau actively represents, protects and advances the social and economic interests of farm families and California communities by organizing production agriculture to provide group benefits and manage issues which affect our membership.

PURPOSE OF FARM BUREAU

Farm Bureau is a free, independent, nongovernmental, voluntary organization of farm and ranch families united for the purpose of analyzing their problems and formulating action to achieve educational improvement, economic opportunity, and social advancement and, thereby, to promote the national well-being. Farm Bureau is local, statewide, national, and international in its scope and influence and is nonpartisan, nonsectarian, and nonsecret in character.

PHILOSOPHY OF FARM BUREAU

Farm Bureau exists to actively represent, protect, and advance the social, economic and educational interests of farm families and the rural community in California through organized action in a diverse area of activities.

Farm Bureau believes in the American Way, individual freedom, fiscal responsibility, limited government control, the work ethic and fair play for all citizens.

Farm Bureau supports unity in agriculture so that farmers may exert maximum influence on the future of farming in California.

Farm Bureau insists on the responsible stewardship of our land, water and air so that our quality of life is maintained for generations to come.

Farm Bureau believes farmers should be allowed to freely operate in a competitive environment so that competition in the marketplace results in maximum opportunity for farmers and freedom of choice for consumers.

Farm Bureau policy should be developed by active farmers, driven by its grassroots emanating from collective action at the county level because farmers are the best planners of their own destiny.

Farm Bureau believes that voluntary cooperation is a part of the American system, that property rights are essential to the preservation of freedom and that each person should be rewarded according to productive contributions to society.

December, 1989

107. **Cambior, Inc.**
     800, boul. René-Lévesque Ouest; Bureau 850; Montreal, Quebec;
        Canada H3B 1X9
     (514) 878-3166
     Industry: 10—Gold mining

Mission

Cambior is a major mining company that seeks excellence in its operations and growth of its producing assets domestically and internationally in order to provide its investors with a superior return.

Objectives

1 - Maximise return on assets
2 - Increase mining production
3 - Protect revenues

108. **Canadian Airlines International Limited**
     700-2nd Street SW, Suite 2800; Calgary, Alberta; Canada T2P 2W2
     (403) 294-2000
     Industry: 45—Airline

OUR MISSION

To be a leading global airline:
- Safe
- Customer Driven

- Committed to Employees
- Financially Strong
- Responsible Member of the Community

109. Canadian Broadcasting Corporation

1500 Bronson Avenue; Ottawa, Ontario; Canada K1G 3J5
(613) 738 6783
Industry: 48—Broadcasting

THE MISSION OF THE CBC

The responsibility entrusted to the Canadian Broadcasting Corporation is a noble, essential and unique one. The CBC is a cornerstone, not only of the Canadian broadcasting system, but of Canada itself. No other organization has been asked to do what the CBC has been called upon to do. No one else has done it, or can do it, in the way or to the extent that the CBC has done and will continue to do it.

The CBC's mission is rooted in its mandate, as defined in the Broadcasting Act; in the Corporation's own proud traditions; its sense of itself and its place in Canada; its past accomplishments and its future aspirations. Whatever changes take place in Canada or in the Corporation, this mission remains a constant, unifying force to guide the CBC in responding to those changes. This mission can be defined in many different ways. One of them is summarized in the following mission statement.

The Canadian Broadcasting Corporation is Canada's national public broadcasting service, rooted in all parts of the country. It exists for the benefit of all Canadians, recognizing their diversity of expectations, values, interests and needs. It produces, procures and distributes primarily Canadian programming, in English, French and a number of other languages, through its national, regional and local radio and television services, and various domestic and international specialty services.

The mission of the CBC is:
- to inform, entertain and enlighten both general and specialized audiences;
- to contribute to the development of a shared national consciousness and identity;
- to reflect the regional and cultural diversity of Canada, by, among other things, presenting each region to itself and to the rest of the country;
- to contribute to the development of Canadian talent and culture; and
- to reflect the changing realities of the Canadian experience and of the world in which we live, as seen by Canadian eyes, heard by Canadian

ears, investigated by Canadian minds and explored by Canadian imaginations.

THE CBC'S VALUES

Certain fundamental shared values are at the heart of everything the CBC is and does. They are beliefs that unite us, goals that inspire us, and standards against which we can be measured.

The way these core values find expression evolves over time. But the values themselves remain constant. At times of change and challenge, it is particularly important to remind ourselves of what these values are. Here are some of them.

1 **We value Canada** As the national public broadcaster, the CBC is one of the most important forces binding this country together. We are pledged to reflect and celebrate our country, by providing predominantly Canadian programming of the highest possible quality, supplemented by the best the rest of the world has to offer.

2 **We value public service** As the national public broadcaster, the CBC has unique responsibilities. Through the mandate given to us in the Broadcasting Act, we are called upon by the people of Canada to act in the public interest. We believe that public service is a high calling, and we are determined to discharge our responsibilities to the best of our ability.

3 **We value our listeners and viewers** It is for them that we produce and distribute radio and television programs. We listen carefully and respond thoughtfully to their views and opinions. Audience service is of paramount importance to the CBC. It is achieved through a combination of meeting expressed needs and anticipating unexpressed needs.

4 **We value the people who work for and with us** They are our most valuable resource. This includes staff and contract employees, on-air performers, journalists, production and technical people, administrative and support personnel, managers, freelance artists and contributors, independent producers and outside contractors: everyone who contributes to the CBC's programming and operations. It is essential to create an environment in which that contribution can be maximized.

5 **We value creativity** The CBC is a creative organization. Its lifeblood is the imagination and innovation, the skills and experience, of everyone who works for and with it. We are committed to nurture, support, develop and showcase Canadian talent of all kinds, both on and off the air.

6 **We value excellence** The CBC will continue to offer a service which is distinctive from that offered by other broadcasters. We will also continue to play a leadership role in the broadcasting community, by maintaining the highest possible standards of programming, operations and management.

7 **We value diversity** The CBC recognizes and responds to the varying expectations and values of individual Canadians. We offer the widest possible range of services, and make them as widely available as possible. Through its programming, CBC is a vehicle for the free expression of a full range of views and opinions, a forum for the expression of differing views on matters of public concern. We are sensitive to cultural, linguistic and regional needs. We respect the unique characteristics of each segment of our society, while sharing them with all Canadians. We strive to represent the pluralistic nature of Canadian society through equitable employment and portrayal policies and practices.

8 **We value integrity** In order to justify the public trust which has been placed in it, the CBC's programming and operations must remain free from partisan political influence. Our programming must meet rigorous standards of fairness, balance and taste, as defined in our programming and journalistic policies and practices. Likewise, the behaviour of our employees must pass the closest tests of professional propriety and public scrutiny.

9 **We value efficiency** The CBC is the manager of public funds. It is incumbent upon us to use them as economically, efficiently, effectively and productively as possible. The CBC is also the custodian of public resources. To maximize the benefits which Canadians receive from these resources, it is appropriate for us to use them to supplement public funds with other sources of income, in ways which are consistent with our mandate and mission.

10 **We value accountability** The CBC must not only live up to its responsibilities; it must be seen to do so. We are accountable to the people of Canada, both directly and through many duly constituted intermediaries, for fulfilling our mandate and exercising our custodianship of public funds and resources. We welcome this accountability for what we do, which is consistent with our journalistic, creative and managerial independence over how we do it.

Extracted from "MISSION, VALUES, GOALS AND OBJECTIVES", October, 1990

110. **Canadian Commercial Corporation**
50 rue O'Connor Street; Ottawa, Ontario; Canada K1A 0S6
(613) 996-0034
Industry: 91—Government trading program

ROLE AND OBJECTIVES OF THE CORPORATION

Canadian Commercial Corporation (CCC) was established by Act of Parliament in 1946 to, *inter alia*, "assist in the development of trade

between Canada and other nations". The Corporation's continuing objectives are:
- to provide an effective, responsive **government-to-government export contracting service** to the private and public sectors in Canada, at the least cost to the Canadian taxpayer;
- to provide an efficient and effective **contract management service** to foreign governmental customers in order to ensure their satisfaction as to the quality, cost and delivery of Canadian goods and services, thereby enhancing the reputation of the Canadian private sector and the Corporation in the international marketplace.

Except as provided in the Canada/U.S. Defence Production Sharing Agreement, the use of CCC's services is entirely at the option of the Canadian private sector. The Corporation will neither compete nor interfere with the established export marketing and distribution efforts of Canadian firms and trade groups.

Many Canadian firms have found that a combined private sector/CCC initiative can give them a competitive edge, since it often provides an extra measure of assurance to the foreign governmental buyer that contract terms and conditions will be fully met.

The Corporation draws upon the services of other Canadian government departments and agencies concerned with providing assistance to exporters. It also works with provincial ministries and agencies, and with private business organizations—banks, insurance companies, trading houses and others—when a government-to-government arrangement will contribute to their export efforts.

Annual Report 1991–1992

111. **Canadian National Railway Company**
Box 8100; Montreal, Quebec; Canada H3C 3N4
(514) 399-5388
Industry: 40—Railroad

MISSION

To meet customers' transportation and distribution needs by being the best at moving their goods on time, safely and damage free.

VISION

As we accomplish our mission, CN will be a long term business success by being:
- Close to our customer
- First in service
- First in quality
- First in safety

- Environmentally responsible
- Cost competitive and financially sound
- A challenging and fulfilling place to work

OUR VALUES

They describe our company as we want it to be. That means every decision and action on the job demonstrates these values.

Values, when integrated into our business plans, programs and performance reviews, and strategies are essential for our long-term success.

CN Leadership participants got down to work and determined which values should guide employees and were most important to CN. After much discussion and review the following six values were finalized:

1 **We deliver satisfaction to the CUSTOMER . . .**

We value our customers, whether they are other businesses, government, or one another. Our success depends upon full customer satisfaction through the profitable delivery of a high quality service that must meet agreed-upon standards.

2 **We value CN PEOPLE . . .**

We treat each other with respect, recognizing the many contributions that come from the diversity of ideas and individuals. Expectations of work performance must be communicated and people should know how they're doing. Teamwork, openness, challenge and development is the desired work environment.

3 **We are responsible for the QUALITY of our work . . .**

Quality has been and continues to be essential to our success, whether it's work produced by employees or by our chosen suppliers. We constantly strive for improvement through the establishment of clear-cut goals, constant monitoring of performance, and recognition of achievements. Each of us is responsible for the quality of our work and the delivery of an excellent product.

4 **We are a SAFE place to work . . .**

Safety is critically important and will never be compromised. CN intends to be the safest railway, for the benefit of its employees, customers, and the communities it serves.

5 **We provide LEADERSHIP as a company . . .**

Each of us shows leadership in reflecting the mission, vision and values of the company. CN involves its people in providing a vision, direction and a work environment that fosters sound decision-making, safety, customer satisfaction, innovation, creativity and teamwork.

6 **We demonstrate INTEGRITY in all we do . . .**

We exemplify the highest standards of business ethics and personal integrity—honesty, openness, good citizenship—in dealing with customers, employees and the public.

see also CN North America (146)

112. **Canbra Foods**
P.O. Box 99; Lethbridge, Alberta; Canada T1J 3Y4
(403) 329-5500
Industry: 20—Foods

Canbra Foods' Mission

is to be an excellent, fully integrated oilseed processing and food company. We will seek to optimize the financial, product and human resources of the company by . . .

People

. . . Providing an environment for all employees which encourages meaningful opportunities for participation, individuality, respect and self-esteem.

Product

. . . Fulfilling customer needs with quality products and services.

Profit

. . . Investing in the future of the Company while achieving a superior return on our shareholders' investment.

We recognize our responsibility to society and we will enhance our role as a corporate citizen through our continuing commitment to excellence.

Cancarb Limited
see TransCanada Pipelines (573)

113. **Cardinal Distribution Inc.**
655 Metro Place South, Suite 925; Dublin, OH 43017
(614) 761-8700
Industry: 51—Health products distribution

OUR MISSION

Cardinal is a team of dedicated professionals creating and distributing a diversified offering of products and services to the national health care market.

Acting with integrity, our goal is to create the highest value and best return to our customers, suppliers, shareowners and employees.

Annual Report 1992

114. CARE

660 First Avenue; New York, NY 10016
(212) 686-3110
Industry: 83—Social services

THE CARE MISSION

CARE's purpose is to help the developing world's poor in their efforts to achieve social and economic well-being. We support processes that create competence and become self-sustaining over time. Our task is to reach new standards of excellence in offering technical assistance, disaster relief, training, food, other material resources and management in combinations appropriate to local needs and priorities. We also advocate public policies and programs that support these ends.

IV. THE CARE CHARTER

1. We work where the needs are greatest to effect substantial and enduring change.

2. We believe in our partners in the developing world and in their ability to achieve self-reliance. We must always listen to them and respect their values, aspirations and culture.

3. We must constantly be guided by our ultimate goal of helping individuals and families improve their lives and communities. We must be the human face of development and never let the scale of our operations diminish our compassion.

4. We represent and link two groups of people: the developing world's poor and those committed to enabling them to help themselves. We must find innovative ways to meet the needs of both and to enable them to work together as one community. To each we owe respect, integrity and accountability.

5. We must never take a single dollar for granted. Because so few are available. Because so many are needed.

6. We must be our own severest critic and toughest auditor. We guard program effectiveness and fiscal integrity through management and financial practices that are solid, established and ethical.

7. We recognize that everyone at CARE is an integral part of the process, whether based in the field or providing the support to make our programs successful. All of us share in the responsibility and rewards of our work.

8. We realize that excellence requires skilled, diverse, dedicated men and women working in an environment that enables them to thrive. We will find them, keep them and help them to succeed.

Extracted from "The CARE Vision"

115. **Cargill, Inc.**
     P.O. Box 9300; Minneapolis, MN 55440
     (612) 475-7575
     Industry: 20, 51—Food retail and wholesale
We will be the best in improving the standard of living of the five billion people in the world. We will do this by buying, storing, processing transporting and distributing basic raw materials, primarily agricultural materials. We will do this by promoting, innovating and creating competition and efficiencies in this distribution chain. Cargill will pay the producer better prices and sell to the consumer for a little less. This vision will increase purchasing power and/or capital formation for the world population.
     Extracted from "Cargill's Vision: A View to the Future," July 12, 1990

116. **Carnegie Corporation of New York**
     437 Madison Avenue; New York, NY 10022
     (212) 371-3200
     Industry: 67—Charitable foundation

Carnegie Corporation of New York Charter, Constitution, and Bylaws

ARTICLE II

PURPOSE

SECTION I. This corporation is established for the purpose of receiving and maintaining a fund or funds and applying the income thereof to promote the advancement and diffusion of knowledge and understanding among the people of the United States, by aiding technical schools, institutions of higher learning, libraries, scientific research, hero funds, useful publications, and by such other agencies and means as shall from time to time be found appropriate therefor.
     Amended through April 21, 1988

117. **Carolina Freight Corporation**
     P.O. Box 697; Cherryville, NC 28021
     (704) 435-6811
     Industry: 42—Trucking

MISSION STATEMENT

The mission of Carolina Freight Corporation is:
- to provide superior service to our customers.
- to effectively utilize company resources.
- to provide appropriate returns to stockholders.

- to provide meaningful, rewarding, and enduring job opportunities for our employees.
- to continually improve all aspects of our company.
- to act ethically and responsibly in matters affecting public safety and the environment.

Ken Mayhew 1990

118. **Caterair International**
 7811 Montrose Road, Suite 400; Potomac, MD 20854
 (301) 309-2800
 Industry: 51—Preparation and distribution of airline meals

MISSION

To be the airline caterer of choice in the world

VALUES

The fundamental beliefs that will guide us on our mission, and bring us closer to our vision

Customer Driven

- Being the best in the eyes of our customers is our #1 job
- Treat each customer as if he or she is our *only* customer
- There is no small customer or small customer issue
- All airline employees are our customers
- Exceeding customer expectations in all we do
- Solve customer problems . . . *fast!*
- Prevent problems from recurring
- Make and meet every customer commitment
- Do the customer's work as if you were doing it for yourself
- Recognize improvements that lead to customer satisfaction

People Are Our Greatest Asset

- Treat all people with respect, honor, dignity and fairness—take care of the people
- Live the Caterair Guarantee of Fair Treatment
- Recognize a job well done
- Help people feel free to ask questions
- Supply people with the tools they need to do their work
- Supply people with the information they need to do their work
- Make and meet commitments to all our people
- Increase our people's knowledge and skills
- Encourage advancement and promotion
- Increase confidence, self-esteem, pride, and professionalism
- Seek out highly motivated people to join the team

Teamwork

- Teamwork is an attitude, not a collection of players
- Communicate team goals
- There are no wins without the team winning
- Solve problems as a team
- Recognize team accomplishments, not just individual accomplishments
- Argue among ourselves but act with one voice
- Think of the next person down the line as your customer
- Think of yourself as the customer of the next person up the line
- Pitch in and help others, even if it's outside your usual work

Empowerment

- Respect our people's knowledge
- Solicit problem-solving ideas from our people
- Encourage unsolicited problem-solving ideas
- Listen to ideas different from your own
- Respond in a timely way to 100% of people's suggestions
- Put decision-making power in the hands of the person who knows the most about the task
- Give people the authority to act when they must
- Back up the person to whom you gave the power
- Find out *why* a mistake happens, learn from it, and prevent it from recurring
- Forgive honest mistakes
- Provide guidance, encouragement, and training

Continuous Improvement

- Communicate the need—the intense competition in the airline business is making our customers demand more from us for the same money
- Continually improve all that we do and how we do it—not only in big steps, but mostly in lots of little steps
- Relentlessly pursue perfection—strive for zero defects
- Don't think that you're the best because it's the enemy of getting better
- Find ways to prevent problems before they happen
- Replace "we don't do it that way" with "let's try it"
- Continuous improvement requires continuous learning

Global Mindset

- Communicate that fact that the airline business has become a world-as-a-single-market business

- Every unit is a member of the Caterair global team
- Remember that one unit's performance affects the success of all other units on the global team
- Pursuing the world market offers the opportunity to grow and further secure our livelihoods
- Maintain a Caterair world standard of quality
- Pursue business opportunities with every airline
- Look forward to and accept career opportunities throughout Caterair's world

119. **Catholic Medical Center of Brooklyn and Queens, Inc.**
    88-25 153rd Street; Jamaica, NY 11432
    (718) 657-6800
    Industry: 80—Hospital

MISSION STATEMENT

Strengthened and nourished by the vision and courage of the congregations of religious women who pioneered Catholic health care in the Diocese of Brooklyn, the Catholic Medical Center was formed through the inspiration and team work of men and women who were willing to be risk-takers and who, in uncertain times, forged the first multi-hospital system in New York State.

We are the heirs of this vision and commit ourselves to continue the healing ministry of Jesus by participating in the mission of the Roman Catholic Church and by adhering to its teachings. We believe that each person is made in the image and likeness of God, and thus we pledge to deliver quality health care to all our patients and to serve with special reverence those who are newly conceived or near death.

We seek to foster within each of our institutions a spirit of excellence, genuine caring, Christ-like compassion, and mutual respect for patients, families and staff. Our ministry to the sick involves caring for the physical, emotional and spiritual needs of each patient. Because we believe that health care is a basic human right, our ministry to the local community involves working to shape public policy to ensure that the root causes of ill health and suffering are addressed and eradicated.

We pledge to continue developing programs that reach those most in need—the poor, the alienated, the aged—all those who struggle for full dignity within our society.

We commit ourselves to be responsible stewards of our resources. We strive to promote a supportive environment where each person, regardless of position, is viewed as important to the proper functioning of the Catholic Medical Center. We seek to create a work environment that embodies the social teachings of the Church. Thus, each person is respected, every idea is appreciated, and each one's labor is valued.

We, who are

The Catholic Medical Center, exist

... To heal,

... To offer hope, and

... To witness

To the presence of a compassionate God

Who dwells among us.

Approved October, 1988

120. **Catholic Relief Services**
     209 West Fayette Street; Baltimore, MD 21201-3443
     (410) 625-2220
     Industry: 83—Social services

MISSION STATEMENT

Catholic Relief Services was founded in 1943 by the Catholic Bishops of the United States to assist the poor and disadvantaged outside this country. It is administered by a Board of Bishops selected by the Episcopal Conference of the United States and is staffed by men and women committed to the Catholic Church's apostolate of helping those in need. It maintains strict standards of efficiency and accountability.

The fundamental motivating force in all activities of CRS is the Gospel of Jesus Christ as it pertains to the alleviation of human suffering, the development of people and the fostering of charity and justice in the world. The policies and programs of the agency reflect and express the teaching of the Catholic Church.

At the same time, Catholic Relief Services assists persons on the basis of need, not creed, race or nationality.

Catholic Relief Services draws its basic financial, material and moral support from the Catholic community in the United States, but it also reaches out for support to individuals of many faiths and to governments and community organizations, foundations, corporations, and to student groups. The agency cooperates with governments and ecumenical groups in programs consistent with its objectives and practices.

Catholic Relief Services gives active witness to the mandate of Jesus Christ to respond to human needs in the following ways:

- by responding to victims of natural and man-made disasters;
- by providing assistance to the poor to alleviate their immediate needs;
- by supporting self-help programs which involve people and communities in their own development;

- by helping those it serves to restore and preserve their dignity and to realize their potential;
- by collaborating with religious and non-sectarian persons and groups of good will in programs and projects which contribute to a more equitable society; and
- by helping to educate the people of the United States to fulfill their moral responsibilities in alleviating human suffering, removing its causes, and promoting social justice.

Effective January 1, 1992

CBN

see Christian Broadcasting Network Inc. (139)

121. **Cedars-Sinai Medical Center**
8700 Beverly Boulevard; Los Angeles, CA 90048-1869
(310) 855-5000
Industry: 80—Hospital

MISSION STATEMENT

Cedars-Sinai Medical Center is an independent, not-for-profit community supported university-affiliated academic medical center. It is committed to excellence in patient health care services delivery, expanding the horizons of medical knowledge through biomedical research and its subsequent application to clinical care, educating physicians and other health care professionals, and providing community services. The ethical and cultural precepts of the Judaic tradition inspire devotion to the art and science of healing, and are the basic guidelines for the humanistic treatment afforded patients.

The Medical Center is committed to leadership as a nationally renowned institution whose excitement, magnetism and values attract highly skilled physicians, nurses, scientists, and other health professionals. Cedars-Sinai Medical Center provides advanced and excellent clinical care in a sensitive environment, solicitous of each patient's dignity and needs.

Cedars-Sinai Medical Center will, within its resources, provide health education, emphasizing disease prevention and early diagnosis, as well as health care to the indigent population of the local community. It will establish a regionally integrated health care delivery system, as defined in the Institution's Strategic Plan.

Drafted 1991

122. **Celestial Seasonings, Inc.**
4600 Sleepytime Drive; Boulder, CO 80301-3292
(303) 530-5300
Industry: 20—Teas

BELIEFS

Our Quest for Excellence

We believe that in order to make this world a better place in which to live, we must be totally dedicated to the endless quest for excellence in the important tasks which we endeavor to accomplish.

Our Products

We believe in marketing and selling healthful and naturally oriented products that nurture people's bodies and uplift their souls. Our products must be superior in quality, of good value, beautifully artistic, and philosophically inspiring.

Our Consumers and Customers

We believe that our past, current and future successes come from a total dedication to excellent service to those who buy our products. Satisfying our customer and consumer needs in a superior way is the only reason we are in business, and we shall proceed with an obsession to give wholeheartedly to those who buy our products. Our customers and consumers are king, and we are here to serve them.

Our Growth

We believe in aggressive, steady, predictable and well planned growth in sales and earnings. We are intent on building a large company that will flourish into the next century and thereafter.

Dignity of the Individual

We believe in the dignity of the individual, and we are totally committed to the fair, honest, kind, and professional treatment of all individuals and organizations with whom we work.

Our Employees

We believe that our employees develop a commitment to excellence when they are directly involved in the management of their areas of responsibility. This team effort maximizes quality results, minimizes costs, and allows our employees the opportunity to have authorship and personal satisfaction in their accomplishments, as well as sharing in the financial rewards of their individual and team efforts.

We believe in hiring above average people who have a "hands on" approach to work and quest for excellent results. In exchange, we are committed to the development of our good people by identifying, cultivating, training, rewarding, retaining and promoting those individuals who are committed to moving our organization forward.

Our Environment

We believe in fostering a working environment which promotes creativity and encourages possibility thinking throughout the organization. We plan our work to be satisfying, productive, and challenging. As such, we support an atmosphere which encourages intelligent risk taking without the fear of failure.

Our Dream

Our role at Celestial Seasonings is to play an active part in making this world a better place by unselfishly serving the public. We believe we can have a significant impact on making people's lives happier and healthier through their use of our products. By dedicating our total resources to this dream, everyone profits: our customers, consumers, employees, and shareholders. Our actions are building blocks in making this world a better place now and for future generations.

123. **CENEX**
Farmers Union Central Exchange, Inc.
P.O. Box 64089; St. Paul, MN 55164-0089
(612) 451-5151
Industry: 51—Agricultural cooperative

CENEX PURPOSE

To enhance the economic well-being of our member-owners.

OUR MISSION

To anticipate and meet market needs of farmers, ranchers, and rural communities.

To be the preferred supplier of selected products and services through local cooperatives.

To be a financially strong cooperative system.

Developed 1989
Annual Report 1991

Central Intelligence Agency
see United States Central Intelligence Agency (585)

124. **Central Louisiana Electric Company, Inc.**
2030 Donahue Ferry Road; P.O. Box 5000; Pineville, LA
71361-5000
(318) 484-7400
Industry: 49—Electric cooperative

MISSION STATEMENT

Central Louisiana Electric Company is in business to provide customers with quality electric utility services at competitive prices and shareholders with an attractive return on investment. We will strive to conduct business such that employees are provided a safe and challenging working environment.

VALUES

At CLECO we value:
- Ethical business conduct.
- Competitively priced quality service.
- A superior return for shareholders.
- Fair and courteous treatment of customers and employees.
- Safety of employees and the public.
- Protection and preservation of the environment.
- Motivated, conscientious, competent employees.
- Teamwork and loyalty.
- Good corporate citizenship.
- Effective leadership.
- Open communications.

Extracted from CLECO "STRATEGIC PLAN, 1992+"

125. Champion International Corporation
One Champion Plaza; Stamford, CT 06921
(203) 358-7000
Industry: 24, 26—Wood and paper products

The Champion Way Statement

Champion's objective is leadership in American industry. Profitable growth is fundamental to the achievement of that goal and will benefit all to whom we are responsible: shareholders, customers, employees, communities, and society at large.

Champion's way of achieving profitable growth requires the active participation of all employees in increasing productivity, reducing costs, improving quality, and strengthening customer service.

Champion wants to be known for the excellence of its products and service and the integrity of its dealings.

Champion wants to be known as an excellent place to work. This means jobs in facilities that are clean and safe, where a spirit of cooperation and mutual respect prevails, where all feel free to make suggestions, and where all can take pride in working for Champion.

Champion wants to be known for its fair and thoughtful treatment of employees. We are committed to providing equality of opportunity for all people, regardless of race, national origin, sex, age, religion, disability, or veteran status. We actively seek a talented, diverse, enthusiastic workforce. We believe in the individual worth of each employee and seek to foster opportunities for personal development.

Champion wants to be known for its interest in and support of the communities in which employees live and work. We encourage all employees to take an active part in the affairs of their communities, and we will support their volunteer efforts.

Champion wants to be known as a public-spirited corporation, mindful of its needs to assist—through volunteer efforts and donated funds—non-profit educational, civic, cultural, and social welfare organizations which contribute uniquely to our national life.

Champion wants to be known as an open, truthful company. We are committed to the highest standards of business conduct in our relationships with customers, suppliers, employees, communities, and shareholders. In all our pursuits we are unequivocal in our support of the laws of the land, and acts of questionable legality will not be tolerated.

Champion wants to be known as a company which strives to conserve resources to reduce waste, and to use and dispose of materials with scrupulous regard for safety and health. We take particular pride in this company's record of compliance with the spirit as well as the letter of all environmental regulations.

Champion believes that only through the individual actions of all employees—guided by a company-wide commitment to excellence—will our long-term economic success and leadership position be ensured.

Revised June, 1992
Copyright © 1986 Champion International

126. **Champlin Foundations**
    410 South Main Street; Providence, RI 02903
    (401) 421-3719
    Industry: 67—Charitable foundation

The Foundations are established for the purpose of making grants to qualified organizations for such purposes "as will relieve the suffering and want of the poor, the sick, the young, the aged, the incompetent and the helpless, alleviate the privation and distress resulting from any sudden or unusual event or catastrophe, promote science, health, recreation, religion and education and benefit and improve the living conditions and the physical, mental and moral well-being of humanity, regardless of race, color or creed."

Charles Levy Company
    see Chas. Levy Company (131)

127. **Charles Schwab Corporation**
     101 Montgomery Street; San Francisco, CA 94104
     (415) 627-7000
     Industry: 62—Securities brokerage

The Vision And Values of Our Company

Back in the early Seventies, I started our company with high ideals, traditional values, and a vision of providing investors with the most useful and ethical brokerage services in America. My personal values were, and continue to be, very straightforward:

- Be fair, empathetic and responsive in serving our customers,
- Respect and reinforce your fellow employees and the power of teamwork,
- Strive relentlessly to improve what we do and how we do it,
- Always earn and be worthy of our customer's trust.

I hope this vision and these values will guide each of you in your daily lives at Schwab. By guarding our values closely, I know that we will have no limits in the pursuit of our vision.

Charles R. Schwab, June 25, 1991

The Mission Statement For Our Company

Our mission as a company is to serve the needs of investors. We have all kinds of customers: individuals, professional, money managers, companies and their employees. We know our customers have many different needs in meeting their own financial goals. We will focus our resources on the financial services that best meet our customers' needs, whether they are transactional, informational, custodial services, or something new. We will strive to deliver to our customers:

- High quality, reliable, ethical products and services at a fair price,
- Superior service from the best team of trained, motivated, and ethical employees, supported by the best technology,
- A strong company, financially viable under any circumstance.

Copyright © 1991 The Charles Schwab Corporation

128. **Charles Stark Draper Laboratory, Inc.**
     555 Technology Square; Cambridge, MA 02139-3563
     (617) 258-2868
     Industry: 87—Research laboratory

VISION STATEMENT

To contribute to the National Interest by *Pioneering in the Application* of Science and Technology.

MISSION STATEMENT

Draper is a state-of-the-art engineering and applied research laboratory committed to developing practical solutions to problems of national interest in the areas of instrumentation, measurement, information processing, and control; to transferring that technology to industry; and to promoting education.

We apply the research and engineering capabilities of the laboratory to provide our customers with solutions to challenging problems on schedule and within cost.

We demonstrate those solutions through engineering prototypes.

We transition those technology applications and processes to industry for production and provide follow-on support.

We provide unbiased evaluations through simulation, analysis, and testing.

We promote and support practical technical education.

CORPORATE VALUES

We require the highest standards of ethical behavior in everything we do.

We strive for excellence in everything we do.

We maintain a stimulating and satisfying work place where our talented people can continue their record of superior achievement.

We strive to continuously improve performance.

We support our local community.

Updated October 8, 1992

129. **Charter One Bank, F.S.B.**
Subsidiary of Charter One Financial, Inc.
1215 Superior Avenue; Cleveland, OH 44114
(216) 566-5300
Industry: 60—Federal savings bank

CORPORATE MISSION

The mission of Charter One Bank, F.S.B., is to:
- Provide financial returns to Charter One Financial, Inc., to enable the Bank's holding company to provide its stockholder meaningful long-term financial rewards,
- Maintain its viable existence and the safety of depositors' and shareholders' investments,
By placing maximum emphasis on the Bank's financial strength, and
   By prudent control of credit and interest-rate risks, and
   By diversification and expansion of its services.
- Promote thrift,

By providing a convenient and safe method for people to save, and
By providing ancillary financial services that meet the needs of the
general public.
- Make sound investments,
    By providing financial services to individuals and families, and
    By providing for the sound and economical financing of homes,
    and
    By investing in service corporations that serve to provide
    additional diversification and expansion of services.
- Provide financial services to businesses,
    By providing depository and loan services to local businesses.
- Contribute to the well being of the communities served,
    By providing gainful, equal and motivating employment
    opportunities, and
    By helping to maintain the viability of neighborhoods, and
    By encouraging participation in worthwhile charitable, civic and
    professional activities.

1992

130. **Chase Manhattan Bank, N.A.**
     1 Chase Plaza; New York, NY 10081
     (212) 552-2222
     Industry: 60—Banking

The Chase Manhattan Vision

PURPOSE

We provide financial services that enhance the well-being and success
of individuals, industries, communities and countries around the world.

MISSION

Through our shared commitment to those we serve, we will be the best
financial services company in the world.
- Customers will choose us first because we deliver the highest quality
  service and performance.
- People will be proud and eager to work here.
- Investors will buy our stock as a superior long-term investment.

VALUES

To be the best for our customers, we are team players who show respect
for our colleagues and commit to the highest standards of quality and
professionalism.
- Customer focus
- Respect for each other
- Teamwork

- Quality
- Professionalism

Chase Values

CUSTOMER FOCUS

- We believe it. We live it. The customer always comes first.
- A customer's problem is everyone's problem. The solution starts with me.
- We don't sell our customers just what they ask for . . . no, we want to provide what they need, with new ideas, better ways, all day, every day.
- I don't know. But it's my job to find out and have Chase get back to you today.

RESPECT FOR EACH OTHER

- We treat our colleagues like respected clients. We respond with integrity, courtesy, candor and urgency.
- Our colleagues are special. They have unique talents. They make special contributions. We recognize and applaud their commitment.
- We recognize that our colleagues have personal lives and we respect that.

TEAMWORK

- Chase first, my unit second.
- I get help—when I need it.
- We share Chase's successes, rewards and failures.
- We build on each other's strengths.
- Each of us makes the team happen.

QUALITY

- I can make a difference. Quality starts with me.
- I strive for 100% satisfaction: I stand behind whatever I do.
- We make it easy to do business with Chase.
- P.D.C.A.: We plan it. We do it. We check it. We act.

PROFESSIONALISM

Customers and colleagues count on me because:
- I'm committed.
- I have high standards.
- I get the job done.
- I'm knowledgeable.
- I act with a sense of urgency.
- I take every opportunity to sharpen my talents and skills.

131. **Chas. Levy Company**
   1200 N. North Branch Street; Chicago, IL 60622

(312) 440-4401

Industry: 51—Wholesale entertainment products

CORPORATE MISSION STATEMENT

The Chas. Levy Co. is a wholesale distributor and rack-jobber of mass market information and home entertainment products. We seek superior performance in all of our businesses:

- By providing a high degree of service and flexibility,
- By meeting the needs of our customers and suppliers efficiently, and
- By using technology to gain efficiency.

We seek continued growth by pursuing related opportunities that add value to our core businesses in order to provide:

- A stimulating workplace,
- Entrepreneurial opportunities for employees, and
- A fair return to our shareholders.

The company is privately held, and plans to remain so.

We believe strongly in contributing actively to the public interest; particularly as it relates to our employees, the business sectors we service and the communities in which we work.

132.   **Chemical Leaman Tank Lines, Inc.**
       102 Pickering Way; Exton, PA 19341-0200
       (215) 363-4200
       Industry: 42—Motor carrier

OUR MISSION

CHEMICAL LEAMAN TANK LINES provides the highest quality bulk motor carrier transportation and associated services available. We represent the first and final step in our customers' efforts to deliver and receive products consistently. Our services meet or exceed customer expectations at a profitable and competitive price.

OUR CORE VALUES

Equal in importance to the achievement of our mission is how we pursue it. The core values we believe in and practice are the foundation of our success. The core values are:

SHAREHOLDER VALUE Enhancement of shareholder value is critical to ensure the success and well-being of Chemical Leaman Tank Lines' employees, associates, shareholders, and customers. We strive to provide our shareholders with a fair return on their invested capital over time, recognizing that long-term stability and growth take precedence over short-term profits.

CUSTOMER EXCELLENCE We believe our future depends on the success of our customers and our ability to recognize and satisfy their requirements. We focus our efforts to continuously improve the services we provide our customers. We create value for our customers through innovative solutions to their needs and by delivering unsurpassed quality service.

PEOPLE EXCELLENCE We endeavor to be the preferred employer of those individuals who take pride in the high quality of their performance and will provide an environment where demonstration of high quality performance is appreciated, nurtured, and rewarded. Our employees are encouraged to set their own strategies and objectives to achieve clearly stated company goals.

HEALTH, SAFETY, AND ENVIRONMENTAL EXCELLENCE As a responsible member of the community, we comply with all applicable laws and regulations governing our industry, and in a more general sense, with the laws of society.

Continuous Improvement Drives Our Success

133.   **Chesapeake Corporation**
       1021 East Cary Street; Richmond, VA 23219
       (804) 697-1110
       Industry: 24, 26—Paper and wood
       . . . Chesapeake's operating philosophy includes wide utilization of incentive-based pay for performance and programs to encourage stock ownership by employees. Employees are encouraged to be creative while looking for ways of continuously improving quality and service that meet the needs of customers. This philosophy facilitates the company's mission, which is to increase the wealth of its stockholders while fulfilling with integrity its responsibility to its employees, customers, suppliers and the public.

Annual Report 1991

134.   **Chevron Corporation**
       225 Bush Street; San Francisco, CA 94104-4289
       (415) 894-7700
       Industry: 13, 29—Integrated petroleum

MISSION

Chevron is an international petroleum company. Our mission is to achieve superior financial results for our stockholders, the owners of our business.

VISION

Our vision is to be Better than the Best, which means:
- All employees are proud of their work.
- Competitors respect us.
- Customers and Suppliers prefer us.
- Investors are eager to invest in us.
- Communities welcome us.

Continuous Quality Improvement is the process we will use to achieve our vision.

VALUES

How we pursue our mission, building on our basic values, is as important as the mission itself.
- Employees—the key to success—providing the fundamental strength, vitality and reputation of our Company.
- Customers—our basic focus—achieving a lasting partnership means a commitment to excellence in everything we do.
- Community—the respect of the community is critical—requiring the highest ethical standards of business, social and environmental responsibility.

January, 1992

Chicago Art Institute
see Art Institute of Chicago (53)

135. **Children's Defense Fund**
25 E Street, NW; Washington, DC 20001
(202) 628-8787
Industry: 83—Social service

About CDF

The Children's Defense Fund (CDF) exists to provide a strong and effective voice for the children of America who cannot vote, lobby, or speak for themselves. We pay particular attention to the needs of poor, minority, and disabled children. Our goal is to educate the nation about the needs of children and encourage preventive investment in children before they get sick, drop out of school, suffer family breakdown, or get into trouble.

CDF is a unique organization. CDF focuses on programs and policies that affect large numbers of children, rather than on helping families on a case-by-case basis. Our staff includes specialists in health, education, child welfare, mental health, child development, adolescent pregnancy prevention, family income, and youth employment. CDF gathers data and disseminates information on key issues affecting children. We monitor the development and implementation of federal and state policies. We provide information, technical assistance, and support to a network of state and local child advocates, service providers, and public and private sector officials and leaders. We pursue an annual legislative agenda in the U.S. Congress and litigate selected cases of major importance. CDF's major initiatives include our adolescent pregnancy prevention program and a prenatal care and child health campaign. CDF educates hundreds of thousands of citizens annually about children's needs and responsible policy options for meeting those needs.

Copyright © Children's Defense Fund

136. **Children's Hospital Medical Center**
Elland and Bethesda Avenues; Cincinnati, OH 45229-2899
(513) 559-4411
Industry: 80—Hospital

OUR MISSION

Children's Hospital Medical Center is dedicated to serving the health-care needs of infants, children and adolescents and to providing research and teaching programs that ensure delivery of the highest quality pediatric care to our community, the nation and the world.

OUR VALUES

Excellence

We will strive to excel in every aspect of our services, recognizing that people are our greatest strength in all our accomplishments and achievements. We will respect and acknowledge the dignity and worth of each patient, family member and employee.

Integrity

We will follow the highest standards of ethical conduct, truth, moral principles and ideals in providing patient care, teaching, research, and all related support services.

Innovation

We will encourage change, creativity and the exploration of new ideas. We will reward the efforts of all we seek and share new knowledge and wisdom that contribute to the advancement of pediatric science and health care.

OUR GOALS

Commitment to People:

-      To demonstrate our commitment to our patients and their families, our employees and colleagues, and the community at large by treating each person with respect, fairness, compassion, and concern.

-      To affirm the indispensable contributions of our employees by employing, promoting and retaining the best-qualified individuals without regard to race, gender or any other differences unrelated to performance.

-      To foster an environment that gives each employee opportunities for individual and team achievement, personal reward and attainment of maximum potential.

Delivering Patient Care:

-      To strive for the highest level of health for children through family-centered care and support in the hospital and in the home, and through education and wellness programs in the community.

-      To sustain excellence in service by providing modern technology and comfortable, well-maintained facilities that meet patient, family and staff expectations and needs.

Research and Teaching:

-      To encourage a lifelong love of learning, to pursue and extend the boundaries of knowledge, and to share all we learn in order to prevent and treat illnesses, diseases and disorders of children.

-      To teach the truth as we know it, to honor honesty, confidentiality, humility, and selflessness and to relate our reverence for life to a thoughtful response to ethical issues of the present and future.

Providing Leadership:

-      To make the most effective use of all resources, within a framework of financial responsibility and quality performance, so as to ensure our ability to provide leadership in pediatric health care, teaching and research for future generations.

137.   **Children's Hospital of Philadelphia**
       One Children's Center; 34th Street & Civic Center Boulevard;
          Philadelphia, PA 19104
       (215) 596-9100
       Industry: 80—Hospital

STATEMENT OF CHILDREN'S HOSPITAL'S MISSION

The Children's Hospital of Philadelphia, the oldest hospital in the United States dedicated exclusively to pediatrics, strives to be the world leader in the advancement of health care for children by integrating excellent patient care, innovative research and quality professional education into all of its programs.

Directly or in partnership with others, the Hospital seeks to provide accessible, fiscally responsible, comprehensive, innovative, high quality medical and surgical care to children in Pennsylvania, New Jersey, Delaware, and other states and countries.

The Hospital focuses its educational mission on physician and allied health professionals at all levels, with an emphasis on training future leaders who are devoted to the care of children. As a means of achieving this mission, the Hospital forges relationships with other institutions that include education and research among their goals.

The Hospital improves the general health of children and demonstrates world leadership by generating new knowledge through its commitment to basic and clinical research.

Revised 1989

138. Chiquita Brands International
250 East Fifth Street; Cincinnati, OH 45202
(513) 784-8011
Industry: 20—Food products

Chiquita's mission is to deliver long-term growth in earnings per share and shareholder value as a global leader in premium branded foods.

Annual Report 1991

139. Christian Broadcasting Network Inc.
CBN Center; Virginia Beach, VA 23463
(804) 424-7777
Industry: 48—Broadcasting

CBN's mission is to prepare the United States of America, the nations of the Middle East, the Far East, South America and other nations of the world for the coming of Jesus Christ and the establishment of the kingdom of God on earth.

We are achieving this end through the strategic use of mass communication, especially radio, television and film; the distribution of cassettes, films and literature, and the educational training of students to relate biblical principles to those spheres of human endeavor that play a dominant role in our world.

We strive for innovation, excellence and integrity in all that we do. We aim always to glorify God and His Son Jesus Christ.

Excerpt from "CBN Mission Statement"

140. **Christian Children's Fund**
     2821 Emerywood Parkway; P.O. Box 26227; Richmond, VA 23261-6227
     (804) 756-2700
     Industry: 83—Social services

MISSION:

Under the Judeo-Christian ethic of helping our neighbor without regard to race, creed, nationality or sex, Christian Children's Fund and its international associated organizations are dedicated to serving the needs of children worldwide—primarily through person-to-person programs, in the context of the family and community, and using a developmental approach through national and local partners.

141. **Chugach Electric Association, Inc.**
     5601 Minnesota Drive; P.O. Box 196300; Anchorage, AK 99519-6300
     (907) 563-7494
     Industry: 49—Electric cooperative

Mission Statement

To meet the energy needs of members and customers by providing competitively-priced, reliable, safe energy and services today and into the future through prudent and responsible planning, maintenance and management of the assets of the cooperative.

Corporate Goals

1. To generate, transmit, and distribute electrical energy in harmony with the environment while working closely with other utilities, municipal, state and federal agencies, cogenerators, and independent power producers (IPPs) to best utilize the resources available in the region.

2. To provide high-quality service and to develop and maintain lasting member relationships by a dedication to preserving cooperative principles through the member election of our board of directors.

3. To implement effective resource management programs that will ensure system stability and reliability for the future.

4. To provide a working environment that offers challenge, a place to work with pride, as well as a place for personal growth, development and career opportunity.

5. To provide continuing education, competitive wage and salary programs, and a responsive human resources program so that we can properly manage our most valuable resource, our employees.

6. To strive for community and statewide leadership in business and economic development.

7. To provide information on the safe and beneficial uses of electricity as well as information on energy management.

8. To provide reliable electrical power at fair and competitive rates and cooperate with other entities on projects and issues that are mutually beneficial.

9. To lead in Generation and Transmission (G&T) planning for the Railbelt and provide planning resources for wholesale as well as retail customers as required.

10. To maintain leadership in the electric utility industry by setting the standards for quality electric service which provides a foundation for the economic growth and stability of our service area.

11. To ensure the continuing viability of Chugach by providing adequate and sufficient, competitively-priced, reliable electrical power to our members and customers through careful planning for controlled growth, equipment maintenance, and prudent management of the assets of the cooperative.

Spring 1990

CIA
see United States Central Intelligence Agency (585)

142. CITGO Petroleum Corporation
P.O. Box 3758; Tulsa, OK 74102
(918) 495-4000
Industry: 29, 55—Petroleum refining and marketing

VISION

To be the best refining, marketing, and transportation company in the U.S. petroleum industry.

MISSION

- To serve customers and meet the owner's strategic needs.

- To market quality, environmentally acceptable fuels, lubricants, petrochemicals and industrial products to core customers who can be served efficiently and competitively through CITGO's supply network.

- To provide stable and adequate earnings from existing core businesses, maintain a positive cash flow from operations and provide an acceptable return on investment.

- To grow the company through internal growth of core businesses, strategic acquisitions of competitor networks and redeployment of assets.

- To manage CITGO's marketing, refining, lubricants, supply, transportation, terminalling and financial assets to provide safe, environmentally sound, and cost efficient operations and maintain maximum market value.

- To attract, develop and retain quality people to safely operate and manage the businesses.

STATEMENT OF VALUES

We, the employees of CITGO Petroleum Corporation, are committed to satisfying our customers, suppliers, and the general public's need for quality service and product performance. To this end, we will conduct our business according to the following core values:

- CITIZENSHIP—We are committed to being an active and supportive citizen and in being a positive example in community endeavors.
- CORPORATE PRIDE in our accomplishments is encouraged—We strive for pride among our employees and for customers who are proud of doing business with CITGO.
- ECONOMIC PROFITS allow us to promote societal well-being; we are dedicated to managing prudently and to earning a good return from our assets.
- ENVIRONMENTAL STEWARDSHIP is important to our corporate existence; we care about our neighbors and our successors. In our products and at our facilities, we will protect the environment, public health and safety.
- INTEGRITY is integral to all our activities; we behave honestly and ethically, caring how results are achieved.
- LEADERSHIP is respected when combined with integrity, energy and enthusiasm.
- OPENNESS is crucial in promoting our way of business—we express ideas, concerns and beliefs about our activities; constructive challenge, inquisitiveness and creativity are encouraged.
- QUALITY is critical in the products and services we provide; we are committed to the process of continuous improvement.
- SAFETY in our operations is primary; we strive to create and maintain injury-free and healthy work places.
- TEAMWORK enhances results—we cooperate, collaborate and support one another in all our efforts.

143.   Upon review of entry, organization declined to participate.

Clark, Edna McConnell Foundation
   see Edna McConnell Clark Foundation (208)

144. **Clay Electric Cooperative, Inc.**
P.O. Box 308; Keystone Heights, FL 32656-0308
(904) 473-4911
Industry: 49—Electric cooperative

Mission Statement

To be the utility of choice by meeting or exceeding our customer/ member expectations for reliable and efficient electrical service in a socially responsible manner. To provide a safe and rewarding workplace for employees. To demonstrate that the cooperative enterprise is the most desirable method for providing/receiving electric service.

Vision Statement

To become widely recognized as a customer oriented, socially responsible, financially strong, successful competitor in the evolving electric energy business.

Drafted July 15–17, 1992

CLECO
see Central Louisiana Electric Company (124)

145. **The Cleveland Foundation**
1422 Euclid Avenue, Suite 1400; Cleveland, OH 44115-2001
(216) 861-3810
Industry: 67—Charitable foundation

The Cleveland Foundation exists to enhance the quality of life for all residents of Greater Cleveland. Using funds entrusted to its stewardship by thousands of people of various means, the Foundation makes grants to nonprofit organizations and governmental agencies to address the community's needs and opportunities. Since only the income generated by investments is ordinarily used for grantmaking, a gift to The Cleveland Foundation helps build a permanent endowment for the benefit of the community. Since its creation in 1914 as the nation's pioneer community trust, The Cleveland Foundation has been one of the great resources of this community. It has served as the model for some 400 community foundations in the United States and a growing number worldwide. Although known chiefly for its grantmaking, The Cleveland Foundation plays many other roles: convenor of funders and community leaders around specific issues; catalyst for the creation of new programs and organizations when warranted; project manager; and philanthropic leader, both locally and nationally. Whether you live, work, or visit here, you undoubtedly have been touched by one or more of the many programs supported by The Cleveland Foundation in the areas of social services, education, health, housing and neighborhood development, economic development, and the arts.

146. **CN North America**
     Subsidiary of Canadian National Railway Co.
     1333 Brewery Park Boulevard; Detroit, MI 48207
     (313) 396-6000
     Industry: 40—Railroad

Mission & Vision

At CN Rail, our mission is to meet our customers' transportation and distribution needs by being the best at moving their goods on time, safely and damage-free.

As CN Rail accomplishes this mission, it will become a long-term success by being:
- Close to its Customers
- First in Service
- First in Quality
- First in Safety
- Environmentally Responsible
- Cost Competitive and Financially Sound
- A Challenging and Fulfilling Place to Work

see also Canadian National Railway Company (111)

CN Railway
   see Canadian National Railway Company (111)

147. **Cobb Electric Membership Corporation**
     P.O. Box 369; Marietta, GA 30061
     (404) 424-1504
     Industry: 49—Electric

Our Mission

Cobb Electric Membership Corporation shall provide safe, adequate and reliable electric and other related energy services to its members/consumers. Our primary focus will be to provide superior service through a professional staff, competitive rates and sound business principles. The organization further dedicates itself to being a corporate citizen within the community and a recognized leader in the utility industry.

Annual Report 1991

148. **Colonial Williamsburg Foundation**
     Goodwin Building #9161; P.O. Box C; Williamsburg, VA 23185
     (804) 229-1000

Industry: 67—Charitable foundation

MISSION

TO PRESERVE, RESTORE, RE-CREATE, AND INTERPRET EIGHTEENTH-CENTURY WILLIAMSBURG.

To preserve, restore, and re-create eighteenth-century Williamsburg, where Virginia colonists and their leaders chose revolution and transformed this British colonial possession into a free commonwealth.

TO TEACH THE HISTORY OF EARLY AMERICA.

To teach American history, using the setting of Williamsburg to help visitors understand the relationship of the Virginia colonists to the king and mother country, to the other colonies, and to each other and the culture, economy, and politics of eighteenth-century America—before it was America, through the transition, and as a new nation.

VALUES

STEWARDSHIP

What we do matters. We are the guardians of a legacy from the past and of a trust for the future.

We are stewards of this historic site. We are responsible for defining and teaching the ideas and the ideals it represents and for maintaining the high standards established by our predecessors.

We are entrusted with safekeeping this heritage so that future generations may learn from the past.

EXCELLENCE

We strive to exceed the expectations of every visitor. We are proud of Colonial Williamsburg's reputation for excellence and value, but we know we must earn it anew every day. In our work, as individuals and together, we continuously strive to improve the programs and services offered by Colonial Williamsburg.

HOSPITALITY

We work to build a lifelong relationship with every visitor. By welcoming visitors—our guests—warmly and exceeding their expectations, we encourage them to return again and again to learn more about Colonial Williamsburg and to enjoy our hospitality.

RESPECT FOR PEOPLE

Colonial Williamsburg's people are its most important resource. We, individually and together, are the stewards. We provide the excellence and hospitality that distinguish Colonial Williamsburg.

Our knowledge, skills, and caring attitudes—toward visitors, neighbors, and one another—enable us to achieve our mission and to make Colonial Williamsburg the best place to work.

In all of our relationships we are guided by integrity, truthfulness, fairness, and respect for the dignity of the individual. We treat others as we wish to be treated.

Updated June, 1992

149. **Colorado National Bankshares, Inc.**
      P.O. Box 5168; Denver, CO 80217
      (303) 629-1968
      Industry: 60—Banking

Mission Statement:

The purpose of this banking organization is to preserve and enhance the value of its shareholders' investment through asset and dividend growth. The business of the company shall be conducted in a legal and ethical manner guided by conservative principles which include prudent stewardship of depositor funds, judicious and constructive extension of credit, proper discharge of responsibility of trust, quality service to our customers, equitable employee relations, and awareness of community development and social needs.

150. **Columbia Gas System, Inc.**
      Columbia Gas System Service Corporation
      20 Montchanin Road; P.O. Box 4020; Wilmington, DE 19807-0020
      (302) 429-5261
      Industry: 49—Gas utility

Mission Statement

The Columbia Gas System, Inc., through its subsidiaries, is active in pursuing opportunities in all segments of the natural gas industry and related energy resource development.

Exemplified by Columbia's three-star symbol, these separately managed companies strive to benefit: **System stockholders**—through enhancing the value of their investment; **customers**—through efficient, safe, reliable service; and **employees**—through challenging and rewarding careers.

151. **Commerce Bancshares, Inc.**
      1000 Walnut Street; P.O. Box 13686; Kansas City, MO 64106
      (816) 234-2470
      Industry: 60—Banking

Mission Statement

Our goal is to be the premier provider of targeted financial products and services by offering distinctive value, quality, convenience, dependability, and security. We will seek to generate an attractive, long-term, risk-adjusted return for shareholders.

THE NATURE OF OUR BUSINESS

Our corporate goal is to be the premier provider of targeted financial products and services in our marketplace by offering distinctive value, quality, convenience, dependability, security, and other benefits to our customers. Our products and services will be designed to be market driven, cost competitive, and prioritized to enhance our Company's long term profitability. We will pursue sound growth while maintaining our asset quality, our capital strength, and superior rates of return on assets and equity.

OUR MARKETS AND CUSTOMERS

Geographically, our marketplace is the central Midwest; in that market, we will provide products and services to a diversified base of financially responsible retail and commercial customers. Our customers and target prospects encompass: (1) a broad economic spectrum of retail customers where we can sell profitable financial services, and (2) middle market and community businesses and institutions where we can provide value added services. We will focus on the development of relationships with our customers which are long term and broad based in nature.

OUR PEOPLE

Our people are the most critical resource in fulfilling our corporate mission. We will recruit and retain people who are highly motivated, customer oriented, and share a vision of our common goals. We will provide a working environment which encourages personal development, equal opportunity, recognizes and compensates our people based upon performance, and promotes a sense of ownership and pride in the Company and in each person's work product. Our cultural environment will place a high priority on strong management at all levels with superior communication skills and a commitment to developing and implementing long range plans for the benefit of our customers, stockholders, and employees.

OUR COMMUNITY ROLE

We will invest in and contribute to the well-being of the communities we serve with our financial and personnel resources, recognizing that our own growth and prosperity depends upon the social and economic health of our marketplace. In our role as stewards of our customers' financial resources, we will conduct our business to strengthen the long term economy of our marketplace.

OUR FINANCIAL OBJECTIVES

We will seek to generate attractive, long term, risk adjusted rates of return for our shareholders. We will plan to achieve top quartile performance when measured against our competitors and comparable peer group indices, prioritizing our efforts in terms of asset quality, earnings, efficiency, and growth. Such efforts should result in consistent earnings per share and dividend growth.

Drafted 1991

152. **Commonwealth Edison Company**
One First National Plaza; P.O. Box 767; Chicago, IL 60690-0767
(312) 294-4321
Industry: 49—Electric utility

VISION STATEMENT

Commonwealth Edison will be the supplier of electric service that best meets customers' needs.

Our customer base is one of our greatest assets. To protect that base and outperform our competitors, we will create loyal customers by meeting our customers' needs as they define them. Toward that end, we will become a flexible and responsive organization. We will provide superior value by responding to customers' varying needs for quality, reliability, and cost.

To meet these objectives, we must maintain the health and support the growth of the entire Company. Accordingly, we will become the nation's premier utility, stressing superior performance in all aspects of our operations. We will redefine how we work and deploy resources to improve our performance. We will assess every activity in terms of its contribution to customer satisfaction, and we will measure ourselves against customer-defined performance goals.

We will also serve our customers in non-traditional ways by using skills and assets to encourage and support electricity-related enterprises that respond to the emerging needs of our customers.

Success will create an excellent company that is valued by its customers; rewards its shareholders; recognizes the contribution of its employees; and is respected by regulators, competitors, and peers.

Adopted 1989

Comp-U-Card
see CUC International (171)

153. **Cone Mills Corporation**
   1201 Maple Street; Greensboro, NC 27415-6540
   (919) 379-6462
   Industry: 22—Textiles

Cone's Mission Statement

Identify consumer needs (opportunities) that match Cone's capabilities to add value. Select the ones that fit and deliver the products and services that provide value to our customers and an appropriate return to investors in an environment that is responsible to employees and society.

Drafted May, 1992

Conrail
   see Consolidated Rail Corporation (155)

154. **Conseco, Inc.**
   11825 North Pennsylvania Street; P.O. Box 1911; Carmel, IN 46032
   (317) 573-6100
   Industry: 63—Life and health insurance

Conseco's Mission:

Conseco is dedicated to leading the process of change in the insurance industry by setting new standards for operating efficiency, product innovation, product profitability and active investment management. We believe strongly that this process assures the best products and services for our customers, the highest value for our shareholders and the most rewarding careers for our employees.

Adopted 1990

155. **Consolidated Rail Corporation**
   Six Penn Center Plaza; Philadelphia, PA 19103-2959
   (215) 977-4000
   Industry: 40—Railroad

Our future depends on our ability to totally please our customers with service that meets their changing needs. To that end, in 1990, Conrail developed its Vision, Guiding Principles and key corporate Goals. Together they represent the course that Conrail will follow to become "the carrier of choice in every transportation market we serve."

Vision

We, the employees of Conrail, are dedicated to making our company the carrier of choice in every transportation market we serve. We promise safe, reliable and innovative services that meet or exceed customers' expectations. We are committed to continuous quality improvement as a means of providing superior service to our customers, developing and recognizing excellence in one another, enhancing value for our shareholders and being worthy of the public's trust.

Guiding Principles

- *Safety First.* The safety of employees, the public, the environment and customer shipments are in our trust. We will strive for accident free work and commit to continuous and measurable decreases in safety-related incidents.

- *Customer Focus.* The customer is the key to our success. We are committed to understanding, anticipating and responding to every customer's requirements with service excellence.

- *Leadership By Example.* Visible leadership will be practiced at all levels of the organization through open communication, integrity and respect for each employee. Management will ensure availability of cost-effective resources and promote empowerment of employees to achieve our vision.

- *Employee Involvement.* We will create an environment which makes every employee a team member and encourages participation in achieving our goals. We will provide the needed training and opportunity for personal growth that develops each employee's full potential to contribute.

- *Partnerships.* All key stakeholders in our business—customers, employees, suppliers, shareholders, communities, governments and business peers—will be treated as partners. We will build long-term relationships founded on mutual respect and trust.

- *Commitment to Quality.* We will work together, combining our ideas and skills to continuously improve the quality of our work. We will strive for prevention, rather than correction, by using fact-based problem solving methods. Work processes will be benchmarked against leading companies and measurable goals will be set to become the best at everything we do.

Goals

- To be the safest carrier.
- To provide total customer satisfaction as measured by the customer.
- To achieve seamless service through cooperation with others.
- To create an environment that motivates and develops all employees to fully meet the needs of the customer.
- To achieve best business practices.
- To achieve growth in the markets we serve.
- To achieve an operating ratio of 80%.
- To achieve a return on assets exceeding the cost of capital.

Annual Report 1990

156. **Consumers Gas Co. Ltd.**
500 Consumers Road; Willowdale, Ontario; Canada M1K 5E3
(416) 495-6184
Industry: 49—Gas distribution

Mission

Consumers Gas primary business is the distribution of natural gas.

The Company will strengthen and develop this business and will develop existing ancillary business ventures and other opportunities related to its primary business.

Goals

1. To serve our customers with integrity, sensitivity and fairness, at reasonable cost, and in a manner that fosters customer satisfaction, loyalty and employee pride.

2. To provide a fair return to the shareholders comprising dividend yield and increases in share value, which is competitive with alternative investment opportunities.

3. To provide stable employment with just compensation in a safe working environment, which recognizes both the performance and the dignity of the individual and provides opportunity for achievement.

4. To conduct our affairs in a manner that is sensitive and responsive to community need.

Strategies

1. The Company will continue to focus strongly on understanding and meeting the evolving needs of its customers.

2. The Company will maintain a high profile in the marketplace and will work toward attaining increased market share and investment, through profitable expansion, in all markets.

3. The Company will intensify its efforts to provide excellent service to its customers and ensure that this commitment is reflected in day to day operations and future planning. In all its endeavors the Company will strive for innovation and operational excellence.

4. The Company will maintain its financial self-sufficiency and market attractiveness to investors as well as enhancing the value of its shareholders investment.

5. The Company will identify and evaluate business opportunities which complement its primary business.

6. The Company will be pro-active in influencing the social and political environment in which it operates.

7. The Company will focus its efforts on creating a leadership style at all levels of the organization and in all aspects of the business which will

motivate management and employees to strive for organizational excellence and quality in all its undertakings.

8. The Company will conduct all of its operations in an environmentally sensitive manner.

9. The Company will promote natural gas as an environmentally preferred energy source.

10. The Company will strive for continuous improvement and will ensure that all work undertaken is productive and required for effective operations.

11. The Company will evaluate and adopt appropriate new technologies to meet stakeholder needs and contribute to improved productivity.

12. The Company will maintain positive relationships with its regulators and ensure effective planning and execution of its regulatory proceedings.

157. **Consumers Union**
    101 Truman Avenue; Yonkers, NY 10703-1057
    (914) 378-2000
    Industry: 27—Publishing

Mission Statement

Consumers Union advances the interests of consumers by providing information and advice about products and services and about issues affecting their welfare, and by advocating a consumer point of view.

158. **Continental Airlines, Inc.**
    P.O. Box 4607; Houston, TX 77120
    (713) 834-5000
    Industry: 45—Airline

CRITICAL FACTORS NEEDED FOR SUCCESS:

- Create and maintain customer-driven culture
- Create and deliver a UNIQUE, higher quality service than competition
- Recognize that employee treatment determines customer treatment
- Provide appropriate employee support and incentives
- Commit necessary resources

CORPORATE VISION:

To be recognized as the best airline in the industry by our customers, employees and shareholders.

KEY CORPORATE VALUES

- Integrity
- Commitment
- Caring
- Quality

Formulated March, 1992

159. **Continental Medical Systems, Inc.**
600 Wilson Lane; P.O. Box 715; Mechanicsburg, PA 17055
(717) 790-8300
Industry: 80—Health care

The mission of Continental Medical Systems, Inc. (CMS), is to lead the industry in the provision of medical rehabilitation services through delivery of the highest quality care by the most competent team of professionals. CMS' goal is to ensure that patients achieve their greatest functional outcome in the most cost effective manner.

Annual Report 1992

160. **Cooper Industries**
P.O. Box 4446; Houston, TX 77210
(713) 739-5400
Industry: 35, 36—Industrial and electrical equipment

Cooper Industries is a diversified, worldwide manufacturer of electrical products, electrical power equipment, tools and hardware, automotive products, and petroleum and industrial equipment. Annual revenues are approximately $6 billion. The company operates 170 manufacturing plants in 41 states and 36 foreign countries. It employs 54,000 people.

Our fundamental objectives are:

- to provide the best value delivered to our customers;
- to provide our shareholders with a superior investment over the long term; and
- to do both of these things while performing as a responsible employer and good corporate citizen.

Among the basic strategies for accomplishing these objectives, we have identified the following:

- Put customer satisfaction above all other criteria as the measure of manufacturing and product success;
- Progressively improve return on investment through a carefully designed program of diversification, cost reduction and cash flow management;
- Treat employees with fairness and respect; and

- Strive to be the kind of corporate citizen that people want to have in their communities.

We have established a return on equity objective of 12% plus the current rate of inflation, and a dividend payout of approximately 30% of share earnings. Our strategy for accomplishing these goals is based on:
- Superior results as a value-added manufacturer;
- Market leadership in each of our businesses;
- A strong cash flow;
- Positioning Cooper as a world-class competitor; and
- An active program of management development and succession planning.

We expect to perform as a good corporate citizen in each of our communities. This is expressed by a wide range of practices, from strict adherence to local, state and federal laws and regulations to the way we maintain the appearance of our buildings and grounds, and includes a number of pro-active programs such as cash contributions, matching gifts, encouraging employee volunteerism, support for education; and a dedication to employee safety and environmental responsibility.

1993

161. **Cooper Tire & Rubber Company**
      P.O. Box 550; Findlay, OH 45840
      (419) 423-1321
      Industry: 30—Tires and rubber

It was in 1926 that I. J. Cooper expressed our Company's Business Creed with these words:

"It wouldn't be called a plan or a policy by a highpowered modern business expert because it is not complicated enough. In fact, it is very simple. Our platform of business conduct has only three planks in it:
- Good merchandise
- Fair play, and a
- Square deal

Good merchandise because it doesn't pay to make, sell or use an inferior article. Fair prices that satisfy the user, leave the dealer with a profit and the maker with a margin to cover his labor, thought and investment. And a square deal to everyone, every time, because you can't beat a natural law and still progress and prosper."

These words were true then, are true today, and will remain true tomorrow.

For over three-quarters of a century Cooper Tire & Rubber Company has been building its reputation for quality products and customer service. We express sincere thanks to our dedicated employee team, our loyal customers, our suppliers and our stockholders for making our success possible.

162. Corning Inc.
Houghton Park; Corning, NY 14831
(607) 974-9000
Industry: 28, 33, 38—Chemicals, glass, and analytic equipment

WHO WE ARE

Our Purpose

Our purpose is to deliver superior, long-range economic benefits to our customers, our employees, our shareholders, and to the communities in which we operate. We accomplish this by living our corporate values.

Our Strategy

Corning is an evolving network of wholly owned businesses and joint ventures.

Our strategy is to grow profitably by building upon our strengths and experiences. These include the markets we know, the specialty glass and ceramics technology in which we are pre-eminent, and our unique ability to make joint ventures work successfully.

We choose to compete in four global business sectors: Specialty Materials, Consumer Housewares, Laboratory Sciences and Telecommunications. In these sectors, our combined market, technical and management skills allow us to be worldwide leaders.

Within each sector we use varying organization and ownership structures, including partnerships with other companies, to best meet the requirements of our customers and to compete more effectively.

Our corporate network adds value beyond that created by its single parts. It is bound together by a dedication to total quality, a commitment to technology, shared financial resources, common values, and management links.

WHAT WE VALUE

We have a set of enduring beliefs that are ingrained in the way we think and act. These values guide our choices, defining for us the right courses of action, the clearest directions, the preferred responses. Consistent with these values we set our objectives, formulate our strategies and judge our results. Only by living these values will we achieve our purpose.

Quality

We insist that Total Quality be the guiding principle of our business life. This means new ways of working together. It means knowing and meeting the requirements of our customers and our co-workers. It means doing it right the first time, on time, every time.

Integrity

We demand honesty, decency, fairness. Respect must characterize all internal and external relationships.

Performance

We hold ourselves and each other, as individuals and as an organization, accountable for our results.

Leadership

We are a leader, not a follower. This extends to the markets we serve, our multiple technologies, our manufacturing processes, our management practices, and our financial performance. The goods and services we produce must never be ordinary and must always be truly useful.

Independence

We cherish our corporate freedom. This condition has fostered the innovation and initiative that makes our company great.

Technology

We lead primarily by technical innovation. This belief in the power of technology is common to all our parts. It is the glue that binds us together. We are committed to translating our specific expertise into goods and services, to expanding the range of our scientific competence, and to linking these abilities with new market needs.

The Individual

We know in the end that the commitment and contribution of all employees will determine our success. Open relationships with each other and with our customers are essential. Therefore, each employee must have the opportunity to participate fully, to grow professionally, and to develop to his or her highest potential.

Extracted from "Values" brochure

163. **Costco® Wholesale Corp.**
      P.O. Box 97077; Kirkland, WA 98083-9777
      (206) 828-8100
      Industry: 59—Specialty retailing
      Costco's mission is to continually provide our members with quality goods and services at the lowest possible prices. In order to achieve our mission we will conduct our business with the following four responsibilities in mind:
      1. Obey the law
      2. Take care of our customers

3. Take care of our employees
4. Respect our vendors

If we do these four things essentially in the order listed we will accomplish our overall goal of taking care of our shareholders.

164. Countrymark Cooperative, Inc.

950 North Meridian Street; Indianapolis, IN 46204-3909
(317) 685-3000
Industry: 20, 51—Food production and wholesale

Mission Statement

Serve Countrymark Co-op members by using profitable and financially sound practices to supply and market important products and services that will enhance long-term member and farmer-patron profitability.

165. Covenant House

346 West 17th Street; New York, NY 10011-5002
(212) 727-4000
Industry: 83—Social services

OUR MISSION STATEMENT

We who recognize God's providence and fidelity to His people are dedicated to living out His Covenant among ourselves and those children we serve, with absolute respect and unconditional love. That commitment calls us to serve suffering children of the street, and to protect and safeguard all children. Just as Christ in His humanity is the visible sign of God's presence among His people, so our efforts together in the Covenant community are a visible sign that effects the presence of God, working through the Holy Spirit among ourselves and our kids.

Annual Report 1991

166. Cox Enterprises, Inc.

P.O. Box 105357; Atlanta, GA 30348
(404) 843-5000
Industry: 27, 48—Publishing and broadcasting

Positioned For The Future

Cox Enterprises is postioned to meet the challenges of the future with an operating philosophy based on these principles:

Our employees are the Company's most important resource. We encourage individual initiative and entrepreneurship at every level. We value and reward achievement.

Our customers are the Company's lifeblood. We are dedicated to building lasting relationships with them, and to meeting their needs with high-quality service beyond their expectations.

We embrace new technology to give our customers the variety and quality of services they demand.

With a mixture of caution and initiative, we invest in new business opportunities to enhance our growth.

We believe it's good business to be good citizens of the communities we serve through volunteerism and financial support.

We are committed to helping shape a better world. We do this by using our media to educate the public about important issues, such as the environment, and through responsible company and individual actions.

Annual Report 1991

167. **Cray Research, Inc.**
     1440 Northland Drive; Mendota Heights, MN 55120
     (612) 452-6650
     Industry: 35—Computers

MISSION

Cray Research creates the most powerful and highest quality computational tools for solving the world's most challenging scientific and industrial problems.

Published February, 1992

168. **C.R. Bard, Inc.**
     730 Central Avenue; Murray Hill, NJ 07974
     (908) 277-8000
     Industry: 38—Medical equipment

BARD'S CREED

Our **Mission** is to profitably develop, manufacture and market higher technology health care products to assist the health care professional in caring for the patient.

Our **Values** are characterized by a dedication to:

Quality, Integrity and Service

Quality —We are dedicated to marketing high quality products that help professionals help their patients.

Integrity —We are dedicated to being open and honest in our dealings with one another, and with everyone outside the Company.

Service —We are dedicated to taking care of the customer's needs in the most timely fashion possible.

Our **Philosophy** is summed up in these words:

Decentralization, Concentration and Innovation

Decentralization—Allows us to manage complex businesses and to continue to add new businesses by bringing good managers close to problems and their solutions.

Concentration—Focuses management and resources on these businesses to achieve the number one or number two market share position by listening to, and taking care of, our customer.

Innovation—Allows us to maintain and improve market share through new and improved products.

Annual Report 1991

OUR CORPORATE CHARTER

C.R. Bard, Inc. is in the business of serving:

- the patient;
- the professions who care for the patient;
- the dealers who serve the professions;
- the employees who carry out our service;
- the communities in which our employees live and work;
- the shareholders who provide the capital to sustain all of the above.

Our mission in each of these is:

1. To serve the patient by using our human and financial resources to develop and make the finest quality products of which we are capable. To recognize that we can't serve the patient with every kind of hospital product so to concentrate our activities in those specialties where our competence is greatest.

2. To serve the professions by clearly defining the specialties we're in and by working closely with the professionals in those specialties to be sure we are developing the products that will serve them best and informing them of the advantages our products offer in patient care.

To understand that we are presently serving the professions in the fields of urology, cardiology, surgery, radiology, critical care, medication delivery, home health care and that our prime contribution to the professionals will be in the advancement of product technology in these fields. That new ventures of C.R. Bard, Inc. will be into fields as special as these.

3. To serve the dealers by carefully choosing those who can best aid us in our service to the patient and the professions. To clearly explain our policy to dealers. To fairly compensate them for the contribution they make to our overall service system. To recognize that Bard dealers' contributions are as a service partner, not a sales partner, to our divisions.

4. To serve our employees by recognizing that they deserve good management practices in each of our units so they will understand where we

want to go and the part they are to play in getting us there. To see that each employee of Bard is fairly compensated for the contribution he or she makes to our progress. To maintain Bard's leadership in anticipating employee benefit needs and caring for them as quickly as financially feasible. To create an overall work atmosphere of fairness, urgency and pleasantness in each of our units.

5. To serve the communities in which we work and live by helping them with our time and, where possible, our money; understanding that the strength and vigor of the community contribute to the strength and vigor of the unit operating there.

6. To serve the shareholders by increasing the size and value of C.R. Bard, Inc. and reinforcing its financial strength and stability through all of the foregoing. We believe the shareholders' interest is best served by careful handling of today's business and close attention to planning for logical, solid growth of strongly built product franchises in the future.

169. **Crestar Financial Corporation**
      P.O. Box 26665; Richmond, VA 23261-6665
      (804) 782-5000
      Industry: 60—Banking

Crestar's mission is to provide the maximum economic return to our shareholders over the long term, and to contribute to the economic vitality and quality of life of the communities we serve. We believe this is accomplished by providing an organizational environment that encourages the individual potential of our employees and emphasizes the highest quality financial services for our customers.

Annual Report 1991

170. **CSX Corp.**
      P.O. Box C-32222; Richmond, VA 23261
      (804) 782-1400
      Industry: 40, 44—Railroad and water transportation

CSX MISSION STATEMENT

CSX is a transportation company committed to being a leader in railroad, inland water and containerized distribution markets.

To attract the human and financial resources necessary to achieve this leadership position, CSX will support our three major constituencies:

- For our customers, we will work as a partner to provide excellent service by meeting all agreed-upon commitments.
- For our employees, we will create a work environment that motivates and allows them to grow and develop and perform their jobs to the maximum of their capacity.

- For our shareholders, we will meet our goals to provide them with sustainable superior returns.

171. **CUC International**
707 Summer Street; P.O. Box 10049; Stamford, CT 06904-2049
(203) 324-9261
Industry: 73—Buyer's club and financial services

COMP-U-CARD MISSION STATEMENT:

To provide our members the best value in consumer services through superior quality, significant savings and uequalled convenience.

172. **Cullen/Frost Bankers, Inc.**
100 West Houston Street; P.O. Box 1600; San Antonio, TX 78296
(512) 220-4011
Industry: 60—Banking

Cullen/Frost will strive to be the 'preferred place to do business' for our target customer segments in the markets we serve. We will achieve this by being the premier local bank in those markets and by being recognized for our unrivaled service to our customers and commitment to our communities. This unique market positioning, coupled with corporate-wide commitments to asset quality, sound banking practices and cost containment will generate sustainable improvements in operating performance and enhance shareholder value.

D

173. Dahlin Smith White, Inc.

4 Triad Center, Suite 400; Salt Lake City, UT 84180

(801) 364-0919

Industry: 73—Advertising

DSW's mission is to grow by taking complex and often technical issues and turning them into compelling communications programs for market-leading clients.

August, 1992

Dairy Queen

see International Dairy Queen, Inc. (307)

174. Dakota Electric Association

4300 220th Street West; Farmington, MN 55024

(612) 463-7134

Industry: 49—Electric cooperative

Mission Statement

Provide safe, adequate, reliable electric energy and service at a competitive nonprofit rate in the spirit of a member-owned cooperative.

Meaning of Our Mission Statement

DEA must provide electric energy and service to fulfill our mission.

"Safety" must be our foremost consideration, safety for our employees, our members and the general public.

"Adequate" means to assure a supply of electric energy well into the future provided in the most economical manner.

"Reliable" means to maintain our goal of providing electric service 99.98 percent of the time, on the average, to our members.

"Service" extends beyond keeping the lights on; we must be ready to answer questions, educate our members on the latest technical developments, and then put these developments to use, to extend service to new consumers in a polite, timely manner. Our minds must remain open to accept the change that is demanded of us.

"Competitive Nonprofit Rate"—A major goal is to maintain existing, or lower our rates as time goes on so as to again be the low cost suppliers of electricity in our area.

"Spirit of a Member-Owned Cooperative" can best be defined by reading the "Rochdale Principles" which were developed to govern the first cooperative established in Rochdale, England in 1844. We have to market our cooperative, first by providing the best service, highest quality power in our area and, second, by providing knowledge of a cooperative's philosophy.

Created April, 1990
Revised February, 1991

175. **Dana Corporation**
P.O. Box 1000; Toledo, OH 43697
(419) 535-4500
Industry: 30, 37—Rubber products and auto parts

The Philosophy & Policies of Dana

The Dana philosophy is our basic thinking of how we view the world in which we operate—our fundamental values of how we interact with our people, our customers, and the communities where we live and work. This philosophy is the basis for our policies shown in this folder.

Since our policies represent basic beliefs and values, they will change very slowly and over a long period of time. Any change will only be in the form of a revision necessitated by the growth and development of Dana. The Policy Committee is responsible for our philosophy and our policies.

EARNINGS

The purpose of the Dana Corporation is to earn money for its shareholders and to increase the value of their investment. We believe the best way to do this is to earn an acceptable return by properly utilizing our assets and controlling our cash.

GROWTH

We believe in steady growth to protect our assets against inflation. We will grow in our selected markets by implementing our market strategies.

PEOPLE

We are dedicated to the belief that our people are our most important asset. Wherever possible, we encourage all Dana people within the entire world organization to become shareholders, or by some other means, own a part of their company.

We believe people respond to recognition, freedom to participate, and the opportunity to develop.

We believe that people should be involved in setting their own goals and judging their own performance. The people who know best how the job should be done are the ones doing it.

We believe Dana people should accept only total quality in all tasks they perform.

We endorse productivity plans which allow people to share in the rewards of productivity gains.

We believe that all Dana people should identify with the company. This identity should carry on after they have left active employment.

We believe facilities with people who have demonstrated a commitment to Dana will be competitive and thus warrant our support.

We believe that wages and benefits are the concern and responsibility of managers. The Management Resource Program is a worldwide matter—it is a tool that should be used in the development of qualified Dana people. We encourage income protection, health programs, and education.

We believe that on-the-job training is an effective method of learning. A Dana manager must prove proficiency in at least one line of our company's work—marketing, engineering, manufacturing, financial services, etc. Additionally, these people must prove their ability as supervisors and be able to get work done through other people. We recognize the importance of gaining experience both internationally and domestically.

We believe our people should move across product, discipline, and organizational lines. These moves should not conflict with operating efficiency.

We believe in promoting from within. Dana people interested in other positions are encouraged to discuss job opportunities with their supervisor.

Managers are responsible for the selection, education and training of all people.

All Dana people should have their job performance reviewed at least once a year by their supervisors.

We believe in providing programs to support the Dana Style. We encourage professional and personal development of all Dana people.

PLANNING

We believe in planning at all levels.

The Policy Committee is responsible for developing the corporate strategic plan.

Each operating unit within its regional organization is responsible for a detailed five-year business plan. These business plans must support the corporate strategic plan and market strategies. These plans are reviewed annually.

Commitment is a key element of the Dana Management Style. This commitment and performance will be reviewed on a monthly basis by the appropriate regional operating committee and on a semi-annual basis during Mid-Year Reviews.

ORGANIZATION

We discourage conformity, uniformity and centralization.

We believe in a minimum number of management levels. Responsibility should be pushed as far into the organization as possible.

Organizational structure must not conflict with doing what is best for all of Dana.

We believe in an organizational structure that allows the individual maximum freedom to perform and participate. This will stimulate initiative, innovation, and the entrepreneurial spirit that is the cornerstone of our success.

We believe in small, highly effective, support groups to service specialized needs of the Policy Committee and the world organization at large as requested. We believe in task forces rather than permanent staff functions.

We do not believe in company-wide procedures. If an organization requires procedures, it is the responsibility of the manager to create them.

CUSTOMERS

Dana is a global company focused on markets and customers. We compete globally by supplying products and services to meet the needs of our customers in our selected markets.

We are dedicated to the belief that we have a responsibility to be leaders in our selected markets.

We believe it is absolutely necessary to anticipate our customers needs for products and services of the highest quality. Once a commitment is made to a customer, every effort must be made to fulfill that obligation.

It is highly desirable to outsource a portion of our production needs. Outsourcing increases our competitiveness and protects the stability of employment for our people. It also protects our assets and assures performance to our customers.

Dana People throughout the organization are expected to know our customers and their needs.

COMMUNICATION

We will communicate regularly with shareholders, customers, Dana people, general public, and financial communities.

It is the job of all managers to keep Dana people informed. Each manager must decide on the best method of communication. We believe direct communication with all of our people eliminates the need for third party involvement. All managers shall periodically inform their people about the performance and plans of their operation.

CITIZENSHIP

The Dana Corporation will be a good citizen worldwide. All Dana people are expected to do business in a professional and ethical manner with integrity.

Laws and regulations have become increasingly complex. The laws of propriety always govern. The General Counsel and each General Manager can give guidance when in doubt about appropriate conduct. It is expected that no one would willfully violate the law and subject themselves to disciplinary action.

We encourage active participation of all our people in community action.

We will support worthwhile community causes consistent with their importance to the good of Dana people in the community.

Revised December 1, 1987

176. **Daughters of Charity National Health System**
     East Central Region; 9404 New Harmony Road; Evansville,
     IN 47720-8909
     (812) 963-3301
     Industry: 80—Hospital

MISSION STATEMENT

The Daughters of Charity National Health System (DCNHS) advances and strengthens the healing mission of the Catholic Church through the tradition of service established by St. Vincent de Paul, St. Louise de Marillac and St. Elizabeth Ann Seton.

DCNHS is an integrated structure of local, regional and national health-related organizations. Members may be sponsored or co-sponsored by the Daughters of Charity or affiliated with DCNHS. Our purpose is to contribute toward improving the health status of individuals and the communities we serve by providing patient-centered, economical health services with a special concern for the sick and the poor.

Our vision is to be a values-driven health system which serves the health needs of the total individual—body, mind, and spirit. We will promote a healthy and just society through community-based networks and collaboration with those who share our values.

We are compelled to these ends by our Core Values Statement:

"The Charity of Christ urges us to:

Respect, Quality Service, Simplicity, Advocacy for the Poor, and Inventiveness to Infinity."

August, 1992

177. **David Mitchell & Associates, Inc.**
2345 Rice Street, Suite 205; St. Paul, MN 55113
(612) 482-0011
Industry: 87—Consulting
Bringing world class excellence to business and information solutions.

178. **Davis Distributing Limited**
7171 Jane Street; Concord, Ontario; Canada L4K 1A7
(416) 738-6226
Industry: 51—Grocery wholesale

DAVIS' BUSINESS MISSION

Davis Distributing is a leading Canadian Wholesale distributor dedicated to acting as a partner in helping its retail customers succeed in their increasingly competitive businesses.

In business for over 60 years, Davis also offers the comparable services of the "controlled/dedicated" distributors, with the flexibility to customize services for its Customers—each of whom has unique needs.

DAVIS FOCUS ON THE CUSTOMER ALLOWS US TO PROVIDE:

- Customized Support Programs and Services to help Customers successfully meet the demands of their market area. These include a variety of modern and electronic ordering methods; group programs; special deals; store set up, support and supplies; management reports.

- A product range to service every customer by providing a single supply source for competitively priced goods. Product categories include: frozen and refrigerated products, tobacco, confectionary, Health & Beauty Aids, Grocery, Paper and Sundries.

- Experienced Staff in both the buying and selling departments to ensure the highest quality of Product and Service support.

IN GUIDING ALL ITS ACTIONS DAVIS WILL:

- Have a **Customer First** Philosophy.
- Work with Customers as **Partners** in their businesses.
- Give every Customer **direct access to a Customer Service Representative** to help with special needs.
- **Provide ongoing training of our people** to enable us to improve every aspect of our business.
- **Maintain commitments** to work with the following groups:
- **Employees**—to provide safe and rewarding working conditions;

- **Suppliers**—to offer the best products at the best prices;
- **Community**—to contribute to, and support community needs;
- **Environment**—to operate in an environmentally conscious way.

- Provide sales support in order that Customers can benefit from Davis' industry expertise.

- Keeps its ear to the ground to offer the products and prices which will allow our Customers to meet their goals.

179. **Deere & Company**
    John Deere Road; Moline, IL 61265-8098
    (309) 765-5290
    Industry: 35—Tractors and heavy equipment

VISION STATEMENT

The purpose of Deere & Company is to create GENUINE VALUE for all of our constituents.

Our constituents include customers, employees, shareholders, and the global community. Our customers have invested in our products; our employees have invested their energy and creativity; our shareholders have invested capital; and the global community has invested the use of its environment.

The foundation of the John Deere Vision has always been quality. As a result of the globalization of business, our constituents now have a greater variety of choices than ever before. Such a variety means that quality alone is not enough to guarantee our success in creating GENUINE VALUE. Quality must now be coupled with lower cost and enhanced resource utilization.

GENUINE VALUE for our customers means providing them with products of superior value based upon a blend of price, quality and after-sales support.

GENUINE VALUE for our employees means providing them with excellent opportunities for job satisfaction. In addition to direct pay and benefits, job satisfaction is a combination of the prospects for personal growth and advancement, and the opportunity to add value.

GENUINE VALUE for the Company means profitable growth. Profitable growth occurs when constituents increase their investments in companies where they receive GENUINE VALUE.

GENUINE VALUE for the global community means our being environmentally responsible and efficient in the use of resources which are a part of our business process.

GENUINE VALUE is sustained only when the finest quality becomes finer, the lowest cost becomes lower, and the best utilization of resources becomes better. It is only by creating GENUINE VALUE that profitable growth is assured.

Hans W. Becherer, Chairman
April, 1992

180. Delmarva Power & Light Company
800 King Street; P.O. Box 231; Wilmington, DE 19899
(302) 429-3011
Industry: 49—Electric utility

CORPORATE MISSION STATEMENT

The mission of Delmarva Power is to provide gas, electricity and energy-related services to our customers in a safe, reliable and customer-focused manner at competitive prices consistent with an adequate return to investors.

CORPORATE STRATEGY STATEMENT

The major corporate focus is providing electric and gas service on the Delmarva Peninsula. In all business activities the corporation will emphasize customer service, operational efficiency, and environmental responsibility, recognizing that the customer is the ultimate judge of value. The wise use of energy by customers and employees will be promoted to produce more efficient use of Company resources and result in more competitive prices. Employees through teamwork, participation, skill development, and safe work practices will focus on continuing improvement of our performance, providing Delmarva with a competitive advantage.

Extracted from "Strategy, Principles, & Mission Statements:
Delmarva Power", March, 1991

(This booklet also includes mission statements for individual company departments and units.)

181. Destec Energy, Inc.
Subsidiary of Dow Chemical Company
2500 Citywest Boulevard #1700; P.O. Box 4411; Houston, TX 77210-4411
(713) 735-4000
Industry: 49—Cogeneration

DESTEC'S CORPORATE VISION

We will be the premier independent power company.

BASIC BELIEFS

Technology

We will be a leader in combustion turbine, combined cycle, and syngas technologies and the application of these power generation technologies. We will acquire or develop new technologies to meet our strategic business objectives.

Business

We will participate in technologically state-of-the-art energy projects which are economically efficient, reliable and which meet the highest environmental standards economically feasible.

Customers

We will create solutions to important customer problems in order to contribute added value. We will seek and develop long-term relationships with key customers who offer potential for multiple major projects. We will strive to be recognized by our partners and customers as their highest quality partner or supplier.

Organization

We will have an organization with a minimum of managerial layers. We will expand and develop our staff, first through internal promotion, and, if a qualified person is not available through Destec, by attracting highly qualified and experienced people from outside sources. We will delegate authority and responsibility based on talent and experience.

People

We will acknowledge our employees as the source of our success. We will treat our employees with respect, promote teamwork, and encourage personal freedom and growth. Specifically we will: emphasize individual employee development; recognize individual initiative in the achievement of team success; and, encourage entrepreneurism. We will provide quality performance through the commitment of all employees to seek continuous improvement in all their activities. We will reward employees based on experience and performance and will provide incentives to encourage exceptional performance. We will strive to have fun!

Citizenship/Ethics

We will conduct ourselves responsibly by demonstrating a deep concern for ethics, safety, health and the environment. We will be good citizens in each community where we operate. We will be pro-active in the development of energy and environmental public policies that are beneficial to society and which will help achieve our Corporate Vision.

Financial Results

We will set financial growth and return goals that will demonstrate our leadership in the industry. We will utilize conservative accounting principles. We will manage risk in relationship to profit potential. We will maximize long-term shareholder value.

182. **Devtek Corporation**
100 Allstate Parkway, Suite 500; Markham, Ontario; Canada
L3R 6H3
(416) 477-6861
Industry: 37—Aerospace

Mission Statement

In partnership with employees and shareholders, Devtek will be a leading progressive company committed to continuous growth and profitability. We will focus our efforts on satisfying our customers worldwide with products of the highest quality and value. We accept our accountability for safety and the environment. We will be a respected corporate citizen and will conduct our business with integrity.

Drafted 1989

183. **DeWitt Wallace-Reader's Digest Fund**
261 Madison Avenue, 24th Floor; New York, NY 10016
(212) 953-1208
Industry: 67—Charitable foundation

Vision Statement

The DeWitt Wallace-Reader's Digest Fund believes that America's future depends on providing opportunities for all youth to fulfill their educational and career aspirations.

To help achieve that vision, the Fund invests nationwide to: improve elementary and secondary schools, encourage school and community collaboration, strengthen organizations that serve youth, and support programs that increase career, service and education opportunities for young people. Approved annual grants exceed $60 million.

In general, the Fund's grantmaking activities are designed to:
- Build the staff and management capacity of schools and other organizations that serve youth.
- Develop and institutionalize model programs that can be replicated throughout the nation.
- Support public policy initiatives that promote youth development.

September, 1992

see also Lila Wallace-Reader's Digest Fund, Inc. (342)

184. **Dexter Corporation**
     One Elm Street; Windsor Locks, CT 06096
     (203) 627-9051
     Industry: 28—Specialty chemicals

OUR MISSION

To be recognized as an important and environmentally responsive specialty materials company that derives superior growth and returns from quality products and responsive services based on proprietary technology and operating excellence that provides genuine benefit to customers worldwide, rewards talented and dedicated employees, and satisfies shareholder expectations.

OUR BELIEFS

- We are all employed to serve our customers.
- We are focused on markets which recognize and reward superior quality of products and services.
- Our company is composed of strong people, skilled in their work who treat each other with dignity and respect.
- We recognize and reward distinguished performance.
- We will communicate openly without fear or threat.
- We are a decentralized organization that encourages an entrepreneurial attitude and technical innovation.
- We are committed to total quality in everything we do.
- We differentiate ourselves on the basis of proprietary technology and prompt, superior technical service.
- We compete in global markets that require world-class manufacturing processes.
- We seek partnerships with suppliers and reward those that meet our quality standards.
- We strive for continuous improvement in the safety of our operations.
- We will work to safeguard the environment.
- We will conduct our business with the highest standard of ethical behavior.
- We will work to create steady growth in shareholder value.
- We will be involved citizens in the communities in which we work and the world at large.

Drafted 1988

185. **Dial Corporation**
     1850 North Central Avenue; Phoenix, AZ 85004
     (602) 207-4000

Industry: 28—Personal care products

The Dial Corporation's Mission and Objectives

To assure long-term continually enhanced shareholder value though prudent application of The Dial Corporation's resources to develop and produce quality products and services that offer real value to customers

Maintain an organizational atmosphere and a work environment which encourages innovative, creative and entrepreneurial efforts and which offers opportunity for the advancement and career growth of employees.

Achieve outstanding financial results.

Increase internally generated sources of cash.

Establish an overriding commitment to quality and excellence.

Improve the Corporation's access to and cost of capital by improving its financial quality.

Provide an environment which attracts, retains, and motivates exceptional people.

Increase the proportion of growth opportunities in the corporate portfolio of businesses.

Develop a strong sense of social responsibility and high ethical standards.

Provide wages, incentives and benefits which are competitive and equitable for employees and cost effective to The Dial Corporation and its subsidiaries.

Establish a management structure which will enable efficient and effective execution of the Corporation's strategy.

Assign responsibility for and encourage key corporate and line managers to be responsive to and involved in representing their business interests in relevant forums.

Link key management personnel incentives to the accomplishment of their respective objectives in achieving the overall corporate goals.

Fulfill the Corporation's social responsibilities, by affirmative and aggressive recruitment and individual development programs to achieve full utilization of minority, female and handicapped employees and veterans.

(Each subsidiary formulates a mission statement and objectives for itself and its employees.)

Business Principles

The Dial Corporation and its subsidiaries adhere to the highest standards of ethics in the conduct of their business. The following represent the policy of these companies.

The Dial Corporation and its subsidiaries comply with both the letter and the spirit of the laws of the United States and any other country in which they operate.

The highest standards of integrity and honesty are observed by all personnel at all times.

The Dial Corporation and its subsidiaries remain dedicated to increasing shareholder value and providing quality products and services to customers.

Consideration is given to the potential social and economic benefits to the communities in which we operate when establishing business objectives and strategies.

All business is conducted openly and fairly at all times.

We will always conduct business with a sense of responsibility to shareholders, employees, communities, governments, customers, partners, and suppliers.

Extracted from "Our Corporate Concern—Its Mission, Objectives, Values, and Ethics" booklet, September, 1989

186. **Diebold, Incorporated**
      818 Mulberry Road, SE; P.O. Box 8230; Canton, OH 44711-8230
      (216) 489-4000
      Industry: 35—Financial processing equipment

Vision

We share a vision of Diebold as a worldwide team of people who are:
- *Motivated* to pursue the path to excellence through continuous improvement in all we do;
- *Empowered* to act locally and to think globally as we address the true needs of our markets;
- *Inspired* to provide our customers with products, service and support so outstanding that we will be the natural supplier of choice; and
- *Committed* to provide employment growth opportunities by achieving consistent financial performance.

Mission Statement

Diebold and its associates have a common goal to *meet customer requirements* and to *exceed their expectations* in the markets we serve.

We provide *quality* security, self-service payment transaction and information solutions through state-of-the-art products, software, systems and service.

Values

We will establish the true value of our company by:

- *Earning our leadership position* in all markets we serve by continuing to develop innovative products and services, and by meeting and surpassing our customers' expectations;
- *Maintaining* a steadfast commitment to *excellence* in every product and every service we provide as a means of earning the confidence and loyalty of our customers;
- *Serving* our customers' global needs by offering them our heritage of world support;
- *Encouraging* personal and team *ownership* of responsive problem identification, prevention and solutions;
- *Creating* a climate of *trust* and *respect* which empowers our people to develop to the fullest, while sharing in the responsibilities of success and the rewards of achievement;
- *Keeping* each individual and function *informed* about Diebold, its customers, suppliers and competitors;
- *Forming* lasting, mutually beneficial *relationships* with our customers and suppliers, based on fairness and *integrity*;
- *Achieving* the growth and profit levels that *guarantee* our financial stability and competitive strength to *maximize* the long-term return to shareholders; and
- *Fulfilling* our responsibilities as a good corporate citizen by being a *positive, powerful force* in our communities worldwide and helping *conserve* our natural environment.

Operating Principles

Diebold will maintain *an environment in which all associates are empowered* to *cause actions* which will positively *impact customer satisfaction, encouraged to participate* as team members, and *rewarded* for their contributions to the company's mission.

Diebold will provide *ongoing training* for all associates in order to facilitate *continuous improvement* in everything it does.

Diebold associates will always conduct business with *uncompromising integrity* and the *highest ethical standards*.

Diebold will be a good *corporate citizen* in all communities in which the company operates.

On behalf of Diebold stakeholders, all of our associates will *demonstrate their commitment* to the execution of these principles in the day-to-day conduct of their responsibilities.

Extracted from "Our Vision" brochure

187. **Dime Savings Bank of New York, FSB**
589 Fifth Avenue; New York, NY 10017
(212) 326-6093

Industry: 60—Savings bank

The secret of our growth lies in the fact that we have not tried to please ourselves, but to please our customers. There is no chill formality here, but friendliness, courtesy and an obliging spirit.

DIME "Statement of Condition," July 1, 1923

OUR VISION

We aspire to be a truly great bank—the one stop choice of all our customers, an oasis of superb service, a neighborhood institution with a human touch. We want to be an organization where every job has worth, where every person has dignity . . . and where each of us, working together as a team, can make a difference. We intend to become very profitable, because only a profitable company can secure its future. We are committed to providing our shareholders with a consistently superior return.

OUR PHILOSOPHY

THE DIME's destiny is in our hands. We can begin to realize our vision for the future if we adhere to these fundamental principles:

1. **The customer comes first.** This means that:
   - the primary test of every decision is: will it attract and hold customers and broaden the use of our services?
   - all jobs exist to serve the customer or support those serving customers.
   - every officer needs to spend meaningful time with customers.

2. **Outstanding service is our competitive advantage.** Truly superior service requires:
   - courteous, responsive treatment of *every* person we deal with.
   - a commitment by each of us to become a master at our job—merely good isn't good enough.
   - an environment characterized by warm, friendly, caring people.

Management pledges to invest in the technology and training necessary to deliver superior service.

3. **Our dominant style and approach will be teamwork.** We believe that:
   - we are stronger working together.
   - the foundation for teamwork is trust and management must earn that trust.
   - there is no place in THE DIME for those who think first of themselves.
   - we are all in it together to serve our customers.
   - teamwork is necessary to compete effectively.

4. **Open, honest communication is a key to our success.** We believe that:
- people respond best when they understand.
- a free flow of information leads to better decisions.
- management must seek input, provide feedback and above all, be very good at listening.

5. **We are committed to and dependent upon our people.** THE DIME will:
- respect the dignity and worth of each individual.
- offer staff the training and development necessary for them to excel at their jobs.
- encourage each individual to advance as far as their talent and commitment will take them.
- provide fully competitive pay and benefits, tied to results.

6. **We want THE DIME to be a rewarding place to work,** where each individual:
- feels like a valued member of THE DIME team.
- has human ties throughout the organization.
- is able to realize their personal dreams.
- gets fulfillment and joy from their work and work relationships.

7. **THE DIME has to be a lean and efficient company.** This means that we will:
- minimize bureaucracy.
- encourage the development and cross utilization of personnel.
- have the fewest possible management levels.
- expect our people to be better than the competition.

8. **We will be forward thinking, not reactive, in managing the business.** This requires:
- a planning framework that fosters quicker decisions.
- solid contingency planning to enable us to respond to inevitable change.
- the patience and consistency to see our strategies through.

9. **THE DIME must become a fiercely competitive company.** This requires:
- an attention to detail and a commitment to results.
- constantly improving standards of performance.
- winning customer loyalty by being better than the best of their other choices.
- each staff member to be a salesperson.

10. **Finally, we will become a highly profitable bank.** Profits are essential to:

- make the investment we need to grow and to provide superior service.
- provide job stability and career potential.
- enable us to compete in a land of giants.

Fundamentally, of course, we owe our investors a superior return if we wish to merit their continued support.

Extracted from "Vision and Business Philosophy"

188. **Dofasco Inc.**
P.O. Box 2460; Hamilton, Ontario; Canada L8N 3J5
(416) 544-3761
Industry: 33—Steel

OUR MISSION. . . .

Dofasco is committed to being the leader in:
- providing our shareholders the best investment opportunity in our business
- providing our customers the best "total value" package of high quality flat rolled steel products
- enhancing our employees' career experience and personal development in an open and participative environment
- contributing in a positive way to community and environmental needs

DOFASCO

Our product is steel.
Our strength is people.

Drafted April, 1992

189. **Dollar General Corporation**
104 Woodmont Boulevard, Suite 500; Nashville, TN 37205
(615) 386-4000
Industry: 53—Discount stores

OUR MISSION

Neighborhood stores our customers count on for value in quality, basic merchandise.

GROUP MISSIONS

Human Resources—Human assets empowered for fullest development and productivity.

Merchandising—Increasing the value of our stores for our customers and shareholders.

Distribution—"Count On Us" for quality, efficient flow of merchandise from vendor to customer.

Store Operations—Friendly, well-merchandised neighborhood stores our customers count on for value every day.

Finance—Control which guides and inspires for maximum total return.

OUR PHILOSOPHY

WE BELIEVE that each person in our company should have:
- commitment to moral integrity,
- an enthusiastic sense of mission,
- mature self-assessment and a sense of humor,
- respect of everyone's potential creativity, and
- full commitment to the development of human potential sustained, of course, by self-development!

WE BELIEVE in the creativity of a team committed to participative management. Yet, the leader is responsible for decisive, timely action of the team.

WE BELIEVE in the dignity of the person and the work. Our productivity is, therefore, attained by emphasizing strengths, not by dwelling on weaknesses.

WE BELIEVE that any success is short-lived if it does not involve mutual gain.

190. **Dominion Bankshares Corporation**
P.O. Box 13327; Roanoke, VA 24040-0001
(703) 563-7000
Industry: 60—Banking

STRATEGIC OBJECTIVE

Dominion will strive to create maximum shareholder value through our commitments to strong asset quality, sound banking practices, continuous employee development, and being the preferred provider of financial products and services in the markets we serve. We will attain this position as the preferred provider by being market focused, customer driven, and committed to quality in everything we do.

Plan Organization

The Strategic Plan is organized into four sections that describe how we will achieve our Strategic Objective. These sections are:
1. **Market Strategies**: Describes our business philosophy, the nature of the customer relationships we want to build and the initiatives needed to enhance our market penetration and earnings production.

2. **Management Strategies**: Describes our management philosophy and the management initiatives needed to enhance long-term performance.
3. **Financial Strategies**: Describes the financial results that our Market and Management Strategies must achieve to generate improvement in shareholder value.
4. **Implementation**: Describes how the Dominion Bankshares Corporation Strategic Plan will be used to guide planning of each of our lines of business and support units.

The objective of this plan is to create a vision for the company of how we will restore asset quality and financial strength, and how we will build the strong franchise that will ensure future profitability. This vision will then be utilized by each of our line of business and support unit managers to plan for and manage their businesses.

Market Strategies

As outlined in our Strategic Objective, the primary themes driving our market strategies are providing high quality, value-added service to our customers and focusing on serving the needs of our customers in our markets. Our success will be measured by the number, depth, profitability and longevity of our customer relationships, and our customers' satisfaction with the quality of our products and service delivery.

Dominion will strive to develop comprehensive and long-standing relationships with our customers. We will seek to do business with customers who value our style of doing business and who are receptive to the deep, broad, and lasting relationships we strive to develop. We will continue to broaden our product and service offerings and generally improve our ability to profitably sell, develop, and service these types of relationships. It is these relationships that provide the cornerstone for our future success.

Management Strategies

As outlined in the Strategic Objective, the primary themes driving our Management Strategies are our commitments to service and asset quality, broad based relationships, sound banking practices and employee development. Our success will be measured by our ability to generate sustainable improvements in performance thus enhancing shareholder value. Initially, our Management Strategies will focus on enhancing asset quality, improving management information and controls, and enhancing near term performance. Over time, these Management Strategies will focus on creating the environment needed to ensure strong and stable long-term performance.

Financial Strategies

First and foremost, our financial imperative is to maximize the value of Dominion to our shareholders. This can only be achieved by establishing a sound financial foundation for sustainable improvements in operating performance.

Implementation

This Strategic Plan sets forth the business principles, market strategies, management strategies, and financial strategies that will guide the day-to-day management of our company. Our collective challenge is to:

1. Achieve the near-term objectives outlined in the plan while positioning Dominion to achieve the longer-term objectives; and
2. Apply this Strategic Plan to each of our lines of business and support units to maximize the effectiveness of the entire organization.

Extracted from "Strategic Plan—1993–1995"
Compiled July 28, 1992

191. **Dominion Resources, Inc.**
P.O. Box 26532; Richmond, VA 23261
(804) 775-5700
Industry: 49—Electric utility

Now and for the future we are committed to increasing shareholder value by:

- providing excellent service for our utility customers
- maintaining safe and superior generating unit operations
- meeting future electric power needs economically and efficiently
- protecting the environment and
- building on the successes of our nonutility companies.

Annual Report 1991

192. **Dominion Textile Inc.**
1950 Sherbrooke Street West; Montreal, Quebec; Canada H3H 1E7
(514) 989-6305
Industry: 22—Textile

The mission of Dominion Textile Inc. is to serve worldwide markets profitably with quality textiles and textile-related products. The fundamental goal of the Corporation is to attain and sustain leadership positions in selected market segments on an international basis, concentrating on total value to customers.

1990

193. **Domino's Pizza, Inc.**
30 Frank Lloyd Wright Drive; P.O. Box 997; Ann Arbor, MI
48106-0997

(313) 930-3030

Industry: 58—Pizza delivery

Domino's Pizza has led the industry by dedicating its attention, energy and resources to one mission: To safely deliver a hot, quality pizza to the customer's door in 30 minutes or less at a fair and a reasonable profit.

Extracted from "Domino's Pizza: Over 30 Years of Leadership"
[At press time this was being revised by Domino's.]

Donnelley, RR & Sons Company
see RR Donnelley & Sons Company (493)

194. Dover Corporation
280 Park Avenue; New York, NY 10017-1292

(212) 922-1640

Industry: 35—Elevators and industrial equipment

Dover's business goal is to be the leader in all the markets we serve. We earn that status by applying a simple philosophy to the management of our businesses. This requires us to:

Perceive the customer's real needs including products, support, and, especially in government business, complete compliance with all regulations.

Provide better products and services than the competition.

Invest to maintain our competitive edge.

Ask our customers to pay a fair price for the extra value we add.

Service to our customers, product quality, innovation and a long-term orientation are implicit in this credo. Pursuit of this market leadership philosophy by all our businesses, plus . . . value oriented acquisitions of companies that share this philosophy, plus . . . a decentralized management style that gives the greatest scope to the talented people who manage these companies . . . have combined to produce impressive financial results featuring:

- Long-term earnings growth.
- High cash flow.
- Superior returns on stockholders' equity.

Annual Report 1991

195. Downey Savings and Loan Association
3501 Jamboree Road; P.O. Box 6000; Newport Beach, CA 92658

(714) 854-3100

Industry: 60—Savings and loan

MISSION STATEMENT

Downey Savings seeks to maximize shareholder return. In order to effect this mission, Downey will provide its customers competitive and fairly priced products, primarily mortgage loans and deposits, delivered with superior service while serving the communities in which it conducts business and maintaining its current well-capitalized status. This requires the development and retention of competent, motivated staff capable of delivering superior customer service.

Draper Laboratory

see Charles Stark Draper Laboratory, Inc. (128)

196. Dresser Industries, Inc.

P.O. Box 718; 1600 Pacific Avenue; Dallas, TX 75221
(214) 740-6946
Industry: 35—Energy industry equipment

MISSION

Our mission is to be a profitable, growing multinational manufacturer and marketer of value-added products. We are dedicated to excellence and innovation, and to developing superior technology with market-focused products and services.

We will remain a strong, successful organization by:
- Achieving sustainable competitive leadership in our markets of choice.
- Earning an above-average return on investment for our shareholders and steadily increasing the value of their holdings in the Company.
- Developing and motivating our employees with a culture and operating environment that enables each individual to make positive contributions and to maintain a sense of pride in the Company.
- Acting as a responsible and ethical corporate citizen.

DRIVING FORCE

We will maintain our strong technological capabilities, adapting them to meet the changing market needs. We will serve markets from a position of strength with a dedication to our customers.

GOALS AND OBJECTIVES

Business: Our objective is to grow profitably by understanding and addressing market and customer needs. We believe our technological, manufacturing and marketing expertise can be used most effectively to meet those needs better than our competitors. We will maintain a competitive advantage to become the preferred supplier in those markets.

To sustain our growth and profitability, we will continually develop new opportunities, either internally or by acquisition or licensing while selectively divesting mature and declining products and services.

Financial: Our primary objective is to build long-term shareholder value. We will do this by earning a return on invested capital that exceeds the cost of the capital while operating under the corporate capital structure and resource guidelines. On a continuing basis, we also aim to achieve above-average financial performance (return on investment, earnings per share and revenue growth) for our industry, while maintaining a positive cash flow for the Company.

Human Resources: Our employees are our most important asset. We can maintain our successful organization only by employing excellent people motivated to do excellent work.

Recruiting, developing and motivating employees is an integral part of our managers' responsibilities, with the ultimate goal of improving productivity to sustain the Company's business and financial objectives.

CUSTOMERS AND SUPPLIERS

We offer customers innovative, quality products and services that fill their needs and provide lasting value. We stress to our customers reliability of supply, consistency of quality, superiority in service, and fairness and integrity in our dealings.

We listen to our customers, respond quickly to their current needs and anticipate their future needs. In return, we ask our customers to treat us with the same measure of fairness, integrity and responsibility that they have come to expect from us.

We are committed to quality. This commitment extends into every phase of our operations, both before and after the sale. Total commitment to quality entails doing a job right the first time, every time.

We consider our suppliers as "partners" in business and we expect the same quality and service commitment from them as we pledge to our customers.

We will be consistent in our sales and purchasing policies. We prefer and seek to build long-term relationships based on a commitment to deal fairly and reasonably with both our customers and suppliers.

COMPETITION

We have a reputation as a vigorous, ethical and fair competitor in the marketplace. We will continue to conduct ourselves in this manner to gain and maintain the respect of our competitors.

HUMAN RESOURCES

Our most critical resource is our employees. We believe that quality products are essential, but impossible without quality people who will keep us at the top of the markets we serve and provide a continuing resource for development of new products and capabilities.

We are committed to creating an environment that enables each employee to identify clearly with our purposes, to make an important contribution, and to maximize his or her career potential.

Recruiting, developing, motivating and rewarding employees are key parts of our managers' job and a part of managerial performance evaluations. We are committed to the concepts and practice of equal opportunity. We select, place, promote and reward employees with a broader perspective and knowledge of our operations and, at the same time, strive to help further enhance their skills.

We treat all individuals with respect, dignity, and integrity. Our employees are entitled to participate in setting their goals and judging their own performance with regular reviews. We encourage open communication throughout the organization. Creativity and reasonable risk-taking is fostered. We give priority to providing our employees stable, secure employment consistent with the long-term success and growth of the Company.

ORGANIZATION

We are an adaptive, market-driven organization that is flexible, innovative and entrepreneurial consisting of independent decentralized business divisions. These divisions have a substantial amount of freedom, within corporate and divisional policy guidelines, to develop and implement their own strategies and plans to achieve stated objectives. Operating decisions will be placed at the level in the organization where they can be most effectively implemented.

COMMUNICATION

We must communicate effectively and on a regular basis with our employees, customers, suppliers, shareholders and others. Effective communication requires commitment to the process at all levels of management. Through such communication, we can develop a better understanding of our organizational goals and how we operate and minimize any uncertainty and confusion.

We believe that effective communication is the essence of strong relationships with our employees and leads to greater motivation and understanding of our objectives and, ultimately, to better performance. All our managers are responsible for keeping our employees informed and listening to them. We will provide our employees the opportunity to ask "why" and offer them direct, accurate responses.

For our suppliers and customers, better communication fosters better understanding and will improve our long-term positions with these groups. The same is true for all other groups with which we interact.

CITIZENSHIP

We will continue to be a responsible corporate citizen worldwide, conducting business in a professional and ethical manner and abiding by existing governmental laws and regulations. We will remain socially conscious at all times. We will practice responsible stewardship of all materials and products we use, manufacture, market and dispose of and will uphold our responsibility to protect our employees, customers and the communities and environment in which we work and live.

Released November, 1992

197. **Dr Pepper/Seven-Up Companies, Inc.**
P.O. Box 655086; Dallas, TX 75265-5086
(214) 360-7000
Industry: 20—Beverages

MISSION STATEMENT:

Dr Pepper/Seven-Up Companies, Inc. will set standards for the soft drink industry for maintaining high-quality trademark brands and positive bottler/customer relations. The company will provide a profitable return to shareholders and sustain a professional focus on market share development of our products and growth opportunities for our employees.

STANDARDS OF PERFORMANCE:

The company will establish and measure its performance standards to enhance its
- **Bottler/customer relations**
- **Quality of trademarks**
- **Profitability**
- **Professionalism**
- **Employee relations**

STANDARDS WILL BE ACHIEVED FOR:

Bottler/customer relations by extending superior support services to create the industry's best possible bottler/customer orientation.

Quality of trademarks by continuous development of our trademark equities through innovative product positioning, advertising and promotion. The essence of our success also depends on our ability to promote and protect the highest standards in the manufacture of concentrate, syrups and extracts and vigilant quality assurance.

Profitability by maximizing shareholders' and employees' value through economies of scale, increased efficiencies and productivity.

Professionalism by demonstrating unceasing integrity in dealing with our many publics that include customers, consumers, investors and employees. Management will continue to increase its knowledge of our many products in order to compete successfully in a dynamic marketplace.

Employee relations by fair and honest treatment of our human resources. The company will provide challenging and rewarding work in an enjoyable, quality environment and offer training for development and growth opportunities.

198. **DUAL Incorporated**
      2101 Wilson Boulevard, Suite 600; Arlington, VA 22201
      (703) 527-3500
      Industry: 87—Engineering

CORPORATE MISSION STATEMENT

DUAL Incorporated is a technical services and manufacturing firm providing software engineering; systems integration; hardware/software simulator engineering; engineering, test, and logistics; management systems; and training support and custom products to the military, civilian government agencies, and commercial organizations. Corporate direction is established by our Board of Directors and Executive Team and governed by corporate-wide commitments to performance, employees, and business viability.

Commitment to Performance

Superior performance is essential to achieving success in the competitive marketplace. We meet—even exceed—customer expectations for quality services and products delivered on time and at reasonable cost. Through consistent performance, we build customer confidence, maintain credibility, and further the company's reputation for reliability and excellence.

Commitment to Employees

Employees are the mainstay of our business since their collective skills and experience are our major offering in the marketplace. To attract and retain highly qualified personnel, we compensate equitably for level of responsibility and reward promptly for outstanding contributions. We encourage teamwork while recognizing individual capabilities. We maintain a working environment that emphasizes job security, allows free expression of ideas and concerns, supports strong professional attitudes and behavior, and provides ample opportunities for growth and development. Through actions that are consistent, fair, ethical, and free of prejudice, we gain the best efforts and respect of our employees. Only through their ongoing commitments to participation, performance, and cooperation can we continue to improve the company's competitive position and maintain our integrity.

Commitment to Manage Our Business for Continued Viability

Keeping our business strong allows us to meet current obligations to customers and employees while we build for the future. We manage our existing resources wisely. We encourage innovation, continuously identify targets of opportunity, and work proactively to expand existing markets and to open new ones. We take time to review last year, visualize next year, and plan how to improve our overall performance every year. Through ensuring, to the best of our abilities, a reasonable return on all investments, we serve customers and support employees today while we capitalize the company's growth and development for tomorrow.

February, 1988

199. **Ducks Unlimited Inc.**
     One Waterfoul Way; Memphis, TN 38120-2351
     (901) 758-3825
     Industry: 86—Membership organization

MISSION STATEMENT

The mission of Ducks Unlimited is to fulfill the annual life cycle needs of North American waterfowl by protecting, enhancing, restoring and managing important wetlands and associated uplands. Since its founding in 1937, DU has raised over $700 million which has contributed to the conservation of nearly six million acres of prime wildlife habitat in all fifty states, each of the Canadian provinces and in key areas of Mexico. In the U.S. alone, DU has over 1,000 individual habitat enhancement projects completed or under way. Some 600 species of wildlife live and flourish on DU projects, including many threatened or endangered species.

First Copyrighted in 1991

200. **Duke Power Company**
     422 South Church Street; Charlotte, NC 28242-0001
     (704) 373-4011
     Industry: 49—Electric utility

Our Shared Vision

We will be the supplier of choice by our customers, the employer of choice by our co-workers and our communities, the investment of choice by our owners and the model of integrity and excellence for business and industry.

Our Mission

We produce and supply electricity, provide related products and services and pursue opportunities that complement our business. We will continually improve our products and services to better meet our customers' needs and expectations, helping our customers, employees, owners and communities to prosper.

Our Guiding Principles

We pursue excellence in all we do.

We strive continually to improve our products and services, our human and community relations, the safety of our operations and our financial performance.

Customers are our focus.

We anticipate, understand and meet our customers' changing needs and expectations.

Involved employees are our most important asset.

We give our best and work to create an environment that provides each of us the opportunity to reach our potential.

Financial success keeps us in business.

To prosper, both as employees and as a corporation, we maintain the financial strength of our company and provide a competitive return to our owners.

We are involved, responsible citizens.

We maintain our tradition of citizenship and service through actions that demonstrate our care for the people and environment around us.

Teamwork is our way of life.

We work in partnership with our co-workers, and with our customers, suppliers, owners and governments to achieve mutual goals. Trust and respect are the foundations of our team approach.

Integrity is never compromised.

Our actions and decisions reflect the highest ethical and professional standards.

Du Pont

see E.I. Du Pont De Nemours & Company Incorporated (210)

E

201. Earth Care Paper
P.O. Box 14140; Madison, WI 53714-0140
(608) 223-4022
Industry: 26—Paper

Our Vision

To improve the world by educating and empowering our customers through our products and services

Our Mission

- Produce and market paper and related products which: educate and empower consumers to improve society and the environment; reflect, from cradle to grave, responsible use of natural and human resources; and, through creative artistic presentation, express values of importance to our customers.

- Provide a workplace where we work together to realize our full potential, share in the success of our efforts, and achieve our mission in a fun, fulfilling, and productive manner.

- Create relationships with the local and world community and provide financial support which enhances society and the environment.

- Market our products through direct mail catalogs, retail stores, school fundraising programs, and other avenues to individuals, organizations, and businesses.

- Operate with excellence regarding service to our customers, internal operations, and quality of products.

- Use our financial success to further accomplish the mission of the company; measure our success by our positive impact on ourselves, society, and the environment.

September, 1991

202. East Coast Computer Systems, Inc.
One Sheila Drive; Tinton Falls, NJ 07724
(908) 747-6995
Industry: 35—Computer equipment

Mission Statement

To be a quality and profitable provider of unique mass storage enhancement products and Open Systems-based networked computing solutions.

203. **Eastern Enterprises**
   9 Riverside Road; Weston, MA 02193
   (617) 647-2300
   Industry: 44, 50—Barges and distribution

MISSION STATEMENT

Eastern Enterprises' primary objective is to maximize total return to its shareholders, by investing in companies which provide their customers with quality products and services, and managing those businesses in a manner that achieves, over time, sustainable earnings growth and an above average return on invested capital.

July 9, 1992

204. **Eastman Kodak Company**
   343 State Street; Rochester, NY 14650
   (716) 724-4000
   Industry: 28, 38—Chemicals and photographic equipment and supplies

KODAK VALUES

Building Blocks for Company Success

Quality

. . . to strive for continuous improvement in all we do through both personal contributions and teamwork to provide products and services that are world-class in value.

Integrity

. . . requiring honesty in relationships with each other and with customers, shareowners and suppliers—so that all know and trust the name Kodak.

Trust

. . . throughout the organization—characterized by fair treatment of and confidence in each other, treating everyone with respect and dignity.

Ethical Behavior

. . . consistent and invariable in all aspects of business and in all that we do, so that we can earn and always deserve a reputation that is beyond question.

Teamwork

... through open communication that gives everyone a sense of personal involvement in our company's performance.

Job Satisfaction

... fostered by an environment that promotes individual opportunity and self-fulfillment, encouraging people to grow to their full potential in skills and responsibilities.

Creativity

... by creating an atmosphere that challenges everyone in all parts of the business to seek new solutions and to take intelligent risks.

Flexibility

... recognizing the need—as a company and as individuals—to anticipate and respond to changing economic, social, competitive and market conditions.

Winning Attitude

... in knowing that through hard work, pride and confidence, Kodak people make up a world team of deep capability, carrying forward a reputation that is unique and invaluable.

Reprinted courtesy of Eastman Kodak Company
Copyright © Eastman Kodak Company

205. **Eaton Corporation**
     Eaton Center; Cleveland, OH 44114-2584
     (216) 523-4541
     Industry: 34, 37—Auto parts and related equipment

MISSION

Producing the highest quality products at costs which make them economically practical in the most competitively priced markets.

J. O. Eaton, 1911

VALUES

To be achieved by our global commitment to:
- Customer satisfaction
- Profitable growth
- Total quality leadership
- Continuous productivity improvement
- The Eaton philosophy of excellence through people
- Concern for our communities and environment, and
- The highest standard of integrity

ECCS, Inc.
see East Coast Computer Systems, Inc. (202)

206. **Ecolab Inc.**
Ecolab Center; 370 Wabasha Street, N; St. Paul, MN 55102
(612) 293-2233
Industry: 28—Specialty chemical products

"Quest for Excellence: Our Mission, Philosophy and Standards of Performance"

Our Mission. Our business is to be a leading innovator, developer and marketer of worldwide services, products and systems, which provide superior value to our customers in meeting their cleaning, sanitizing and maintenance needs, while conserving resources and preserving the quality of the environment and providing a fair profit for our shareholders.

Our Shareholders. We will be a growth company. We will provide our shareholders with a 15% annual growth in per share earnings while continually investing in product research and business development to assure a reliable future. Dividends will be consistent and recognize shareholders' needs for an adequate return and the company's need for growth capital. Our financial objectives also include a minimum 20% return on beginning of the year shareholders' equity and an "A" rated balance sheet.

We intend to remain an independent company. We believe that, to effectively maximize our shareholders' equity, positive customer service attitudes are critical to our success. This can best be provided in a flexible and entrepreneurial environment.

We encourage all employees to be long-term shareholders.

Recognizing that the quality of our shareholders' investment is built and measured over time, we will not sacrifice long-term growth in sales and earnings for short-term results.

Employees. We are dedicated to the belief that the most important resource is people who respond positively to recognition, involvement and opportunities for personal and career development. We are most productive and fulfilled in an environment where we empower and are empowered to act. We will address problems and mistakes constructively, learn from them and contribute to their solution. We encourage a team approach with mutually supportive relationships based on objectivity, integrity, openness and trust.

We will judge ourselves on our ability to be self-critical and to provide an atmosphere encouraging open and constructive communication. We will share the information needed to do our jobs and provide a sense of direction and purpose required to face up to problems and take appropriate actions and risks. We will communicate our goals clearly, assure that decisions are made by those people closest to the situation, and encourage and support them in those decisions.

Our workplace will be functional, clean and safe. Our working environment will foster mutual values, goals and goodwill. We will constantly strive for excellence, satisfaction and, occasionally, joy. Enthusiasm at all levels of our company is important to us.

People will be hired, paid and promoted based on qualifications, teamwork and performance. We believe that everyone benefits when the most capable person is promoted. People will be compensated fairly and rewarded well for their extra contributions to the company's success. We will not need a third party to protect our fair rights and interests.

People are encouraged to participate in setting their own goals and judging their own performance with regular supervisory reviews. We prefer promotion from within and support active programs of training and self-development that complement the corporation's philosophies and objectives.

We seek talented, action-oriented people who are enthusiastic, honest, open and hardworking, who want to do their jobs well and who expect their co-workers to do likewise. We want men and women who use the company's equipment and money as carefully as if it were their own, who suggest ways to be more productive and who help each other. We want and will encourage people to go the extra mile, work the added hour, make the additional call! Above all, we want associates who accept responsibility and accountability for their own growth, behavior and performance.

Our Customers. The company that fails its customers, fails! We will be superior to our competitors in providing the highest value to our customers at a fair price. We will constantly listen to our customers, respond quickly to their current needs and anticipate future needs.

We will stay close to our customers, tell them the truth and earn their business every day. Superior service built this company. Superior service will continue to be our central policy and philosophy. We will be vigorous, tough, ethical competitors.

We will supply our customers with superior services, specialty products and systems that are safe and reliable. We will advertise and promote our services and products in a professional and ethical manner and support them with well-trained people.

Our Organization. We seek an organization that is flexible, innovative, responsive and entrepreneurial. To accomplish this, we will create decentralized business units which have great freedom, within corporate strategy and policy limits, to develop their own business strategies and plans and to achieve agreed upon objectives. Actions will be judged on the extent to which they promote the overall good of the corporation over the separate interests of groups.

We will anticipate a changing environment. We are committed to the concept of continual improvement.

We seek to concentrate our efforts on providing services and products which have measurable benefits over state-of-the-art.

We will organize around the needs of our business units and provide only those central services which are essential to our growth, the protection of our corporate assets or provide significant advantages in terms of quality and cost.

We will observe uniform accounting practices and prompt disclosure of operating results, with no surprises.

We favor simplicity; we want action. We are results-oriented. We favor substance over form and quality over quantity. We believe in the free flow of candid, objective information, up, down and across organizational lines. We insist on "homework" and planning. We want overachievement.

Our Society. We recognize the importance of service to society and will contribute positively to the communities in which we operate. Our company's business will be conducted in accordance with the law and stated corporate and societal standards of conduct.

This statement is an expression of our mission and shared values, the achievement of which is an ongoing challenge and a never-ending process. It requires us to respond effectively to an ever-changing environment. It requires pragmatism and dreams, courage and confidence, trust and commitment—our mutual Quest for Excellence.

Copyright © 1987 Ecolab Inc.

Vision

- To be the acknowledged world leader in the cleaning and sanitizing markets
- Recognized for its excellence in quality, service, product development, environmental stewardship, and financial performance
- For its leading market shares and harmonious and caring organization
- To achieve a consistent shareholder return in excess of the S&P 500
- To be world class!

207. **Edison Electric Institute**
701 Pennsylvania Avenue, NW; Washington, DC 20004-2696
(202) 508-5000
Industry: 86—Trade association

Mission

The Edison Electric Institute is the association of the United States investor-owned electric utilities and industry affiliates worldwide. The Institute leads, represents, and serves the industry by:

ADVOCATING PUBLIC POLICIES that foster adequate, reliable, economical, and environmentally sound electricity supply and efficient electricity use.

AIDING MEMBER COMPANIES to generate and sell electric energy at a value commensurate with customer choice, energy efficiency, environmental quality, competitive forces, and the interests of customers, investors, and employees.

OFFERING QUALITY SERVICES tailored to meet member companies' changing needs in an increasingly competitive environment.

PROVIDING FACTUAL INFORMATION, data, and statistics relating to electric energy and its value to the well-being of individuals and the economic progress of society.

First written in 1980

Vision

Our Vision sets forth what we strive to achieve in the performance of our Mission. The Vision should be consistent with our values and should determine the content of our strategic and operating plans.

The Vision should impart a sense of dynamic and positive change and should provide the high level benchmarks by which the success of the organization can be measured relative to achieving the Vision.

EEI will be THE BEST trade association.

We will be **the best** because we are committed to knowing our members and their needs; we will provide leadership and deliver services which consistently meet or exceed their expectations.

We will be **the best** because we will attract and retain employees who have the ambition to serve and will empower them to work effectively as individuals and in teams.

Above all, we will be **the best** trade association because, in the tradition of Thomas Edison, we will make a significant and positive contribution to the long-term success of the electric utility industry in its vital mission to provide electricity to foster economic progress and improve the quality of life.

Core Values

Core Values are those intrinsic guiding standards and principles that collectively define and determine the character of our organization.

These values are, in short, what we always stand for and what we will never compromise in the performance of our Mission and in the pursuit of our Vision.

INTEGRITY—Our actions and decisions reflect the highest set of ethical standards and professionalism.

SERVICE ETHIC—We have an ambition to serve and believe that providing excellent service is the noblest endeavor.

STRONG SENSE OF PUBLIC SERVICE—We maintain a strong tradition of corporate citizenship through actions that demonstrate care for our community.

EMPATHY—We work with and involve all customer groups (members, the public, employees) in a caring, courteous, and individualized manner.

CONTINUOUS IMPROVEMENT—We believe that our ability to provide excellent service depends on becoming better today than we were yesterday.

STEWARDSHIP—We will never compromise our responsibilities in the management and use of resources.

DIGNITY—We encourage innovativeness, creativity, and energy of employees, allowing greater individual influence and control over our work.

Operating Principles

Operating Principles are action-oriented and essential rules of conduct and behavior that are derived from our Core Values. Taken together, they define our attitude and orientation. They, in short, describe the parameters of our everyday activities and how we will work to achieve our Mission.

CUSTOMERS—EEI employees will recognize that EEI's primary "customers" are the EEI member company employees who participate in EEI activities. In a larger sense, the customers of EEI member companies and the general public are also EEI's customers. And, in the context of EEI's internal operations, EEI employees are also customers.

CUSTOMER FOCUSED—Every EEI employee will work to meet customers' needs through understanding their expectations, creating cost-effective services consistent with those needs, delivering a quality service in a positive and professional manner and, in every sense, exceeding the customer's expectations every time a service is provided.

RESULTS FOCUSED—EEI employees set priorities, seek results and will devise, manage, and use creative and economical ways to define and measure our success in achieving those results, both short and long-term.

VALUE ORIENTED—EEI employees will provide service of high value in every instance—that is, employees will understand that the value of the service will be correlated with the cost and demand for that service and that all employees are responsible for choosing, providing, and communicating value.

QUALITY SERVICE—EEI employees are motivated to provide service that is prompt, responsive, accurate, and credible.

EMPOWERED EMPLOYEES—EEI employees will take individual initiatives and informed risks and accept accountability in meeting the needs of customers and fellow employees.

TEAMWORK—EEI employees endorse fully the concept of teamwork as achieved through effective communication, mutual respect, trust, creation of a sense of camaraderie and cooperation on tasks to meet the customers' needs.

SATISFIED EMPLOYEES—EEI employees will work together to create a work environment that makes EEI a good place to work and fosters personal growth.

Written 1990
Reproduced courtesy of Edison Electric Institute

208. **Edna McConnell Clark Foundation**
       250 Park Avenue; New York, NY 10177-0026
       (212) 986-7050
       Industry: 67—Charitable foundation

Purpose

The Edna McConnell Clark Foundation works to improve conditions for people who are poorly served by the established institutions of society.

Through its grants, the Foundation assists nonprofit organizations and public agencies committed to practices and policies that might materially improve people's lives. We seek projects that show promise for changing the ways institutions respond to the needs of the disadvantaged. We especially look for projects that have not received adequate support, where our contribution will make a difference.

1992

209. **Educational Broadcasting Corporation**
       Thirteen/WNET
       356 West 58th Street; New York, NY 10019
       (212) 560-2000
       Industry: 48—Broadcasting

Thirteen/WNET has forged strong partnerships with the many individuals and institutions that share its commitment to making a unique contribution to people's lives. This support enables Thirteen to fulfill its mission to:

Be a leading provider of educational, informational and cultural products and services, using all media, which:
Reflect and respect a diverse and complex world
Serve the underserved—new Americans, high school dropouts, illiterate populations, and urban youth
Foster lifelong learning opportunities
Offer cultural enrichment
Facilitate responsible citizenship
Adhere to the highest standards of artistic and editorial integrity
Create opportunities for experimentation
Thirteen/WNET is the partnership that makes a difference.

Annual Report 1990–1991

Edwards, A.G.
see A.G. Edwards & Sons, Inc. (4)

210. **E.I. Du Pont De Nemours & Company Incorporated**
1007 Market Street; Wilmington, DE 19898
(302) 774 1000
Industry: 13, 28, 29—Chemicals and petroleum

Our Mission . . .

Du Pont is a diversified chemical, energy and specialty products company with a strong tradition of discovery. Our global businesses are constantly evolving and continually searching for new and better ways to use our human, technological and financial resources to improve the quality of life of people around the world.

The mission that drives us in ongoing and challenging . . . to increase the value of the company to customers, employees and shareholders by profitably providing beneficial products and services to worldwide markets.

In doing so, each of our businesses must deliver financial results superior to those of its leading competitors . . . for we consider ourselves successful only if we return to our shareholders a long-term financial reward comparable to the better performing, large industrial companies.

While much of our growth occurs through discovery and development of new products, energy resources and services, our success depends ultimately upon our total commitment to serving the needs of the marketplace. This requires that we work in full partnership with our customers . . . not only in understanding and meeting customer needs, but in anticipating their problems as well.

Above all, we recognize that the degree of our success is in direct proportion to the quality and dedication of our people.

To be more successful than our competitors, we must never be satisfied with the status quo . . . we must be calculated risk takers with a compulsive curiosity . . . the curiosity to seek the most innovative answers to the most complex problems . . . bringing better things for better living to the marketplace.

Our Principles . . .

A significant factor contributing to our success is adherence to a distinctive set of guiding principles and commonly shared values.

CUSTOMER ORIENTATION

We must focus our energies on customers and markets, constantly striving for excellence in understanding, anticipating and serving their needs faster and better than our competitors.

COMPETITIVE POSITION

We must serve those markets in which we can be the best . . . markets where our human, technological and financial strengths give us opportunities to establish and maintain leadership positions and achieve profitable growth. Further, we must be aggressive in both acquiring and divesting businesses to enhance those positions.

MANAGEMENT STYLE

We must manage our diverse businesses with organizational structures, systems and policies that enable them to excel in the markets they serve. In so doing, calculated risk taking must be encouraged to maximize returns, and barriers that inhibit achievement of full business and individual potential eliminated.

INDIVIDUAL OPPORTUNITY

We must treat each other fairly, with respect for individual dignity, while developing our talents and skills to their full potential to increase our contributions to the success of the businesses we serve. Our recognition, rewards and advancement must be based on the value of those contributions as we strive for continuous improvement in the quality of everything we do.

ETHICAL BEHAVIOR

We must conduct our business affairs with the highest ethical standards and work diligently to be a respected corporate citizen worldwide.

SAFETY

We must adhere to the highest standards for the safe operation of facilities and the protection of the environment, our people and customers, and the citizens of the communities in which we do business.

211. **Electric Power Research Institute**
3412 Hillview Avenue; P.O. Box 10412; Palo Alto, CA 94303
(415) 855-2000
Industry: 87—Research and development

OUR MISSION

To discover, develop, and deliver advances in science and technology for the benefit of member utilities, their customers, and society.

TECHNICAL DIRECTIONS

MEETING INDUSTRY OBJECTIVES

Align strategic R&D objectives with utility issues . . . allocate primary resources to pursuit of objectives . . . evaluate technical progress against objectives.

INDUSTRY ISSUES/STRATEGIES

Electricity Value
- Enhance the value of electricity in creating products, processes, and services to benefit utility customers and society.

Environmental Health and Safety
- Investigate emerging health and environment issues; develop products and strategic options to help reduce risks in the most cost-effective yet socially responsible manner.

Sustainable Energy Future
- Expand future energy system options.
- Develop cost-competitive supply, delivery, and demand-side technologies and strategies that mitigate resource, safety, and environmental risks.

Cost Control
- Improve efficiency, reliability, and productivity of utility resources.

OPERATIONAL DIRECTIONS

DEVELOPING QUALITY STAFF, EFFECTIVE ORGANIZATION

Align staff and resources with objectives and results . . . recognize and reward achievement of valued results . . . develop and streamline operations to maximize cost efficiencies.

OPERATIONAL GOALS, OBJECTIVES

High-Caliber Staff
- Attract, hire, and challenge staff of highest caliber.
- Provide professional and personal growth opportunities for employees.

Organizational Effectiveness
- Design the organization, planning processes, resource allocations, and business practices to maximize flexibility and efficiency.
- Emphasize a total quality approach in all products and services, from discovery and development through commercial market entry.
- Maintain timely and open internal communications.

Individual Leadership
- Develop leaders who create a climate for inspired, cooperative performance.
- Measure performance based on results.
- Tie rewards to performance: innovation, prudent risk-taking, effective team performance, and successful commercialization.

Motivational Culture
- Create a flexible, productive, business-like organization.
- Establish and maintain an interactive, motivating work environment that fosters openness, trust, decisiveness—one that seeks and values individual diversity.

Extracted from "New Directions" brochure
Published 1991
Copyright © 1991 Electric Power Research Institute

212. **Electrohome Limited**
809 Wellington Street North; Kitchener, Ontario; Canada N2G 4J6
(519) 744-7111
Industry: 36, 48—Electronics and broadcasting

Our Mission:

To provide creative and competitive product and service solutions to meet customer needs in selected world Electronics and Broadcast markets.

Our Commitments:

To provide quality services or products that conform to specific consumer needs. This is accomplished by establishing state-of-the-art capabilities and by prudent investment in R & D, capital equipment and facilities.

To operate profitably on a business segment basis with a blend of mature and growing sectors that address well defined markets.

To remain a Canadian controlled public company.

To provide an adequate return to shareholders, plus benefits to our employees and the communities in which we are located, through the mutual efforts of the Company and its most important asset: our people.

Annual Report 1991

213. **Empire Company Limited**
115 King Street; Stellarton, Nova Scotia; Canada B0K 1S0
(902) 755-4440
Industry: 54—Grocery stores

MANAGEMENT PHILOSOPHY AND BUSINESS PRINCIPLES

BUSINESS DEFINITION

Empire Company is a diversified investment management company whose foundation is the Sobeys food retail and distribution business. Controlled by the Sobey family, Empire's business is to support our wholly-owned subsidiaries and manage a diversified portfolio of investments.

BUSINESS GOAL

Empire's goal is to prudently build shareholder value over the long term through asset appreciation and meaningful cash flow generation. We will do this by: keeping our core operating businesses strong; leveraging and allocating our resources effectively; and investing in businesses with superior management and excellent fundamentals. Toward this end we will be influenced by the following:

BELIEFS AND GUIDING PRINCIPLES

We believe that the value and success of our core operating businesses and our investments is directly related to the quality of our senior managers. In every case, we will seek out and support leadership with a demonstrated track record of creating value, and with personal and business values that we feel are compatible with our own.

We will be conservative in our approach to financing and risk, investing thoughtfully, limiting our exposure in any single investment, and ensuring a prudent debt structure. Our preferred approach to taking on financial leverage is at the subsidiary level, always limiting the amount of structured debt at the corporate level.

Our preference is to invest in businesses we understand, and where we can add value. When assessing opportunities in industries where we have considerable expertise, we will leverage that knowledge and experience to effectively evaluate and access the opportunity When assessing opportunities which appear interesting in industries where we lack experience, we will gather the best available outside expertise. In every case, we will always invest cautiously, building our confidence in the future potential of the enterprise before committing significant amounts of capital.

We believe there is a real and necessary benefit to having Board representation in our significant investments and friendly, constructive open relationships with all our management partners. As such, we will only make investments in situations where these conditions exist.

As a general rule, we do not involve ourselves in the day-to-day operations of our investments, but rather seek and support superior management. Through our active involvement at the Board level, we will influence the companies' values, leadership choices, financial structure, and strategic direction.

Our interest always has been, and continues to be, in investing for the long term. This provides us with the best climate in which to work with our partners and managers as the companies go through their natural cycles. If we become uncomfortable with the fundamentals, we may, after consultation with our partners, choose to sell our position.

We believe that insightful information about each company's direction, competitive environment, and performance is critical to our ability to support our investments. As such, we will ensure that each company with which we have a significant involvement sets a deliberate strategy, tracks critical information, and shares these with us.

A key responsibility of Empire leadership is to balance management's desire to build the asset base over the longer term with shareholders' desire for dividends. As such, significant attention will be paid to ensuring that the cash generated by the business is effectively and satisfactorily shared between keeping the operating entities strong and growing and satisfying the shareholders.

Annual Report 1992

214. **Engelhard Corporation**
101 Wood Avenue; Iselin, NJ 08830-0770
(908) 205-5000
Industry: 28, 33—Chemicals and metals

ENGELHARD CORPORATION . . .

OUR COMMITMENT

We uphold five basic commitments that arise from a shared view of what the Company is and what its responsibilities must be. These commitments guide our daily conduct as representatives of Engelhard Corporation, and they guide the Company's course in an ever more competitive and global marketplace. They recognize our responsibility to provide a safe workplace for our employees, to offer safe products to our customers and to protect the environment. Our strength as a company flows directly from our determination and our ability to fulfill these commitments in all our operations around the world.

Commitment to Customers To anticipate the dynamics of our customers' markets and to respond to our customers' changing needs with superior quality products, processes and services, faster and more effectively than our competitors.

Commitment to Product Excellence To ensure that the Engelhard name is the guarantor of quality and product excellence on a global basis through continuous scientific and market research and new product development that provides innovative solutions to customer needs and market opportunities.

Commitment to Employees To recognize Engelhard employees as the key to our success and to promote teamwork in our daily operations so that all employees can attain their full potential in a challenging environment that benefits the Company worldwide.

Commitment to Shareholders To manage and direct the Company and its businesses in order to maintain satisfactory growth in revenues and profitability and to provide shareholders with the highest possible long-term returns on investment compatible with such business growth.

Commitment to the Community To act responsibly and work to be a positive economic and social force in all the communities in which we operate throughout the world.

Copyright © 1991 Engelhard Corporation

EPRI
see Electric Power Research Institute (211)

215. **Equifax Inc.**
1600 Peachtree Street, NW; Atlanta, GA 30309
(404) 885-8000
Industry: 73—Credit reporting services

Equifax is in the business of helping business and consumers do business together.

216. **Ethix Corporation**
12655 SW Center Street; Beaverton, OR 97005-1600
(503) 641-1111
Industry: 64—Health insurance services

To enhance the value of healthcare services, and the interrelationships of providers, buyers and users. Important underlying principles include:
- Professionalism
- Service
- Client satisfaction
- Innovation
- Value of our fees
- Rewards to our employees
- Profitability

217. **Ethyl Corporation**
330 South Fourth Street; P.O. Box 2189; Richmond, VA 23217
(804) 788-5000
Industry: 13, 28—Petroleum and chemicals

OUR VISION

To Be At The Top of Customers' Lists of Suppliers

In the markets we serve, Ethyl's family of companies will be at the top of existing and potential customers' lists of companies from which they will choose to do business.

To achieve this vision, we will operate according to the following values:

Respect for People

Achieving our vision depends entirely on the ability of Ethyl's people to contribute individually and collectively, to develop new skills, to work in the environment that fosters pride and to share in the contributions they make toward the success of the company. This success requires a culture that makes it possible for Ethyl people to achieve full potential. Such a culture is based on mutual trust and respect.

Unquestionable Integrity

Personal and corporate integrity are the foundations for all our activities. Integrity is a cherished possession we want never to lose.

Continually Improving Quality

Quality means satisfying customers' needs now and in the future. To do this, we must continually improve the quality of everything we make or do.

Our Partners—Customers and Suppliers

To be at the top of customers' lists, we must become their partners. This means we must share their business goals, champion their interests and link our resources to theirs in anticipation of their future needs. We need and will encourage the partnership of our suppliers in support of our customers' needs and goals as well.

Safety and Environmental Responsibility

It is Ethyl's goal to provide workplaces for employees that are safe, healthy and environmentally sound. Likewise, our presence in communities will not adversely affect the safety, health or environment of our neighbors. Finally, we will participate in ongoing activities, like Responsible Care®, that improve the health, safety and environment of the world.

Good Citizenship

We intend to be good citizens wherever we have a presence throughout the world. Good citizens do more than simply comply with laws; they support causes that help to improve the community. We will support such causes as a corporation and encourage Ethyl people to take active roles in answering community needs.

Economic Viability

To realize this vision, Ethyl must be an economically viable and profitable organization. As we operate according to our vision and values, Ethyl will enjoy long-term growth with continually improving performance.

218. **Evangelical Health Systems**
2025 Windsor Drive; Oak Brook, IL 60521
(708) 572-9393
Industry: 80—Hospitals

PHILOSOPHY

Evangelical Health Systems is a multifaceted health care organization. It is committed to develop the resources and structure to provide quality, cost-effective health care to meet the needs of individuals, families and our society.

This commitment grows from a Christian belief that a faithful response to the ministry of Jesus Christ requires us to minister to the whole person, to promote the wellness of body, mind and spirit. Through our actions, we affirm the worth and dignity of each human being.

From this philosophy come seven basic tenets that govern our mission and goals.

- We believe each person is created in the image of God, and that we have an obligation to serve people without regard to race, religion, sex, age or disability.

- We will seek to assure the spiritual freedom of all people and not impose our beliefs upon them.

- Our faith inspires us to rise above self-interest to minister to individuals as well as address the health care problems of society.

- We have an obligation to recognize medical-ethical issues from a faith perspective and assist individuals and professionals in their resolution of them.

- Our concern for whole persons and their families extends beyond our patients and includes our employees, physicians and volunteers.

- In ministering to individuals and society, we have a commitment to effectively organize and direct our resources to provide quality, cost-effective health care delivery systems.

-    We support the voluntary, not-for-profit concept in hospital care as an expression of our dedication to the communities we serve. In addition, we fully recognize that we must maintain an economically viable organization if we are to successfully carry out the tenets of our philosophy and mission.

MISSION

The mission of Evangelical Health Systems is to provide for the effectiveness and efficient delivery of quality health care and health-related services in areas of identifiable need, for the benefit of individuals, families and society. In keeping with its heritage and philosophy, Evangelical Health Systems is committed to maintain a Christian emphasis in all its endeavors.

1983
Copyright © Evangelical Health Systems

219.   **E.W. Scripps Company**
       P.O. Box 5380; 1100 Central Trust Tower; Cincinnati, OH 45201
       (513) 977-3825
       Industry: 27, 48—Publishing and broadcasting

The company aims at excellence in the products and services it produces and responsible service to the communities in which it operates. Its purpose is to engage in successful, growing enterprises in the fields of information and entertainment. The company intends to expand, to develop and acquire new products and services and to pursue new market opportunities. Its focus shall be long-term growth for the benefit of its stockholders and employees.

Annual Report 1991

F

220. F&C International, Inc.
11260 Chester Road; Cincinnati, OH 45246
(513) 782-5019
Industry: 20—Flavors and fragrances

Mission Statement

It is the purpose of F&C International to create and manufacture the best proprietary flavors, fragrances and natural chemicals possible to assure customer satisfaction, employee pride and shareholder value.

Annual Report 1992

221. Farm & Home Savings Association
10100 North Executive Hills Boulevard; Suite 400; Kansas City, MO 64153-1396
(816) 891-7778
Industry: 60—Savings and loan

Mission Statement

To increase shareholder revenue by creating a dependable, consistent and growing stream of earnings. Our strategy to achieve this goal is to fulfill the vision of the Association as being a segment driven, community bank with an expanding regionally oriented mortgage bank.

Farmers Union Central Exchange, Inc.
see CENEX (123)

222. Father Flanagan's Boys' Home
14100 Crawford; Boys Town, NE 68010
(402) 498-1300
Industry: 83—Social service

Father Flanagan's Boys' Home is a non-profit, non-sectarian, charitable, educational and medical corporation organized and existing under the laws of the State of Nebraska.

Its purpose is to provide food, clothing, shelter, medical care and treatment, education and spiritual development to homeless, abused, neglected and handicapped boys and girls.

To this end, and in accordance with its Articles of Incorporation, as amended, Father Flanagan's Boys' Home maintains residential care facilities and schools for youth to prepare them to lead useful lives; maintains a national hospital which provides health evaluation and treatment for youth who have, or are suspected of having, communication disorders and related disabilities and undertakes applied research; develops relevant programs of education, research, information, evaluation and training for youth insofar as these promote and carry out the Home's central objectives and purposes; in addition, as permitted under Nebraska law, does all things necessary and convenient to effect any and all of the purposes for which the corporation was organized.

Revised 1985

223. Federal Express Corp.
2005 Corporate Avenue; Memphis, TN 38132-1702
(901) 369-3600
Industry: 47—Package delivery

MISSION STATEMENT

Federal Express is committed to our People-Service-Profit philosophy. We will produce outstanding financial returns by providing totally reliable, competitively superior global air-ground transportation of high priority goods and documents that require rapid, time certain delivery. Equally important, positive control of each package will be maintained utilizing real time electronic tracking and tracing systems. A complete record of each shipment and delivery will be presented with our request for payment. We will be helpful, courteous and professional to each other and the public. We will strive to have a satisfied customer at the end of each transaction.

224. Federal-Mogul Corporation
P.O. Box 1966; Detroit, MI 48235
(313) 354-7700
Industry: 35, 37—Industrial machinery and equipment

Mission Statement

Federal-Mogul's primary strategic focus is the manufacturing and distribution of products into the global vehicular and industrial aftermarket. The company is committed to providing these markets with world class quality products and adding value through the interdependence of our manufacturing and distribution operations.

We will also continue our history of support to the original equipment market. In fact, we will strive to be a leader in all OEM products in which the company participates.

Through this integrated approach, we will create sufficient value to be rewarded by our customers. This unique value created will result in profits for our investors, and help meet our commitment of providing job satisfaction and a pleasant work environment for all our employees.

Our product development, manufacturing and distribution systems will be designed for flexibility, high quality and fast customer response. This will create Federal-Mogul's time-based competitive advantage of supplying low volume/high variety products.

Corporate Strategy

The elimination of time in dealing with the development, manufacturing, distribution and administrative needs of our customers is our major priority.

Guiding Principles

1. Quality

Complete customer satisfaction in products and service is crucial to our continued survival in a global environment.

2. Customer Response

Our customers are our reason for being. All our efforts must be directed towards providing them with the best products and services.

3. Continuous Improvement

We must never be satisfied with our performance. We must strive to provide the very best in products, services and value.

4. Respect for all Individuals

Employee involvement means trust and respect for each other as members of a team.

5. Ethical Conduct

Our integrity in the marketplace and with each other must never be compromised. Our conduct must be socially responsible. We are committed to equal opportunities for all individuals.

225. **Federated Department Stores, Inc.**
7 West Seventh Street; Cincinnati, OH 45202
(513) 579-7000
Industry: 53—Department stores

Management Philosophy

Federated clearly recognizes that the customer is paramount, and that all actions and strategies must be directed toward providing an enhanced merchandise offering and better service to targeted consumers through dynamic department stores.

Careful and thorough planning, as well as aggressive implementation of strategies, will provide Federated's department stores a competitive edge.

Federated is committed to open and honest communications with employees, shareholders, vendors, analysts and the news media. The company will be pro-active in sharing information, and in keeping these audiences up-to-date on important developments.

Management Objectives

The corporate management objectives of Federated Department Stores, Inc. are:

- To return the company to performance levels that are consistent with the results produced by the nation's top department store retailers;
- To produce improved results through a more coordinated, centralized and common approach to running the business, and through disciplined, consistent and undiverted attention to execution in all aspects of the company's department store operations.

Issued July 1992

226. Fiesta Mart Inc.

P.O. Box 7481; 5235 Katy Freeway; Houston, TX 77248-7481
(713) 869-5060
Industry: 54—Supermarkets

Fiesta Mission Statement

Our customer provides for our success. It is our responsibility to work together to provide customer satisfaction through service, selection, value in the most effective way possible.

In order to continue the traditions that have made Fiesta 'a great place to shop,' to provide jobs and a better future for all our employee/owners and management, we support the following goals:

1. Become the **Number 1** Hispanic/Ethnic supermarket in whichever market we choose to operate.
2. Treat each other fairly.
3. Open lines of communication.
4. Be honest in dealing with customers, employee/owners and vendors.
5. Be team players.

Drafted January, 1991

227. **Firstar Corporation**
777 East Wisconsin Avenue; Milwaukee, WI 53202
(414) 765-5235
Industry: 60—Banking

CORPORATE PURPOSE STATEMENT

A statement of corporate purpose is important to ensure that all of us affiliated with Firstar Corporation thoroughly understand our goals, enabling us to orient our daily tasks toward their achievement. It is essential that our corporate purpose be compatible with the aims of society, for no society will long tolerate any institution that does not serve the wants and needs of a majority of its members.

Firstar Corporation, as a publicly owned provider of financial services, recognizes that the following groups have a vital interest in our organization and each have specific needs and desires as they relate to it.

A. Customers and prospects desire:
  1. Safety and confidentiality
  2. Quality products
  3. Equitable and competitive prices
  4. Considerate, prompt, efficient, and convenient service
  5. Continuity of customer contact personnel
B. Employees desire:
  1. Challenge and opportunity
  2. Recognition and participation
  3. Fair compensation
  4. Individual dignity
  5. Job security
C. The community as a whole desires:
  1. Concern and support for its economic, social, cultural and environmental well-being
  2. Ethical conduct
D. Stockholders desire:
  1. Maximum return on their investments
  2. Adequate information to facilitate investment decisions
  3. Marketability

We accept the wants of these groups as our own, and the satisfaction of meeting these wants constitutes our Corporate Purpose.

We realize that the only way we can achieve this purpose is through a financially strong, consistently profitable, and growing institution. Hence, as we prioritize our activities, soundness is first, then profitability, and, finally growth. We will not sacrifice financial soundness for the sake of profits; nor will we sacrifice consistent profitability for growth.

For the Corporation to accomplish its Corporate Purpose, this statement must be understood, accepted, and supported by all of us. We sincerely solicit that support from every employee.

February, 1992

228. FirsTier Financial, Inc.
1700 Farnam Street; P.O. Box 3443; Omaha, NE 68103-0443
(402) 348-6000
Industry: 60—Banking

Mission

The mission of FirsTier Financial, Inc., is to provide high quality financial services to our customers while maximizing shareholder value. We intend to remain an independent financial services corporation and to strengthen the company's market position as a premier provider of high quality, profitable financial services to corporate, retail, and trust customers, primarily in Nebraska and contiguous states. We will be responsive to the needs of our customers, communities and employees. FirsTier will operate as one banking company delivering uniform products and services, with a commitment to quality, customer service and sales.

Annual Report 1991

229. First Tennessee Bank National Association
P.O. Box 84; Memphis, TN 38101
(901) 523-4444
Industry: 60—Banking

Mission Statement

Be **the** best at serving our customers, one opportunity at a time.

230. First Union Corporation
First Union Plaza; Charlotte, NC 28288
(704) 374-6444
Industry: 60—Banking

STATEMENT OF VALUES

WITH RESPECT TO CUSTOMERS:

- Provide absolute customer satisfaction.
- Always exceed customers' expectations.
- Over time, enhance our customers' financial well being.

WITH RESPECT TO SHAREHOLDERS:

- Outperform our peers in building long-term shareholder value.
- Be a sound well-managed, innovative corporation.

WITH RESPECT TO COMMUNITY:
- Conduct our business with a dedication to the highest ethical standards.
- Provide financial support that stimulates development throughout all our communities and improves the quality of life.
- Encourage employee participation in community improvement activities.

WITH RESPECT TO EMPLOYEES:
- Be candid, open and honest in all of our interactions.
- Ensure that all employees understand and embrace the corporate vision as well as the strategies and individual roles that support it.
- Foster and reward teamwork at all levels throughout our company.
- Create a participative environment for setting goals, seeking input, meeting personal objectives, and encouraging individual responsibility.
- Be an enjoyable place to work.
- Satisfy the individual needs of employees for recognition, rewards, self esteem and personal growth.
- Have the best, most efficient, and highest motivated employees compensated at the upper range of our peer group.
- Promote programs and policies that encourage employees to balance their work and family life and assist them in being effective in both roles.

Copyright © 1990 First Union Corporation

231. **Fiserv Inc.**
P.O. Box 979; Brookfield, WI 53008-0979
(414) 879-5000
Industry: 73—Data processing

This Is The FIserv Vision.

Together, as FIserv, we will be known worldwide for our advanced service quality and held in the highest esteem by our clients, employees, service partners, industry and communities.

This Is The FIserv Mission.

To be the leading provider of data processing and information management products and services to the financial industry.

To deliver products and services that help our clients grow their business and enhance service to their customers.

To enable our people to achieve outstanding job performance and personal growth.

To produce a favorable level of earnings and consistent earnings growth for our company.

232. **Fishery Products International Limited**
      70 O'Leary Avenue; P.O. Box 550; St. John's, Newfoundland;
          Canada A1C 5L1
      (709) 570-0000
      Industry: 09—Fisheries

CORPORATE PHILOSOPHY OF EXCELLENCE

Corporate Values

FPI is committed to the values of quality, honesty, innovation and teamwork.

Customer Quality

FPI is committed to providing the highest value to all of its customers by responding as an innovative team to their needs for quality and service.

Employee Quality

FPI is committed to achieving a spirit of employee teamwork which will result in a highly motivated, healthy, skilled and safe workforce with a sense of well-being.

Shareholder Quality

FPI is committed to earning a quality return for its shareholders as the undeniable result of its commitment to total quality for its customers and employees.

Our Goal—To be the best at everything we do and in so doing to be recognized as a quality partner by our employees, customers and shareholders.

                                                    Annual Report 1991

233. **Fluor Daniel**
      Subsidiary of Fluor Corp.
      3333 Michelson Drive; Irvine, CA 92730
      (714) 975-2000
      Industry: 15, 16—Construction

MISSION

As Fluor Daniel employees, our mission is to assist clients in attaining a competitive advantage by delivering quality services of unmatched value.

PRINCIPLES

To add value to our services, these principles are emphasized:
- We are client focused.

- We are innovative and flexible in meeting client needs.
- We deliver quality.
- And above all, we do every task safely.

PHILOSOPHY

Our philosophy is based upon ethical conduct, mutual trust and teamwork. To ensure continuous improvement, we challenge, test, reevaluate and continually raise our standards of excellence.

As a service organization, our success depends upon the combined capability and contribution of all employees.

Fluor Daniel is dedicated to fostering a work environment which challenges, enriches and rewards each individual.

Extracted from company brochure

234. **Food Lion Inc.**
P.O. Box 1330; Salisbury, NC 28145-1330
(704) 633-8250
Industry: 54—Supermarkets

FOOD LION MISSION

The Food Lion **team** will **work hard** using our **talents** and **resourcefulness** to provide all customers with **friendly service, high quality products**, and **Extra Low Prices**.

235. **Ford Motor Company**
The American Road; P.O. Box 1899; Dearborn, MI 48121
(313) 322-3000
Industry: 37—Automobiles and trucks

MISSION

Ford Motor Company is a worldwide leader in automotive and automotive-related products and services as well as in newer industries such as aerospace, communications, and financial services. Our mission is to improve continually our products and services to meet our customers' needs, allowing us to prosper as a business and to provide a reasonable return for our stockholders, the owners of our business.

VALUES

How we accomplish our mission is as important as the mission itself. Fundamental to success for the Company are these basic values:

- **People**—Our people are the source of our strength. They provide our corporate intelligence and determine our reputation and vitality. Involvement and teamwork are our core human values.

- **Products**—Our products are the end result of our efforts, and they should be the best in serving customers worldwide. As our products are viewed, so are we viewed.
- **Profits**—Profits are the ultimate measure of how efficiently we provide customers with the best products for their needs. Profits are required to survive and grow.

GUIDING PRINCIPLES

- **Quality comes first**—To achieve customer satisfaction, the quality of our products and services must be our number one priority.
- **Customers are the focus of everything we do**—Our work must be done with our customers in mind, providing better products and services than our competition.
- **Continuous improvement is essential to our success**—We must strive for excellence in everything we do: in our products, in their safety and value—and in our services, our human relations, our competitiveness, and our profitability.
- **Employee involvement is our way of life**—We are a team. We must treat each other with trust and respect.
- **Dealers and suppliers are our partners**—The Company must maintain mutually beneficial relationships with dealers, suppliers, and our other business associates.
- **Integrity is never compromised**—The conduct of our Company worldwide must be pursued in a manner that is socially responsible and commands respect for its integrity and for its positive contributions to society. Our doors are open to men and women alike without discrimination and without regard to ethnic origin or personal beliefs.

236. **Frisch's Restaurants, Inc.**
     2800 Gilbert Avenue; Cincinnati, OH 45206
     (513) 559-5208
     Industry: 58—Restaurants

Mission Statement

Our mission is to be a respected leader in the food service and hospitality industries. We guarantee our customers quality products that provide real value, with the service they expect, in clean, pleasant surroundings. We dedicate ourselves to sound management practices and effective human relations, while returning maximum earnings to our stockholders.

Our customers can expect:
- Respect
- Quality products

- Warm hospitality
- Excellent service
- Value

Our employees can expect:
- Self satisfaction
- Company pride
- Opportunities to grow
- Fair treatment

The community can expect:
- Economic strength
- Neighborhood involvement
- Employment opportunities

The stockholder can expect:
- A fair return on their investment
- Pride in their business
- Increased revenue

Drafted 1990

Fuller, H.B. Company
see H.B. Fuller Company (273)

G

237. Gale Group Inc.

111 North Orlando Avenue; Winter Park, FL 32789
(407) 621-4253
Industry: 22—Lawn and garden products

MISSION . . .

One team, together, balancing innovative solutions for your home environment with our planet's fragile and finite resources.

VISION . . .

Our Focus

Our focus is to create products which enhance the quality of life in and around the home environment. Many times, in this pursuit, we develop unique technologies which have great commercial applications. These products, through merchandising, advertising and recommendations, must develop a consumer or commercial brand awareness which speaks of quality, integrity, value, and caring.

Market Knowledge Program Design

It is essential that we are the true leaders of our industry in consumer and market knowledge and that we keep this information in a form that is current and easily accessible to all who need it. It is important to all in our organization to realize that from this information—not from our individual tastes and desires—we create and position our services, products and programs.

Research and Development

We are a company that dominates most of its products' niches. Therefore, we must be our own best competition; constantly challenging our own categories, brands and products. Only then will we be able to assume the leadership mantle in each industry category.

Change

We are not committed to just keeping up with change in our industry. We are dedicated to be a catalyst within our chosen field, which constantly challenges the rate of change to increase. Only then are we truly able to influence it.

Our People Their Customers

Our Number 1 commitment is to our people. We commit to an environment where our people can be challenged and grow, where they can succeed and prosper. This environment encourages our people to make their customers their Number 1 commitment.

Market Position

Each category, brand or product must dominate its field. Domination is when our market share equals the sum of the next two competitors. It is acceptable just to lead only if we see market domination a distinct medium term possibility and that the desire and belief is shared by the team.

Quality and Productivity

Our operations task is to achieve and then surpass quality to productivity parity with the best in our chosen field. This means, at the quality level we choose to select our use of human and capital resources is as efficient, if not better, than the best.

Our Team

We, as a team, share this vision and work as one, side-by-side, together. We are a team of ordinary people accustomed to delivering extraordinary results.

Drafted December, 1991

238. Gandalf Technologies, Inc.

130 Colonnade Road South; Nepean, Ontario; Canada K2E 7M4
(613) 723-6500
Industry: 36—Communications equipment

Business Charter

Our mission is to supply, connect and manage local and long distance networks in partnership with our customers.

Copyright © 1992 Gandalf Technologies, Inc.

239. Gannett Co. Inc.

1100 Wilson Boulevard; Arlington, VA 22234
(703) 284-6000
Industry: 27, 48—Publishing and broadcasting

GANNETT'S BASIC GAME PLAN

To create and expand products through innovation and continue to make acquisitions in news, information and communications and related fields that make strategic and economic sense.

To get a positive return on new and acquired products in a reasonable period of time, while recognizing those with high growth potential may take more time.

To emphasize as priorities:
- Increased profitability and increased return on equity and investment over the long term.
- Enhanced quality and the editorial integrity of our products, recognizing that quality products ultimately lead to higher profits.
- Respect for and fairness in dealing with employees.
- A diverse environment where opportunity is based on merit.
- Commitment and service to communities where we do business.
- Customer satisfaction.
- Disposing of assets that have limited or no potential.

August 24, 1992

240. **Gates Rubber Company**
Subsidiary of Gates Corporation
900 South Broadway; P.O. Box 5887; Denver, CO 80217
(303) 744-1911
Industry: 30—Rubber products

Gates Quality Commitment

Everyone in every function involved, empowered, and committed to continuous quality improvement using systematic approaches and processes.

Quality Definition

Meet or exceed customer expectations with products, services, and experiences that are superior to the competition.

Gates Rubber Company Values

At the Gates Rubber Company, we value . . .
- ethical behavior,
- quality and service to our customers, both internal and external,
- open and effective communication,
- innovation,
- contribution of both the individual and the team,
- results,
- continuous improvement in everything we do,
- being the best in all we do, and
- trusting and respecting all stakeholders
   . . . in working with our customers, suppliers, each other; and our communities.

The Mission of The Gates Rubber Company

- Satisfy our customers' expectations around the world by manufacturing and marketing engineered products used in fluid and mechanical power transmission, fluids handling, and molded goods applications in both original equipment and replacement markets.

- Continually improve all business processes by involving all employees in the Gates Quality Commitment.

- Grow faster than our markets by introducing better products and systems, producing them consistently in our factories, and marketing them aggressively to the marketplace.

- Be recognized for our quality values by our customers, suppliers, employees, shareholders, and in the communities in which we operate.

- Generate profits sufficient to provide adequate capital for growth, adequate reward to employees, and an acceptable return on invested capital.

The Vision of The Gates Rubber Company

The vision we have for The Gates Rubber Company as we progress into the 21st century:

- CUSTOMER SATISFACTION:

an innovative, technological leader dedicated to customer satisfaction with constantly improving products and services of superior quality and value.

- HUMAN RESOURCES:

a progressive and open place to work which views the individual as the most important asset for success, thereby continually improving the individual's capabilities through training, systems improvements and empowerment, stressing a teamwork environment while also recognizing individual contribution, providing consistent personnel policies and populated by highly skilled individuals with a perspective of being the best in all they do.

- VALUES:

a successful, prudent, efficient company with ethical standards, recognized as a quality leader.

- COMPETITIVENESS:

a competitive company striving to be the best in the industry, controlling costs while growing in sales and profits, constantly expanding product offerings, serving customers on a global basis, and being the highest value and most responsive producer.

- PUBLIC IMAGE:

an ethical and environmentally conscious manufacturer responsive to customers, employees, and community, recognized internally and externally for quality and value, welcome wherever we go, and constantly striving to improve.

- FINANCIAL:

a financially sound institution with the financial strength necessary to support the strategic direction, emphasizing long-term benefits of investments and recognized as the best value company by all stakeholders.

241. **Gaz Métropolitain, Inc.**
       1717, du Havre; Montreal, Quebec; Canada H2K 2X3
       (514) 598-3767
       Industry: 49—Gas utility

THE MISSION

Gaz Métropolitain is defined by its mission, goal and values. They in turn determine the Company's strategic plan, code of ethics, policies, programs and action plans which establish the parameters of corporate activities.

The Company's operations are defined by its MISSION:

Gaz Métropolitain is a natural gas distributor in Quebec. In addition, it provides related goods and services.

The Company's vision is defined by its GOAL:

To be the best energy distributor in Quebec and the best Canadian gas distributor.

Properly executed work and respect for its employees and other publics are the heart of the interdependent VALUES which guide corporate actions.

Gaz Métropolitain:

- grows with its employees by allowing them to attain excellence;
- outperforms competitors in meeting the energy needs of customers;
- meets the expectations of its shareholders in terms of growth and returns;
- maintains loyal relationships with suppliers and intermediaries and selects them on the basis of their commitment to excellence;
- lobbies governments to promote development of natural gas;
- acts as a good corporate citizen and maintains harmonious relations with regulatory bodies;
- contributes to social well-being and development.

                                                            Annual Report 1991

GCIU
    see Graphic Communications International Union (255)

242. **GEICO Corporation**
One Geico Plaza; Washington, DC 20076-0001
(301) 986-3000
Industry: 63—Property and casualty insurance

Government Employees Insurance Company Mission Statement

GEICO's mission is to market quality personal insurance services at a price advantage to preferred risks through direct response mechanisms, and through General Field Representatives where appropriate.

First prepared 1976

243. **GenCorp**
175 Ghent Road; Fairlawn, OH 44333-3300
(216) 869-4200
Industry: 30—Rubber and defense products

MISSION STATEMENT

Our mission is to continuously improve the company's value to shareholders, customers, employees, and society.

STRATEGY STATEMENT

We will pursue our vision through focused growth based on our technologies and our strong positions in aerospace, automotive, and polymer products.

This strategy of focused diversification will be implemented through effective management processes which assure that consistent corporate interests and values are brought to decentralized decisions.

VALUES STATEMENT

We are committed to this set of core values:
- Quality is our primary objective in everything we do. We will strive for quality in our products, people, technology, financial results, management processes, and our relations with all of our constituents.
- We will respond effectively to our customers' needs by—
Pursuing continuous improvement.
Encouraging innovation.
Delivering what we promise.
Valuing our suppliers.
- The people of GenCorp will determine our success by—
Maintaining the highest ethical standards.
Placing primary emphasis on safety.
Involving all employees by creating an environment which enhances teamwork, personal growth, achievement, and re-cognition.
Treating each other with respect and trust.

Integrity will govern our conduct.

- We will demonstrate respect for the environment and our neighbors by—

Meeting our responsibilities as citizens.

Operating our facilities in an environmentally responsible manner.

VISION STATEMENT

GenCorp will be one of the most respected diversified companies in the world.

244. General Mills, Inc.
P.O. Box 1113; Minneapolis, MN 55440
(612) 540-2311
Industry: 20—Food processing

STATEMENT OF CORPORATE VALUES

CONSUMERS

Consumers choose General Mills because we offer competitively superior products and services.

EMPLOYEES

Employees choose General Mills because we reward innovation and superior performance and release their power to lead.

INVESTORS

Investors choose General Mills because we consistently deliver financial results in the top 10 percent of all major companies.

Our heritage and commitment to outstanding accomplishment has made General Mills "The Company of Champions." Each of us at General Mills must strive to exemplify the values that distinguish us as a unique and special company.

PRODUCTS AND SERVICES

We will provide competitively superior products and services to our customers and consumers. This superiority will be measured by rigorous, comparative testing versus the best competitive offerings and by growth in market shares.

Providing championship products and services is a never-ending job requiring continuous improvement ahead of competition.

PEOPLE AND ORGANIZATION

General Mills' people will be the best in our industries—people who are winners, ever striving to exceed their past accomplishments. Exceptional performance is the result of these people working together in small and fluid teams on those issues where success will clearly widen our competitive advantage.

We value diversity and will create workplaces where people with diverse skills, perspectives, and backgrounds can exercise leadership and help those around them release their full power and potential.

We will minimize organizational levels and have broad spans of responsibility. We will drive out bureaucracy and parochialism. We will trust each other and have the self-confidence to challenge and accept challenge.

INNOVATION

Innovation is the principal driver of growth. Innovation requires a bias for action. To be first among our competitors, we must constantly challenge the status quo and be willing to experiment. The anticipation and creation of change, both in established businesses and in new products and services, is essential for competitive advantage.

We recognize that change—and risk—are inherent to innovation. Our motivation system will strongly reward successful risk-taking, while not penalizing an innovative idea that did not work.

SPEED

We will be the fastest moving and most productive competitor. We will set specific goals to improve our speed and productivity each year compared to our own past performance and to the competition.

COMMITMENT

Our commitment to our shareholders is to deliver financial results that place us in the top 10 percent of all major companies. This can only be accomplished with the personal commitment of each of us.

The persistency to bounce back from disappointments, the intensity to pursue the exceptionally difficult, and the reliability to deliver promised results are all part of our commitment to our shareholders, to each other, and to our pride in "The Company of Champions." This commitment is demonstrated by substantial and increasing levels of employee stock ownership.

CITIZENSHIP

We will have significant positive impact on our communities. We will focus on specific projects where our efforts will make a difference in direct philanthropy, in our corporate investment in nonprofit ventures, and through our own personal involvement in civic and community affairs.

245. General Motors Corporation
3044 West Grand Boulevard; Detroit, MI 48202

(313) 556-5000

Industry: 37—Automobiles and trucks

MISSION

The fundamental purpose of General Motors is to provide products and services of such quality that our customers will receive superior value, our employees and business partners will share in our success, and our stockholders will receive a sustained, superior return on their investment.

GUIDING PRINCIPLES

-    We will establish and maintain a Corporation-wide commitment to excellence in all elements of our product and business activities. This commitment will be central to all that we do.

-    We will place top priority on understanding and meeting our customers' needs and expectations.

-    General Motors is its people. We recognize that GM's success will depend on our involvement and individual commitment and performance. Each employee will have the opportunity, environment, and incentives to promote maximum participation in meeting our collective goals.

-    We recognize that a total dedication to quality leadership in our products, processes, and workplaces is of paramount importance to our success.

-    We are committed to sustained growth which will enable us to play a leading role in the worldwide economy.

-    We will continue to focus our efforts on transportation products and services, both personal and commercial, but will aggressively seek new opportunities to utilize our resources in business ventures that match our skills and capabilities.

-    We will offer a full range of products in the North American market and participate with appropriate products in other markets on a worldwide basis.

-    We will maintain strong manufacturing resources at the highest levels of technology and be cost competitive with each manufacturing unit.

-    We will operate with clearly articulated centralized policies with decentralized operational responsibilities to keep decisions as close to the operations as possible.

-    We will participate in all societies in which we do business as a responsible and ethical citizen, dedicated to continuing social and economic progress.

246. **Geo. A. Hormel & Company**
      P.O. Box 800; Austin, MN 55912
      (507) 437-5611

Industry: 20—Meat products
Mission Statement
To be a leader in the food field with highly differentiated quality products that attain optimum share of market while meeting established profit objectives.

Drafted 1983

247. Gerber Plumbing Fixtures Corp.
4656 West Touhy Avenue; Chicago, IL 60646
(708) 675-6570
Industry: 34—Plumbing fixtures

GERBER'S MISSION

To be the supplier of choice to the wholesale plumbing distribution channel by designing, manufacturing, and marketing high quality fixtures, faucets and fittings for the U.S. and selected international markets, and to provide a satisfactory financial return to the company.

GERBER'S GUIDING PRINCIPLES

We are committed to:
1. Focusing on customer satisfaction in everything we do.
2. Providing exceptional value to our customers.
3. Never compromising our integrity.
4. The profitable growth of the company and the people associated with it.
5. A trusting partnership with our employees, suppliers, customers, and sales representatives.
6. An environment in which all involved feel a sense of family and company commitment.

248. Gerber Products Company
445 State Street; Fremont, MI 49413
(616) 928-2000
Industry: 20—Food products

CORPORATE MISSION

The human, physical and financial resources of Gerber Products Company are dedicated toward:
- Establishing Gerber as the premier brand of food, clothing and care items for children from birth through age three.
- Giving our customers and consumers what they want all the time, every time, on time.
- Continuously pursuing improvements in all phases of our business.
- Seeking intelligent risks that will build shareholder value.

- Providing long-term shareholders with superior returns.
- Creating opportunities for all associates to achieve their full potential.
- Maintaining the Gerber heritage as the authority in the field of infant and child nutrition and care.

249. **Gibson Greetings, Inc.**
2100 Section Road; P.O. Box 371804; Cincinnati, OH 45222-1804
(513) 841-6600
Industry: 27—Greeting cards

OUR MISSION

Our mission is to provide the highest quality products that communicate personal expression; to support our retailers' business objectives through innovation, responsiveness and productivity; and to achieve the goals of our shareholders and our associates.

OUR VALUES

WHO WE ARE AND WHAT WE STAND FOR:

- We are a TEAM committed to achieving our mission.
- We strive to be the best in everything we do.
- We seek open communication and feedback by listening and responding to our customers, our shareholders and our associates.
- We adhere to a stringent code of honor and integrity.
- We trust, respect and care for each other.
- We mutually establish clear accountability and goals.
- We seek to attack the problem and not the person.
- We encourage our associates to become prudent risk takers, to grow, to contribute and to accomplish.
- We take satisfaction from winning and having fun in the process.

Copyright © Gibson Greetings, Inc. Reprinted with Permission of Gibson Greetings, Inc., Cincinnati, Ohio 45237. ALL RIGHTS RESERVED.

250. **Gillette Company**
Prudential Tower Building; Boston, MA 02199
(617) 421-7000
Industry: 28, 34—Personal care products

Mission

Our mission is to achieve or enhance clear leadership, worldwide, in the existing or new core consumer product categories in which we choose to compete.

Current core categories are:

- Male grooming products including blades and razors, electric shavers, shaving preparations, and deodorants and antiperspirants.

- Selected female grooming products including wet shaving, hair removal and hair care appliances, deodorants and antiperspirants and party plan skin care and cosmetic products.

- Writing instruments and correction products.

- Certain areas of the oral care market including toothbrushes, interdental devices and oral care appliances.

- Selected areas of the high-quality small household appliance business, including coffeemakers and food preparation products.

- To achieve this mission, we will also compete in supporting product areas that enhance the company's ability to achieve or hold the leadership position in core categories.

Values

In pursuing our mission, we will live by the following values:

People. We will attract, motivate and retain high-performance people in all areas of our business. We are committed to competitive, performance-based compensation, benefits, training and personal growth based on equal career opportunity and merit. We expect integrity, civility, openness, support for others and commitment to the highest standards of achievement. We value innovation, employee involvement, change, organizational flexibility and personal mobility. We recognize and value the benefits in the diversity of people, ideas and cultures.

Customer Focus. We will invest in and master the key technologies vital to category success. We will offer consumers products of the highest levels of performance for value. We will provide quality service to our customers, both internal and external, by treating them as partners, by listening, understanding their needs, responding fairly and living up to our commitments. We will be a valued customer to our suppliers, treating them fairly and with respect. We will provide these quality values consistent with improving our productivity.

Good Citizenship. We will comply with applicable laws and regulations at all government levels wherever we do business. We will contribute to the communities in which we operate and address social issues responsibly. Our products will be safe to make and to use. We will conserve natural resources and we will continue to invest in a better environment.

We believe that commitment to this mission and to these values will enable the Company to provide a superior return to our shareholders.

251. **Golub Corporation**
     P.O. Box 1074; Schenectady, NY 12301
     (518) 355-5000
     Industry: 54—Supermarkets

     CORPORATE MISSION

     Our primary mission is to serve our customers by selling goods and services through retail outlets in a manner which increases shareholder value.

     Engage in support activities that will strengthen the primary mission.

     Evaluate and engage in profitable opportunities arising from activities which are conducted as a support function of the primary mission.

Goodrich, BF
     see BFGoodrich Company (80)

252. **Gordon Food Service**
     333 Fiftieth Street, SW; P.O. Box 1787; Grand Rapids, MI
         49501-1787
     (616) 530-7000
     Industry: 51—Food wholesale

     OUR PURPOSE AND PHILOSOPHY

     Our purpose is to serve at home and away from home consumer markets, utilizing innovative systems to provide food service products and services of highest quality to major regional markets in the midwest.

     OUR PHILOSOPHY IS SIMPLE:

     ON CHANGE:

     We believe that change is a way of life; we should welcome it, we should look forward to it; we should create and force change. We should not wait to react to change created by others.

     ON GROWTH:

     We believe in controlled permanent growth for both the company and the individual. We will only grow as a company if we grow individually. Further, we believe that each person's contribution is meaningful and that each person helping us grow is entitled to share in such growth through:
     - Sharing in company profits
     - Meaningful individual incentives based on individual performance

     ON BUSINESS CONDUCT:

     We believe in complete integrity with each other, our customers, our suppliers and our community. Most important is the complete openness of information, and the ability for everyone to accept constructive ideas from each other.

ON THE RACE OF LIFE:

We believe that to be complete people we must:
- Succeed and not fail
- We must not drift aimlessly and without purpose
- That the race will indeed be won by the swift.

Accordingly, each of us, and therefore our company, must be among the swift.

FINALLY:

We believe in God, who sent his son, Jesus Christ, to earth to show us himself, and for us to be complete people, we must accept him by faith.

CORNERSTONE VALUES
- Customer is King
- Networking organization
    - initiative, teamwork, decision making
- Everyone is important
    - focus on individual excellence
- Rewards for performance
    - financial incentives, recognition
- "War Room" mentality
    - low cost producer, emphasis on results
- Integrity
    - customers, employees, suppliers
- Philosophy of sharing
    - ideas, profit sharing

Gore, W.L. & Associates, Inc.
see W.L. Gore & Associates, Inc. (618)

253. Goulds Pumps, Inc.
240 Fall Street; Seneca Falls, NY 13148
(315) 568-2811
Industry: 35—Pumps

TOTAL QUALITY POLICY:

Goulds Pumps, Inc. is committed to being a Total Quality Company. Each employee will strive to meet the agreed upon requirements of all internal and external customers the first time and every time. This will be accomplished by continuous improvement through education, training, teamwork, and innovation.

VISION:

All of us at Goulds Pumps will create a very special Company committed to achieving complete Customer Satisfaction. We will become a place where all our customers, external and internal alike, feel that we really care and know that we will relentlessly seek to meet their expectations and exceed them when possible. This will be accomplished by an absolute commitment to Total Quality and the practice of its principles— everywhere, every time, by everyone of us.

We are proud of our independent heritage and intend to strengthen it as we continuously improve performance. Our intense effort to satisfy customers will lead us to superior financial performance which will provide the resources to realize our full potential as an organization and as individuals.

We will be an innovative, growing, worldwide Company built not just with our hands and minds, but with our hearts as well. A place where everyone of us matters . . . where our individual differences are valued and our efforts, ideas and enthusiasm are sought out. All of our efforts, focused as a team with a common vision, become our strength.

MISSION:

As a Total Quality Company our Mission is:

- To become our Customer's first choice. Customer satisfaction will be the focus of everything we do.

- To be the preferred place to work. Through increased education, training and development, we will empower all employees to contribute and achieve their full potential. A measure of our success will be the increase in profits produced by each and everyone of us.

- To achieve profitable growth and increased market share on a global basis through customer focused planning, development, and implementation.

- To set the industry standard for Product Development, Manufacturing Processes and Business Systems. We recognize the importance of our customers and suppliers as partners in our progress.

- To have financial performance as the means by which we meet our shareholders' expectations. Continuous improvement in return on sales and return on equity will be our indicators of success.

We will evaluate our progress by measuring our results against our goals, objectives and benchmarks.

VALUES:

People are and always will be the strength of our Company. All of us have the right to be respected, valued, understood and supported.

Values provide a common understanding of what is to be provided and expected of us on a daily basis. We embrace the following values as the basis for individual behaviors and attitudes in our work:

- **Integrity:** We feel accountable for our word and honor our commitments. Honest and ethical conduct is the only acceptable behavior.

- **Communication:** Everyone has the right to receive and the obligation to give clear, straightforward communication . . . openess, honesty, and courtesy are essential to our sense of well-being.

- **Teamwork:** We all want to belong to a group with purpose, and feel wanted . . . and needed. Teamwork, based on cooperation and trust, makes the best of our individual strengths, and rewards us with superior results.

- **Diversity:** We recognize that our strength as a company is built upon the worth of each individual. We welcome, respect and seek unique and talented people from varied backgrounds and experience.

- **Individual Performance and Growth:** Our goals will be clearly stated and our individual performance will be measured. Recognition and rewards will be tied to achievement of our goals.

Our full potential is realized in an atmosphere which encourages initiative, risk-taking, and acceptance of ownership and accountability. We are committed to achieving this through continuous learning, growth and development.

- **Leadership:** Our actions speak louder than our words. We will expect behavior consistent with our vision, mission and values . . . regardless of position or title in the organization.

We will be ever mindful of our social and environmental responsibilities and will seek to balance the demands of our personal and work lives. We must have patience and understanding as we seek new behaviors. Our commitment is to continually close any gaps between existing practices and these values. We will take satisfaction from our accomplishments, celebrate achievements, enjoy friendships and have fun.

Copyright © Goulds Pumps, Inc. 1992

Government Employees Insurance Company
 see GEICO Corporation (242)

Grand Trunk Corporation
 see CN North America (146)

254. **Granite Broadcasting Corporation**
 One Dag Hammarskjold Plaza; New York, NY 10017
 (212) 826-2530
 Industry: 48—Broadcasting

Granite's Mission Statement

First, we want Granite stations to be "revenue driven." (i) The sales force in each of Granite's markets should have the reputation as the most aggressive, creative and well-trained. (ii) The sales effort must be integrated into all phases of station operations. (iii) Granite's sales people must be marketing-oriented with an emphasis on helping our customers achieve goals. (The customer's success story is our best sales tool.) (iv) Our sales people must understand and believe in the power of television as a critical and effective investment of their client's budget. (v) We believe our revenue potential is not determined solely by the success or failure of the other television stations in the market but is a function of our achieving an appropriate share of local and national spending on all forms of media, marketing and promotion. (vi) The better our financial performance the more we can invest in our sales and marketing operations.

Second, we expect our employees to be cost conscious and profit oriented. (i) Profitability allows us to better serve our employees, advertising customers, viewers, and investors. (ii) The better our financial performance the less our cost of debt.

Third, we want Granite stations to be the clear audience leader in local news. (i) Our news audience should be loyal beyond the popularity of our network affiliation or syndicated lead-in programming. (ii) The investment made at each station in equipment, promotion and people should be heavily skewed toward achieving dominance in our local news product. (iii) The better our financial performance the more we can invest in our news product.

Fourth, the communities we serve are diverse in terms of gender, ethnicity, religion and racial background, and our local news coverage, community affairs involvement, syndicated and other local programming, and employee base must explicitly recognize that variety of population. (i) We have a federally granted license under which we are mandated to serve these communities. (ii) Our stations should be in the forefront of utilizing the enormous power of our airwaves to the benefit of the local community. (iii) Our managers must encourage involvement in the local community by all our employees. (iv) Our definition of the community must be broad enough to encompass its diversity. (v) The better our financial performance the more we can invest in community service projects.

Fifth, we expect that Granite will grow through the acquisition of new stations and other forms of media. (i) We expect to provide our managers and employees with an opportunity to advance in the Company based on performance. (ii) The better our financial performance the sooner we can make additional acquisitions.

Finally, we want our key managers and employees to have an opportunity to benefit from the growth of Granite. (i) Over time, we expect to implement further employee benefit plans and invest more in the professional training of our staffs. (ii) Our ability to do this is highly dependent on the financial performance of the Company.

February 22, 1990

255. **Graphic Communications International Union**
1900 L Street, NW; Washington, DC 20036
(202) 462-1400
Industry: 86—Labor union

The objectives of the International Union shall be:

a. to unite all workers, regardless of race, color, creed, national origin, sex or age, eligible for membership, employed within its jurisdiction.

b. to advance and extend the economic and other welfare interests of its members, including their job security and job opportunities by the establishment and implementation of laws and policies designed to accomplish such results and by continued improvement in the terms of collective bargaining agreements.

c. to establish and regulate sound systems of apprenticeship so that high standards of workmanship may be maintained, and to create training and educational programs for its members in respect to new and advanced techniques and processes so that they may adapt to changing technologies and maintain and improve their skills and job proficiency.

d. to establish and continue plans, programs and special funds covering and relating to the health and welfare, pension and mortuary needs of its members and in cases of unemployment whether due to strikes, lockouts or otherwise, to protect, promote, and advance the welfare and interests of its members by such other actions, consistent with the Constitution, as may be necessary and appropriate.

e. to engage in legislative, political, civic, social, and other activities to promote and safeguard the well-being of the membership and their dependents.

256. **Great Western Bank**
9200 Oakdale Avenue; Chatsworth, CA 91311
(213) 852-3411
Industry: 60—Federal savings bank

PRIMARY LONG-TERM OBJECTIVE

Enhance Great Western's position as a strong, multi-state, mortgage-oriented consumer banking institution with cyclical earnings growth and steady dividend increases.

Greyhound Corporation
see Dial Corporation (185)

257. **Groupe Laperrière & Verreault Inc.**
3100, rue Westinghouse; Parc Ind. No 2; Trois-Rivières, Quebec;
Canada G9A 5E1
(819) 373-5733
Industry: 17, 87—Construction and design services

Corporate Mission

Groupe Laperrière & Verreault Inc. (GL&V) supplies a selective range of equipment and services to its clients. At GL&V, manufacturers throughout North America will find a technologically and economically optimal solution. More importantly, GL&V will deliver it faster than any other major supplier.

GL&V employees are considered partners whose ingenuity and dynamism are essential to achieving corporate objectives. Therefore, GL&V pledges to foster an environment favorable to initiative and autonomy where each individual is rewarded for his/her own contribution to the success of the organization.

Profits earned by GL&V will maintain the company financially stable and generate further returns to investors comparable to those of similar investments.

January 20, 1990

258. **Group Health Cooperative of Puget Sound**
521 Wall Street; Seattle, WA 98121
(206) 448-6460
Industry: 80—Health care

GROUP HEALTH'S MISSION

Group Health Cooperative is a consumer-governed organization whose mission is to enhance the well-being of patients and other customers by providing quality, cost-effective, pre-paid healthcare.

GROUP HEALTH'S VISION FOR THE FUTURE

- By the year 2000, Group Health Cooperative will be the nation's best managed-healthcare organization.
- We will have the most-satisfied customers.

- Our customer governance structure will be a national model for the collaborative delivery of cost-effective, quality healthcare.
- We will be the Northwest's most-desirable healthcare system in which to work.
- We will deliver and be recognized nationally for delivering quality healthcare to all segments of our population.

GROUP HEALTH'S VALUES

In support of our mission, we believe in:

1   A partnership of consumers, medical staff and employees committed to quality in all aspects of our endeavors.

2   Providing services that are professional, caring, efficient and appropriate for all our patients and other customers.

3   Meeting the needs of our patients and other customers, constantly trying to ensure their satisfaction and well-being.

4   Maintaining a diverse work force in an environment that is safe, rewarding and stimulating.

5   Providing an integrated system of comprehensive managed care, primarily through our staff model, as the most effective way of meeting healthcare needs.

6   Striving to protect enrollees from undue financial risks associated with the cost of healthcare.

7   The right and responsibility of individuals to participate in decisions affecting their own health.

8   Health promotion, education and prevention as key elements in our services.

9   Assuming a leadership role in our society in:
   - ensuring access to appropriate healthcare for all, and
   - supporting research and innovation to improve healthcare and its delivery.

10   Participating in community affairs and charitable activities.

Extracted from brochure "Group Health Cooperative:
Model For The Future"

259.   **Grumman Corporation**
1111 Stewart Avenue; Bethpage, NY 11714-3580
(516) 575-0574
Industry: 37—Aerospace and defense

Mission

We are a major company satisfying the world-wide needs and expectations of our customers in the design, development, production and servicing of large-scale systems solutions demanding excellence in systems management, engineering, integration and production, and quality in all phases of the product life-cycle.

Our primary business emphasis is to serve the security needs of the United States and friendly nations. This emphasis extends from strategic, tactical and operational products and services for defense to also serve the needs associated with the internal capabilities of governments at all levels and for selected commercial markets/customers. The protection and development of the core competencies and capabilities to perform this mission also facilitate our participation in related markets.

This mission is accomplished through understanding and anticipating our customers' needs and by advancing technology and transforming it in chosen markets into competitively attractive products and services that provide the best value to customers.

We strive to carry out this mission by benefiting our customers, the users of our products and services, and the regions and communities in which we operate while assuring that we enhance the value of our company for its shareholders and employees. [At press time Grumman was being acquired by Northrop (421).]

GTE Corporation
    see GTE Mobile Communications (260)

260. **GTE Mobile Communications**
      Used by Contel Cellular and GTE Mobilnet
      Subsidiary of GTE Corporation
      245 Perimeter Center Parkway; Atlanta, GA 30346
      (404) 391-8000
      Industry: 48—Cellular communications

   MISSION

   To provide innovative, high quality, technologically advanced personal communications products and services in a cost effective manner that maximizes shareholder value and return on investment, inspires employee pride and enthusiasm and establishes GTE Mobile Communications as the industry leader in the eyes of our customers.

   MAJOR GOALS

   Increase market penetration and maintain market share leadership through acquisition and retention of customers
      Maximize revenue by adding value to the services we provide
      Develop a total quality approach to our business
      Be a leader in technological innovation

Establish the foundation for long-term profitability while achieving short-term profit commitments

GTE VALUES

These seven values are enduring and are meant to guide employees in their daily work

Quality: Delivering products and services which fully meet the requirements and expectations of external and internal customers.

Benchmarking: Collecting competitive data and comparing our performance to the most effective competitors.

Employee Involvement and Teamwork: Managing in a way which emphasizes teamwork, sharing information, creating opportunities to contribute ideas and participating in problem solving.

People: One of GTE's greatest strengths is the quality and commitment of our men and women. Because future success depends upon their continued pride and enthusiasm, GTE will strive to maintain a motivating and rewarding work environment.

Innovation: Generating new ideas, new products and services, and new ways of doing things; stimulating and promoting innovation among all our employees.

Technology: Effectively developing and applying technology to achieve and maintain a competitive technological position across our diverse businesses.

Market Sensitivity: Constantly focusing on the needs and requirements of customers and awareness of competitive activity.

261. **Guilford Mills, Inc.**
P.O. Box 26969; Greensboro, NC 27419-6969
(919) 292-7550
Industry: 22—Fabrics and textiles

Corporate Covenant

We dedicate our combined efforts and abilities to foster our commitment to excellence and to the continued growth of Guilford Mills as a world-wide textile company.

And for the individual . . . continue to support the values that inspire personal growth, job satisfaction, peer recognition, promotion and a stable future.

As we share our visions and strive for new goals, we will embrace the highest of personal values—ethical decision making, leadership, dedication, and commitment to success—ever mindful, that an organization is its people.

Drafted October, 1986

262. **Gulf States Utilities Company**
     P.O. Box 2951; Beaumont, TX 77704
     (409) 838-6631
     Industry: 49—Electric utility

MISSION STATEMENT

The mission of Gulf States Utilities Company is to meet responsibly the needs of the public it serves and its investors; to provide reliable customer service at the most reasonable rates practicable; to develop fully and to utilize its human resources; to provide an environment which is safe and free of unnecessary hazards; to adapt to the evolving business climate created by changing technology, economic conditions, and environmental constraints; to conduct all of its affairs in an open, ethical and lawful manner; and to provide leadership in programs that help improve the quality of life in the area served.

To carry out this mission, management will:

MANAGE the company's resources in such a manner as to earn a fair return on investment and maintain the respect and confidence of investors.

SET clearly defined performance goals which include reliability of service, resource justification, cost optimization, responsiveness to public and investor needs; and demonstrate the cost effective attainment of these objectives.

ENCOURAGE innovative and progressive ideas that will result in maintaining and improving high standards of service at reasonable costs to the customer.

EMPLOY, develop, motivate and reward employees who provide the talents, knowledge and experience required to maintain our role as a leader in the industry.

DEVELOP programs and policies that will emphasize the conservation and wise use of energy.

STRIVE for excellence in all facets of the company's business.

In order to transform this mission statement into concrete terms, management will develop and maintain five-year objectives which give specific direction to the use of our resources.

H

263. Halliburton Company
3600 Lincoln Plaza; 500 North Akard Street; Dallas, TX
75201-3391
(214) 978-2600
Industry: 13, 16, 63—Oilfield services, insurance, and construction

Mission Statement

The world needs energy resources and commercial and industrial facilities to fulfill the need of its communities in a safe and environmentally sound manner.

Halliburton Company is dedicated to leading the way in meeting this need through demonstrated excellence in providing a broad spectrum of services and products for finding and developing energy resources; designing, constructing, operating and maintaining facilities; and protecting the environment.

We will afford our employees opportunities to contribute to our Company's success. Through their skills and abilities, we will continuously improve the quality of services and products we supply our customers.

We will provide a fair return for our shareholders and good opportunities for our business partners and suppliers, and be good citizens of our communities.

Annual Report 1991

264. Hallmark Cards, Inc.
2501 McGee; Kansas City, MO 64108
(816) 274-5111
Industry: 27—Greeting cards

THIS IS HALLMARK

We believe:

That our *products and services* must enrich people's lives and enhance their relationships.

That *creativity and quality*—in our concepts, products and services—are essential to our success.

That the *people* of Hallmark are our company's most valuable resource.

That distinguished *financial performance* is a must, not as an end in itself, but as a means to accomplish our broader mission.

That our *private ownership* must be preserved.

The values that guide us are:

Excellence in all we do.

Ethical and moral conduct at all times and in all our relationships.

Innovation in all areas of our business as a means of attaining and sustaining leadership.

Corporate social responsibility to Kansas City and to each community in which we operate.

These beliefs and values guide our business strategies, our corporate behavior, and our relationships with suppliers, customers, communities and each other.

265. Handleman Company
500 Kirts Boulevard; P.O. Box 7045; Troy, MI 48007-7045
(313) 362-4400
Industry: 50—Distribution of entertainment products

Mission Statement

Our mission is to create customers for our customers. To do this, we must understand consumers so well that we can anticipate their buying decisions. When consumers change their buying habits, Handleman will be the first to know and will be the first to make change work for our customers.

Helping our customers succeed is what we must do every day.

Vision

In a time of accelerating change, we will help customers succeed in the marketplace of the 1990's. Working in partnership with retailers and suppliers, Handleman will provide the specialized marketing services to bring consumers the products which best satisfy their wants for home entertainment.

266. H&R Block, Inc.
4410 Main Street; Kansas City, MO 64111
(816) 753-6900
Industry: 72—Tax preparation services

H&R Block Corporate Values

Mission Statement

H&R Block has a mission in our society to save tax dollars for the American taxpayer. We believe that no taxpayer should pay more taxes than is required by law. Only by providing a quality service affordable to most taxpayers can we assure that our mission is accomplished.

Our mission as a company makes H&R Block the leader in the tax preparation industry. Three key values support our mission: A quality product, excellent service, and a reasonable fee.

No one of these characteristics alone makes our Company unique. There are others in the industry who can and will provide a quality tax return, although often at a higher fee. We have competitors who provide personalized service, again with various levels of quality and fee ranges. We know that there are those in the industry that will charge lower fees than does H&R Block, but rarely are they able to match the consistent level of product quality and service that we provide.

It is all three aspects of our business—consistently high quality of product and service at a reasonable fee—that allow H&R Block to maintain the leading edge in the tax preparation field.

Statement of Values

Quality Product

H&R Block takes pride in providing every client with a tax return that establishes the lowest possible tax and is mathematically accurate.

To live up to the confidence placed in our service, we must look for *every* possible tax saving for every client and ensure that the most beneficial tax treatment is used for every transaction. Just as our clients place their confidence in us, we have confidence in our clients' desire to provide accurate information, thus allowing us to devote our attention to assertively saving our clients' tax dollars.

A quality product is also measured by the mathematical accuracy of the tax return. An accurate return meets the minimum standards for client confidence and Company pride in our product. The checktape and the math check that is provided with every return are critical quality control measures the Company has instituted to ensure these standards are met.

We expect every individual involved in producing a tax return to feel the same pride in our product.

Excellent Service

High quality and service are closely intertwined as Company values.

The objective of many of H&R Block's policies and procedures is the provision of unparalleled service. Emphasizing the Company's dedication to service, these policies and procedures have been developed over the years to meet customer needs. These procedures, however, are only the parts that make up the whole. Underlying all of them is H&R Block's philosophy of consistent excellence in service.

H&R Block is dedicated to serving millions of taxpayers across a wide spectrum, rather than only a select few. Just as there is no average tax return, there is no average client. We recognize that the spectrum includes clients with many different motivations for using our service, with varying levels of sophistication, and with diverse attitudes toward tax return preparation and tax preparers in general.

Our challenge is to let every one of these clients know that we are on his or her side and will do everything possible to make the filing of the tax return as pleasant and convenient as possible. The hallmark of our professionalism as a Company is our ability to treat every client in this varied spectrum with respect and hospitality.

A Reasonable Fee

We believe that quality tax preparation must be affordable, allowing many taxpayers to obtain professional help. We must keep our fee structure within reasonable limits to maintain the value that we offer to society.

H&R Block has a strong financial history with a good profit record. At the same time, ours has remained an affordable service, offering value to the American taxpayer. We are not willing to pass unnecessary expenditures on to our client, nor are we willing to lower the standards our stockholders have come to expect.

To maintain an affordable fee structure while meeting our obligation to our shareholders, it is incumbent on all levels of the organization to operate as efficiently as possible. Our Company has always held the ethic of operating lean, with our largest expenditures focused toward improving our ability to meet the needs of our clients. A continuing strength of our Company is the dedication of all members of the organization to make maximum use of our resources to deliver the quality product and service of which we are proud.

We believe that these three factors, quality product, excellent service, and a reasonable fee, keep H&R Block a leader in the field, further our mission, and guarantee our continued success.

Harland, John H. Company
   see John H. Harland Company (315)

267. **Harley-Davidson, Inc.**
     3700 West Juneau Avenue; P.O. Box 653; Milwaukee, WI 53201
     (414) 342-4680

Industry: 37—Motorcycles

OUR VISION

Harley-Davidson, Inc. is an action-oriented, international company—a leader in its commitment to continuously improve the quality of profitable relationships with stakeholders (customers, employees, suppliers, shareholders, government and society). Harley-Davidson believes the key to success is to balance stakeholders' interest through the empowerment of all its employees to focus on value-added activities.

268. **Harris Bankcorp, Inc.**
P.O. Box 755; Chicago, IL 60690-0755
(312) 461-2121
Industry: 60—Banking

THE HARRIS MISSION

Our goal is to be the most customer-responsive, relationship-oriented provider of financial services in those markets where we choose to compete.

THE HARRIS VALUES

The core of our corporate values is "honesty and fair dealing," first articulated by our organization's founder, N. W. Harris, in 1882.

Over the years, those four words have come to mean integrity, professionalism and honorable, moral conduct. This heritage is in our guardianship, and it is our responsibility to preserve and enhance it.

Adhering to these principles, Harris has earned and will maintain its reputation for high quality service.

The world of financial services has changed a great deal since 1882, but the formula for a successful institution remains the same: Determine values to guide the organization and apply them every day in relationships with customers, employees and communities.

Our customers can expect from the Harris:
- quality products and services
- outstanding professional skills
- advanced technological capabilities
- creativity and innovation

Customers can expect a relationship of uncommon value, working with employees who listen and respond to their needs.

Our employees can expect:
- caring, respect and attention to their needs
- a relationship of mutual trust
- open and honest communication
- equality of opportunity

- clear corporate and individual goals
- courtesy and cooperation
- fair, competitive compensation
- opportunities for advancement with preference for promotion from within
- opportunities for personal and professional development

Harris expects from its employees:

- superb service to customers
- teamwork, shared values and enthusiasm
- hard work and quality performance
- open and honest communication
- a relationship of mutual trust
- compliance with corporate policies and ethics

Our communities can expect:

- Harris to help make communities better places to live and work, and to encourage our employees to do the same

Our shareholder can expect:

- excellence in everything we do
- a financially sound and profitable institution
- a proud reputation built on quality service by outstanding people

THE HARRIS STYLE

Our customers come first.

The primary purpose of every job in our organization is to assist in the delivery of quality products and services to our customers. That requires us to listen to our customers so that we can satisfy their needs.

Our management style emphasizes teamwork with delegated authority and responsibility to help encourage initiative and innovation. Performance is measured and rewarded against specific goals.

We assume risk when it can be managed effectively and when the level of risk assumed is appropriate to the expected reward.

We are proud of our organization. We have a sense of shared ownership for its success.

And at the Harris, we care about one another.

269. **Harsco Corporation**
       P.O. Box 8888; Camp Hill, PA 17001-8888
       (717) 763-7064
       Industry: 29, 30, 34—Diversified manufacturing

Mission

The Mission of Harsco Corporation is to be a **World Class** competitor in the domestic and international manufacturing and marketing of diverse goods and industrial services, principally for defense, industrial, commercial and construction applications. The Corporation is committed to providing innovative engineering solutions to specialized problems, emphasizing technology and close attention to customer service. In accomplishing its Mission, the Corporation will build upon the base of experience acquired during its long association with manufacturing and industrial services. Growth will be achieved through acquisition and internal development within a framework that balances risk of diversification against continued prudent management of current businesses.

Operating Principles

Harsco will continue to make major commitments of resources to further enhance its understanding of the markets that it serves and the technologies associated with its businesses. Harsco aggressively develops new products and services. Harsco will seek constantly to install the most efficient manufacturing systems. For these purposes, Harsco will continually strengthen its resources of people with technical, marketing and entrepreneurial skills. Harsco's resources will be deployed in a balanced fashion in both mature and developing markets, in the United States and select foreign countries, with concentration on products and services that offer superior opportunities. The Corporation will divest itself of products and services that fail to contribute to its Mission. Harsco will maintain a strong financial competence, characterized by professional skill, conservative and tangible asset values, good liquidity, moderate debt leverage and high quality of earnings.

Written 1983; Revised 1991
Annual Report 1991

270. **Hartford Steam Boiler Inspection and Insurance Co.**
One State Street; Hartford, CT 06102
(203) 722-1866
Industry: 63, 87—Insurance and engineering services

Corporate Purpose

To provide technical and professional services which contribute to the safety, reliability and efficiency of property and equipment in the best interests of society.

271. **Harvard Community Health Plan**
10 Brookline Place West; Brookline, MA 02146

(617) 731-8210

Industry: 80—Health care

MISSION STATEMENT

We serve people in all segments of the community with excellent prepaid, integrated health care at a reasonable cost. Member satisfaction is the primary measure of our success.

We continually evaluate and improve what we do. We innovate and pursue new initiatives that support our central mission. We seek motivated and skilled staff and recognize and reward their accomplishments.

Our strong service program also supports teaching, research and community service. These activities, which we fund through the Harvard Community Health Plan Foundation, enhance our organization and serve others.

November, 1987

272. **Haworth, Inc.**

One Haworth Center; Holland, MI 49423-9576

(616) 393-3000

Industry: 25—Furniture

GLOBAL BUSINESS STRATEGIES

1992

TOTAL CUSTOMER SATISFACTION

PRESIDENT'S MESSAGE

"It is Haworth's mission to become the world's leading manufacturer and seller of office furniture, and to be recognized for excellent products and services."

OUR PRIORITIES

- Know and exceed our customers' needs and expectations
- Offer goods and services of the highest quality and value
- Involve all members in the pursuit of total customer satisfaction
- Improve processes and eliminate waste through cycle time reduction
- Compete through anticipating, innovating and creating in all aspects of our business
- Expand our worldwide business operations to service customers everywhere
- Build upon the values expressed in the Haworth Creed

HOW WE MEASURE SUCCESS

Our success will be measured by the orders our customers place with us. The goals of Haworth will be surpassed through the outstanding performance of each of our members.

Adapted from poster

273. **H.B. Fuller Company**
2400 Energy Park Drive; St. Paul, MN 55108-1591
(612) 645-3401
Industry: 28—Chemicals

Mission Statement

The H.B. Fuller corporate mission is to be a leading and profitable worldwide formulator, manufacturer and marketer of quality specialty chemicals, emphasizing service to customers and managed in accordance with a strategic plan.

H.B. Fuller Company is committed to its responsibilities, in order of priority, to its customers, employees and shareholders. H.B. Fuller will conduct business legally and ethically, support the activities of its employees in their communities and be a responsible corporate citizen.

The words of the company's mission statement provide operational guideposts for company management and employees as they make daily business decisions, thereby keeping people and programs focused on the achievement of strategic objectives.

Establishment of such a statement, and the thoughtful consideration that went into its drafting, reflect the company's commitment to the adherence to a strict set of ethical, operational and strategic standards. In fact, the statement is formally reviewed by senior management as the first step of the annual strategic planning process.

274. **Health Net**
21600 Oxnard Street; Woodland Hills, CA 91367
(818) 719-6775
Industry: 80—Health maintenance organization

CORPORATE MISSION

It is the mission of Health Net to promote good health while providing, as a federally qualified Health Maintenance Organization, a quality health care delivery system to the greatest number of people in California at the most reasonable, competitive cost by sharing the financial risk among the medical community, the employer groups and the members.

HEALTH NET PHILOSOPHY

- We are dedicated to serving all of our constituencies: our members, our employer groups and our provider network.

- We believe that our strongest resources are the people who work here, and we are dedicated to maintaining a challenging work environment that brings personal as well as career fulfillment to our Associates.

- We promote good health by encouraging positive lifestyle choices and quality preventive medicine.

- We continually search for ways to improve and grow.

- We are driven to find new and innovative ways to meet marketplace demands.

- We are committed to providing quality health care at the most reasonable, competitive cost.

Extracted from company brochure

275. **HealthTrust, Inc.**
4525 Harding Road; Nashville, TN 37205
(615) 383-4444
Industry: 80—Health care services

OUR GUIDING PRINCIPLES

The guiding principles for HealthTrust, Inc., are a reflection of our corporate goals and values. Each individual's commitment to these four important principles will ensure the strength and vitality of our company.

HealthTrust, Inc., is dedicated to meeting the expectations of those we serve by providing compassionate, quality, cost effective health services.

HealthTrust is in business to meet the needs of several customer groups, including physicians, patients, families, purchasers of health services and the community as a whole. As we balance the different interests, we will keep three criteria in mind. First, we will provide services with compassion and treat people as individuals. Second, we will produce quality health services, recognizing that excellence in primary care has its place separate from the more sophisticated services of large medical centers. Third, our services must be cost effective relative to a combination of local and national standards. This means emphasizing efficiency in hospital services, and working with our medical staffs on practice patterns and disease prevention in our communities.

HealthTrust Inc., will operate in an environment of encouragement and challenge; innovation and continuous improvement; teamwork and collaboration; honesty and integrity.

How we conduct our business is important. We will set high expectations for ourselves in three areas. First, we will demand continuous improvement in all we do. This will be ingrained in our operating culture, and people will be encouraged to be innovative in how they perform their jobs. Second, teamwork within HealthTrust is important to our success. Teamwork includes working relationships within hospitals, across hospitals, and between hospitals and corporate. We will ensure that we are working together, pursuing the same ends and not working at cross-purposes. We will also collaborate with our medical staffs, employers who purchase health benefits, suppliers and others, always striving to improve the cost effectiveness and quality of our health services. Third, we will promote and encourage honesty and integrity in all areas of our professional, business, and personal contacts.

HealthTrust, Inc., will provide leadership in the communities we serve.

We believe health services will increasingly be delivered through regionalized networks and systems. We will be proactive in our communities in both facilitating the development of and securing a place in these regional medical networks. This will mean different agendas in different markets based on services needed and the opportunity to collaborate with market leaders.

HealthTrust, Inc., will conduct its business in a manner that preserves financial viability and creates shareholder value.

Profits will follow if we meet our customers' needs in the way we have outlined. It is our duty to operate in a fiscally responsible manner in order to maintain our hospitals' ability to meet the needs of the communities we serve. Only by being fiscally sound can we ensure appropriate financial support to meet hospital facility and technology needs, future opportunities, continued employment for HealthTrust employees, and the long term success of the company.

Principles developed beginning in December, 1991.

Heinz
   see H.J. Heinz (283)

276. **Henry Ford Health System**
   600 Fisher Building; Detroit, MI 48202-3012
   (313) 876-8700
   Industry: 80—Health care services

MISSION, VISION, AND COMMITMENT TO QUALITY

Mission

Henry Ford Health System is dedicated to developing and providing the highest quality, compassionate health care to serve the needs of the southeastern Michigan community. The System's services will be the most comprehensive, efficient and clinically effective in the region, supported by nationally recognized Henry Ford education and research programs.

Vision

Henry Ford Health System will:

- Evolve into the highest quality, most comprehensive and integrated health system in the region.

- Develop a Center for Health Sciences which will be engaged in leading-edge tertiary care, research and teaching.

- Provide virtually all the health care needs of the population served, from primary care to highly specialized tertiary care.

- Offer a range of health insurance and managed care programs that meet the diverse needs of the population and payors.

- Think of itself as an entity to which the users of its services belong. Administrative systems will emphasize the ease and convenience of use by the members.

- Be a responsible member of the community and assume leadership in developing sound health care policies at the local, state and national level.

277. **Hercules Incorporated**
Hercules Plaza; Wilmington, DE 19894-0001
(302) 594-5000
Industry: 28—Specialty chemicals

Corporate Vision and Strategy Statement

VISION THROUGH THE NINETIES

Hercules will build a major position in advanced materials, and related systems and structures. It will be a leader in key materials for markets which include the space, defense, and transportation industries. Chemical technology and materials engineering will be the foundation on which Hercules will build a future that includes high-performance composites, adhesives, sealants, ceramics, coatings, structural polymers, and additives. Hercules will aggressively expand its position in flavors and food ingredients. Hercules will maintain leadership positions in its core business.

VALUES AND PHILOSOPHIES

In pursuing its vision, Hercules will strive for consistently high profitability by

- Maintaining safety as our highest priority
- Giving our people the opportunity and support to achieve their potential contribution
- Stressing individual and group accountability for success in all parts of the corporation
- Maintaining high standards of ethical behavior
- Managing business risk through an appropriate mix of global businesses by market and product line
- Emphasizing high-value-added applications and low capital intensity
- Achieving continuous productivity improvement
- Stressing Excellence in Marketing as an imperative for all businesses
- Making Quality a fundamental cornerstone for all management and business systems
- Continuously improving and building our Technology to support our present business and be a base for growth of the company
- Continuing to maintain Processes and Technologies in our plants at appropriate state-of-the-art as a vital element for capitalizing on our growth opportunities.

COMMITMENT

Underlying this vision is a commitment to our stakeholders, including:

Our Customers—to improve continuously the value received;

Our Employees—to provide a safe, challenging, participative work environment that will allow them to maximize their contribution and share in the rewards which that contribution creates;

Our Stockholders—to provide continuous growth in the value of their investment; and

Our Communities—to be socially, ethically and environmentally responsible.

Drafted 1988
Annual Report 1988
Copyright © 1989 Hercules Incorporated

278. **Hermann Hospital**
6411 Fannin; Houston, TX 77030-1501
(713) 797-4011
Industry: 80—Health care services

HERMANN HOSPITAL MISSION STATEMENT

The mission of Hermann Hospital is to fulfill the spirit and intent of the will of its founder, George H. Hermann, through offering state-of-the-art health care to all patients. Hermann Hospital is committed to carrying out this mission while keeping pace with the dynamic health care environment, to ensure that the institution will endure for all times.

The hospital maintains its long-term fiscal viability and mission through providing a whole range of services to all socioeconomic groups, and serving as a base for physicians in private practice. Hermann Hospital is dedicated to serving poor and indigent persons in Harris County through its Charity Care Program.

By serving as a primary teaching affiliate of The University of Texas Medical School at Houston, Hermann Hospital benefits the entire Houston community through attraction of faculty physicians and delivery of quality health care to all patients. The hospital and the medical school work in concert toward shared goals of exemplary patient care, innovative teaching and community service, and productive research.

Hermann Hospital is committed to a philosophy of caring and consistent service to its patients and their families, as well as to its physicians and employees. Its historic role continues to evolve to meet the changing needs of contemporary times and its community, while the heart of the mission of Hermann Hospital remains dedicated to the vision of George H. Hermann.

September, 1987

HERMANN CHILDREN'S HOSPITAL MISSION STATEMENT

The mission of Hermann Children's Hospital is to fulfill the spirit and intent of our founder, George H. Hermann, with regard to the special needs and interests of children.

Hermann Children's Hospital is more than a hospital where doctors treat children for illness and injury—it is an institution with a total commitment to children's health. The complete care and treatment of children is our priority; the nurturing of sick and challenged children is our responsibility. We strive to constantly acknowledge and respond to the special world in which children live.

Our commitment to children's health is enhanced by our affiliation with The University of Texas Medical School at Houston; our research in areas of pediatric interest; our specialized programs for children; our facilities and environment, adapted to the unique nature of children's care; our community service; and our concentration of comprehensive care for children with special problems. Hermann Children's Hospital works in concert with The University of Texas Medical School at Houston toward shared goals of exemplary care of children, innovative teaching and community service, and productive research.

Hermann Children's Hospital embraces the mission and vision of its companion institution, Hermann Hospital. Hermann Children's Hospital is committed to a philosophy of caring and consistent service to patients, their families, physicians and fellow employees, and is dedicated to providing quality care and a wide range of services to children of all socioeconomic groups. The institution continues to develop and evolve in order to meet the changing health care needs of the child—now and for all time.

November, 1989

279. Hernandez Engineering Inc.
17625 El Camino Real, Suite 200; Houston, TX 77058
(713) 280-5159
Industry: 87—Engineering

HEI'S CORE VALUES

We are committed to:
- Meeting our customers' needs,
- Maintaining the highest standards of ethics and integrity,
- Achieving long lasting business and community relations,
- Providing a rewarding work environment,
- Working as a team, and
- Accepting entrepreneurial risk to achieve sustained growth and profit.

MISSION STATEMENT

Hernandez Engineering, Inc. will efficiently provide the highest quality engineering and technical services to support our customers in achieving success.

1991

Hewlett, William and Flora Foundation
see William and Flora Hewlett Foundation (614)

280. Hillcrest Medical Center
1120 South Utica; Tulsa, OK 74104
(918) 584-1351
Industry: 80—Hospital

MISSION STATEMENT

The primary purpose of the Hillcrest HealthCare System is to serve the communities of Tulsa and northeastern Oklahoma by providing high quality healthcare services that meet the physiological, psychological and spiritual needs of those who come to us during some of the most vulnerable times of their lives. In pursuit of this worthy mission, we are building an organization founded on a value system that embodies an ongoing quest for overall excellence, pride in service, respect for human dignity, recognition of the importance of meaningful work as it relates to employee empowerment and development, synergistic teamwork, innovation, financial integrity and an ethic of fair and honest dealing in all our endeavors.

July, 1992

281. **Hillenbrand Industries**
     Highway 46; Batesville, IN 47006-9166
     (812) 934-7000
     Industry: 25, 38—Caskets medical equipment

THE HILLENBRAND VISION

Hillenbrand Industries is a diversified international company that invests in highly skilled, inquisitive, honest and motivated people who are personally involved in making and keeping our businesses the leaders in the markets we serve.

We create superior, long-term shareholder value by building *exceptional* relationships with our customers. We enhance our customers' businesses and exceed their expectations by providing superior products and services as measured against worldwide competitors.

We manage for cash flow and reinvest our cash to create long-term shareholder value. Our investment priorities are: 1) Invest in our companies to make sure they remain strong leaders in the markets they serve; 2) Invest in add-on products lines that leverage our existing companies; 3) Invest in new ventures that enhance our existing companies; 4) Acquire companies that conform to our acquisition criteria; 5) Buy back Hillenbrand Industries' stock.

Our Vision has four fundamental, interrelated and equally weighted principles that serve as our foundation for value creation:

I. NICHE MARKET LEADERSHIP:
   We maintain a disciplined focus on carefully chosen market segments. We are the leaders in these market segments because we provide superior value to our customers.

II. TOTAL CUSTOMER SATISFACTION:
   We strive to understand our customers' needs, build lasting relationships with them and consistently exceed their expectations.

III. CONTINUOUS IMPROVEMENT:
   We will only do work that creates or adds value. We strive for daily improvements in all areas of our business.

IV. INDIVIDUAL WORTH:

We can only create value by being personally involved and committed. We insist on a safe and productive workplace, challenging and rewarding work, and performance-based rewards and recognition. We will continually improve our skills, satisfy our internal and external customers, and be accountable for our work.

These principles are not new. They have always been our basis for managing for cash flow to create long-term value for our shareholders, customers and employees.

"Our vision is to serve our customers better than any competitor and to exceed our customers' expectations. This is a commitment to excellence and to the continuous improvement of everything we do."

Extracted from "Hillenbrand Vision" brochure
Copyright © 1992 Hillenbrand Industries, Inc.

282. Hilton Hotels Corporation

9336 Civic Center Drive; P.O. Box 5567; Beverly Hills, CA 90209
(213) 278-4321
Industry: 70—Lodging

Hilton's Corporate Mission

To be recognized as the world's best first-class hotel organization, to constantly strive to improve, allowing us to prosper as a business for the benefit of our guests, our employees, and our shareholders.

Fundamental to the success of our mission are:

PEOPLE

Our most important asset. Involvement, teamwork, and commitment are the values that govern our work.

PRODUCT

Our programs, services and facilities. They must be designed and operated to consistently provide superior quality that satisfies the needs and desires of our guests.

PROFIT

The ultimate measure of our success—the gauge for how well and how efficiently we serve our guests. Profits are required for us to survive and grow.

With this mission comes certain guiding principles:

QUALITY COMES FIRST

The quality of our product and services must create guest satisfaction, that's our No. 1 priority.

VALUE

Our guests deserve quality products at a fair price. That is how to build business.

CONTINUOUS IMPROVEMENT

Never standing on past accomplishments, but always striving—through innovation—to improve our product and service, to increase our efficiency, and profitability.

TEAMWORK

At Hilton, we are a family, working together, to get things done.

INTEGRITY

We will never compromise our code of conduct—we will be socially responsible—we are committed to Hilton's high standards of fairness and integrity.

1985

283. **H.J. Heinz**
P.O. Box 57; Pittsburgh, PA   15230-0057
(412) 456-5700
Industry: 20—Food processing

Mission Statement

Dissemination of pure products and nutritional services.

284. **H.J. Russell & Company**
504 Fair Street, SW; Atlanta, GA   30313
(404) 330-1000
Industry: 15—Construction

MISSION STATEMENT

To continue as a profitable enterprise that:
Is known for delivering quality services and products;
Is recognized within the community by its efforts to enhance the quality of life;
Earns the loyalty of its employees through demonstrated commitment to the development of superior human resources.

285. **Hoechst Celanese Corporation**
Route 202–206; P.O. Box 2500; Somerville, NJ   08876-1258
(908) 231-2000
Industry: 22, 28—Textiles and chemicals

Mission

We are a large, international company based in the United States. We operate a broad spectrum of chemistry-related businesses within the worldwide Hoechst organization.

We will be the recognized leader in our target markets.

We will be the preferred employer in our industry.

We recognize that people are our most valuable asset.

We will be the partner of choice for customers, suppliers, and other creators of innovative concepts.

We will be a major contributor to and take full advantage of the strong technological base of the Hoechst Group.

We will continually increase the long-term value of our company.

We operate in a decentralized manner, allowing each business to develop within our Values.

286. **Holland Mark Martin**
Formerly Database Marketing Corp.
174 Middlesex Turnpike; Burlington, MA 01803-4467
(617) 270-3500
Industry: 73—Advertising

At Holland Mark Martin our mission is as follows:

To become a world class marketing agency whose efforts are validated by long-term customer relationships and motivated employees.

By world class marketing agency, we mean that our agency combines outstanding strategic, creative, technical products with flawless execution.

Written 1993

Corporate Goals:

1. Focus on the Customer
2. Do Things Right the First Time
3. Have Fun
4. Be Innovative
5. Be Profitable

In existence since 1986

287. **Holnam Inc.**
6211 Ann Arbor Road; P.O. Box 122; Dundee, MI 48131
(313) 529-2411
Industry: 32—Cement and concrete

Mission Statement

Holnam Inc. is a leader in the production of cement and related construction materials.

We continually work toward fulfilling commitments to our employees, neighbors, customers, and shareholders.

Product integrity, fiscal responsibility, and protection of the environment are more than goals—they are the foundation of our business.

Annual Report 1991

288. **Home Oil Company Limited**
1600 Home Oil Tower; 324 Eighth Avenue SW; Calgary, Alberta,
   Canada T2P 2Z5
(403) 232-7100
Industry: 13, 29—Petroleum

Mission Statement:

To be a geographically and geologically focused full business system exploration and production, pipeline and marketing company.

Adopted February, 1992

289. **Honeywell Inc.**
Honeywell Plaza; P.O. Box 524; Minneapolis, MN 55440-0524
(612) 951-0111
Industry: 34, 35, 38—Electrical equipment

Our Mission

Honeywell. We are a publicly owned, global enterprise in business to provide control components, products, systems and services. These are for homes and buildings, aviation and space, industrial processes and for application in manufactured goods.

For the future: We are committed to sustaining our focus on the controls business as we grow and change, and to being the global leader in the markets we serve.

Our Guiding Values

As a business, we have responsibilities to all of our stakeholders: customers, shareholders, employees, suppliers and communities. Balancing these responsibilities requires a value system, and ours comprises the following:

Integrity To practice the highest ethical standards.

Quality To strive for total quality to set the pace for our industry and satisfy our customers' current and future needs.

Performance To achieve and reward outstanding results through continuous improvement, personal and organizational commitment, and accountability.

Mutual Respect To employ teamwork, trust, involvement and open communication as the foundation of our working relationships.

Diversity To attract, develop and retain individuals with diverse backgrounds and capabilities.

Hormel

see Geo. A. Hormel & Company (246)

290. **Hospital Corporation of America**
One Park Plaza; Nashville, TN 37203
(615) 327-9551
Industry: 80—Hospitals

Mission

To attain international leadership in the health care field.

To provide excellence in health care.

To improve the standards of health care in communities in which we operate.

To provide superior facilities and needed services to enable physicians to best serve the needs of their patients.

To generate measurable benefits for:

The Community

The Employee

The Medical Staff

and, most importantly,

The Patient

Philosophy

We believe the following principles to be true and timeless:

1. We will continue to develop an organization that will deliver quality health care at a reasonable cost in accordance with each community's needs while generating a reasonable return on investment.

2. We attribute our success to, and recognize that our future success is dependent upon, developing and utilizing our greatest asset—people.

3. We have great confidence in our employees and will relate to and build upon their strengths.

4. We will maintain a compensation policy which closely relates performance and rewards.

5. We will make sure that employees clearly understand their duties and responsibilities and their authority to discharge them.

6. We are committed to an effective communication system that will provide appropriate and timely interchange of information.

7. We believe in decentralized management whereby professional leadership will provide a climate of high expectation, trust and integrity.

8. Management will be encouraged to work with physicians to effectively deliver health care without conflict of interest.

9. We are committed to participate in personal and corporate activities benefiting the community, state and nation.

10. We are committed to a thorough and thoughtful planning process which will guide the destiny of HCA.

11. We will maintain a strong, viable financial position which will continue to deserve the respect of and give confidence to the financial and investment communities.

12. We are committed to conducting our business with integrity and rendering our services always on a high, ethical level.

291. **Household International**
       2700 Sanders Road; Prospect Heights, IL 60070
       (708) 564-5000
       Industry: 61—Lease and finance

Our Mission

The business objectives and strategies of Household International are established within the framework of our corporate mission: "We will be a premier financial services organization meeting the needs of individuals and companies through consumer banking, consumer finance, commercial finance, insurance, investments and related services.

We will treat our customers with dignity and respect as we deliver the best service in the industry. We will develop and maintain long-term relationships with our customers by offering a broad line of high quality products and services which meet their needs. We will be vigorous, innovative and a leading participant in the markets we serve.

We view our employees as our greatest resource and will provide every opportunity for them to achieve their hopes, goals and career aspirations. We will encourage our employees to be involved in the civic affairs of their communities.

We will be exemplary corporate citizens, always conducting ourselves in an ethical and honest manner.

We will accomplish these goals while providing our shareholders with superior returns on their investment."

Annual Report 1991

292. **Houston Lighting & Power**
       Subsidiary of Houston Industries Incorporated
       P.O. Box 1700; Houston, TX 77251
       (713) 228-9211
       Industry: 49—Electric utility

CORPORATE VISION

Houston Lighting & Power will be counted among the best electric utilities in the nation by providing highly valued services to our customers.

In meeting this challenge, we will conduct our business so that we are recognized as a valued and respected member of the community, a considerate employer who demands and rewards excellence, and a rewarding investment opportunity for all who share our vision and choose to grow with us.

293. **Howard Hughes Medical Institute**
6701 Rockledge Drive; Bethesda, MD 20817
(301) 571-0200
Industry: 80—Health care

The Howard Hughes Medical Institute (HHMI) was founded in 1953 by the aviator-industrialist Howard R. Hughes. Its charter reads, in part:

The primary purpose and objective of the Howard Hughes Medical Institute shall be the promotion of human knowledge within the field of the basic sciences (principally the field of medical research and medical education) and the effective application thereof for the benefit of mankind.

HHMI is a scientific and philanthropic organization whose principal purpose is the direct conduct of biomedical research. Its laboratories are located in outstanding academic medical centers, hospitals, universities, and other research institutions throughout the United States. The research of HHMI investigators is concentrated in five broad areas: cell biology and regulation, genetics, immunology, neuroscience, and structural biology. Through its philantropic grants program, the Institute supports various aspects of education in the sciences, from elementary school through postgraduate training, and the research of outstanding biomedical scientists in selected countries outside the United States. HHMI is governed by its Trustees, a group of nine prominent citizens. The Institute's operations are the responsibility of the president, who is the chief executive officer. HHMI's executive offices are located in Bethesda, Maryland.

Annual Report 1991

294. **Humana Inc.**
The Humana Building; 500 West Main Street; P.O. Box 1438;
Louisville, KY 40201-1438
(502) 580-1000
Industry: 80—Hospitals

The mission of Humana is to achieve an unequaled level of measurable quality and productivity in the delivery of health services that are responsive to the needs and values of patients, physicians, employers and consumers.

Annual Report 1991

295. Humiston-Keeling, Inc.
233 East Erie Street, Suite 200; Chicago, IL 60611
(312) 943-6066
Industry: 51—Wholesale pharmaceuticals

Mission Statement

We are committed to quality and ethical service to the health care community.

We dedicate ourselves to being the trusted leader in our field.
- Innovative in our methods
- Respectful and appreciative of our employees' contributions and ideas
- Responsive to the changing needs of our customers now and in the future

While setting the standard of excellence unsurpassed in our industry.

Drafted 1990

296. Husky Oil
707 8th Avenue, SW; P.O. Box 6525, Station D; Calgary, Alberta; Canada T2P 3G7
(403) 298-6111
Industry: 13, 29—Petroleum

Values & Beliefs

1   We believe each employee is key to a successful company.
2   We value an open, honest and trusting environment.
3   We value learning, initiative and creativity.
4   We value each other's expertise and decision-making capabilities.
5   We value commitment and best efforts.
6   We value each employee's contribution.
7   We believe in cooperation and teamwork.
8   We believe in the opportunity for career development for each employee.
9   We believe people want to do their best.

Desired Interpersonal Behaviors

COMMUNICATION

1 Multi-Directional Communication

Feedback is given and received. Dialogue is balanced with parties taking responsibility to state what is on their mind and active listening.

2 Firm but Fair

Let individuals know where they stand, treat them fairly and equitably, but recognize the need for flexibility.

3 Visible Interactive Management

Management sets aside time to spend with each employee to establish and keep open lines of communication.

4 Positive Recognition

Frequent and meaningful praise and recognition.

5 Conflict Resolution

Conflicts and problems are addressed in a timely manner utilizing constructive feedback. Focus on issues, not on personalities.

LEADERSHIP

6 Decision Making

Emphasis is on optimizing employee involvement. Our decision-making process recognizes the situation and selects the most appropriate approach from among directive, consultative, participative, and delegative styles.

7 Receptive to Ideas

Solicit, encourage and support ideas and creativity. Blend new ideas with successful past practices.

8 Bias for Action

Take responsibility to promote your own ideas. It is everyone's responsibility to make things better.

9 Lead by Example

Everyone leads by example utilizing the Desired Interpersonal BehaviorS.

GOAL SETTING

10 Corporate Goals

Clearly define corporate goals and objectives which are well communicated and understood as objectives for everyone.

11 Individual and Team Goals

Everyone participates in setting goals and objectives for themselves and their teams, which are consistent with corporate goals.

TEAMWORK

12 Teamwork

Encourage a team approach. Team members are responsible to make their views, concerns, and level of support known, and to deal with the views and concerns of other team members. Teamwork is a resolution process that deals with all issues and earns support.

13 Cooperation Among Teams

Recognize the need to consult with and involve other teams in actions and decisions. Responsibility and recognition are shared.

14 Planning

Anticipate and set reasonable goals and deadlines with those affected. Everyone exhibits the same degree of commitment to meeting deadlines.

15 Career Development

Encourage and support the development of individuals for current and future positions.

16 Job Function Definition

Ensure that everyone's role and job function is clearly defined and fully understood.

17 Balance Between Work and Personal Life

Recognize and show consideration for the balance between work and personal life.

297. Hydro-Québec

75 Ouest Boul Réne Lévesque; Montreal, Quebec; Canada H2Z 1A4
(514) 289-2211
Industry: 49—Hydroelectric utility

Hydro-Québec Vision

Between now and the year 2000, Hydro-Québec wants to become recognized by its customers as the foremost electric utility in Canada for the quality of its services. Hydro-Québec also wants Quebecers to recognize it as a major partner in the sustainable development of Québec. To achieve these objectives, the utility will make the most of its employees' know-how and Québec's hydroelectric resources.

I

IDA
see Institute for Defense Analyses (304)

IFH
see Alex Lee, Inc. (10)

IIE
see Institute of International Education (305)

298. **Illinois Power Company**
500 South 27th Street; Decatur, IL 62525-1805
(217) 424-6600
Industry: 49—Electric utility

CORPORATE MISSION

Illinois Power will one of the top companies providing **quality** energy services to its customers.

CORPORATE COMMITMENT

Illinois Power will achieve its mission through a commitment to the following:
- Customer satisfaction
- Encouragement and recognition of employee professionalism
- Shareholder value
- Honesty in communication and excellence in performance
- Enhancement of service territory
- Integrity and social responsibility

Drafted and reviewed 1992

299. **IMC Fertilizer Group, Inc.**
2100 Sanders Road; Northbrook, IL 60062
(708) 272-9200
Industry: 28—Fertilizers

We have a mission to make and keep IMC Fertilizer the world's most responsible and reliable supplier of quality crop nutrients to world agriculture. To achieve that mission or objective, the company has, since its creation, carried out a series of strategic measures to build the fertilizer industry's most effective combination of production, distribution and marketing capabilities. Technical advances, innovative financial and product management, market-specific agronomic and customer services, and an ongoing forward planning process that insures adequate in-the-ground reserves for future growth . . . all these things have supported the mission in the past, and will continue to do so in the years ahead.

WE HAVE A MISSION

1. To maintain low-cost production through efficient operations which recognize the company's ongoing commitment to meet or surpass established environmental standards.

2. To attract and retain world-class employees by providing a safe work environment and maintaining competitive compensation and benefit programs.

3. To manage financial functions responsibly to assure positive near-term results and sustain profitable growth.

4. To develop marketing programs promoting high-yield, environmentally sound agricultural practices.

5. To build distribution systems maximizing transportation economies.

April, 1991

300. Immunex Corporation

51 University Street; Seattle, WA 98101
(206) 587-0430
Industry: 28—Pharmaceuticals

Immunex Corporation is a biopharmaceutical company focused on the discovery, development, manufacture and marketing of products to treat immune system disorders. Immunex is dedicated to bringing new and important drugs to market to provide substantial health care benefits to patients, professional challenge and satisfaction to its employees and significant returns to its stockholders.

Our core values are the key to accomplishing our corporate mission and providing an environment in which we strive for continued success.

INNOVATION

Creative Solutions

We are proud of our intellectual curiosity and our willingness to support and reward risk-taking in the pursuit of our mission. We seek innovative solutions to complex problems and continually strive to excel in our business.

ACHIEVEMENT

Active Pursuit of Excellence

We have built our success on a foundation of scientific excellence, intellectual honesty and ethical conduct. We will continue to apply these high standards in all aspects of our business and in our contacts with patients, customers, co-workers, collaborators and shareholders. We build maximum long-term value for our shareholders based on our fundamental technological strengths and responsible financial management of all company assets.

RESPECT FOR PEOPLE

Immunex is its People

The quality, diversity and dedication of our people are Immunex's greatest assets. We are committed to providing a challenging, rewarding, informal, open and safe environment for all employees. We encourage individual initiative and teamwork, and provide opportunities for professional growth and development.

COMMUNICATION

Vital to Success

We are all responsible for cultivating an environment of open and honest communication. We strive to understand each other's roles. Each employee's ideas are recognized as valid and worthy of consideration. Teamwork and collaboration are our goals, and personal communication is the foundation of this endeavor.

QUALITY

Extraordinary Products

We manufacture and market products of the highest quality. We provide our customers with service of the highest caliber. We take pride in knowing that the products we bring to market satisfy the needs of our customers and make a positive impact on health care.

COMMUNITY SERVICE

Committed to Involvement

We recognize our responsibilities as concerned and caring citizens. We manage our business affairs with sensitivity to society and the environment. We seek opportunities to share the rewards of our success with the communities in which we live and work through civic, charitable, educational and scientific contributions.

1992

301. **Information Resources, Inc.**
      150 North Clinton Street; Chicago, IL 60661-1416
      (312) 726-1221
      Industry: 73—Software and market research

Our primary goal is to help improve our client's decision making through the application of actionable and innovative technologies. Achieving that goal dictates a certain type of company. We must be perceptive to market forces, finding those unique opportunities which match our clients' needs. We must pursue unsurpassed excellence in our people, maintaining a rare blend of analytical, technical and communication skills. We must have the self-confidence and business daring necessary to step forward first with new commercial solutions. We must have the service commitment and the people who can make these solutions work for our clients. Above all, we must be an active agent for change, an industry leader, not just another follower.

302. **Inova Health Systems**
      8001 Braddock Road; Springfield, VA 22151
      (703) 321-4000
      Industry: 80—Health Care Services

IHS Vision:

To develop a comprehensive integrated health care system that will provide services superior to those available from any other source.

IHS Mission:

The primary mission of Inova Health System is to serve the community as a not-for-profit organization through the provision of a full spectrum of health maintenance and restoration services. These services are provided through owned organizations and partnerships with other health care providers, including physicians, hospitals, and insurers, and include risk-sharing and management of care. Additionally, IHS participates in educating health care professionals and engages in research activities. The nature of these education and research programs includes both the intrinsic value of education and the creation of new knowledge as well as the positive effect they have on the quality of services provided.

Core Values:

Caring for and about people
Innovation
Community responsibility

Quality Policy:

Quality is doing those things necessary to meet the needs and expectations of those we serve and doing those things right every time. We will continuously improve the ways we do our work and strive to eliminate barriers to the improvement of quality.

303. **Insilco Corporation**
P.O. Box 1919; Midland, TX 79702
(915) 686-5967
Industry: 24, 33, 36—Lumber products, metal fabrication, and electronics

INSILCO CORPORATION MISSION STATEMENT

Driven to Exceed Customer Expectations

INSILCO CORPORATION COMMITMENT

Value

We are committed to providing our customers with maximum **value,** through continuous, long term improvements in quality, service and technology.

Exceed Expectations

We will exceed our customers' expectations with a close relationship that **anticipates** their future requirements through innovation, creativity, flexibility, and sensitivity to the changing business environment.

Customers

This commitment to our **customers,** includes not only our trade customers and end users, but also our "internal and other customers" which include employees, vendors and shareholders.

INSILCO CORPORATION MEASURE OF SUCCESS

We will measure our success in terms of continuous growth in Revenues and Operating Profits while achieving above industry average Returns on Assets thus providing increasing value to our customers, employees, vendors and shareholders.

304. **Institute for Defense Analyses**
1801 North Beauregard Street; Alexandria, VA 22311-1772
(703) 845-2500
Industry: 87—Research and development
The primary mission of the Institute for Defense Analyses, a federally funded research and development center, is to assist the Office of the Secretary of Defense, the Joint Staff, the Unified and Specified Commands,

and Defense Agencies in addressing important national security issues. IDA also works for other federal agencies, such as the Department of Justice and the National Aeronautics and Space Administration, when our skills and experience are appropriate to their uses and when the work is likely to be synergistic with that done for the Department of Defense.

305. **Institute of International Education**
     809 United Nations Plaza; New York, NY 10017-3580
     (212) 984-5425
     Industry: 82—Educational services

Purpose

By enabling outstanding men and women to study, conduct research, receive practical training, or provide technical assistance outside their own countries, IIE works to:
- foster mutual understanding;
- build global problem-solving capabilities;
- create international networks of individuals and institutions that serve as the foundation for greater international cooperation;
- strengthen the international competence of U.S. citizens and their capacity to interact with other societies.

Goal

IIE believes international study and training will help to:
- solve international problems that demand global solutions—poverty, disease, economic instability, and the degradation of the environment;
- assist developing nations and emerging market economies in managing the process of economic and social change;
- strengthen U.S. economic competitiveness;
- maintain U.S. leadership abroad and encourage appreciation of democratic values.

              Extracted from "Institute of International Education Fact Sheet"
                                                        Developed Spring 1991

Institutional Food House, Inc.
     see Alex Lee, Inc. (10)

306. **Intermountain Health Care, Inc.**
     36 South State Street, 22nd Floor; Salt Lake City, UT 84111-1486
     (801) 533-8282
     Industry: 80—Hospitals

OUR MISSION

Excellence in the provision of health care services to communities in the Intermountain region.

OUR COMMITMENTS

- Excellent service to our patients, customers, and physicians is our most important consideration.
- We will provide our services with **integrity**. Our actions will enhance our reputation and reflect the **trust** placed in us by those we serve.
- **Our employees are our most important resource.** We will attract exceptional individuals at all levels of the organization and provide fair compensation and opportunities for personal and professional growth. We will recognize and reward employees who achieve excellence in their work.
- We are committed to **serving diverse needs** of the young and old, the rich and poor, and those living in urban and rural communities.
- We will reflect the **caring and noble** nature of our mission in all that we do. Our services must be high quality, cost-effective, and accessible, achieving a balance between community needs and available resources.
- It is our intent to be a **model health care system**. We will strive to be a national leader in nonprofit health care delivery.
- We will maintain the **financial strength** necessary to fulfill our mission.

307. **International Dairy Queen, Inc.**
P.O. Box 39286; Minneapolis, MN 55439-0286
(612) 830-0200
Industry: 20, 58—Food products and restaurants

MISSION STATEMENT

We are in the business of managing diverse franchise systems, with current emphasis on those in the fast-food, treat and snack areas.

It is our intention to continue to grow in the franchising business, providing financial, management, marketing, operational, training, equipment, engineering, insurance and supply systems to franchisees. We will continue to expand within the food franchise industry through the growth of existing systems, and the acquisition of systems which complement the existing systems, and outside that industry through franchise systems in non-food categories.

We will maintain strong financial standards which will facilitate enhanced return to our stockholders, capital for our future business growth and market growth for our franchisees.

In each system we manage, we will be as professionally informed and skilled as the best operators within the category, so that the revenues we earn result from leadership, innovation, and genuine service to our franchisees.

We will operate our business professionally and ethically, with appropriate concern for our franchisees, employees and the communities in which we conduct business.

308. **International Game Technology**
P.O. Box 10580; Reno, NV 89510-0580
(702) 688-0100
Industry: 39—Coin-operated gambling equipment

IGT MISSION STATEMENT

IGT is in business to provide for the needs of our customers, our employees, and our shareholders, while recognizing our responsibility to the communities in which we operate.

IGT is committed to providing our customers with quality products at a competitive price which, together with excellent service and support, will assist them in maximizing their profitability.

IGT is committed to providing our employees with a stable and rewarding work environment, the opportunity to grow to the extent of their talents, and the opportunity to share in the success of the company which they make possible.

IGT is committed to providing our shareholders with an above average return on their investment, since our ability to serve the needs of our customers and employees is made possible only through their support.

IGT is committed to being a responsible corporate citizen in the communities in which we operate, and encourages our employees to individually be an asset to the community in which they live.

309. **IPSCO Inc.**
P.O. Box 1670; Regina, Saskatchewan; Canada S4P 3C7
(306) 924-7700
Industry: 33—Steel

IPSCO's long-term goals are to:
- be the predominant supplier of carbon hot rolled steel, and reinforcing bars and shapes in Western Canada and the neighboring states;
- become a major player in certain special steel markets, especially tubular products and alloy steels, in North America;
- earn at least 15 percent return on shareholders' equity;
- be a reliable employer with excellent working conditions; and

- be a good corporate citizen in the communities in which it operates.

Irvine, James Foundation
see James Irvine Foundation (311)

310. **ISO Commercial Risk Services, Inc.**
2 Sylvan Way; Parsippany, NJ 07054
(201) 267-0359
Industry: 64—Risk services

CRS MISSION

We provide high quality specific location information to facilitate profitable decision making for our customers.

February 29, 1992

J

311. James Irvine Foundation
One Market Plaza, Spear Tower, Suite 1715;
San Francisco, CA 94105
(415) 777-2244
Industry: 67—Charitable foundation

THE JAMES IRVINE FOUNDATION MISSION STATEMENT

The James Irvine Foundation is dedicated to enhancing the social, economic, and physical quality of life throughout California, and to enriching the State's intellectual and cultural environment.

Within these broad purposes, the Foundation supports community services, the cultural arts, health programs, higher education, and youth programs, and is guided in its grantmaking by the following goals:

- To enhance equal opportunity and support the values of a pluralistic, interdependent society
- To improve the economic and social well-being of the disadvantaged and their communities, foster self-sufficiency, and assist ethnic minorities to function more effectively as full participants in society
- To encourage communication, understanding, and cooperation among diverse cultural, ethnic, and socio-economic groups
- To promote civic participation, social responsibility, public understanding of issues, and the development of sound public policy
- To enrich the quality and diversity of educational, cultural, health, and human service programs throughout the State

Jaycees
see United States Junior Chamber of Commerce (586)

312. JCPenney Company, Inc.
P.O. Box 10001; Dallas, TX 75301-0001
(214) 591-1000
Industry: 53—Department store

Company Mission

Our mission at JCPenney has changed little since Mr. Penney founded the Company in 1902: it was, and is, to sell merchandise and services to consumers at a profit, primarily but not exclusively in the United States, in a manner that is consistent with our corporate ethics and responsibilities.

This statement covers our current activities and potentially many others. It includes stores and catalog, as well as our financial services, drugstore, and specialty retailing operations.

Corporate Objectives

Objectives express the kind of company we want to be—within the framework of the Company mission.

At the corporate level, objectives tend to be broad and primarily financial. Each division has its own objectives, which are consistent with and support those of the Company.

In setting corporate objectives, we are guided by two concepts. The first is **leadership**. We are one of the world's largest retailers, a unique presence in consumer markets, an innovator—in short, a leader. We recognize that leadership does not necessarily equate with size. It does equate with our ability to fulfill the needs and expectations of all those who have some stake in our activities as a Company.

Stakeholders (or constituencies) are the second basic concept for setting objectives. Our principal stakeholders are **customers, associates, suppliers, investors, government**, and the **public** at large. If we serve these "constituencies" to their satisfaction, we will earn a reputation for outstanding value with commensurate goodwill and financial rewards. Our reputation will give us access to the resources required for profitable growth: human, material, financial. We compete with all other enterprises for these resources.

In accordance with these concepts of leadership and stakeholders, we have developed the following corporate objectives:

1. To achieve and maintain a position of **leadership** in the businesses in which we compete.
2. To be a positive force that enhances the interests of our **customers, associates, suppliers, investors, government,** and the **public** at large.
3. To be an attractive **investment** for our shareholders and creditors, and for this purpose:

   a. To achieve a **return on equity** in the top quartile of major competitors for the Company as a whole and for each operating division.

   At the present time, this will require us to achieve an after-tax return on equity of a minimum of 16%.

b. To achieve consistent growth in **earnings** at a rate required to meet or exceed the return on equity objective.

To achieve the minimum 16% ROE will require a consistent earnings growth of 11%.

c. To maintain consistency and growth in **dividend** payout through increased earnings.

At the current time our objective is a payout in the range of 35–40% of net income.

d. To maintain a **capital structure** that will assure continuing access to financial markets so that we can, at reasonable cost, provide for future resource needs and capitalize on attractive opportunities for growth.

Specifically, we will maintain a minimum of A1/A+ ratings (Moody's/Standard & Poor's) on senior long-term debt and the A1/P1 ratings on commercial paper.

e. To ensure that **financing** objectives governing the amount, composition, and cost of capital are consistent with and support other corporate objectives.

All performance objectives will be reviewed at least once a year and, if necessary, revised to reflect the results required to be in the top quartile of our major competitors.

Capital Resources Allocation

JCPenney Stores and Catalog, the two largest operating divisions, are currently the principal users of capital resources. As they achieve their objectives, they will become net providers of capital for future Company growth.

As funds become available for other purposes, they will be deployed where they can achieve the highest rate of return consistent with the Company's mission and financial objectives.

Funds will be made available for expansion or improved profitability where they generate the highest rate of return in excess of the cost of capital and where they support corporate objectives and strategies.

1990

313. **Jewish Hospitals, Inc.**
     3200 Burnet Avenue; Cincinnati, OH 45229
     (513) 569-2000
     Industry: 80—Hospitals

MISSION STATEMENTS

Jewish Hospitals, Inc.

Jewish Hospitals, Inc. is the parent holding company of Jewish Hospital of Cincinnati, Inc., Jewish Hospital Kenwood, and Jewish Hospital

Services, Inc. whose purpose is to support, promote, advance, and strengthen its subsidiary corporations through the provision of physical facilities, financial strength, and broad policy level direction.

Jewish Hospital of Cincinnati

Jewish Hospital of Cincinnati, Inc., in partnership with our physicians, seeks to meet the unique health care needs of our customers by providing quality care and service which will differentiate us from the competition, enhance our market position, and ensure a positive financial contribution.

"Strategic Plan, Executive Summary," December, 1990–91

Jewish Hospital Kenwood

Jewish Hospital Kenwood, in partnership with its medical staff, strives to be a provider of quality osteopathic and allopathic acute care through diagnostic and treatment services on an inpatient and outpatient basis, in an efficient manner.

"Strategic Plan," 1990–91

John Deere & Company
see Deere & Company (179)

314. **John Hancock Financial Services**
P.O. Box 111; Boston, MA 02117
(617) 572-6000
Industry: 63—Insurance

John Hancock Mission Statement

The mission of John Hancock Financial Services is to be the highest quality financial services company.

We offer a broad range of financial products and services nationally and internationally to meet the needs of our customers, and provide our customers with the highest quality service.

We maintain superior financial strength, offering those products and services that provide attractive rates of return, competitive product value and expectations for growth.

We offer challenging career opportunities and personal development for all associates, enable all associates to contribute to their fullest potential and promote open and cooperative relationships among all associates, customers and the public.

In all that we do, we exemplify the highest standards of business ethics and personal integrity; and recognize our corporate obligation to the social and economic well-being of our community.

Core Values

Customers are the reason we are in business. In order to establish lasting relationships, we provide the best customer service in the financial services industry.

We care about the dignity of each person in this organization. In order to be successful, we treat others with the same respect we seek for ourselves.

Annual Report 1992

315. **John H. Harland Company**
P.O. Box 105250l; Atlanta, GA 30348
(404) 981-9460
Industry: 27—Check printing

THE JOHN H. HARLAND COMPANY MISSION STATEMENT

THE JOHN H. HARLAND COMPANY WILL:

-    Provide quality products and services to satisfy the funds transfer and other related needs of the financial community;

-    Pursue predictable repeat business utilizing its existing technology and resources,

-    Seek new businesses with growth compatible with its financial objectives.

IN PURSUING THESE OBJECTIVES, THE JOHN H. HARLAND COMPANY WILL:

-    Market products and services at a fair price to benefit our customers and as well as the company;

-    Give shareholders a premium return on their investment,

-    Offer employees a work environment and wage/benefit program conducive to long tenure in an open relationship with management.

316. **John S. and James L. Knight Foundation**
One Biscayne Tower, Suite 3800; 2 South Biscayne Boulevard;
Miami, FL 33131-1803
(305) 539-0009
Industry: 67—Charitable foundation

STATEMENT OF PURPOSE

The John S. and James L. Knight Foundation was established in 1950 as a private foundation independent of the Knight brothers' newspaper enterprises. It is dedicated to furthering their ideals of service to community, to the highest standards of journalistic excellence, and to the defense of a free press.

In both their publishing and philanthropic undertakings, the Knight brothers shared a broad vision and uncommon devotion to the common welfare. It is those ideals, as well as their philanthropic interests, to which the Foundation remains faithful.

To heighten the impact of their grant making, Knight Foundation's trustees have elected to focus on four programs, each with its own eligibility requirements: Community Initiatives, Journalism, Education and Arts and Culture.

In a rapidly changing world, the Foundation also remains flexible enough to respond to unique challenges, ideas and projects that lie beyond its identified program areas, yet would fulfill the broad vision of its founders.

None of the grant making would be possible without a sound financial base. Thus, preserving and enhancing the Foundation's assets through prudent investment management continues to be of paramount importance.

317. **Johns Hopkins Health System**
     600 North Wolfe Street; Baltimore, MD 21205
     (301) 955-5000
     Industry: 80—Health care services

THE JOHNS HOPKINS HOSPITAL AND HEALTH SYSTEM

MISSION STATEMENT

In 1873 Johns Hopkins charged the first trustees of the hospital which bears his name, in part:

". . . [to] provide for a Hospital, which shall, in construction and arrangement, compare favorably with any other institution of like character in this country or in Europe."

"[to care for] the indigent sick of this city and its environs, without regard to sex, age or color, who may require surgical or medical treatment . . . and the poor of this city and State, of all races, who are stricken down by any casualty, shall be received into this hospital, without charge, for such periods of time and under such regulations as you may prescribe."

". . . [to] secure for the service of the Hospital surgeons and physicians of the highest character and greatest skill."

". . . [to] bear constantly in mind, that it is my wish and purpose that this institution shall ultimately form a part of the Medical School of that University for which I have made ample provision in my will."

The Johns Hopkins Hospital has established missions and goals which have incorporated and elaborated upon the charges from the Hospital's founder and its trustees. The Johns Hopkins Health System was conceived and created by the Hospital trustees in 1986 and exists today to support and to facilitate the operations of the Johns Hopkins Hospital. The missions and goals of the Hospital have been subsumed into those of the Health System and are one and the same. The Johns Hopkins Endowment Fund was created to receive and manage funds donated to the Hospital and apply the same to the missions of the Hospital.

The Trustees of these Institutions, working together, are charged with the duty of effecting these goals with managerial skill and fiscal responsibility. The goals of specific affiliates may vary according to the function of each affiliate, but the missions of the Johns Hopkins Health System taken as a whole, and Johns Hopkins Hospital are identical.

GOALS AND OBJECTIVES

Patient Care

- To render patient care that is the best in the world at the lowest possible cost consistent with quality.

- To provide medical care to those who are unable to pay or unable to pay to full cost.

- To provide a full spectrum of health services with particular emphasis on those specialties in which we have extraordinary skills or potential.

Research and Education

- To support the mission of the faculties of the Johns Hopkins University in research and education in the health professions and development of new diagnosis, treatment and prevention strategies for human illness.

Staff

- To recruit and train health care specialists who excel in their profession.

- To create a working environment that will enable the Johns Hopkins Health System to attract and retain a work force of superior quality.

Facilities and Equipment

- To provide facilities and equipment to enable the Johns Hopkins Health System to remain in the forefront of medicine and to deliver health care services in a manner that is efficient and attractive to patients and health care professionals.

Financial Responsibility

- To provide the financial stability needed to meet the above goals and objectives. This will require generating revenues from patient care, other activities and charitable contributions that enable the Johns Hopkins Health

System to build, maintain, staff and operate a medical complex for patient care of world renown.

June, 1990

Johnson, Robert Wood Foundation
see Robert Wood Johnson Foundation (486)

318. **Johnson & Higgins**
125 Broad Street; New York, NY 10004-2400
(212) 574-7000
Industry: 64—Insurance brokerage

The purpose of Johnson & Higgins is to be the best in everything we do—insurance and reinsurance, risk management, actuarial and human resource consulting, and related services—for our clients throughout the world.

We achieve this purpose through the cooperative efforts of professional people who are excited about what they do, imbued with a keen sense of urgency, dedicated to Quality, and committed to meeting or exceeding our clients' expectations.

Consistent with attaining this purpose is our dedication to the highest ethical standards in the conduct of our business, the continued support of our communities' worthy institutions, and the preservation of the independence made possible by our private ownership.

Essential to all of this is the maintenance of an environment that will attract and motivate people of outstanding character and ability and encourage their personal growth and professional fulfillment.

By doing these things well, we assure our continued steady growth and profitability, as well as our position of global leadership.

Published June, 1992

319. **Johnson & Johnson**
One Johnson & Johnson Plaza; New Brunswick, NJ 08933
(201) 524-0400
Industry: 28, 38—Consumer products and medical supplies

OUR CREDO

We believe our first responsibility is to the doctors, nurses and patients, to mothers and fathers and all others who use our products and services. In meeting their needs everything we do must be of high quality. We must constantly strive to reduce costs in order to maintain reasonable prices. Customers' orders must be serviced promptly and accurately. Our suppliers and distributors must have an opportunity to make a fair profit.

We are responsible to our employees, the men and women who work with us throughout the world. Everyone must be considered as an individual. We must respect their dignity and recognize their merit. They must have a sense of security in their jobs. Compensation must be fair and adequate, and working conditions clean, orderly and safe. We must be mindful of ways to help our employees fulfill their family responsibilities. Employees must feel free to make suggestions and complaints. There must be equal opportunity for employment, development and advancement for those qualified. We must provide competent management, and their actions must be just and ethical.

We are responsible to the communities in which we live and work and to the world community as well. We must be good citizens—support good works and charities and bear our fair share of taxes. We must encourage civic improvements and better health and education. We must maintain in good order the property we are privileged to use, protecting the environment and natural resources.

Our final responsibility is to our stockholders. Business must make a sound profit. We must experiment with new ideas. Research must be carried on, innovative programs developed and mistakes paid for. New equipment must be purchased, new facilities provided and new products launched. Reserves must be created to provide for adverse times. When we operate according to these principles, the stockholders should realize a fair return.

320. **Johnson Controls, Inc.**
  P.O. Box 591; Milwaukee, WI 53201-0591
  (414) 228-1200
  Industry: 30, 38—Automobile parts, controls

THE JOHNSON CONTROLS CORPORATE VISION

CORPORATE CREED

We believe in the free enterprise system. We shall consistently treat our customers, employees, stockholders, suppliers and the community with honesty, dignity, fairness and respect. We will conduct our business with the highest ethical standards.

OUR MISSION

Continually exceed our customers' increasing expectations.

WHAT WE VALUE

Integrity: Honesty and fairness are essential to the way we do business and how we interact with people. We are a company that keeps its promises. We do what we say we will do, and we will conduct ourselves in accordance with our code of ethics.

Customer satisfaction: Customer satisfaction is the source of employee, shareholder, supplier and community benefits. We will exceed customer expectations through continuous improvements in quality, service, productivity and time compression.

Our employees: The diversity and involvement of our people is a foundation of our strength. We are committed to their fair and effective selection, development, motivation and recognition. We will provide employees with the tools, training and support to achieve excellence in customer satisfaction.

Improvement and innovation: We seek continuous improvement and innovation in every element of our business.

Safety and the environment: Our products, services and workplaces reflect our belief that what is good for the environment and the safety and health of all people is good for Johnson Controls.

OBJECTIVES

Customer satisfaction: We will exceed customer expectations through continuous improvements in quality, service, productivity and time compression.

Technology: We will apply world-class technology to our products, processes and services.

Growth: We will seek growth by building upon our existing businesses.

Market leadership: We will only operate in markets where we are, or have the opportunity to become, the recognized leader.

Shareholder value: We will exceed the after-tax, median ROE of the S&P 400 Industrials.

CUSTOMER SATISFACTION: AN OVERVIEW OF JOHNSON CONTROLS COMMITMENT

PHILOSOPHY

Johnson Controls mission is to "continually exceed our customers' expectations."

This commitment is founded on our belief that customer satisfaction is the source of employee, shareholder, supplier and community benefits. Satisfied customers enable us to employ people, provide a competitive return to shareholders, offer business to suppliers and enhance a community's standard of living.

Striving to exceed the expectations of customers, rather than just meeting their requirements, is consistent with our corporate objective to be a market leader. We also recognize that customer expectations are always increasing; continuous improvement, therefore, is essential.

Every employee has customers. Internal customers are other employees who use our work output. External customers are people who purchase our products and services. While each customer may have specific expectations, all expect quality, value and timeliness. So our focus is on achieving continuous improvement in quality, service, productivity and time compression.

Only Johnson Controls employees can ensure that we exceed customer expectations. Management is responsible for involving all employees in the continuous improvement process and providing them with the education, training, time and resources to enable us to fulfill our mission.

Extracted from Company brochure

321. **Jordan Motors**
     609 East Jefferson Boulevard; Mishawaka, IN 46545
     (219) 259-1981
     Industry: 55—Auto dealerships

THE JORDAN GROUP'S MISSION

We, the management and staff of the Jordan Group, pledge our continuing efforts to provide the best service, selection, satisfaction, and value for each and every customer, whether the need be large or small. We also commit ourselves to customer education in sales and service, to allow our customers to make informed decisions regarding their transportation needs. Management pledges to help every employee know the importance of his or her contribution in attaining this goal, and work in partnership to be the very best we can be. From paperwork to parts, service to sales, let the "Jordan Family" serve *your* family, now and in the future.

322. **Jostens, Inc.**
     5501 Norman Center Drive; Minneapolis, MN 55437
     (612) 830-3300
     Industry: 23, 39—Jewelry and promotional items

Mission Statement

Jostens, Inc. will focus on providing high quality products and services for the youth, education, sports award and recognition markets. The Company's product development and acquisition efforts will be closely related to these areas.

Important factors that have contributed to the Company's long-term success will continue to be stressed. These include:
- **The sales structure** of the Company will rely primarily on a direct sales organization of highly trained sales professionals.
- **The marketing strategy** of the Company will be based on increasing market share and building product leadership.

- **The corporate culture** will encourage and support participative management, open communication, the Quality Involvement Process and community service.
- **The management emphasis** of the Company will be on increasing shareholders' value over the long term, as reflected by the growth trend in earnings per share.

The Company will strive to keep its mission and focus simple and direct, so they are easily understood by employees, sales representatives, investors and other stakeholders.

March 1, 1988

K

323. Kaiser Foundation Health Plan, Inc.
One Kaiser Plaza; Oakland, CA 94612
(510) 271-5910
Industry: 80—Health care services

Kaiser Permanente's Mission

The Kaiser Permanente Medical Care Program seeks to improve and maintain the health of its members by providing accessible, affordable, comprehensive health care of high quality on a prepaid basis.

324. Kash n' Karry Food Stores
6422 Harney Road; P.O. Box 11675; Tampa, FL 33680
(813) 621-0200
Industry: 54—Supermarkets

MISSION STATEMENT

We operate supermarkets for value-conscious and time-sensitive customers. Our stores provide quality products at lower overall prices than our competition.

We provide efficient services and easy-to-shop stores while operating with consistently high standards of performance and achieving excellent financial returns.

We deal ethically with customers, vendors, and one another.

Adopted 1988

325. Kaufman and Broad Home Corporation
10877 Wilshire Boulevard; Los Angeles, CA 90024
(213) 443-8000
Industry: 15—Home builders

MISSION STATEMENT

"We build homes to meet people's dreams."

Our Business

Our primary business is to provide well designed, quality homes and communities to home buyers in California, France and Canada. Innovative commercial developments and residential investment properties, presold to major institutional investors, enhance the company's growth and market presence in Europe. Competitive mortgage financing programs provide a critical marketing edge in our California housing operations.

Objectives

We are fiercely determined to continue to succeed. We intend to provide the best quality housing for our customers, a superior return to our shareholders, and a chance for every employee to make a difference and share in our success.

Vision

We strive to be the premiere real estate developer in each market in which we operate. We intend to lead the way in home building well into the 21st century.

Core Values

It is our intention to deliver a quality product . . . 100% of the time.

We believe the true test of quality is customer satisfaction. There are no good excuses.

We treat each customer specially and each situation individually.

We strive to be at the cutting edge of product development and innovative design.

We reward innovation and encourage reasonable and prudent risk taking.

We don't just build homes, we build neighborhoods. We expect our presence will enhance long term values.

This business is built around people. We want self-directed winners who have high personal integrity.

This is a team business where we depend on one another. We expect each person to make a contribution.

All people at Kaufman and Broad have clout. We all work for the same ultimate boss, our customers.

Our subcontractors and suppliers are our partners. We demand a lot from them, especially high quality work. We expect to grow and prosper together.

We respect the dignity of those with whom we deal. We always try to be fair.

While we are committed to steady growth and improved earnings, we will not over-emphasize short-term results.

Our growth is ensured through substantial land resources. We view land as a raw material for use in the building process, not as a speculative investment.

We believe in long-range planning. It is nonsense to say you can't plan the future in this business.

Our company's success is built on conservative financial policies, a strong capital base and superior earnings capacity. We believe a sustained level of solid profitability is critical to our future.

Autonomous regions are the cornerstone of our operational success. We have pioneered a divisional structure that links entrepreneurial executives with a lean headquarters group.

We are constantly striving to conduct our business in a way that will enable us to prosper in both good times and the occasional lean years.

Kellogg, W.K. Foundation
see W.K. Kellogg Foundation (617)

326. Kellogg Company
One Kellogg Square; P.O. Box 3599; Battle Creek, MI 49016-3599
(616) 961-2000
Industry: 20—Food products

"We are a company of dedicated people making quality products for a healthier world."—W. K. Kellogg

OUR MISSION

Kellogg is a global company committed to building long-term growth in volume and profit and to enhancing its worldwide leadership position by providing nutritious food products of superior value.

OUR WORKING ENVIRONMENT

The challenge of an increasingly competitive global marketplace requires an environment within our Company which encourages personal initiative and enables Kellogg people to contribute to their full potential. This environment must promote a free exchange of information, the generation of new ideas and the continued accumulation of knowledge.

To meet this challenge, we will:

Exhibit a high level of personal integrity and fairness which respects the individual and our cultural diversity.

Demonstrate leadership which encourages teamwork, open communication and mutual trust.

Approach our work with a focus on results, a sense of urgency and a healthy dissatisfaction with the status quo.

OUR SHARED VALUES

- Profit and growth
- People

- Consumer satisfaction and quality
- Integrity and ethics
- Social responsibility

Revised March, 1992
Extracted from "Kellogg Company Philosophy" brochure
Copyright © 1992 Kellogg Company

327. **Kemper Corporation**
Kemper Center; One Kemper Drive; Long Grove, IL 60049-0001
(708) 540-2000
Industry: 63—Diversified insurance

Mission Statement

Kemper Corporation is a financial services company that gathers, manages and protects the assets of individual, corporate and institutional clients and generates attractive returns and long-term appreciation for its stockholders. We plan to achieve this mission by developing and distributing high-quality products and services and operating in a highly professional and ethical manner.

Drafted Fall 1991
Annual Report 1991

328. **Keystone International, Inc.**
9600 West Gulf Bank Road; Houston, TX 77040
(713) 466-1176
Industry: 34—Valve products

Mission—Serving the Customer

Keystone's mission is to profitably expand its leadership position on a worldwide basis for flow control equipment and systems that meet the requirements of the customers.

Purpose

For the Customer: To provide high quality and technically advanced products, systems and service on a global scale.

For the Employee: To furnish a climate of growth so that each will have the opportunity to develop and advance, and be adequately rewarded for his or her performance.

For the Shareholder: To give a worthwhile return on his or her investment in the form of cash dividends and increases in the value of stock ownership.

For the Company: To be a good corporate citizen in every country in which it operates.

Copyright © Keystone International, Inc.

329. **Kmart Corporation**
   3100 West Big Beaver Road; Troy, MI 48084-3163
   (313) 643-1000
   Industry: 53—Discount stores

Mission Statement:

Kmart will be a symbol to Americans—the place which helps them to attain the quality of life guaranteed in the American dream—sooner, better and more conveniently than anyone else.

Drafted November, 1989
Mission Statement included with the permission of Kmart.

Knight, John S. and James L. Foundation
   see John S. and James L. Knight Foundation (316)

330. **Knight-Ridder, Inc.**
   One Herald Plaza; Miami, FL 33132-1693
   (305) 376-3800
   Industry: 27, 48—Publishing and broadcasting

THE KNIGHT-RIDDER PROMISE

No individual or single group can assure Knight-Ridder's continued success. All who care about this company and count upon its healthy future are dependent on one another. Therefore, we make these promises . . .

To Our Customers . . . We promise to put you first. Unless we satisfy you, we cannot succeed. We are committed to meeting your needs and expectations—and exceeding them whenever possible. You can count on our honesty and fairness, our professionalism, our responsiveness, our courtesy, our dedication to quality—and our passion to serve you well.

To Our Employees . . . We promise to help you achieve your full potential. We promise personal respect, fair pay, a clean and safe workplace. We promise equal opportunity for reward and advancement. We promise a role in a great enterprise that is central to our society—and recognition and appreciation for a job well done.

To Our Shareholders . . . We promise to work hard, in all parts of our company, to make your investment in Knight-Ridder an attractive one. We are committed to seeing that your money is invested in operations with sound economic prospects. We are committed to consistent growth in profits and a fair return on investment—and not just when the economy is robust.

To Our Communities . . . We promise to be good citizens, to contribute to the quality of life and civic betterment of the communities that sustain us. We will do that through searching and sensitive journalism that fully meets our public service obligations, through ethical and enlightened business practices, through civic participation and financial support.

To Our Society . . . We know that ours is not just another business, but one that requires special fidelity to the principles of democracy. We promise to be faithful to those principles and to act always in vigorous support of a free press, freedom of speech and a free flow of information around the globe.

A Statement Of Values

Knight-Ridder is one of the world's leading publishing and information companies. Our enterprise is both a business and a public trust, built on the highest standards of ethics and integrity. We are rooted in our founders' conviction that high-quality newspapers—fair, independent, probing, relevant and compassionate—are indispensable to our free society.

Our moral obligation is to excel in all that we do. We recognize that change is inevitable. We welcome change and intend to benefit from it. Our values, though, do not change. We intend that the name of Knight-Ridder shall be forever synonymous with the best in newspaper publishing, the delivery of business and professional information, and all other activities in which we choose to participate.

331. **Knights of Columbus**
   One Columbus Plaza; New Haven, CT 06510-3326
   (203) 772-2130
   Industry: 86—Membership organization
   The purposes for which said corporation is formed are the following: (a) of rendering pecuniary aid to its members, their families and beneficiaries of members and their families; (b) of rendering mutual aid and assistance to its sick, disabled and needy members and their families; (c) of promoting social and intellectual interaction among its members and their families, and (d) of promoting and conducting educational, charitable, religious, social welfare, war relief and welfare, and public relief work.
   Extracted from "Section A: Corporate Strategy and Direction"

Kodak
   see Eastman Kodak Company (204)

332. **Kohl's Department Stores**
   N54 W13600 Woodale Drive; Menomonee Falls, WI 53051
   (414) 783-5800
   Industry: 53—Department stores

KOHL'S MISSION

To be a value oriented family store that services our customers' wants and needs through clear, dominant, value-driven assortments.

333. **The Kroger Company**
      1014 Vine Street; Cincinnati, OH 45202
      (513) 762-4000
      Industry: 54—Supermarkets

The Kroger Co. Corporate Mission Statement

Our principal objective is to be a leader in the distribution and merchandising of food, health, personal care, and related consumable products and services. In achieving this objective, we will satisfy our responsibilities to shareowners, employees, customers and the communities we serve.

-    We will conduct our business to produce financial returns that encourage and reward investment by shareowners and allow the company to grow. Investments in retailing, distribution and processing will be continually evaluated for their contribution to our corporate return objectives.

-    We will constantly strive to satisfy consumer needs as well as, or better than, the best of our competitors. Operating procedures will increasingly reflect our belief that the organization levels closest to the consumer are best positioned to serve changing consumer needs.

-    We will treat our employees fairly and with respect, openness and honesty. We will solicit and respond to their ideas and reward meaningful contributions to our success.

-    We will encourage our employees to be active and responsible citizens and will allocate resources for activities which enhance the quality of life for our customers, our employees and the general public.
                 Extracted from "The Kroger Co. Policy on Business Ethics"

334. **KZF Incorporated**
      655 Eden Park Drive; Cincinnati, OH 45202
      (513) 621-6211
      Industry: 87—Architectural and engineering services

THE KZF MISSION

We are committed to excellence in the design of the built environment.

Quality leadership, open communication and the creative interaction of clients and staff are keys to fulfilling this objective.

We encourage personal development, individual and team responsibility as well as mutual support through positive recognition and constructive criticism.

We are dedicated to a challenging and stimulating workplace in which we strive for the highest level of professional service, continued profitability and client satisfaction.

Drafted 1988

L

335. Lands' End, Inc.
1 Lands' End Lane; Dodgeville, WI 53595
(608) 935-9341
Industry: 59—Mail order clothing

THE LANDS' END PRINCIPLES OF DOING BUSINESS.

Principle 1.

We do everything we can to make our products better. We improve material, and add back features and construction details that others have taken out over the years. We never reduce the quality of a product to make it cheaper.

Principle 2.

We price our products fairly and honestly. We do not, have not, and will not participate in the common retailing practice of inflating mark-ups to set up future phony "sale."

Principle 3.

We accept any return, for any reason, at any time. Our products are guaranteed. No fine print. No arguments. We mean exactly what we say: GUARANTEED. PERIOD.®

Principle 4.

We ship faster than anyone we know of. We ship items in stock the day after we receive the order. At the height of the Christmas season the longest time an order was in the house was 36 hours, excepting monograms which took another 12 hours.

Principle 5.

We believe that what is best for our customer is best for all of us. Everyone here understands that concept. Our sales and service people are trained to know our products, and to be friendly and helpful. They are urged to take all the time necessary to take care of you. We even pay for your call, for whatever reason you call.

Principle 6.

We are able to sell at lower prices because we have eliminated middlemen; because we don't buy branded merchandise with high protected mark-ups; and because we have placed our contracts with manufacturers who have proved that they are cost conscious and efficient.

Principle 7.

We are able to sell at lower prices because we operate efficiently. Our people are hard working, intelligent and share in the success of the company.

Principle 8.

We are able to sell at lower prices because we support no fancy emporiums with their high overhead. Our main location is in the middle of a 40-acre cornfield in rural Wisconsin. We still operate our first location in Chicago's Near North tannery district.

Copyright © 1992, Lands' End, Inc.

336. **Lee County Electric Cooperative, Inc.**
P.O. Box 3455; North Fort Myers, FL 33918-3455
(813) 995-2121
Industry: 49—Electric cooperative

VISION

LCEC will be a leader in providing innovative, market-driven and customer-driven energy services.

MISSION

To provide cost competitive and reliable electricity and related services in Southwest Florida.

Drafted May, 1992

337. **Lee Enterprises, Incorporated**
400 Putnam Building; 215 North Main Street; Davenport, IA
52801-1924
(319) 383-2172
Industry: 27, 48—Publishing and broadcasting

MISSION

Through a combination of content, formats and conduits, we will concentrate on creating, processing, selling and distributing information and entertainment products and services to customers and create audiences for advertisers.

We will manufacture and distribute equipment, supplies and provide services related to graphic arts.

SHARED VISION

At our best . . . Lee Enterprises is people who care about customers and care for each other. We are passionate about quality and success and take pride in each person making a positive difference.

October, 1991

338. **Leo Burnett Company, Inc.**
35 West Wacker Drive; Chicago, IL 60601
(312) 220-5959
Industry: 73—Advertising

LEO BURNETT CORPORATE MISSION

The mission of Leo Burnett Company is to create superior advertising.

In Leo's words: "Our primary function in life is to produce the best advertising in the world, bar none."

"This is to be advertising so interrupting, so daring, so fresh, so engaging, so human, so believable and so well-focused as to themes and ideas that, at one and the same time, it builds a quality reputation for the long haul as it produces sales for the immediate present."

February 28, 1955

Lever Brothers Company
see Unilever United States, Inc. (577)

339. **Levi Strauss & Co.**
Levi's Plaza; P.O. Box 7215; San Francisco, CA 94120
(415) 544-6000
Industry: 23—Clothing

MISSION STATEMENT

The mission of Levi Strauss & Co. is to sustain profitable and responsible commercial success by marketing jeans and selected casual apparel under the Levi's brand.

We must balance goals of superior profitability and return on investment, leadership market positions, and superior products and service. We will conduct our business ethically and demonstrate leadership in satisfying our responsibilities to our communities and to society. Our work environment will be safe and productive and characterized by fair treatment, teamwork, open communications, personal accountability and opportunities for growth and development.

ASPIRATION STATEMENT

We all want a Company that our people are proud of and committed to, where all employees have an opportunity to contribute, learn, grow and advance based on merit, not politics or background. We want our people to feel respected, treated fairly, listened to and involved. Above all, we want satisfaction from accomplishments and friendships, balanced personal and professional lives, and to have fun in our endeavors.

When we describe the kind of LS&CO. we want in the future what we are talking about is building on the foundation we have inherited: affirming the best of our Company's traditions, closing gaps that may exist between principles and practices and updating some of our values to reflect contemporary circumstances.

340. **Levitz Furniture**
6111 Broken Sound Parkway, NW; Boca Raton, FL 33487
(407) 994-6006
Industry: 57—Furniture retailing

CORPORATE MISSION STATEMENT

Our mission is to satisfy the needs and expectations of our customers with quality products and services.

EMPOWERMENT QUESTIONS:

1. Is it the right thing for the customer?
2. It is the right thing for Levitz?
3. Is it something I'm willing to be accountable for?
4. Is it consistent with Levitz' basic beliefs?

Levy, Chas. Company
see Chas. Levy Company (131)

341. **Liberty National Bank and Trust Company**
P.O. Box 32500; Louisville, KY 40232
(502) 566-2000
Industry: 60—Banking

Statement of Corporate Values

Corporate Mission

The mission of Liberty National Bancorp, Inc., is to be the strongest independent financial institution in this region and to be second to none in the excellence and ethical application of our services. In order to achieve this goal, we must be creative in maintaining a full range of financial services on a profitable basis; achieve an excellent rate of return for our shareholders; develop a loyal staff and recognize our responsibilities to them; and maintain a relationship with each of the communities we serve that is beyond reproach.

Corporate Values

Employees share a belief in the following values which make up the basis of corporate strategy.

- Every Liberty employee accepts individual responsibility to other Liberty stakeholders, i.e., customers, shareholders, the community and other employees.
- Every Liberty employee strives to do the best job possible.
- Liberty conducts its business ethically and with individual and corporate integrity.
- Liberty maintains superior long-term profitability in order to create value for shareholders and employees.
- Liberty strives for unmatched customer service excellence in all aspects of its business.

Guiding Principles

The principles which shape day-to-day decisions and influence individual behavior on the job.

- Liberty and its employees focus on serving customers and exceeding their expectations.
- Liberty recognizes and respects the individual employee and customer.
- Liberty empowers employees through proper training, continuous communication and proper reward and recognition.
- Liberty seeks to be a good corporate citizen through corporate and individual leadership and involvement.
- Liberty is innovative and creative in its support of internal and external customers.
- Liberty seeks employee involvement, fosters teamwork and promotes continuous improvement in all its operations.

Revised and updated September, 1992

342. **Lila Wallace-Reader's Digest Fund, Inc.**
      261 Madison Avenue, 24th Floor; New York, NY 10016
      (212) 953-1200
      Industry: 67—Charitable foundation

Vision Statement

The Lila Wallace-Reader's Digest Fund believes that a vibrant and thriving cultural life adds vitality to our nation and provides enriching experiences for people in communities across the country.

To help achieve that vision, the Fund invests in programs and partnerships that:

- Create greater understanding of the arts and America's rich cultural heritage.
- Encourage people to participate in and contribute to the cultural life of their communities.
- Bring artists and audiences together in local communities to interact and learn from each other.
- Increase adult literacy so that people can participate effectively in the life of their communities.
- Improve the quality of life in urban neighborhoods through revitalization of parks, gardens and other community resources.

The Fund supports programs in the performing, visual, literary and folk arts; adult literacy; and urban parks. With annual grants of more than $30 million, the Fund is the largest private funder of arts and culture in the United States.

October, 1992

see also DeWitt Wallace-Reader's Digest Fund (183)

LILCO

see Long Island Lighting Company (345)

343. **Lillian Vernon Corporation**
510 South Fulton Avenue; Mount Vernon, NY 10550-5067
(914) 699-4131
Industry: 59—Mail order

LILLIAN VERNON CORPORATION MISSION STATEMENT

Lillian Vernon Corporation is a leader in the mail order industry. We provide a time and cost efficient means to shop ideally suited for the lifestyles of busy women.

Products from the Lillian Vernon catalogs are:
- unique
- excellent value
- top quality

Lillian Vernon shops the world to find merchandise that cannot be found elsewhere.

Lillian Vernon helps build and promote American businesses by discovering their products and introducing them to the marketplace.

Products in the Lillian Vernon catalog are things Lillian wants to own or give herself. Products are designed to make our customer's lives easier, more fun and enable them to live better for less.

Lillian Vernon Corporation is staffed by friendly, yet highly professional individuals with a strong commitment to customer service.

344. **Lilly Endowment Inc.**
     2801 North Meridian Street; P.O. Box 88068; Indianapolis,
       IN 46208
     (317) 924-5471
     Industry: 67—Charitable foundation

LILLY ENDOWMENT MISSION

Lilly Endowment strives to be an institution that builds community—an environment in which consensus about values can develop and partnerships can be forged.

The Endowment clings to a profound belief in democratic values and individual human potential, both of which are elevated through education.

At the heart of our interest in community and individual dignity is an abiding conviction that we are guided, not only by contemporary human experience, but by religious traditions of lasting power.

1992

345. **Long Island Lighting Company**
     175 East Old Country Road; Hicksville, NY 11801
     (516) 933-4590
     Industry: 49—Electric utility

LILCO'S MISSION STATEMENT

The people of LILCO are dedicated to providing unparalleled service to every customer. Through the establishment of a working environment that promotes excellence, communication and cooperation, we are committed to achieving the highest level of customer satisfaction.

346. **Long John Silver's Inc.**
     P.O. Box 11988; Lexington, KY 40579
     (606) 263-6000
     Industry: 58—Fast food restaurants

LONG JOHN SILVER'S

OUR MISSION

OUR PROMISE

We will provide each guest great tasting, healthful, reasonably priced fish, seafood and chicken in a fast, friendly manner on every visit.

OUR GUESTS

We rely on our guests to help us keep this promise. If you have a suggestion, opinion or complaint, please discuss it with the manager or call the toll-free Long John Silver's Guest Hotline at 1-800-880-FISH.

OUR GOAL

We want to be America's best quick-service restaurant chain.

OUR CULTURE

We will maintain a work environment that encourages team members to put forth their best efforts to serve our guests.

We will respect each team member as we work together to achieve excellence.

The participation of team members in our success is an essential part of our culture. Many team members share in our Equity or Financial Incentive programs. Our goal is to increase the value of these programs and extend equity ownership to more team members.

Drafted November 13, 1990
Copyright © Long John Silver's

Lowe's Food Stores, Inc.
see Alex Lee, Inc. (10)

347. **LSI Industries Inc.**
10000 Alliance Road; P.O. Box 42728; Cincinnati, OH 45242
(513) 793-3200
Industry: 36—Lighting fixtures

Philosophy of Business

LSI's mission is to penetrate the lighting and commercial graphics markets with responsive, quality products and services.

We believe that a business enterprise succeeds only when the interests of its customers, suppliers, employees, and investors are served equitably and the condition of each is improved as a result of the undertaking.

We are committed to growth in all aspects of our business operations. Because this growth is qualitative as well as quantitative, it represents dedication to the improvement of our Company. It is important that growth be planned and directed toward niche markets which are consistent with the Mission of the Company. We apply the "80/20 Rule" to each aspect of our business as this provides focus for our actions, promotes efficiency, and maximizes the potential return to our investors.

We accept the responsibility to design and manufacture quality products at a price that constitutes a value. Our commitment to service underscores our desire for long-term relationships with our customers, our suppliers, and our sales representatives, and provides LSI with an important competitive edge.

Employees sharing common values and an entrepreneurial spirit are the essence of our Company. Money, plant, and equipment are worthless without utilization by people. Employees give the Company integrity and purpose, and they alone enable the Company to serve its customers and investors. In turn, the Company must compensate them fairly, concern itself with the development of each and provide a safe working environment.

The investment of the shareholders constitutes for the management a trusteeship, and entitles the shareholders to a fair return on their investment. To protect the shareholders' investment, management is fiscally conservative and strives to avoid unnecessary risk. We believe that profits are essential for serving the interests of customers and employees as well as investors.

Finally, we are determined to earn and retain a reputation for honesty and integrity in the conduct of our affairs. We wish to be seen as a Company that extolls products, people, and profits—a truly interdependent triad.

348. **Lukens Inc.**
       50 South First Avenue; Coatesville, PA 19320-0911
       (215) 383-3100
       Industry: 33, 87—Steel and architectural engineering services

Vision

Lukens' vision for the next decade is to grow as an innovative, world-class industrial organization providing products and services which exceed customer expectations for quality and value, thereby benefiting all stakeholders.

Mission

Lukens will exceed customer expectations for quality, innovation and value while providing carbon and specialty steels, industrial products and services to diverse global markets. Growth, an essential element of Lukens' long-range strategies, will be accomplished through internal and external programs that are closely aligned with our strengths. Success will be measured by how effectively we achieve excellence in customer satisfaction, develop our employees, create a climate conducive to continuous improvement and provide value to our shareholders.

Values and Beliefs

1. Customer Satisfaction

Exceeding the expectations of both internal and external customers is the primary responsibility of each of us. We will strive to establish long-term partnerships with our customers for our mutual benefit. Customer-driven quality will be viewed as a competitive advantage in achieving our vision of being the preferred supplier in our industry.

2. Employee Development

We recognize that employees are the key to Lukens' success in achieving our vision. To build on that key strength, individuals will be treated with dignity and respect and provided with a safe place to work. We are committed to providing an open environment in which all employees will be involved in achieving our vision. Individual growth will be accomplished and reinforced through teamwork, training, communication and recognition.

3. Public Responsibility

We will maintain the highest standards of ethical business practices and exercise due care for the environment. We will work to improve the quality of life in the communities in which we operate.

4. Leadership

Management is primarily responsible for creating an environment conducive to continuing improvement. To create this environment and achieve our vision, management must be personally involved in planning for improvement, review of performance and recognizing employees for achievement. Lukens' management must serve as a role model to reinforce our beliefs.

5. Management by Fact

Achieving the goals of the company will require that all key business processes be managed based upon timely and reliable information. The solution of chronic problems and achievement of permanent improvement will be based on data and analyses that uncover root causes.

6. Quality by Design

Identifying, understanding and quantifying market and customer needs and expectations underlie the successful development and production of quality products and services. Key business and manufacturing capabilities will be designed to exceed customer expectations.

7. Continuous Improvement

To become a world-class competitor, all key business processes will be continuously improved using a systematic approach. While all improvement is valued, that which is strongly aligned to our strategic business plan will be promoted. Continuous improvement will focus on preventive measures taken at the earliest stages in the process.

8. Supplier Focus

We will develop mutually beneficial partnerships with suppliers who share our commitment to achieving continuous improvement in quality, value, on-time delivery and technology.

9. Shareholder Value

To be a world-class organization, Lukens must provide superior value to its shareholders. The ultimate measure of success in our efforts to exceed customer expectations, develop our employees and create a climate conducive to continuous improvement is our long-term growth in shareholder value.

M

349. Maclean Hunter Limited
777 Bay Street; Toronto, Ontario; Canada M5W 1A7
(416) 596-5000
Industry: 27, 48—Publishing and broadcasting

CORPORATE PLAN

We will stay exclusively within the communications business, primarily in North America and Europe.

All investments that fall into the normal-risk category will achieve a minimum after-tax return on net assets employed of 15%. In lower-risk investments (e.g., in most cable TV operations), a minimum after-tax return of 12% may be more appropriate.

All properties that do not measure up to the corporate plan's objectives will require approval for continuance.

We will own, if not a majority interest, at least effective control of all activities.

The Company has a target of paying 40% of the previous year's after-tax earnings in dividends.

We will manage our growth so that any new venture or acquisition will not jeopardize the future stability of the Company.

Annual Report 1991

350. Magma Copper Company
7400 North Oracle Road, Suite 200; Tuscon, AZ 85704
(602) 575-5600
Industry: 10—Copper mining

VISION STATEMENT

MAGMA will be a growing, low cost producer of copper dedicated to employee involvement and operating in accordance with our guiding principles.

MAGMA'S GUIDING PRINCIPLES

Conduct all aspects of our business with integrity and professionalism.
Commit to provide quality products and service.

Be dedicated to the health, safety and welfare of all employees.

Promote an atmosphere of trust, respect and open communication among all employees.

Encourage creativity and innovation through the development of employees.

Operate our business in an environmentally responsible manner.

Support the communities in which we are located.

Actively encourage and support the professional development and advancement within the organization of minorities and females.

Enhance long term shareholder value by earnings growth and asset appreciation.

June, 1992

Magma Metals Company
Subsidiary of Magma Copper Company

MAGMA METALS COMPANY 1992 STRATEGIC PLAN

VISION STATEMENT

"The World's Best"

MISSION STATEMENT

Magma Metals Company through its empowered, highly-productive employees, will operate a profitable, market driven, world class smelter, refinery, and rod plant, producing value-added copper products and by-products which meet all customer needs and expectations. The company will operate in a safe, environmentally responsible, and technically innovative manner.

June, 1992

Pinto Valley Mining Division
Subsidiary of Magma Copper Company

1992/93 STRATEGIC PLAN

Vision Statement

Team Pinto Valley is committed to being a long-lived profitable contributor to, and key partner in, the success of Magma Copper Company, its employees, unions and shareholders.

Mission Statement

Team Pinto Valley's vision shall be accomplished through commitment to the following:
- Fostering an environment of trust through clear and concise communication
- Actively promoting employee involvement and cooperation

- Continually refining safety, health and environmental goals
- Exploring technological advances and training opportunities
- Seeking innovative leadership that encourages creative thinking and intelligent risk taking
- Uniting customer requirements with service, quality and product development
- Setting measurable and attainable targets reviewed periodically and revised when appropriate

Through continuous improvement Pinto Valley's Team will enhance Magma Copper Company's role as a community minded, highly productive, low cost and internationally competitive world class entity.

June, 1992

Superior Mining Division
Subsidiary of Magma Copper Company

1992/1993 STRATEGIC PLAN

VISION STATEMENT

Superior is committed to being a high performance work team, environmentally responsible and dedicated to the purpose of mining profitably and safely for the benefit of all stakeholders. Total team member participation creates the cutting-edge thinking and drives the innovations that are key for our continuous improvement and success.

June, 1992

San Manuel Mining Division
Subsidiary of Magma Copper Company

MISSION STATEMENT

The San Manuel Mining Division will be a key contributor to the success of Magma Copper Company, its employees, Unions, and shareholders.

This will be achieved through the safe production of copper, utilizing a well-trained, motivated and empowered work force, the most adaptable technological improvements, and continually striving for productivity gains and cost reductions.

VISION STATEMENT

The San Manuel Mining Division will be the premier long-term copper producing operation of Magma Copper Company.

June, 1992

351. **Manitoba Hydro**
P.O. Box 815

Winnipeg, Manitoba; Canada R3C 2P4
(204) 474-3600
Industry: 49—Hydroelectric utility
The Manitoba Hydro Act states that:

"The intent, purpose and objective of this act is to provide for the continuance of a supply of power adequate for the needs of the province, and to promote economy and efficiency in the generation, distribution, supply and use of power."

Manitoba Hydro will interpret this legislative mandate within the context of contemporary values of society and will be responsive to policy direction from the Government of Manitoba.

July, 1989

352. **Manitoba Telephone System**
489 Empress Street; Winnipeg, Manitoba; Canada R3C 3V6
(204) 941-4111
Industry: 48—Telecommunications

MTS MISSION

To meet the telecommunications needs of all Manitobans with the right solutions, outstanding service, and superior products.

MTS CORPORATE GOALS

- To provide customer satisfaction
- To be financially responsible and self-sufficient
- To pursue market opportunities aggressively
- To provide equal opportunities and an environment which develops employee competence, commitment and satisfaction
- To be a good corporate citizen
- To keep the public well informed

353. **March of Dimes**
1275 Mamaroneck Avenue; White Plains, NY 10605
(914) 428-7100
Industry: 83—Non-profit Membership Organization

The mission of the March of Dimes Birth Defects Foundation is to improve the health of babies by preventing birth defects and infant mortality.

354. **Marin Community Foundation**
17 East Sir Francis Drake Boulevard, Suite 200; Larkspur,
CA 94939
(415) 461-3333
Industry: 67—Charitable foundation

Mission

Marin Community Foundation's Continuing Purpose

The Mission of the Marin Community Foundation is to help improve the human condition and to enhance the quality of life of the community, now and for generations to come.

The Foundation carries out its Mission through two sets of interrelated activities:

Program Development:

Developing and maintaining (1) Grants & Loan Programs that address essential aspects of community life; and (2) Community Programs of Technical Assistance, Community Recognition & Awards, Communications, and Service to the Philanthropic Community.

Fund Development and Management:

Encouraging and supporting the philanthropic involvement of individuals and organizations in the community through the establishment of endowments, donor-advised funds, and other vehicles.

355. Marion Merrell Dow, Inc.

9300 Ward Parkway; Kansas City, MO 64114-0480
(816) 966-4000
Industry: 28, 38—Drugs and medical devices

WHO WE ARE

Marion Merrell Dow is a global pharmaceutical organization involved in the discovery, development, manufacture and sale of prescription and over-the-counter products. Most of our sales are in the United States and seven other key markets: Canada, Japan, Italy, France, Germany, the United Kingdom and Australia/New Zealand.

OUR VISION

As reflected in the pictures of patients throughout this report, our vision is to be the best global pharmaceutical company at improving the longevity and/or quality of human life.

BUSINESS UNITS

We have three major divisions with the Pharmaceutical Industry Segment: Prescription Products, Consumer Products and International.

CORPORATE MISSION

Core Through excellence in the fulfillment of customer needs, Marion Merrell Dow will attain global market leadership in prescription and over-the-counter products.

Environment Providing our associates with a performance oriented, safe working environment that stimulates integrity, entrepreneurial spirit, productivity and a sense of social responsibility.

Science Assuring new-product continuity through innovative internal discovery research and the aggressive pursuit of external licensing, acquisition and research opportunities.

Quality Striving for continuous measurable improvement in all functions and elements of our company to provide a level of quality in our products and services that sets the standards for the industry.

Profitability Achieving a continuum of profitable growth that ranks us among the industry leaders.

Reprinted in 1989
1991 Annual Report

356. **Maritz, Inc.**
   1375 North Highway Drive; St. Louis, MO 63099
   (314) 827-4000
   Industry: 73, 87—Market research and consulting

THE MISSION OF MARITZ INC.

Maritz is a privately held company with its principal stockholders being members of the Maritz family and its Management Team. The Maritz Board of Directors consists of eight people, six of whom are from outside both the company and the Maritz family. Maritz Inc. employs 5,500 people worldwide and is headquartered in St. Louis. It is a company with strong values and a proud heritage. It has become a dominant factor in the businesses it has helped pioneer and develop. It has substantial potential for continued growth and service to its clients.

Maritz subsidiary companies in the United States, England and Canada provide: reward-based performance improvement services that help Maritz clients increase productivity and motivate their people to higher levels of achievement; marketing services; business travel; business meetings; business communications; training; and marketing research. Increasingly these services will be offered in combination to major clients. Excellent services will be developed and rendered at a fair price, but the emphasis will be always on excellence rather than on price.

Maritz people will be treated well and rewarded for achievement. In the hiring and treating of its people, Maritz will allow no discrimination based on age, sex, race, national origin or religious preference. Maritz is a people-oriented company and places consideration of its people second only to consideration of its clients.

It is a major objective of Maritz to plan and manage for consistent growth at a rate exceeding the growth of the nation's GNP. Current strategies are aimed at increasing corporate sales volume from approximately 1.2 billion dollars in the fiscal year ending March 31, 1992, to more than 2 billion dollars in the fiscal year ending March 31, 1997, with net earnings improving to between 3 and 4 percent of revenues, and a return on equity of between 25 and 30 percent annually. Maritz is financially strong and will remain so.

A major objective of Maritz Inc. is to be a good corporate citizen of the St. Louis community and other communities in which it has a major concentration of people and facilities. To that end, contribution of corporate funds, as well as the time and effort of its people, will be encouraged to pursue humanitarian, cultural, social and economic community goals.

At all times, Maritz Inc. and its people will adhere to all legal requirements and to the highest moral and ethical standards of business conduct.

Annual Report 1992
Copyright © Maritz Inc., 1992

357. **Marriott Corporation**
Marriott Drive; Washington, DC 20058
(301) 380-9000
Industry: 70—Lodging

MARRIOTT CORPORATION'S MISSION STATEMENT

We are committed to being the best lodging and management service company in the world, by treating employees in ways that create extraordinary customer service and shareholder value.

358. **Mary Kay Cosmetics, Inc.**
8787 Stemmons Freeway; Dallas, TX 75247-3713
(214) 630-8787
Industry: 28—Cosmetics and toiletries

THE MARY KAY VISION

To be preeminent in the manufacturing, distribution, and marketing of personal care products through our independent sales force.

To provide our sales force an unparalled opportunity for financial independence, career achievement, and personal fulfillment.

To achieve total customer satisfaction worldwide by focusing on quality, value, convenience, innovation, and personal service.

We Believe:

INTEGRITY and fairness guides every business decision, using the golden rule and go-give spirit as heartfelt principles.

SERVICE should be thoughtful, prompt, and proactive to provide convenience with a personal touch.

QUALITY in our products and services is of the utmost importance in delivering value and satisfaction to our customers.

ENTHUSIASM encourages a can-do, positive attitude, and provides laughter and inspiration as we work to achieve our goals.

PRAISE encourages everyone to grow and reach their full potential.

TEAMWORK enhances performance because each individual contributes to the success of the organization when he or she is needed and appreciated by others.

LEADERSHIP among our sales force and employees is encouraged and recognized because effective leaders will help us achieve long-term success.

PRIORITIES lead to balanced lives, with God, family, and career in harmony.

The lives of everyone who comes in contact with our Company—employees, sales force, customers, and vendors—should be enhanced by their association with us.

1987 and "modified several times since its inception."

359. Maxtor Corp.
211 River Oaks Parkway; San Jose, CA 95134
(408) 432-1700
Industry: 35—Disk drives

MAXTOR'S MISSION

Maxtor is dedicated to being the leading supplier of high-performance information storage products by offering the highest quality line of high-end to low-cost, high-volume products with the best customer service.

360. Mayo Foundation
200 1st Street, SW; Rochester, MN 55905
(507) 284-2511
Industry: 80—Hospitals

THE MAYO VISION

Mayo aspires to provide the best medical care—through practice, education and research, in a unified, multi-campus system.

THE MAYO PLEDGE

Mayo pledges to conduct its interdependent programs of medical care, research and education in keeping with the highest standards of ethics and quality. Fundamental to this pledge is the absolute need to combine the science and art of medicine and technology with personalized care.

Excellence in all endeavors with respect for the individual—both patient and employee—is the primary goal.

Mayo will achieve this pledge through:
- Comprehensive and compassionate care delivered through an integrated, multi-specialty group practice.
- Superior biomedical research.
- Scholarly educational programs to teach and train medical and scientific professionals for national and Mayo needs and to be a health information resource for the public.

INSTITUTIONAL PRINCIPLES

To realize the vision, and in keeping with the pledge, Mayo has as its principles:

1. To honor the commitment that "the needs of the patient come first."

2. To be local, regional, national and international in service.

3. To emphasize access for patients who may most benefit from Mayo's practice characteristics.

4. To be a unified, integrated medical system in multiple locations offering the Mayo style of group practice, research and education.

5. To recruit and train outstanding people to work as a team in an interdisciplinary setting.

6. To respect the individual contributions of each member of the Mayo family and to reaffirm the importance of "continuing interest by every member of the staff in the professional progress of every other member."

7. To promote cultural diversity and equality of opportunity within the Mayo family.

8. To serve appropriately those patients whose financial circumstances indicate that payment of normal charges would be a difficult burden.

9. To be a leader in conducting our activities in a manner which protects, conserves and reuses natural resources.

10. To consider resource allocation at Mayo within the perspective of a system rather than its individual entities.

11. To conduct our activities in a manner that permits a financial return sufficient to meet present and future requirements, both operational and capital, for its programs in practice, education and research.

12. To measure success in terms of quality and not quantity; service and not self-serving; financial security and not accumulated wealth; system in contrast to individual entity.

Mayo does **not**:

1. Aspire to grow to be the largest medical system.

2. Aspire to create geographically separate groups functioning independently.

3. Have as an objective to maximize profit—any financial surplus is viewed as a means to an end (the accomplishment of our mission), and not an end in itself.

Copyright © 1990 Mayo Foundation

MBIA

see Municipal Bond Investors Assurance Corporation (390)

McCormick, Robert R. Tribune Foundation

see The Robert R. McCormick Tribune Foundation (485)

361. **McCormick & Company, Inc.**
18 Loveton Circle; Sparks, MD 21152-6000
(410) 771-7301
Industry: 20—Spices and flavorings

MISSION

The primary mission of McCormick & Company, Incorporated is to expand its worldwide leadership position in the spice, seasoning and flavoring markets.

This means our efforts are focused on three areas:

- First: Improve the returns from each of our existing operating units—consumer, industrial, food service, international and packaging.
- Second: Dispose of those parts of our businesses which do not or cannot generate adequate returns or do not fit with our business strategy.
- Third: Make selective acquisitions which complement our current businesses and enhance our overall returns.

362. **McKesson Corporation**
One Post Street; San Francisco, CA 94104
(415) 983-8300
Industry: 50, 51—Water and pharmaceutical distribution

McKESSON A CORPORATE VISION

Over the past decade, McKesson has transformed from a broadly diversified conglomerate into a company actively focused on distribution and on providing related support services to its customers and suppliers. McKesson was founded early in the 19th Century, and as we approach the 21st Century we are firm in the belief that our future prospects are enhanced by a sharper focus on our two core businesses.

- Distributing and marketing pharmaceutical and health and beauty care products and providing related retail, hospital and managed prescription care services
- Bottling, marketing and distributing pure drinking water

In addition to these businesses, McKesson also owns a prized asset: an 83% stake in Armor All Products Corporation. McKesson will continue to provide Armor All with a foundation and framework to develop its own independent identity and to reach its full business potential.

We are committed to an aggressive program to build Armor All's long-term future as the premier worldwide distributor of automotive appearance products.

By pursuing this course, we can build value for the shareholders of both McKesson and Armor All.

In the nearly 160 years of McKesson's existence, we have owned and managed a variety of businesses deeply rooted in the U.S. consumer marketplace. From the start, a constant has been our participation in pharmaceutical and health and beauty related products distribution.

PRINCIPLES

Pharmaceutical distribution and pure drinking water, each serving essential human needs and each offering opportunity for steady growth, form the stable, balanced core of McKesson. We believe we will perform best by focusing on these two core businesses. In so doing, we will create superior products and services for our customers and suppliers, and a rewarding and challenging work environment for our employees.

We firmly subscribe to conducting all of our business activities in accordance with the highest ethical standards and in full compliance with both the letter and spirit of the law. Recognizing the critical need to maintain the highest possible quality in our products and services, we will accept no compromise in our operations that endangers human health and safety. Working in conjunction with the McKesson Foundation, we are committed to playing a constructive role in those communities where we operate and to encouraging the participation of our employees in civic and non-profit activities.

In measuring progress toward realizing our vision, we will focus not only on financial success but also on our ability to attract, develop and retain talented people. As a distributor, we appreciate the central role played by employees in providing superior customer service. We will continually rely on these employees—who collectively account for about 20% of our stock—to exercise their distinctive creativity, initiative and dedication.

As we achieve our vision, McKesson should produce superior returns for shareholders. By the second half of this decade, we expect to be positioned in the top quartile of U.S. companies, measured in terms of return on equity and growth and become established as one of the country's most admired service corporations.

Extracted from "A Corporate Vision" brochure

363. **The McKnight Foundation**
     600 TCF Tower; 121 South Eighth Street; Minneapolis, MN 55402
     (612) 333-4220
     Industry: 67—Charitable foundation

The McKnight Foundation has a primary interest in assisting people who are poor or disadvantaged by enhancing their capacity for productive living. The Foundation also seeks to strengthen community and community institutions, to enrich people's lives through the arts and to encourage preservation of the natural environment. The Foundation's primary geographic focus in its human services and arts grantmaking is the state of Minnesota.

The Foundation employs three strategies to pursue this mission: grantmaking that identifies and meets community needs in response to requests from nonprofit organizations; targeted initiatives developed by the Foundation to meet critical challenges; and support for research in selected fields.

Updated December, 1991

364. **McSwain Carpets, Inc.**
     4730 Glendale-Milford Road; Cincinnati, OH 45242
     (513) 554-1600
     Industry: 57—Carpet retail

McSwain Carpets' Statement of Purpose

The goal of McSwain Carpets is to meet the needs and expectations of all our customers by consistently providing quality products and services. Our motto is "to sell every customer more than once." As a company founded on and committed to Christian principles, we will strive to be a responsible member of our industry, as well as an outstanding corporate citizen in the communities we serve. We believe that long-term growth and financial strength will be realized by establishing a reputation for quality, service and integrity, and by maintaining an environment which encourages and rewards personal resourcefulness, dedication and contribution at all levels of the organization.

MDI
     see Alex Lee, Inc. (10)

365. **MDS Health Group Limited**
     100 International Boulevard; Etobicoke, Ontario; Canada M9W 6J6
     (416) 675-7661
     Industry: 38, 80—Medical diagnostic services

MISSION

To be a premier provider of services and products that contribute to the health and well-being of people.

GOALS

CUSTOMERS: To provide services and products which will assist physicians, health care institutions, corporations, government agencies and communities to improve the health and well-being of the people for whom they are responsible.

LEADERSHIP: To demonstrate leadership through an ongoing responsiveness to the changing needs of clients and customers and to carry on our business in conformity with the public policy principles and goals of the jurisdictions in which we operate.

PEOPLE: To maintain a climate of mutual trust which provides employee satisfaction and encourages and rewards competent, caring people to work together to achieve innovative responses to our client and customer needs.

GROWTH: To expand and improve the range of services and products that we offer to each of our customer groupings as well as expanding our customer and client base geographically.

PROFIT: To achieve a level of profitability that will provide an above average return to our shareholders, will allow us to compensate our employees justly and attract financial resources to fund our growth.

THE VALUES OF MDS

Flowing from this corporate perspective are certain values that every employee can identify with, acknowledging that personal commitment to these values has a positive influence on the company as a whole. These values are:

QUALITY—doing the right things the right way;

COMPETENCE—having the appropriate attitudes and abilities;

CARING—showing genuine concern for others;

RESPECT FOR THE INDIVIDUAL—treating people as individuals, with the same understanding and appreciation we seek for ourselves;

MUTUAL TRUST AND OPENNESS—having confidence enough to rely on others and to be open to new and different people and ideas;

INTEGRITY—being reliable and accountable in word and behavior;

TEAMWORK—accepting a "hierarchy of roles with equality of persons" willing to work together as "we";

COMMUNICATION—listening is the key;

BALANCE—keeping home and work in perspective, recognizing that one helps the other;

SIMPLICITY—maintaining humility, humor, and a common-sense approach to work and life.

Fundamentally, these values are based on the premise that if a job has to be carried out in MDS, then the individual who fills that job has a unique contribution to make. That unique contribution should be encouraged and the individual should be listened to with respect.

What is expected of all individuals can be summarized as **Competence and Mutual Trust.**

Extracted from "Perspective: Who We Are & What We Believe" booklet

366. **MDU Resources Group, Inc.**
       400 North Fourth Street; Bismarck, ND 58501
       (701) 222-7900
       Industry: 12, 13, 49—Coal and oil exploration, electric utility

CORPORATE MISSION STATEMENT

MDU is a diversified natural resource company. The company is engaged in exploration, development, production, transportation, conversion, distribution, and customer utilization of various forms of energy.

Through creative and reasoned management, and with due regard for the land and the environment, the company intends to continue the development of natural resources in the Northern Great Plains region, principally natural gas, oil and low sulfur coal, allowing for flexibility and diversity as additional opportunities arise.

Continued growth and maintenance of present markets will be achieved in a variety of ways, including:

- Wholesale and retail sales of natural gas and electricity
- Surface mining of coal and marketing to customers, including the company
- Participation in oil and natural gas acquisition, exploration and development programs
- Participation in alternative energy sources
- Encouragement of commercial, industrial and cultural development in the company's service territory

The enhancement of corporate growth will be achieved through the acquisition or development of businesses that provide reasonable profit opportunity through the extension of selected historic operating strengths. Expansion will be accomplished through the pursuit of regional opportunities in existing or closely related businesses and through the pursuit of national opportunities in similar industries.

The company will emphasize its long-held commitment to the environment while providing customers with reliable and cost-effective energy services commensurate with a reasonable and timely return to its investors. In the management of its business, the company will provide opportunities for the personal and professional growth and development of its employees.

Mission statement for 1992, which is reviewed annually

367. **Mead Corporation**
10 West Second Street; Dayton, OH 45463
(513) 222-6223
Industry: 24, 26, 27, 50, 51—Paper and lumber

OUR MISSION

OUR GOAL

At Mead, our growth and success as a business enterprise depend on how well we satisfy our customers. Therefore, our goal is: To be number one in customer satisfaction in the markets we choose to serve.

OPERATING PRINCIPLES

IN ACHIEVING OUR GOAL, WE WILL:

- interact with our customers to understand their requirements and provide superior value by meeting or exceeding these expectations;
- value the contributions of all employees and provide an environment in which each of us can contribute to the full extent of our talents and aspirations;
- act, at every level in our company, to generate superior returns to share owners over the long term;
- treat our suppliers as essential contributors to our success;
- serve the communities in which we operate by performing successfully as a business enterprise and by being a responsible citizen.

At all times, our conduct will be guided by the ethical standards expressed by George H. Mead: "It is only by dealing honestly and fairly in all things that real success is attainable."

ABOUT OUR GOAL

"At Mead, our growth and success as a business enterprise depend on how well we satisfy our customers. Therefore, our goal is: to be number one in customer satisfaction in the markets we choose to serve."

We believe satisfied customers will determine how large we become, how fast we grow and how successful we become as a business. That's why our goal is to be number in satisfying customers. Mead's goal is based on the belief that if we are number one in customer satisfaction, everything important will follow. Employees will find reward and fulfillment in their work. Our share owners will receive a superior return on their investment. Suppliers will share our success. Our communities will benefit.

Being number one in customer satisfaction requires that we do what we do best and that we do it consistently. It requires that we choose our markets carefully. We must focus our energies on customers with whom our resources and experience give us the best chance for success.

Being number one involves more than **becoming** number one. It requires that we reach the top, and **stay** there. To achieve this we must strive for continuous improvement and must measure our performance over time against our competition.

We will have achieved our goal when we are consistently number one in the eyes of our customers.

ABOUT OUR OPERATING PRINCIPLES:

"Interact with our customers to understand their requirements and provide superior value by meeting or exceeding these expectations."

The ultimate purpose of each of our jobs is to serve Mead's customers. Usually we serve customers directly. Sometimes we serve them indirectly by providing support to fellow employees. The secret to becoming number one is to understand customers' needs as they define them and commit ourselves to meet or exceed their expectations.

Customer needs constantly change and, as confidence in our performance grows, customer expectations become more demanding. Therefore, meeting customer needs requires a never-ending push for higher levels of performance.

"Value the contributions of all employees and provide an environment in which each of us can contribute to the full extent of our talents and aspirations."

Every employee has a role to play in our ability to meet or exceed customer expectations. In fact, Mead's corporate goal is meaningless unless it becomes the personal belief of every employee—a personal belief that directs our daily performance in every job.

Mead is committed to helping all employees develop and participate to their full potential.

"Act, at every level in our company, to generate superior returns to share owners over the long term."

Superior returns are not the **goal** of our daily effort, they are the **result** of it. By consistently meeting or exceeding customer needs, we will create the success that assures a superior return to share owners over the long term.

"Treat our suppliers as essential contributors to our success."

Suppliers are an essential resource in our effort to meet and exceed customer expectations. We need to treat them as teammates whose success is tied inseparably to our own.

"Serve the communities in which we operate by performing successfully as a business enterprise and by being a responsible citizen."

Mead's success in being number one with customers is closely linked with the strength, vitality, and support of the communities in which we operate. Helping assure that our communities are good places to live and work is a strong tradition at Mead.

Being a responsible citizen also means operating safely and in ways in which we are sensitive to the environment.

"At all times, our conduct will be guided by the ethical standards expressed by George H. Mead: 'It is only by dealing honestly and fairly in all things that real success is attainable.'"

Personal integrity is deeply rooted in Mead's culture. Being number one in the eyes of our customers is a position of **trust**. Trust is not easily won. It is earned over time by behaving ethically and fairly in everything we do.

1990
Reproduced with the permission of Mead Corporation

368. **Medica**
Physicians Health Plan of Minnesota
5601 Smetna Drive; Hopkins, MN 55343
(612) 936-1200
Industry: 63—Health insurance plan

Mission Statement

Our Mission is to be the leader in improving the quality, affordability and accessibility of health care.

369. **Medtronic, Inc.**
7000 Central Avenue, NE; Minneapolis, MN 55432
(612) 574-4000
Industry: 38—Medical equipment

Mission

- To contribute to human welfare by application of biomedical engineering research, design, manufacture, and sale of instruments or appliances that alleviate pain, restore health, and extend life.
- To direct our growth in the areas of biomedical engineering where we display maximum strength and ability; to gather people and facilities that tend to augment these areas; to continuously build on these areas

through education and knowledge assimilation; to avoid participation in areas where we cannot make unique and worthy contributions.

- To strive without reserve for the greatest possible reliability and quality in our products; to be the unsurpassed standard of comparison and to be recognized as a company of dedication, honesty, integrity, and service.

- To make a fair profit on current operations to meet our obligations, sustain our growth, and reach our goals.

- To recognize the personal worth of employees by providing an employment framework that allows personal satisfaction in work accomplished, security, advancement opportunity, and means to share in the company's success.

- To maintain good citizenship as a company.

1960

Copyright © Medtronic, Inc. 1992

Merchants Distributors, Inc.

see Alex Lee, Inc. (10)

370. **Merck & Co., Inc.**

P.O. Box 2000; Rahway, NJ 07065

(908) 594-4000

Industry: 28—Pharmaceuticals

Merck's corporate purpose is to provide society with superior products—innovations that produce health and well-being—and to ensure investors a superior rate of return, while also providing Merck people with superior employment and advancement opportunities.

Reproduced with permission of Merck & Co., Inc.

371. **Merrill Lynch & Co., Inc.**

World Financial Center, South Tower; New York, NY 10080

(212) 449-1000

Industry: 62—Securities brokerage

Mission Statement

Our mission is to be a client-focused, worldwide financial services organization, striving for excellence by serving the needs of individuals, corporations, governments and institutions. Our objective is be the acknowledged leader in the value we offer our clients, the returns we offer our shareholders and the rewards we offer our employees.

Realizing Our Mission

In realizing our mission we will be guided by our vision of the future, a focus on our clients and markets, the need for a highly skilled and motivated organizational team, and a commitment to profitability and sound financial management.

Our Vision of the Future

We envision a new financial services world—one of great challenge and equally great opportunity. It will be an era of dynamic change characterized by the globalization of financial markets, instantaneous communication and intense competition. The prospect for growth in our markets is excellent, driven by ever more sophisticated and complex needs of our clients.

More that ever before, ours is becoming a business of risk management. Our ability to take prudent risk, to manage it and turn it to our clients' and Firm's advantage is fundamental to achieving our mission.

Clients and Markets

Our strategies begin and end with our clients. Our progress will be measured by how well we earn the loyalty necessary for long-time client relationships. These relationships provide the foundation for the Firm's success. We will win client loyalty by providing value-added products and services, differentiated by unique expertise and responsiveness.

Success will require new skills and agility to respond competitively to the rapidly changing needs of our clients. We must seek out the most talented people and the newest and most resourceful ideas. We will combine entrepreneurial perspective, technology and discipline in order to focus our resources creatively and efficiently in diverse markets worldwide.

We will compete globally from our investment base in consumer and capital markets. We will focus only on those businesses where we can achieve a leading market position and superior profitability.

Our consumer markets businesses will concentrate on serving the integrated financial service needs of the affluent and very affluent individuals, small businesses, and small institutions, primarily in the United States. Our capital markets businesses will provide financing, advisory and investment services to large corporations, institutions and governments on a worldwide basis.

Organization and Values

Merrill Lynch will organize its separate operations in ways that better enable us to anticipate and respond to changing client needs. Authority and accountability will be placed at levels which allow our professionals to make the best decisions on behalf of our clients and our Firm.

We are "One Firm" with a number of separate but related operations. This enables us to leverage our resources and positions in different markets worldwide in response to specific client needs. The integrating philosophy of our diverse businesses is reflected in shared values and in our approach to managing our people, capital and corporate reputation.

As a Firm we share a powerful sense of identity. We are dedicated to the values on which this identity was built—a winning spirit and a standard of excellence in all that we do. We value integrity, leadership, the entrepreneurial spirit, and hard work. We value the individual.

At the same time, ours is an increasingly complex and competitive world, often requiring multiple perspectives and cooperation among our people. Teamwork is critical. This sharing of knowledge and skills is the common thread that binds our people together in response to specific client needs.

Financial

We are a strategically focused organization. We manage through objectives, guided by formal management systems which measure performance and promote productive use of our resources. The success or failure of our strategy will be measured by the creation of value for our stockholders.

We recognize that, in the long term, only the most efficient organizations will survive, let alone prevail, in an intensely competitive environment. We must rigorously control our costs, improve our productivity—and measure our progress in terms of profit, not volume.

We believe that the Firm's future depends on maintaining sound financial controls, a well-managed and growing capital base, and earnings stability in the face of volatile markets. This, in turn, will protect the Firm's crucial reputation for financial strength.

Merrill Lynch has a solid foundation for accomplishing its mission. The Firm's significant resources, most importantly our people, represent the critical building blocks. We have a strong market position in both consumer and capital markets worldwide and a long-standing reputation for competitive spirit with the courage and understanding to manage risk. This will enable us to successfully build on Merrill Lynch's legacy of leadership in the value we offer our clients, the returns we offer our shareholders and the rewards we offer our employees.

1990
Used courtesy of Merrill Lynch & Co., Inc.

372. **Methodist Hospital of Indiana, Inc.**
1701 North Senate Boulevard; Indianapolis, IN 46206
(317) 924-6411
Industry: 80—Hospital

OUR MISSION/OUR VISION

"A vision without a task is but a dream, a task without a vision is but drudgery, a vision with a task is the hope of the world" (Observed in 1730 on a church wall in Sussex, England.)

As a witness to the love of God as revealed in the spirit and social principles of the United Methodist church, this institution is dedicated to the enhancement of health, dignity, and spirit of those we serve. Therefore, we commit to four basic values:

COMPASSION IN CARE

By listening sensitively to patients and their families and shaping services accordingly.

By meeting patient needs in the areas of diagnosis and treatment and by restoring patients to a maximum level of functioning.

By maintaining a view of health that encompasses body, mind, spirit, and a high level of wellness.

By caring for employees, caregivers, and volunteers with compassion and concern.

By confronting moral and ethical dilemmas and by providing positive support to staff, patients, and families in making difficult medical decisions.

SERVICE TO COMMUNITY

By providing one level of service for all patients.

By continuing access for all persons critically ill or in need of immediate attention.

By collaborating with public health organizations to develop and provide health services to economically disadvantaged persons from the inner city.

By increasing community awareness of health risks and by helping families adopt and maintain health-producing lifestyles.

By expanding medical care to include psycho-social and educational components of service, where appropriate.

EXCELLENCE OF SERVICE

By delivering to patients the the highest levels of health care in a cost-effective manner, to the satisfaction of both patients and buyers of services.

By developing an environment that fosters teamwork.

By attracting and retaining exceptional staff members and providing them with the necessary tools and support for greater effectiveness.

By providing broad-based, advanced diagnostic and therapeutic technology.

By offering a full range of services to the culturally and economically diverse population of central Indiana.

By encouraging inter-specialty and physician/hospital associations and partnerships that enhance and extend services.

By developing multi-institutional affiliations that will enhance services, education, and research.

INNOVATION IN SERVICE, EDUCATION, AND RESEARCH

By continuing our tradition of innovation in health care, research, education, and hospital management.

By providing a broad range of graduate medical opportunities and continuing medical education programs for physicians.

By offering educational opportunities for all employees, clergy, and volunteers.

By conducting clinical research that will advance technological services and that will result in cost effectiveness.

By committing to these basic values and by faithfully following the inherent moral and ethical principles, we serve a cause that is greater than ourselves.

Approved December 21, 1989

373. **Methodist Hospital System**
     5615 Kirby Drive; Houston, TX 77005
     (713) 831-2930
     Industry: 80—Hospital

Statement of Values

Our paramount commitment is to our patients. We are dedicated to providing the finest medical care in the world and being the best service organization anywhere. We will offer the foremost technology and facilities, enhanced by healing skill, a sense of compassion, and an abiding respect for human dignity.

We are further committed to providing leadership. We will maintain our emphasis on education and clinical research so that we contribute to the knowledge and well-being of humankind. We will conduct our business affairs according to the highest ethical principles, making decisions fairly and honestly, so that we set a standard for all. We strive for excellence— delivering the highest value and the finest health care at a reasonable cost.

In all that we do, we will not forget that people are the means and ends of endeavors. We will continue the effective working relationships among our physicians, volunteers, and employees. We will preserve our connection with the United Methodist Church, whose traditional concern for serving God through servicing individuals remains the steadfast framework for our actions.

By honoring our commitments, principles, and values, we will achieve a larger purpose: making a difference, and serving a cause that is greater than ourselves.

374. **Metropolitan Financial Corporation**
6800 France Avenue South, Suite 600; Minneapolis, MN 55435
(612) 928-5014
Industry: 60—Savings and loan

MISSION STATEMENT

Metropolitan Financial Corporation will be the Heartland's premier provider of consumer financial and home ownership services by offering exceptional value to targeted customers, resulting in profitable growth, fulfilling careers and community enhancement.

What Our Mission Means

METROPOLITAN FINANCIAL CORPORATION WILL BE THE HEARTLAND'S PREMIER PROVIDER . . .

Quite simply, everything we do, from answering the phone to recommending financial services and home ownership solutions to our customers, is done with unwavering excellence. After all, it's not just *what* we do that counts to our customers, but *how* we do it. It's the *how* that can make the difference between an ordinary customer transaction and developing a *lasting customer relationship*.

This phrase speaks of *one organization* in America's Heartland. While MFC is made up of separate business units, our goal is to share the values of one company, united in its vision. This will enable us to leverage the strengths of a strategically-unified business while operating decentralized, flexible business units.

. . . OF CONSUMER FINANCIAL AND HOME OWNERSHIP SERVICES . . .

Our products and services include, but are not limited, to:
- consumer savings and investment products;
- checking accounts;
- consumer loans;
- residential mortgages;
- real estate and title services.

. . . BY OFFERING SUPERIOR VALUE TO TARGETED CUSTOMERS, . . .

Our goal is to listen to each customer and improve their lives by helping people attain their financial and home ownership goals. We will focus on those markets and customers who represent the greatest potential for growth, profit, and appreciation for the value we offer.

We will cater to those customers who rely and depend on:
- Convenience
- Swift and dependable service
- "Win/win" problem resolution
- Competitive price/value relationship

Our success in achieving these results will permit MFC to differentiate itself from competitors and to attract and keep profitable customers.

We will design every aspect of MFC to meet or exceed the expressed needs of prospects and customers in our target markets. This has three dimensions:

- *First, our employees will be customer-responsive.* Each of us adds value to customers, either by serving them directly, or by supporting others in the company who do. Every employee will help to identify and satisfy the needs of customers; improve communications inside MFC and outside; and continuously help to improve the effectiveness with which the company satisfies our customers' needs.

- *Second, corporate and local management will identify and commit to market segments we can best serve.* We will identify, through formal and informal means, the needs of each market segment. We will stay close to the customer. We will devote management, marketing, sales, service, and operating resources toward those organizational activities that will *add value* to customers in those market segments.

- Third, we will consciously research, develop, implement, and monitor all internal processes and procedures that allow us to *become more efficient* at delivering value to our customers. This process of continuous improvement in our work processes will maximize employee involvement and take place at the individual, departmental, local, company and corporate levels. To accomplish this, we will devote training and development resources to educate employees on the principles and practices of continuous improvement. We will foster a culture that encourages creativity, risk taking, innovation, and challenging the status quo. We will involve customers in our quality process and reward real, measurable quality improvements as defined by the customer.

We need this market differentiation and must work hard to develop and maintain it. Many segments of the consumer market have a commodity mentality when it comes to choosing a banking relationship. It will be a continual challenge for all of us to sell *value*, not price. It is a challenge we greet enthusiastically.

. . . RESULTING IN PROFITABLE GROWTH, . . .

MFC is committed to long-term growth, which will, from time to time, require us to take measured risks. Our financial goals include performance in several key areas:

- Asset growth
- Capital growth
- Net income growth
- Shareholder value
- Return on equity

Our profit margins must be strong enough to generate the cash flow needed to sustain our growth goals, provide dividends and capital appreciation to our shareholders, and maintain access to the capital markets. Our drive to increase our market share and customer base will be managed, so that existing customers are never compromised as a result of our strong desire to find new customers.

To help assure this, MFC will carefully manage our customer relationships, monitor all costs, and consistently achieve our profitability goals. Our financial strength will provide us with the needed resources to fund our growth, reward deserving employees, provide an attractive return to shareholders and support the communities we serve.

Finally, corporate and business unit plans will be developed in a participatory manner. This will assure that all managers agree with the corporate direction, have a *vested interest* in its success and work together as a unified team toward a common end.

. . . FULFILLING CAREERS . . .

All employees will have the opportunity to develop personally and professionally in a results-oriented and supportive business environment. This will include:

- Fair and competitive compensation
- Recognition for extraordinary achievements
- Opportunity to meet challenging performance standards and truly make a difference as part of a winning team
- Maximum personal growth and the opportunity to feel good about what we do

Through a shared vision, MFC will establish long-term relationships with employees. We will:

- Consistently challenge ourselves and each other to meet and exceed personal and company goals
- Actively listen to each other and encourage a sense of partnership
- Involve everyone in the process of identifying and implementing improvements resulting in maximum value for our customers

- Provide the coaching, training, resources, and tools for each employee to reach their maximum potential
- Reward excellent performance
- Recruit and retain people who will help us fulfill our mission

Together, we will set the standards for our industry and ourselves.

... AND COMMUNITY ENHANCEMENT.

We believe that we must invest financial resources and our individual time to help foster the advancement of our communities. Our financial success and our personal commitment will enable us to make a substantial contribution to the communities we serve. MFC will be held out as an excellent example of a corporation that is concerned about, involved in and committed to the future of our communities.

375. **Metters Industries, Inc.**
      8200 Greensboro Drive, Suite 500; McLean, VA 22102
      (703) 821-3300
      Industry: 73—Computer systems

VISION

Metters Industries in the year 2002 will be a $100 million company that provides diverse products and services to a worldwide market. The Company will accomplish this through the efforts of its highly motivated and well-trained workforce, and by capitalizing on mutually beneficial alliances and partnerships with complementary organizations. Dedication to the highest integrity and principles will allow the Company to enjoy not only consistent long-term profitability but also a reputation as a contributor to human advancement.

MISSION

Our mission is to become a world-class provider of high quality engineering and software products and services. We will distinguish ourselves by focusing on specific lines of business for which we have undisputed competency and an uncommon understanding of our customers' needs and requirements.

September 21, 1992

376. **Michigan Consolidated Gas Company**
      MichCon Gas Company
      500 Griswold Street; Detroit, MI 48226
      (313) 256-5500
      Industry: 49—Gas utility

OUR VISION STATEMENT . . .

The Vision Statement presented here is the result of 262 challenge sessions conducted throughout the company. It is not possible to say precisely how many employees participated in challenge sessions, but we estimate that no less than 75 percent of the MichCon team—approximately 2,600 employees—took part.

In reviewing the many comments made and changes suggested, some were found to be contradictory of others. Some mirrored the concerns expressed by senior management when the original Vision Statement was drafted and, in fact, reinforced it. Still others led to the creation of two new value statements. This brochure attempts to explain the rationale for the changes, which appear in bold type.

1. "We, the employees of MichCon, acknowledge our unique responsibility in providing **services** critical to the quality of life in the communities we serve."

Reasoning: "Services" reflects challenge session concerns that MichCon provides more than natural gas service.

Other suggestions:

- Add ". . . providing *quality* services": Many employees recognized the importance of quality. It was determined that this could be covered more thoroughly in a new value statement.

- Delete "acknowledge" and "unique": Most employees, however, agreed that "acknowledge" represents a thoughtful commitment and that our services are truly different from virtually all other businesses.

- Delete "critical to the quality of life": Employees expressed concern about this statement because customer shutoffs seem contradictory. It was retained because most employees felt even shutoffs were essential for MichCon to provide safe services and maintain financial health in order to serve others.

2. "Therefore, we are dedicated to being a premier organization, **and the best natural gas company**, by continuously improving value to our customers and shareholders."

Reasoning: "Distribution" was deleted from the draft because employees expressed concern that it seemed to limit the statement.

Other suggestions:

Add ". . . improving value to our customers, shareholders and employees": The change was not made because, first and foremost, this is a statement from each of us as an employee. It's not necessary to list us here. Also, 3,259 employees—more than 93 percent of the work force—already are shareholders through participation in various employee benefit plans. Employees own about 2 million shares of MCN Corporation common stock.

3. "Our actions are guided by the following principles:"

Unchanged.

Reasoning: There was broad agreement that "principles" implies a sense of integrity and "guided" indicates we make careful, conscious decisions.

4. "We respect **diversity** and the value of **each** individual."

Reasoning: "Diversity" better captures employees' views of this principle, and "each," as employees said, strengthens the sense of individualism.

5. "**How** we achieve results is as important as the results themselves."

Reasoning: Employees said the emphasis needed to be on the word "how," so the words "we believe," which were not seen as strong enough, were deleted.

6. "We take personal responsibility for our actions **and pride in making a difference.**"

Reasoning: The draft stated, "We take personal responsibility for our contributions and our actions," but employees expressed confusion about the difference between actions and contributions. The change better links responsibility and actions. Also, the term "pride in making a difference" has a down-to-earth appeal and makes a strong statement that we take pride in making a contribution in whatever way we can to the success of MichCon.

7. "We work together as a team committed to open, **candid** communication and mutual support."

Reasoning: Numerous challenge session statements and the employee survey results indicated that communication was a source of deep concern. Statements indicated that information was perceived as power, with individuals reluctant to share that source of power. Statements also indicated that individuals feared being open because their comments might be used against them.

The term "candid" was added to round out the principle. Webster's Ninth New Collegiate Dictionary defines "candid" as: "free from bias, prejudice or malice; indicating or suggesting sincere honesty and absence of deception."

8. "**Our safety and that of our customers and the general public will not be compromised.**"

Reasoning: Completely new, this replaces "We provide safe and reliable service." Employees said the draft principle did not adequately address safety. Challenge session comments also indicated that the terms "provide" and "reliable" were too passive. The new statements puts teeth in our commitment to safety.

9. "**Our successes will be measured by our ability to exceed internal and external customer expectations.**"

Reasoning: Also completely new, this indicates "quality" is achieved when a job performed or service provided surpasses customer expectations. It was developed in response to challenge session inquiries about quality and how it would be measured. It also focuses on our need to improve both **internal** and **external** service.

10. "We act with **honesty** and integrity."

Reasoning: Originally drafted as "we act with uncompromising integrity," most employees felt that "uncompromising" was different for each person. Instead, employees suggested the addition of "honesty," which Webster's defines as "fairness and straightforwardness of conduct" and "implies a refusal to lie, steal or deceive in any way."

11. "We protect **the environment and improve the quality of life** where we **work** and **live.**"

Reasoning: Employees said we could "protect" the natural environment, but not always "improve" it. In addition, employees recommended switching the order of "live" and "work" to put the emphasis on MichCon's business concerns. As revised, the statement acknowledges the traditional meaning of "environment," but also recognizes a broader interpretation when addressing the "quality of life" that we strive to improve.

12. "We are committed to being innovative and creative in our jobs."

Unchanged. No clear consensus regarding any changes emerged from the challenge sessions.

Vision Statement

We, the employees of MichCon, acknowledge our unique responsibility in providing services critical to the quality of life in the communities we serve.

Therefore, we are dedicated to being a premier organization, and the best natural gas company, by continuously improving value to our customers and shareholders.

Our actions are guided by the following principles:

We respect diversity and the value of each individual.

How we achieve results is as important as the results themselves.

We take personal responsibility for our actions and pride in making a difference.

We work together as a team committed to open, candid communication and mutual support.

Our safety and that of our customers and the general public will not be compromised.

Our successes are measured by our ability to exceed internal and external customer expectations.

We act with honesty and integrity.

We protect the environment and improve the quality of life where we work and live.

We are committed to being innovative and creative in our jobs.

377. Mid-American Waste Systems, Inc.
1006 Walnut Street; Canal Winchester, OH 43110
(614) 833-9155
Industry: 49—Solid waste disposal
Mission Statement

Mid-American Waste Systems, Inc. is a nonhazardous solid waste company with integrated operations in selected markets throughout the United States and an ongoing plan for prudent growth, through internal market expansion, profitable acquisitions and public/private partnerships. Our goal is to increase shareholder value by using sound management principles and maintaining the integrity of the environment.

Annual Report 1990

378. Minnkota Power Cooperative, Inc.
P.O. Box 1318; Grand Forks, ND 58206-1318
(701) 795-4000
Industry: 49—Electric cooperative

MISSION STATEMENT

The mission of Minnkota is to assist the associated systems in improving the quality of life of their consumers by continuously improving the value of electric energy to the consumer.

Drafted 1992

Mitchell, David & Associates, Inc.
see David Mitchell & Associates, Inc. (177)

379. Modern Technologies Corp.
4032 Lincoln Avenue; Dayton, OH 45432
(513) 252-9199
Industry: 73—Software

Vision Statement

Our vision is to become recognized for Centers of Excellence, to be the customer's firm of choice providing highest quality technical services and manufactured products, and to achieve continuous improvement through the professional growth and active involvement of all our people.

380. Modular Casework Systems Inc.
377 Kansas Street; Redlands, CA 92373

(714) 793-2706

Industry: 25—Furniture

MISSION STATEMENT

To be recognized as a premier world class manufacturer of laminated cabinetry for institutional markets, and to achieve a level of service to our customers that is above and beyond their expectations.

1992

381. **Mohawk Oil Canada Limited**

6400 Roberts Street #325; Burnaby, British Columbia; Canada V5G 4G2

(604) 299-7244

Industry: 13—Petroleum

Our mission is to serve our customers and to provide a return to shareholders by offering high quality products and related services while leading in renewable, sustainable and environmentally responsible energy alternatives.

382. **Molson Companies Limited**

Scotia Plaza; 40 King Street West, Suite 3600; Toronto, Ontario; Canada M5H 3Z5

(416) 360-1786

Industry: 20—Food and beverages

OUR CORPORATE PHILOSOPHY

We shall respect and honour Molson history and tradition and work to preserve and enhance our unique heritage of two centuries of business success and community contribution.

We shall provide our employees with an environment of equal opportunity for personal growth.

We shall respect and abide by the laws and conventions of the societies in which we conduct business.

We shall be respected for our success, and for the quality and integrity of:

- our products and services
- our principles and actions
- our participation in the community
- our people

We will be the best in everything we undertake to do.

383. **Monenco AGRA Inc.**

Subsidiary of AGRA Industries Ltd.

2010 Winston Park Drive, Suite 100; Oakville, Ontario; Canada
L6H 6A3
(416) 829-5400
Industry: 73, 87—Software and engineering services

Corporate Mission Statement

To be an acknowledged world leader in technology fields related to:
- Engineering,
- Construction,
- Project Development and Management,
- Computer-based Information Systems, and
- Environment.

We provide quality work in all our operations to ensure client satisfaction. Central to our efforts is a challenging, rewarding workplace for all employees, an attractive return for our shareholders and responsible corporate citizenship.

November 9, 1992

see also AGRA Industries Limited (5)

384.   Organization requested entry be withdrawn at press time.

385.   **Moon Lake Electric Association, Inc.**
P.O. Box 278; Roosevelt, UT 84066-0278
(801) 722-2448
Industry: 49—Electric cooperative

CORPORATE MISSION

To provide reliable electric service to all who desire it within the system's service area at the lowest price consistent with the highest standards of service.

386.   **Mosler Inc.**
1561 Grand Boulevard; Hamilton, OH 45012
(513) 867-4000
Industry: 34—Fabricated metal products

MOSLER BUSINESS PHILOSOPHY & CODE OF ETHICS

Since 1867, we have dedicated ourselves to excellence, and serving our customers faithfully, efficiently, honestly, and competently. We anticipate future prosperity through continued dedication to these practices and acting on the beliefs and business principles below.

OUR PURPOSE

At Mosler, our primary purpose is customer satisfaction by providing useful, high-quality products, systems, and services at an adequate profit.

OUR BUSINESS

Providing security to a worldwide market is our base business. Financial institutions will continue to be our primary market. Other important markets are government, commercial businesses, and third party service. Our growth will be in security and closely related technologies and markets.

We will be aggressive in competing to expand our business, but will on no occasion resort to unethical practices to achieve that objective. We shall require our suppliers to provide quality goods and services and will extend to them the same treatment which we wish to receive ourselves. We shall conduct our business in conformity with all federal and local laws to the best of our ability.

OUR PEOPLE

We seek to employ high-quality, self-motivated people, and will tolerate no dishonest or immoral conduct in business matters on the part of anyone we employ. We strive for a professional, participative atmosphere which offers opportunities for our people based on individual creativity and performance. We shall deal with our employees fairly and with full respect for the dignity of the individual in all matters of personal treatment.

OUR OWNERSHIP

The primary assets of Mosler are the education, training, experience and ability of our employees. We believe the rewards of those assets should flow to all employees. We have chosen an Employee Stock Ownership Plan (ESOP) and pension plans to assure this flow. We believe this form of ownership provides the highest degree of quality, productivity, and service.

OUR CITIZENSHIP

As individuals and as a firm, we believe in good personal and corporate citizenship. We endeavor to enhance the quality of life through our professional work and public service. We will actively support our community, our government, and our educational system.

387 Moto Photo, Inc.
4444 Lake Center Drive; Dayton, OH 45426
(513) 854-6686
Industry: 73—Photofinishing laboratories

MISSION STATEMENT

Moto Photo aspires to be the leading specialty retailer of high quality imaging services in North America and selected international markets. The company will market its services through franchised and company-owned stores serving both the consumer and commercial markets.

In the consumer segment, Moto Photo is dedicated to enhancing its customers' enjoyment of their photographic/imaging experience and in the commercial segment, to increasing its customers' imaging communication capabilities.

Moto Photo will achieve its mission by building an organization committed to superior performance within an open, caring, and participative business culture that promotes the growth of all its associates.

388. **Motorola Inc.**
    1303 East Algonquin Road; Schaumburg, IL 60196-1065
    (708) 576-5000
    Industry: 36—Electronic equipment

CORPORATE MISSION STATEMENT

In each of our chosen arenas of the electronics industry, we plan to grow rapidly by providing our worldwide customers what they want, when they want it, with Six Sigma quality and best-in-class cycle time, as we strive to achieve our fundamental corporate objective of Total Customer Satisfaction, and to achieve our stated goals of increased global market share, best-in-class people, products, marketing, manufacturing, technology and service, and superior financial results.

MTS
    see Manitoba Telephone System (352)

389. **Multimedia, Inc.**
    P.O. Box 1688; Greenville, SC 29602
    (803) 298-4373
    Industry: 27, 48—Publishing and broadcasting

Multimedia's mission is to grow and prosper as a corporate organization by:
- Maximizing shareholder value by managing and growing our current businesses most effectively and by capitalizing on new investment opportunities
- Producing and distributing the best news, information and entertainment products for our consumers
- Being the preferred media supplier for our advertising customers
- Providing a workplace where the contributions of our employees are recognized and rewarded to their maximum capabilities

390. **Municipal Bond Investors Assurance Corporation**
    113 King Street; Armonk, NY 10504
    (914) 273-4545
    Industry: 63—Municipal bond insurance

MBIA Mission Statement

Our goal is to be the best and most respected provider of products and services which enhance the efficiency of public finance while selectively expanding our credit enhancement products to other financial obligations.

Our Business—We will make what we do best—enhancing the efficiency of public finance—our blueprint for a successful future. We will continue to build this strong viable business while prudently expanding into new areas where we are able to utilize our existing skills or better serve the changing needs of our traditional customer base.

Our Bondholders—We will provide our securities' holders with a guarantee of unquestioned strength. We will do this by maintaining the most stringent underwriting standards in the industry, by providing the most comprehensive surveillance of our insured credits and by maintaining the financial strength necessary to comfortably meet all of our commitments.

Our Customers—We will provide our customers with innovative value-added solutions and a level of service that is second-to-none.

Our Shareholders—We will achieve strong, sustainable and predictable growth in earnings and in the value of our Company.

Our Employees—We will set high expectations for ourselves and for our business. We will strive to build a culture that is open and treats all fairly. We will create an environment which encourages individual decision-making and working together as a team in the interest of serving our clients and shareholders. We will give of our time, skills and capital to make our community a better place for us all to live and work.

N

391. Nalco Chemical Company
One Nalco Center; Naperville, IL 60563
(708) 305-1000
Industry: 28—Specialty chemicals

Philosophy of Operation

Nalco seeks to find customer needs and fill them through the application of specialty chemicals and technology. We enhance the profitability of our customers' business by providing products and services that add value to their operations and provide them an acceptable return on their investment.

Every Nalco employee is expected to do his or her part to help our quality process achieve continuous improvement and greater customer satisfaction.

In doing so, we intend to make a reasonable profit in an ethical manner so that we can reward our shareholders and employees, invest in our future and enrich or improve life in the communities in which we operate. We strive for leadership and continuous growth in serving industry worldwide through practical applied science.

We intend to produce and sell only those chemicals that can be manufactured, distributed, used and disposed of in a safe manner. We will conduct our operations worldwide in compliance with all applicable laws and regulations; we will make environmental health and safety considerations a priority in order to keep risks at the lowest reasonable level.

No employee shall engage in conduct which results in a conflict of his or her personal interest with that of the company or which reflects unfavorably on the integrity of the company.

All employees are expected to treat one another, suppliers and neighbors within our facility communities with respect. It is our policy that all employees should be able to enjoy a work environment free from all forms of discrimination. In the same fashion, anyone who comes in contact with Nalco should receive the same consideration and fair treatment as though that person were a Nalco employee.

392. **Nash Finch Company**
P.O. Box 355; Minneapolis, MN 55440-0355
(612) 929-0371
Industry: 51—Food wholesaler

NASH FINCH IS . . .

For more than a century, Nash Finch has build a proud achievement-oriented organization firmly based on traditional values . . . one committed to the success of "Our Family" of employees, customers, and vendors. It is these same values which provide the foundation for future prosperity.

MISSION STATEMENT

Our mission is to be the superior distributor of food, related products and services to our customers, and to provide our shareholders an above average long-term return on their investment.

We believe in:
- Continuous improvement.
- Our employees' personal and professional success.
- Close working relationships with all vendors.
- Flexible, innovative and rapid response to change.
- Prudent risk taking to ensure continued financial strength.
- Working hard and productively to accomplish corporate goals.
- Full utilization of available technology.
- Conscientious corporate citizenship.
- Ethical behavior and integrity.

GUIDING PRINCIPLES

To accomplish our Mission, we must . . .
- Be committed to truly understanding our customers' needs and to focus our efforts on meeting those needs . . . *Customer Satisfaction is Always First!*
- Manage performance by setting goals, measuring results, providing ongoing feedback, and rewarding strong performance.
- Act with a sense of urgency . . . pro-active when possible.
- Continually streamline the decision-making process . . . effectively delegating authority to levels as close to the customer as possible.
- Strive for and expect excellence and quality in everything we do.

393. **National Association of Manufacturers**
1331 Pennsylvania Avenue, NW; Suite 1500—North Lobby;
  Washington, DC 20004
(202) 637-3014
Industry: 86—Trade association

NAM MISSION

To be seen as the best national business organization in the public and governmental affairs area and to expand NAM's image and value to all manufacturers.

394. **National Association of Postal Supervisors**
     490 L'Enfant Plaza, SW, Suite 3200; Washington, DC 20024-2120
     (202) 484-6070
     Industry: 86—Labor union

The object of this Association shall be to promote, through appropriate and effective action, the welfare of its members and to cooperate with the United States Postal Service and other agencies of the federal government in a continuing effort to improve the service, to raise the standard of efficiency and to widen the field of opportunity for its members who make the Postal Service or the federal government their life work.

Extracted from "Constitution and Bylaws of the National Association of Postal Supervisors"

395. **National Association of Realtors®**
     430 North Michigan Avenue; Chicago, IL 60611-4087
     (312) 329-8242
     Industry: 86—Trade association

MISSION STATEMENT

The purpose of the NATIONAL ASSOCIATION OF REALTORS® is to enhance the ability and opportunity of its members to conduct their business successfully and ethically, and to promote the preservation of the right to own, transfer and use real property. The NATIONAL ASSOCIATION OF REALTORS®:
- Speaks to and addresses real estate issues
- Supports a legislative environment favorable to its members
- Supports a legal environment favorable to its members
- Represents members in all real estate specialties
- Promotes the highest level of integrity, and fair business practices
- Enhances the public image of its members
- Provides opportunities for professional growth and education
- Communicates information to its members to help them succeed in their business activities
- Identifies, anticipates, and addresses economic and marketing trends in the real estate industry

1993

396. **National Association of Securities Dealers, Inc.**
1735 K Street, NW; Washington, DC 20006-1506
(202) 728-8000
Industry: 86—Trade association

NASD® Mission

Our mission is to facilitate capital formation in the public and private sectors by developing, operating, and regulating the most liquid, efficient, and fair securities markets for the ultimate benefit and protection of the investor.

Annual Report 1992
Copyright © 1993 National Association of Securities Dealers, Inc.

397. **National Audubon Society**
950 Third Avenue; New York, NY 10022
(212) 832-3200
Industry: 86—Membership organization

To effect wise public policy for the environment, especially in major issues that bear on wildlife and wildlife habitat.

Reaffirmed by the Board of Directors, 1989

398. **National Collegiate Athletic Association**
6201 College Boulevard; Overland Park, KS 66211-2422
(913) 339-1906
Industry: 86—Membership organization

1.2 PURPOSES

The purposes of this Association are:

(a) To initiate, stimulate and improve intercollegiate athletics programs for student-athletes and to promote and develop educational leadership, physical fitness, athletics excellence and athletics participation as a recreational pursuit;

(b) To uphold the principle of institutional control of, and responsibility for, all intercollegiate sports in conformity with the constitution and bylaws of this Association;

(c) To encourage its members to adopt eligibility rules to comply with satisfactory standards of scholarship, sportsmanship and amateurism;

(d) To formulate, copyright and publish rules of play governing intercollegiate athletics;

(e) To preserve intercollegiate athletics records;

(f) To supervise the conduct of, and to establish eligibility standards for, regional and national athletics events under the auspices of this Association;

(g) To cooperate with other amateur athletics organizations in promoting and conducting national and international athletics events;

(h) To legislate, through bylaws or by resolutions of a Convention, upon any subject of general concern to the members related to the administration of intercollegiate athletics, and;

(i) To study in general all phases of competitive intercollegiate athletics and establish standards whereby the colleges and universities in the United States can maintain their athletics programs on a high level.

1.3 FUNDAMENTAL POLICY

1.3.1. **Basic Purpose.** The competitive athletics programs of member institutions are designed to be a vital part of the educational system. A basic purpose of this Association is to maintain intercollegiate athletics as an integral part of the educational program and the athlete as an integral part of the student body and, by so doing, retain a clear line of demarcation between intercollegiate athletics and professional sports.

Extracted from "NCAA Constitution, 1992–1993 NCAA Manual"

399. **National Education Association**
1201 16th Street, NW; Washington, DC 20036-3290
(202) 822-7100
Industry: 86—Labor union

NEA STRATEGIC PLAN FOR 1993-94

MISSION STATEMENT

To establish strategic direction and to enhance commitment to a unified vision for the National Education Association, NEA adopts the following mission statement:

To fulfill the promise of a democratic society, the National Education Association shall promote the cause of quality public education; and advance the profession of education; expand the rights and further the interests of education employees; and advocate human, civil, and economic rights for all.

STRATEGIC OBJECTIVES

1. NEA shall expand and protect quality public education as a basic right (preK-G) and secure its adequate and equitable funding.

2. NEA shall achieve the restructuring of public schools and enhance the preparation, practice, and professional standards of education employees to improve student learning.

3. NEA shall achieve a pluralistic education work force, and advance the economic interests, protect the job security, and improve the terms and conditions of employment for all education employees.

4. NEA shall promote equity for all and the elimination of discrimination and other barriers to learning generated by social, economic, and political conditions.

5. NEA shall strengthen its capacity to attract, represent, and serve members in all membership categories.

6. NEA shall maintain the organizational systems essential to fulfill the mission of the Association.

Adopted by the NEA Board of Directors May 2, 1992

400. National Gallery of Art
Constitution Avenue & 4th Street, NW; Washington, DC 20565
(202) 737-4215
Industry: 84—Art museum

MISSION STATEMENT

The mission of the National Gallery of Art is to serve the United States of America in a national role by preserving, collecting, exhibiting, and fostering the understanding of works of art, at the highest possible museum and scholarly standards.

Policies and procedures towards these goals are cumulatively set forth in the Gallery's legislation, bylaws, trustee action and staff guidelines. The following general definitions are intended to explicate the goals of the Gallery.

1. **Preserving.** The Gallery's principal duty is to keep its collections intact for future generations and to pass these on in optimum condition. To carry out this responsibility the Gallery strives to maintain effective programs of security, environmental control, buildings maintenance, and conservation.

2. **Collection.** The Gallery limits its active art collecting to paintings, sculpture, and works of art on paper, from the late middle ages to the present, from Europe and the United States. Trustee policy allows the Gallery to accept, in addition, other significant works of art in conjunction with major donations in the primary areas of the Gallery's collections.

3. **Exhibiting.** The Gallery is dedicated to putting its collections on view in Washington and by loan elsewhere, as well as borrowing works of art for exhibition in Washington. As its collecting field is narrow in comparison to the world's art, the Gallery strives to supplement its own works with exhibitions of material from other times and other cultures. At the same time balance is sought with exhibitions that illuminate and reinforce its own collections. The highest standards of scholarship, maintenance, installation, and interaction with the public all contribute to this critical exhibiting role.

4. Fostering Understanding. The Gallery's role as an institution dedicated to fostering an understanding of works of art operates on a broad spectrum. From advanced research conducted both at its Center for Advanced Study in the Visual Arts and by its curators, to the dissemination of knowledge to its visitors and to the widest possible student and general public, the Gallery is an educative institution. The Gallery also collects materials for research related to its collections, as well as the history and appreciation of art in general. The Gallery recognizes that not only the dissemination of information but the enhancement of the aesthetic experiences are essential to fostering understanding of works of art. Ancillary programs furthering its aesthetic role, such as concerts and changing horticulture displays, have been part of the Gallery's mission virtually since its inception.

401. **National Geographic Society**
     17th and M Streets, NW; Washington, DC 20036
     (202) 857-7000
     Industry: 86—Membership organization

     Mission Statement

     The mission of the National Geographic Society is to increase and diffuse geographic knowledge. Geography is defined in a broad sense: the description of land, sea and universe; the interrelationship of humankind with flora and fauna of earth; and the historical, cultural, scientific, governmental, and social background of people.

402. **National Rifle Association**
     1600 Rhode Island Avenue, NW; Washington, DC 20036
     (202) 858-6000
     Industry: 86—Membership organization

     ARTICLE II

     Purposes and Objectives

     The purpose and objectives of the National Rifle Association of America are:

     1. To protect and defend the Constitution of the United States, especially with reference to the inalienable right of the individual American citizen guaranteed by such Constitution to acquire, possess, transport, carry, transfer ownership of, and enjoy the right to use arms, in order that the people may always be in a position to exercise their legitimate individual rights of self-preservation and defense of family, person, and property, as well as to serve effectively in the appropriate militia for the common defense of the Republic and the individual liberty of its citizens;

2. To promote public safety, law and order, and the national defense;

3. To train members of law enforcement agencies, the armed forces, the militia, and people of good repute in marksmanship and in the safe handling and efficient use of small arms;

4. To foster and promote the shooting sports, including the advancement of amateur competitions in marksmanship at the local, state, regional, national, and international levels;

5. To promote hunter safety, and to promote and defend hunting as a shooting sport and as a viable and necessary method of fostering the propagation, growth, conservation, and wise use of our renewable wildlife resources.

The Association may take all actions necessary and proper in the furtherance of thee purposes and objectives.

Extracted from the "Bylaws" of the National Rifle Association

403. National Westminster Bancorp

Ten Exchange Place; Jersey City, NJ 07302
(201) 547-7571
Industry: 60—Banking

Our Vision

Our Vision for NatWest Bancorp is to be a highly respected, well-capitalized, profitable financial services organization that provides excellence in customer service. NatWest people strive each day to make this vision a reality. To that end, we pledge:

To Our Customers

We will provide true relationship banking based on mutual respect, integrity and stability. We will distinguish ourselves from our competitors by being customer-driven, dedicated to banking that is problem-free. We will express our commitment to our customers by listening to them and responding to their needs with products and services designed for them, priced competitively and delivered in a timely, courteous and efficient manner.

To Our Communities

We recognize that we share a common destiny with our communities and will use our human and financial resources to foster their growth and vitality. We will support our communities with funding and professional expertise, and encourage the volunteer efforts of our employees, particularly in projects that aid education. We will operate in a socially responsible and environmentally sensitive manner.

To Our Parent Organization

We are committed to building a North American presence for our parent that consistently provides an appropriate rate of return on its investment. Through prudent management of our business, we will be a key contributor to the NatWest Group's success and we will enhance its reputation as a respected worldwide financial services organization.

To Ourselves

We will be an organization where trust and respect for the individual prevail, where diversity is valued and where open communication is the norm. Our customer focus will create an environment that is challenging and creative, fosters individual responsibility within a context of teamwork, rewards superior performance and offers the opportunity for professional growth.

404. National Wildlife Federation
1400 Sixteenth Street, NW; Washington, DC 20036-2266
(202) 797-6800
Industry: 86—Membership organization

Mission Statement

The mission of the National Wildlife Federation is to educate, inspire and assist individuals and organizations to conserve wildlife and other natural resources and to protect the Earth's environment.

405. Nationwide Mutual Insurance Company
One Nationwide Plaza; Columbus, OH 43216
(614) 249-7111
Industry: 63—Insurance

Nationwide Property/Casualty Companies Mission Statement

To satisfy the financial protection needs of select risk individuals, families, and businesses through superior service and competitive insurance products while building profitable, growing companies in partnership with our exclusive agents.

Nationwide Life Insurance Company Mission Statement

To provide high quality competitive financial protection products and superior services while building profitable, growing companies.

406. The Nature Conservancy
1815 North Lynn Street; Arlington, VA 22209
(703) 841-5300
Industry: 86—Membership organization

The mission of The Nature Conservancy is to preserve plants, animals and natural communities that represent the diversity of life on Earth by protecting the lands and waters they need to survive.

NatWest Bancorp

see National Westminster Bancorp (403)

NB Power

see New Brunswick Power Corporation (409)

407. Nebraska Municipal Power Pool

521 South 14th Street; P.O. Box 95124; Lincoln, NE 68509
(402) 474-4759
Industry: 49—Electric utility
Our Mission is to provide reliable and economical
- Energy
- Related Services
to our members

NEES

see New England Electric System (410)

408. Nevada Power Company

6226 West Sahara Avenue; P.O. Box 230; Las Vegas, NV 89151-0230
(702) 367-5000
Industry: 49—Electric utility

Our Mission Is To:

Continuously improve customer service, while ensuring an adequate and reliable supply of electricity at reasonable prices.

- Provide shareholders with returns on their investments that build long-term value.

- Create and maintain a working environment where each employee's contribution is valued and each has the opportunity to excel.

- Be a valued corporate citizen and a respected leader in environmental, employee and public safety issues.

Statement of Corporate Values

SERVICE EXCELLENCE

We take pride in our work. We are entrusted with a public service that enhances the quality of life. We are committed to delivering a reliable supply of electricity and excellence in customer service. We achieve service excellence by working with customers to understand their needs, measuring their satisfaction and continuously improving the scope and quality of our services.

INTEGRITY

We are fair in our dealings with others, respectful of confidential information and communicate with one another openly, honestly and without deception. We treat each other with respect. This spirit extends to our relations with customers, shareholders, regulators, government agencies and the community.

TEAMWORK

We clearly communicate our goals and work priorities and each of us has access to the information we need to do our jobs well. We take the initiative to apply ourselves, to seek guidance, to provide feedback and support to others and to make decisions. We share resources, knowledge and ideas. We work as a team to solve problems, improve procedures, and develop necessary policies and programs. We value and respect different skills and perspectives, recognizing that creativity stems from diversity.

CORPORATE CITIZENSHIP

We encourage and support volunteerism and take pride in building effective partnerships with the communities we serve. We promote the safety and well-being of all individuals and we are dedicated to protecting the environment, both today and for generations to come.

BUILDING SHAREHOLDER VALUE

We are committed to providing shareholders with returns that make Nevada Power a secure and attractive long-term investment. We accomplish this by ensuring the cost-effectiveness of our decisions, by providing excellence in customer service, by operating our business with uncompromising integrity, by working as a team to achieve our corporate mission and uphold our values and by building and maintaining an excellent relationship with customers, regulators, government agencies and the community.

November, 1991

409.   **New Brunswick Power Corporation**
       P.O. Box 2000; Frederickson, New Brunswick; Canada E3B 4X1
       (506) 458-4444
       Industry: 49—Electric utility

Mission

To provide a continuous supply of energy adequate for the needs and future development of the province &

To promote economy and efficiency in the generation, distribution, supply, sale and use of power.

Objectives

Our mission will be met by following these objectives:
- ensuring a reliable supply of electricity
- making the best use possible of New Brunswick's energy resources via energy efficiency and conservation
- protecting the environment from the effects of our operations
- satisfying our customers by giving them quality service
- managing the business of the utility such that we maintain the confidence of the financial community and our customers
- contributing to the economic development of the business community and the well being of the people of New Brunswick.

Values

In achieving our mission and our objectives, NB Power expects management and employees to demonstrate the following values:
- honesty
- integrity
- commitment
- productivity
- mutual respect and courtesy
         Extracted from "The Next Decade: NB Power" booklet, 1991

410. **New England Electric System**
     25 Research Drive; Westborough, MA 01582-0001
     (508) 366-9011
     Industry: 49—Electric utility

WHAT QUALITY MEANS AT NEES

NEES VISION

The NEES companies pledge to provide our customers the highest possible value by continuously improving electric service, managing costs, and reducing adverse environmental impacts.

COMMITMENT

The employees of the NEES companies are committed to seeking out the expectations of our customers and consistently satisfying those expectations in our service and attitudes.
- Employee initiative is the key to success,
- continuous improvement is essential,
- cost control is a way of life,
- integrity is never compromised, and

- environmental improvement is our responsibility

NEES QUALITY POLICY

Customer expectations drive all of our efforts.

Our customers are not only those who consume our product and use our services, but also our co-workers, regulators, communities, and shareholders. Satisfying their changing expectations determines our success.

Individual initiative, teamwork, and recognition are the tools for success.

Our accomplishments come from the efforts and teamwork of all employees. We treat each other with trust and respect, and recognize each other's contributions.

Continuous improvement is essential.

Helping customers obtain the highest value from the services we provide is fundamental to our job. Continuous improvement enhances our position in an increasingly competitive industry.

Cost control is a way of life.

We continually manage costs. Controlling the cost of our services helps meet our customers' expectations.

Integrity is never compromised.

We act honestly and responsibly in everything we do.

Environmental improvement is our responsibility.

We adhere to sound environmental practices. We consider the environmental impacts of our daily actions and are reducing the adverse environmental impacts of providing our service.

Extracted from "What Quality Means at NEES" brochure

411. **New England Medical Center Hospitals**
      750 Washington Street; Boston, MA 02111
      (617) 956-5000
      Industry: 80—Hospitals

Mission Statement

We strive to heal, to comfort, to teach, to learn, and to seek the knowledge to promote health and prevent disease. Our patients and their families are at the center of everything we do. We dedicate ourselves to furthering our rich tradition of health care innovation, leadership, charity and the highest standard of care and service to all in our community.

March 10, 1992

412. **New England Mutual Life Insurance Company**
      501 Boylston Street; Boston, MA 02117-9805

(617) 578-2020
Industry: 63—Life insurance

THE MISSION OF THE NEW ENGLAND®

The New England's mission is to create value for our policyholders and customers through insurance and investment.

THE OPERATING PRINCIPLES OF THE NEW ENGLAND

To achieve our mission, we must continue to build on our strengths: quality, distribution, investments, technology, products and services, and business partnerships. We believe these strengths, together with the consistent practice of our operating principles, will ensure our success in creating financial value for our policyholders and customers.

1 We put our obligations to policyholders first.
2 We respect and value all associates—field and home office.
3 We expect field and home office managers to lead effectively.
4 We are dedicated to customer satisfaction.
5 We pursue quality in all we do.
6 We accept responsibility as a corporate citizen.

OUR RESPONSIBILITIES

- To support fully through our actions the goals of our organization and The New England, with particular emphasis on customer solutions
- To exemplify the company's operating principles in all our decisions and actions
- To understand and fulfill, to the best of our ability, all the job responsibilities with which we have been entrusted
- To sustain the integrity of The New England through personal integrity in all we do
- To help recruit the best people by nominating qualified candidates to become associates of The New England

OUR RIGHTS

- A right to understand:
- the mission, operating principles, and strategic directions of the company
- the business plans and associated strategies of the company and of our organization (business unit/agency)
- the expectations associated with our current responsibilities and our career development options
- compensation, bonus, and benefit programs

- A right to a voice in the small and large decisions that may directly or indirectly influence our own careers, our business units, and the future of the company

- A right to a reasonable opportunity to achieve our individual potential

- A right to a meaningful role in which we share responsibility for achievement of the organization's goals

- A right to make a commitment to our job, to go beyond our basic responsibilities and actively seek new challenges

- A right to nonthreatening avenues of appeal to prevent arbitrary decisions

- A right to fair compensation, tied to performance, and recognition for special contributions

Extracted from "Our Mission and Principles" booklet

413. **New Science Associates, Inc.**
One Glendinning Place; Westport, CT 06880
(203) 221-8900
Industry: 87—Consulting

A New Science

A New Approach

In the early 1980s, an information systems architecture with well-defined contours permeated businesses around the world. In the later part of that decade, this architecture began to crack. Now, it is totally fragmented. Without question, a new information systems architecture is emerging that will dominate industry by the late 1990s. Meeting the challenges imposed by this evolution will require a new science.

New Science Associates is the only firm of its kind to focus on information systems architectural change. **Our mission is to facilitate our clients' migration from the IT architecture of the past to the IT architecture of the future.**

As the consultants for IS architectural change, New Science takes an individualized approach to our client relationships. Each client has a senior New Science analyst designated as its primary architecture consultant, backed by the range of expertise of the entire New Science analytical team. We make it our business to know and understand each clients' present IS reality, as well as its future IS requirements. Through on-going consultation, inquiries and meetings, we create and maintain an extensive "portrait" of each client, enabling us to keep abreast of each client's current IS projects, issues, and objectives, and to propose comprehensive solutions and recommendations.

The main difference between New Science Associates and other IS research and consulting firms is:
- New Science focuses on our clients' organizations, rather than on departments or individuals.
- New Science research is driven by emerging architectures, not by past technologies.

414. New York Blood Center, Inc.
310 East 67th Street; New York, NY 10021
(212) 570-3010
Industry: 80—Health care services

Our Mission

- We will provide the safest, best quality transfusion-related products and services at a reasonable cost to those who will benefit.
- We will increase the body and availability of knowledge in transfusion medicine.

Our Values

To achieve its mission, New York Blood Center maintains and promotes certain shared values that guide and inspire everyone associated with our organization. These values are service, quality, innovation and productive growth.

Service: We exist as a service organization, helping the community, blood donors, physicians, hospitals and individual patients who rely on us. Service is our reason for being.

Quality: A cornerstone of the Blood Center, quality can be seen in the care we take to ensure the safety of the blood supply, in the professionalism of our staff, and in our commitment to the well-being of the community we serve.

Innovation: The Blood Center continually strives to improve the quality and effectiveness of our work through the development of new insights, products and techniques that help solve health care problems or expand the level of service we provide.

Productive Growth: Productive growth, the logical result of service, quality and innovation, creates new opportunities for our people and enables the Blood Center to successfully fulfill its expanding role in health care and meet new challenges as they arise.

415. New York Public Library
Fifth Avenue and 42nd Street; New York, NY 10018-2788
(212) 221-7676
Industry: 82—Public library

The New York Public Library is one of the cornerstones of the American tradition of equal opportunity. It provides free and open access to the accumulated wisdom of the world, without distinction as to income, religion, nationality, or other human condition. It is everyone's university; the scholar's and author's haven; the stateman's, scientist's, and businessman's essential resource; the nation's memory. It guarantees freedom of information and independence of thought. It enables each individual to pursue learning at his and/or her own personal level of interest, preparation, ability, and desire. It helps ensure the free trade in ideas and the right of dissent.

The mission of The New York Public Library is to use its available resources in a balanced program of collecting, cataloging, and conserving books and other materials and providing ready access directly to individual library users and to users elsewhere through cooperating libraries and library networks. The New York Public Library's responsibility is to serve as a great storehouse of knowledge at the heart of one of the world's information centers, and function as an integral part of a fabric of information and learning that stretches across the nation and the world.

The Mission of The New York Public Library, Astor, Lenox and Tilden Foundations March, 1980

416. New York State Electric & Gas Corporation
4500 Vestal Parkway East; P.O. Box 3607; Binghampton, NY 13902-3607
(607) 729-2551
Industry: 49—Electric utility

Vision

We put **energy** into action, providing even better quality and value to those we serve. We seek to set the standard for excellence, leadership and integrity in the utility industry.

Mission Statement

NYSEG's diversified business units are committed to . . .
- Pursuing opportunities in existing and emerging markets.
- Providing quality services and products at competitive prices.
- Offering our employees opportunities for personal and professional growth.
- Earning an attractive return for our shareholder.
- Protecting our environment.
- Supporting the needs and visions of our communities.

NYSEG Shared Values

Leadership is the element that provides substance and power to all our shared values. By demonstrating personal and professional leadership, we empower each other with the confidence that "one person can make a difference." Each and every individual must take the responsibility for corporate and personal leadership to make our vision a reality, and back our values with action.

Excellence:

We are committed to professional and operational excellence. We take pride in our work and strive to do it right—the first time—on time—every time.

Specific Behaviors

We strive to be the best and be recognized as such in everything we do.

We promote continuous improvement by creating and accepting challenging goals.

We nurture and promote individual development.

We anticipate and respond to the needs of our customers.

We strive to provide excellence with value.

Innovation:

We understand that growth and success are fostered in a positive environment of continuous improvement, learning and achievement.

Specific Behaviors

We encourage creative thinking, unique ideas and fresh approaches.

We recognize risk taking has the potential for both success and failure and that both provide opportunities for learning.

We exhibit flexibility by focusing on why and how we can, instead of why we can't.

We openly and objectively consider all ideas and provide timely feedback.

Integrity:

Integrity is the bedrock of NYSEG strength; it is never compromised.

Specific Behaviors

We demonstrate the highest ethical and professional standards by always striving to do the "right thing."

We will not compromise safety in rendering service.

We promptly admit mistakes, recognizing the need to adjust and go forward.

We honor our commitments.

Teamwork:

We work in partnership with our co-workers to achieve mutual goals. Trust and respect are the foundations of our team approach.

Specific Behaviors

We provide mutual support and cooperation while constructively participating to achieve common goals.

We willingly share ideas, resources and information.

We listen carefully, initiate and receive feedback willingly and coach each other to higher levels.

We emphasize success through team over individual achievement.

Caring:

We share the concerns of our communities and each other.

Specific Behaviors

We show respect, appreciation, consideration and support in our relationships with each other, our customers and the community.

We keep an open mind and encourage others to share their thoughts and opinions.

We recognize each other as individuals whose contributions are valued, respected and supported.

We are sensitive and understanding of others' feelings, emotions, needs and values.

We actively encourage our co-workers to grow and reach their potential both personally and professionally.

Accountability:

We are responsible for our actions and results. Our accountability encompasses the success of other departments, divisions, units and the entire company.

Specific Behaviors

We give each person the resources and support necessary to accept individual responsibility for the success of the company.

We talk and listen to each other.

We supply the means, knowledge and opportunity to succeed.

We support our co-workers and our company knowing that our actions contribute to their success.

We constantly ask, "What more can I do."

417.   **Niagara Mohawk Power Corporation**
       300 Erie Boulevard West; Syracuse, NY 13202
       (315) 474-1511
       Industry: 49—Electric utility

1993–1995 CORPORATE STRATEGIC PLAN
MISSION

Niagara Mohawk is an energy services company committed to maximizing value to its customers, shareholders and employees.

The Company seeks to satisfy customers' energy needs with high-quality, competitively priced electric and gas energy products and services; increase shareholder value through above average growth in earnings; and provide an atmosphere for employees which promotes empowerment and rewards excellence.

Niagara Mohawk promotes safe and efficient practices in the supply, delivery and use of energy. The Company is committed to a cleaner, healthier environment through an active, positive approach to its environmental responsibilities. The Company supports improvement in the social and economic well-being of the communities it serves and seeks cooperative and constructive relationships with all of its regulators.

Niagara Mohawk's business emphasis focuses on results, aggressive and responsible leadership, responsiveness to customer needs and continuous improvement in operations.

1993–1995 CORPORATE STRATEGIC PLAN
VISION

VISION   CUSTOMERS   EMPLOYEES   SHAREHOLDERS
        ENVIRONMENT

We will become the most responsive and efficient energy services company in the Northeast to achieve maximum value for customers, shareholders and employees.

NMPP Energy
see Nebraska Municipal Power Pool (407)

418. **Noranda Inc.**
181 Bay Street, Suite 4100; P.O. Box 755, BCE Place; Toronto, Ontario; Canada M5J 2T3
(416) 982-7111
Industry: 10, 26—Mining and pulp and paper

Noranda's vision is to be the premier diversified natural resource company.

Adopted 1987

419. **Nordson Corporation**
28601 Clemens Road; Westlake, OH 44145-1148
(216) 892-1580
Industry: 35—Industrial equipment

Corporate Philosophy

Corporate Purpose

Nordson Corporation strives to be a vital, self-renewing, worldwide organization which, within the framework of ethical behavior and enlightened citizenship, grows and produces wealth for our customers, employees, shareholders and communities. Nordson Corporation is an equal opportunity employer.

Corporate Goals

Nordson operates for the purpose of creating balanced, long-term benefits for all of our constituencies: customers, employees, shareholders and communities.

Our corporate goal for growth is to double the value of the company over a five-year period, with the primary measure of value set by the market for company shares. While external factors may impact value, the achievement of this goal will rest with earnings growth, capital and human resource efficiency, and positioning for the future.

Nordson does not expect every quarter to produce increased sales, earnings and earnings per share, or to exceed the comparative prior year's quarter. We do expect to produce long-term gains. When short-term swings occur, we do not intend to alter our basic objectives in efforts to mitigate the impact of these natural occurrences.

Growth is achieved by seizing opportunities with existing products and markets, investing in systems to maximize productivity, and pursuing growth markets. This strategy is augmented through product line additions, engineering, research and development, and acquisition of companies that can serve multinational industrial markets.

Customers

We create benefits for our customers through a Package of Values™ which includes carefully engineered, durable products; strong service support; the backing of a well-established worldwide company with financial and technical strengths; and a corporate commitment to deliver what was promised.

We strive to provide genuine customer satisfaction; it is the foundation upon which we continue to build our business.

Employees

Complementing our business strategy is the objective to provide opportunities for employee self-fulfillment, growth, security, recognition and equitable compensation.

This goal is met through employee training and the creation of on-the-job growth opportunities. The result is a highly qualified and professional management team capable of meeting corporate objectives.

We recognize the value of employee participation in the planning process. Strategic and operating plans are developed by all business units and divisions, resulting in a sense of ownership and commitment on the part of employees in accomplishing company objectives.

Communities

Nordson is committed to contributing an average of 5 percent of domestic pretax earnings to human services, health, education and other charitable activities, particularly in communities where the company has major facilities.

420. **Norfolk Southern Corporation**
Three Commercial Place; Norfolk, VA 23510-2191
(804) 629-2600
Industry: 40, 42—Railroad, van lines

Mission Statement

Norfolk Southern's mission is to enhance the value of our stockholders' investment over time by providing quality freight transportation services and undertaking any other related businesses in which our resources, particularly our people, give the company an advantage.

421. **Northrop Corporation**
1840 Century Park East; Los Angeles, CA 90067-2199
(310) 553-6262
Industry: 37—Aerospace

OUR MISSION

Northrop provides products and services which contribute to the defense and technological strength of our nation. Our goal is to be one of the top two firms in our chosen segments of the military/commercial aircraft and defense electronics markets. Our aim is to satisfy customer needs with innovative, high quality products and services at a competitive price. We are committed to sustained excellence in all dimensions of our business and to providing a fair return for our shareholders. Outstanding performance will provide the resources necessary for Northrop to grow as a world-class aerospace company.

OUR VALUES

We, the men and women of Northrop, are guided by the following values. They describe our company as we want it to be. We want every decision and action on the job to demonstrate these values. We believe that putting our values into practice creates long-term benefits for our shareholders.

We work to deliver CUSTOMER SATISFACTION . . .

We each have valued customers, whether they be government agencies, other businesses, our shareholders or one another. We believe in respecting our customers, listening to their requests, understanding their expectations, and delivering products and services that meet agreed-upon standards.

We value NORTHROP PEOPLE . . .

We treat one another with respect, recognizing the significant contributions that come from the diversity of individuals and ideas. Clear expectations must be communicated and people should know how they are doing. We create an environment of teamwork, openness, challenge, and development.

We regard our SUPPLIERS as essential team members . . .

We owe our suppliers the same type of respect that we show to our customers. Our suppliers deserve fair and equitable treatment, clear agreements and honest feedback on performance. We consider our suppliers' needs in conducting all aspects of our business.

We take responsibility for the QUALITY of our work . . .

We will deliver excellence and continue to strive for improvement. We define Quality as "meeting customer requirements including cost and schedule." Each of us is accountable for the quality of whatever we do.

We demonstrate INTEGRITY in all we do . . .

We are each personally accountable for high standards of behavior, including honesty and fairness in all aspects of our work. We strive to fulfill our commitments, as law-abiding citizens and conscientious employees. We will be responsible and reliable, truthful and accurate, and diligent in the effective use of company and customer resources.

We provide LEADERSHIP as a company and as individuals . . .

Northrop's leadership is founded on advanced technology, innovative manufacturing and sound business management. Our continued success requires developing people and rewarding their achievements. We must each lead through competence, creativity, and teamwork.

September, 1990

[At press time Northrop won a takeover battle to acquire Grumman (259).]

422.   **Northwest Airlines, Inc.**
        5101 Northwest Drive; St. Paul, MN 55111-3034
        (612) 726-2111

Industry: 45—Airlines

Mission

To build together the world's most preferred airline with the best people; each committed to exceeding our customers' expectations every day.

Goals

- Become a great place to work.
- Increase our preference to industry-leading levels.
- Expand our presence in key world markets to industry-leading levels.
- Increase the scope and effectiveness of our sales and distribution systems to industry-leading levels.
- Become one of the world's best managed companies.
- Become an outstanding member of the communities we serve.
- Strengthen profitability to finance growth.

Guiding Principles

These principles provide all of us with guidelines as we work together and make decisions every day:

Never Compromise Safety

Always Put Customers First

- Learn what makes a difference to each customer and deliver it.
- Resolve customer problems on the spot whenever possible.
- Obtain the training and tools we need to serve our customers.

Support and Inspire Each Other

- Work together to achieve common goals.
- Recognize the good work of others.
- Recruit and promote to the highest standards of performance and professionalism.
- Build self-esteem and pride in each other.

Continuously Improve

- Measure against the best.
- Solicit and offer ideas for improvement.
- Search out and break barriers that get in the way.

423. **Northwest Area Foundation**
East 1201 First National Bank Building; 332 Minnesota Street; St. Paul, MN 55101-1373
(612) 224-9635
Industry: 67—Charitable foundation

The mission of the Northwest Area Foundation is to contribute to the vitality of the region by promoting economic revitalization and improving the standard of living for the most vulnerable of its citizens. To accomplish its mission, the Foundation will focus, deepen, and enhance the public dialogue about important regional issues; seek innovative approaches to address these issues; and build the capacity to continue to address them effectively over the long term.

Adopted 1990

424.   The North West Company, Inc.
77 Main Street; Winnipeg, Manitoba; Canada R3C 2R1
(204) 943-0881
Industry: 53, 54—General merchandise and food stores

OUR CORPORATE GOAL

Our goal is to prosper by applying our business skills and shared values to grow existing operations to their full potential, while successfully expanding into similar markets.

OUR SHARED VALUES

In pursuit of our goal, we will:

- Make customer satisfaction our first priority by offering superior value in products and services;

- Demonstrate that an enterprising spirit is a major factor in our success;

- Respect employees as individuals and provide an open and frank environment in which creativity and productivity are encouraged, recognized and rewarded;

- Be a caring and supportive corporate citizen within the communities we serve;

- Recognize suppliers as real partners in our success;

- Create value for shareholders by providing a reasonable return on their investment;

- Conduct business activities with integrity and respect.

Annual Report 1991

425.   Northwestern Memorial Hospital
Northwestern Memorial Corporation; Superior Street & Fairbanks
   Court; Chicago, IL 60611
(312) 908-2000
Industry: 80—Hospital

Our Mission

Northwestern Memorial Hospital is an academic medical center where the patient comes first.

We are an organization of care-givers who aspire to consistently high standards of quality in delivering personalized care with sensitivity to the needs of our patients and their families. NMH is bonded in an essential academic and service relationship with the Northwestern University Medical School. The quality of our services is enhanced through their integration with education and research in an environment that encourages excellence of practice, critical inquiry and learning.

Our Vision

Northwestern Memorial intends to be recognized as the leading health care provider in metropolitan Chicago, as a major Midwestern referral center, and with the Northwestern University Medical School, as one of the nation's pre-eminent academic medical centers.

Extracted from "Strategic Plan 1988–1993" brochure

426. Northwestern Mutual Life Insurance Company

720 East Wisconsin Avenue; Milwaukee, WI 53202

(414) 299-7013

Industry: 63—Life insurance

The ambition of the Northwestern has been less to be large than to be safe; its aim is to rank first in benefits to policyowners rather than first in size. Valuing quality above quantity, it has preferred to secure its business under certain salutary restrictions and limitations rather than to write a much larger business at the possible sacrifice of those valuable points which have made The Northwestern pre-eminently the policyowner's company.

Executive Committee, 1888

427. Norwest Corporation

Norwest Center; Sixth and Marquette; Minneapolis, MN 55479

(612) 667-1234

Industry: 60—Banking

NORWEST CORPORATION AND SUBSIDIARIES MISSION STATEMENT

We seek to: create an environment emphasizing teamwork where employees really care and are committed to doing their best while having fun; promote the long term success of our customers and communities; be our customer's first choice for service and solutions; create stockholder value through strong, consistent growth in our businesses and their profitability; be the best in financial services.

428. **NovaCare Inc.**
      2570 Boulevard of the Generals; P.O. Box 928; Valley Forge, PA
        19482-0928
      (215) 631-9300
      Industry: 80—Health care services

NovaCare IS PEOPLE committed to making a difference . . . enhancing
the future of all patients . . . breaking new ground in our
professions . . . achieving excellence . . . advancing human capability . . .
changing the world in which we live.

WE LEAD THE WAY with our enthusiasm, optimism, patience, drive
and commitment.

WE WORK TOGETHER to enhance the quality of our patients' lives
by reshaping lost abilities and teaching new skills. We heighten
expectations for the patient and family. We rebuild hope, confidence, self-
respect and a desire to continue.

WE APPLY OUR CLINICAL EXPERTISE to benefit our patients
through creative and progressive techniques. Our ethical and performance
standards require us to expand every effort to achieve the best possible
results.

OUR CUSTOMERS are national and local healthcare providers who
share our goal of enhancing the patients' quality of life. In each community,
our customers consider us a partner in providing the best possible care. Our
reputation is based on our responsiveness, high standards and effective
systems of quality assurance. Our relationship is open and proactive.

WE ARE ADVOCATES of our professions and patients through active
participation in the professional, regulatory, educational and research
communities at national, state and local levels.

OUR APPROACH TO HEALTHCARE fulfills our responsibility to
provide investors with a high rate of return through consistent growth and
profitability.

OUR PEOPLE are our most valuable asset. We are committed to the
personal, professional and career development of each individual employee.
We are proud of what we do and dedicated to our Company. We foster
teamwork and create an environment conducive to productive communication among all disciplines.

NovaCare is a company of people in pursuit of this Vision.

NovaCare . . . HELPING MAKE LIFE A LITTLE BETTER

429. **Nowsco Well Service Limited**
      2750, 801-6th Avenue, SW; Calgary, Alberta; Canada T2P 4L8
      (403) 261-2990
      Industry: 13—Oilfield services

MISSION STATEMENT

Nowsco will provide superior growth in shareholder value by providing quality services and engineering to the international energy market. Nowsco will accomplish this by providing the best value to the client through quality management and industry leading solutions delivered with integrity and safety by the best people in the service industry.

NWA

see Northwest Airlines, Inc. (422)

430. NWNL Companies

20 Washington Avenue South; Minneapolis, MN 55401
(612) 372-5432
Industry: 63—Life and health insurance

NWNL's VISION FOR THE 1990s

We will excel as the **leader** in targeted segments of the **personal risk management and employee life, health and retirement benefits** markets by:

- Exceeding customer expectations through **quality products and services**
- Out-executing competitors through clear **business focus** and **efficient operations**
- Building close relationships with **distinctive distribution channels**
- Providing challenge, opportunity, and ownership for **empowered employees**

FOCUS   STRENGTH   DISCIPLINE

April, 1992

431. NYNEX Corporation

335 Madison Avenue; New York, NY 10017
(212) 370-7400
Industry: 48—Telecommunications

MISSION

To be a world-class leader in helping people communicate using information networks and services.

VALUES

- Quality
- Ethics
- Caring for the individual

PRIORITIES
- Customer satisfaction
- Cost-competitiveness
- Earnings growth
- Employee empowerment

Drafted May, 1990

O

432. Ocean Spray Cranberries, Inc.
One Ocean Spray Drive; Lakeville-Middleboro, MA 02349
(508) 946-1000
Industry: 20—Food cooperative

COOPERATIVE MISSION

A company's mission defines its fundamental reason for existence, and serves as the framework for its long-term business objectives.

Our Cooperative's purpose is to protect the long-term financial interests of all grower-owners while insulating returns from short-term cyclical patterns. Ocean Spray Cranberries, Inc. will remain a marketing cooperative for grower-owners of cranberries and grapefruit. Specifically, through the partnership of growers and employees, the organization will:

- Generate the highest reasonable net proceeds on member deliveries consistent with assuring long-term stable markets for Grower-Owner crops,
- Market all crops delivered in an orderly and timely manner, and
- Assist Grower-Owners in maintaining deliveries consistent with meeting the Cooperative's needs.

CORPORATE VISION

A corporate vision is a picture of the future as it should be . . . reflecting business results, as well as personal and corporate standards of excellence. Our vision is:

OCEAN SPRAY QUALITY, EVERYWHERE

Quality means that Ocean Spray people will establish and live a quality level so high that it becomes the "gold standard." This means quality is not only **what** we do, but **how** we do it.

Everywhere means that Ocean Spray beverage products will be available wherever and whenever the consumer has a need.

433. Office Depot, Inc.
2200 Old Germantown Road; Delray Beach, FL 33445

(407) 278-4800

Industry: 59—Office supply stores

MISSION STATEMENT

Office Depot's MISSION is to be the MOST SUCCESSFUL OFFICE PRODUCTS COMPANY IN THE WORLD. We will achieve success by an uncompromising commitment to:

- SUPERIOR CUSTOMER SATISFACTION

A company-wide attitude that recognizes that customer satisfaction is EVERYTHING.

- ASSOCIATE-ORIENTED ENVIRONMENT

An acknowledgment that our associates are our most valuable resource. We are committed to fostering an environment where recognition, innovation, communication and the entrepreneurial spirit are encouraged and rewarded.

- INDUSTRY LEADING VALUE/SELECTION/SERVICES

Offering only the highest-quality merchandise available at everyday low prices, providing customers with an outstanding balance of value, selection and services.

- ETHICAL BUSINESS CONDUCT

Conducting our business with uncompromising honesty and integrity.

- SHAREHOLDER VALUE

Providing our shareholders with a superior Return-On-Investment.

434. **Ohio Casualty Insurance Company**
   136 North Third Street; Hamilton, OH 45025
   (513) 867-3870
   Industry: 63—Property and casualty insurance

The mission of Ohio Casualty is to offer through the independent agents representing our companies the insurance and related products which meet the majority of the current and future needs of the public with a commitment to excellence in our service and in our contracts.

April, 1988

435. **Oklahoma Natural Gas Company**
   Division of ONEOK, Inc.
   100 West Fifth Street; Tulsa, OK 74102-0871
   (918) 588-7568
   Industry: 49—Natural gas utility

Our Mission Statement:

Oklahoma Natural Gas Company will be Oklahoma's preferred energy supplier by providing excellent customer service, preserving the environment, and enhancing shareholder value.

436. **Orlando Regional Healthcare System**
1414 Kuhl Avenue; Orlando, FL 32806
(407) 841-5111
Industry: 80—Hospital

ORLANDO REGIONAL HEALTHCARE SYSTEM

LONG-RANGE STRATEGIC PLAN

I. MISSION: (Why we exist)

The Mission of Orlando Regional Healthcare System is to improve the health and quality of life of the individuals and communities we serve.

II. VISION:

Everyone working together as a team to provide the best quality, comfort and service to our patients and guests in a genuine caring environment.

III. CRITICAL SUCCESS FACTORS

A. PEOPLE

Working together as a team to make the Orlando Regional Healthcare System the best place to work in Central Florida.

B. VALUE

Working together as a team to deliver high quality, cost effective healthcare services.

C. SERVICE

Working together as a team to provide superior customer service by listening and responding to **all** customers. Exceed their expectations.

D. COMMUNITY

Working together as a team to take a leadership role in improving the health and quality of life of our community, while maintaining financial stability.

437. **Outboard Marine Corporation**
100 Sea-Horse Drive; Waukegan, IL 60085-2195
(708) 689-6200
Industry: 34, 35—Marine engines

MISSION

OMC is a global leader in the marketing, design and manufacture of marine products and services.

Our mission is to provide value to our consumers through superior quality products, services and distribution, resulting in above average returns for our shareholders.

This will be achieved by continuous improvement in all aspects of our business through total employee involvement and teamwork.

438. Owens-Corning Fiberglas Corporation
Fiberglas Tower; Toledo, OH 43659
(419) 248-8000
Industry: 30, 32—Fiberglass and building materials

Owens-Corning Fiberglas Corporation is dedicated to expanding its global leadership.

We strive for excellence through our commitment to three guiding principles:
- Customer Satisfaction
- Individual Dignity
- Shareholder Value

By focusing on these ideals and the values they represent, we will build on our proud heritage of innovation and achievement, develop new technologies, launch new products and grow our businesses around the world.

Statement of Values

- Customer Satisfaction

Providing the highest quality products and greatest economic value for our customers.

Using Total Quality Management to understand and meet our customers' needs.

Seeking continuous improvement in all that we do.

Recognizing the value of time and managing it for competitive advantage.

Measuring our success in market share.

- Individual Dignity

Building a reputation as the preferred place of employment.

Developing a culture and environment that attract and retain the very best.

Enabling our people to fulfill their aspirations, regardless of gender, race, creed, religion or national origin.

Operating in a way that safeguards the well-being of our people, our customers and our neighbors.

- Shareholder Value

Rewarding the trust of our shareholders by enhancing the value of our enterprise.

Capitalizing on our market leadership position, customer franchise strengths and technical expertise to continually improve sales and increase profitability.

Respecting the interests of other stakeholders, including suppliers, communities, government and the environment.

P–Q

439. **PacifiCare® Health Systems, Inc.**
5995 Plaza Drive; Cypress, CA 90630-5028
(714) 952-1121
Industry: 63—Health care insurance

MISSION

PHS will maximize long term shareholder value through aggressive asset management, prudent oversight, and innovative development of strategic health care businesses, and by nurturing core competencies that add value and competitive advantage. PHS intends to develop a $2.5 billion family of companies by 1995 with an average ROE in excess of 20%.

VISION

We are an organization of dedicated people committed to improving the quality of those lives we touch.

VALUES

Accountability

We accept personal responsibility for our actions and take ownership of results without blaming others or seeking excuses. We as individuals are challenged to address marginal performance and recognize achievement by providing and accepting coaching and feedback.

Continuous Improvement

We have a sense of urgency in our search for continuous improvement to find better ways of doing everything. We encourage others to try new ideas and measure and recognize results. We are willing to change the status quo to improve.

Customer Driven

Everyone at PHS knows their customer. If you are not serving the customer, your job is to serve someone who is.

Empowerment

We have a bias for action and expect all employees to be proactive in decision-making and problem solving. We delegate authority to match responsibility, expecting decision-making to occur as close to the customer as possible.

Integrity

We adhere to a code of values and make commitments that contribute to the welfare of our constituents. We express ourselves clearly, consistently, and completely and live up to our word.

People

We respect the individual. We believe in recognition of individual business, personal and family aspirations. We celebrate success, and support an environment where it's OK to have fun, where people can enjoy their work and feel ownership in PHS' accomplishments. It is through strong performance of our people that we will achieve our goals.

Teamwork

We work for the good of the team, are accountable for the results of the entire team and together share our successes or failure. We have an atmosphere of openness, honesty, and trust.

Quality

We are a high performance company. Quality is a part of everything we do. Nothing less will be accepted.

440. Pacific Mutual Life

700 Newport Center Drive; Newport Beach, CA 92660-6307
(714) 640-3011
Industry: 63—Life insurance

The fundamental mission of Pacific Mutual is to achieve significant and sustainable growth while maintaining a strong financial position. Our organizational structure operates within centralized corporation direction of a group of separate businesses named strategic business units (SBUs). These seven units are: Individual, Pension Investments, Group Employee Benefits Operation, Multiple Employer Trust, Employee Benefits America, Pacific Financial Asset Management Corporation and Pacific Equities Network.

Each separate business is responsible for developing and implementing its specialized strategy and business plan and does so through control of those functions critical to that implementation.

At the same time, the recognition that Pacific Mutual is a collection of businesses emphasizes the need for centralized corporate direction. Overall cohesiveness is provided by the central corporate organization (CCO), which includes general management, corporate staff support, and centralized service functions.

The people of Pacific Mutual, by working together, have contributed to the financial success of the organization. They have also made it possible for the Company to be a concerned corporate citizen. Today a business must strike a responsible balance between the concept of financial growth and the economic, environmental, and social climates in which it operates. It is the basic and underlying purpose of Pacific Mutual to serve its policyowners and clients well. We believe we can best accomplish this objective if, at the same time, we contribute positively to the quality of life. Ours is an essential contribution—providing financial security to our policyowners and clients. The resulting freedom from financial worry permits individuals to experience a more complete existence now and to celebrate life more fully.

441. **Parker Drilling Company**
Eight East Third Street; Tulsa, OK 74103-3637
(918) 585-8221
Industry: 13—Oil and gas well drilling

Parker Drilling's Mission

- To maintain relationships based on integrity with shareholders, customers and employees.
- To trust in the character, hard-won knowledge, innovative spirit and common sense of our employees.
- To respect the Earth and the safety of its people.
- To keep our sense of adventure as the leader in land drilling technology.
- To be the most profitable global drilling company.
- To listen more than talk.

Annual Report 1992

442. **Parker Hannifin Corporation**
17325 Euclid Avenue; Cleveland, OH 44112
(216) 531-3000
Industry: 35—Industrial equipment
To be a leading worldwide manufacturer of components and systems for builders and users of durable goods. We design, market and manufacture products controlling motion, flow and pressure.

Annual Report 1992

443. **Parkland Industries Ltd.**
4919 59th Street, Suite 236; Riverside Office Plaza; Red Deer,
Alberta; Canada T4N 6C9
Industry: 13, 29—Petroleum production, refining, and marketing
Parkland Industries Ltd. is a diversified petroleum company with refining, retailing and transportation operations and with investments in oil

field services, exploration and production. It is the parent company of a number of wholly owned operating subsidiaries which together form an integrated Western Canadian energy company.

Parkland's goal is to be a growth oriented, healthy, independent oil and gas company providing its shareholders with an above average return on their investment, its employees with a challenging and rewarding workplace and to be a responsible and environmentally aware member of the communities in which it operates.

444. **The Partnership Group, Inc.**
    840 West Main Street; Lansdale, PA 19446
    (215) 362-5070
    Industry: 83 —Provides child and eldercare referral services

VISION

To partner with employers and employees to create a family-friendly workplace.

MISSION

To create beneficial partnerships among employers, employees and their families, and community providers of care through the delivery of innovative, high quality packages of dependent care education, financial assistance, and resource and referral services, including consultation and technical assistance. TPG believes that growth and profitability are essential in order to maintain a position as the quality leader.

Drafted January, 1989; revised January, 1992; reaffirmed September, 1992

445. **Paychex®, Inc.**
    P.O. Box 25397; Rochester, NY 14625-0397
    (716) 385-6666
    Industry: 73—Payroll accounting services

PAYCHEX MISSION STATEMENT

Our mission is to maximize the financial performance of our company through personal achievement in the development of our products and our markets.

1990

Penn, William Foundation
    see William Penn Foundation (615)

Penney, JC Company, Inc.
    see JCPenney Company, Inc. (312)

446. **Pennsylvania Power & Light Company**
Two North Ninth Street; Allentown, PA 18101-1179
(215) 774-5151
Industry: 49—Electric utility

OUR VISION

PP&L will be the energy supplier of choice.

OUR VALUES

PP&L stands for integrity, customer satisfaction, financial strength, excellence, employee fulfillment, equal opportunity, teamwork, safety, environmental commitment and public service commitment.

OUR MISSION

To meet our customers' ongoing needs for economical and reliable electric service in ways that merit the trust and confidence of our publics.

Our Business Philosophy

PP&L will strive to accomplish its mission in conformance with our Standards of Integrity and within the framework of the following philosophy and policies:

- We will be an institution that is humane, responsible and contributive to the betterment of society, with special emphasis on helping to develop both economic prosperity and a better quality-of-life in our service area. We will not compromise safety, public health or environmental quality in carrying out our mission.

- We will maintain an open and full disclosure policy with customers, employees, investors, and others affected by our business.

- We will seek public input in the development and implementation of plans to meet our commitment to provide economical and reliable electric service. We will inform the public about our progress and about probable effects of our plans and actions.

- We will search for new ideas and perspectives so as to anticipate and effectively respond to change.

- We will support the development and application of sound governmental policies that we believe to be in the best interests of our publics.

- We will create and maintain a work environment that attracts and retains capable people, encourages self-development and enables them to take pride and satisfaction in their work.

- We will support improved coordination among interconnected utilities in the planning and operation of generation and bulk power transmission facilities.

- We will strive to earn a fair return on capital provided by investors, maintain a sound credit standing and have the financial strength required to raise needed capital at reasonable costs.

- We recognize our responsibility to be good stewards of the resources entrusted to us. We will utilize those resources efficiently and effectively to carry out our mission. We will promote the wise use of electricity and provide excellent customer service.

- We will constantly look for methods to improve the operating efficiency of the electric supply system, search out cost-effective programs to improve continuity of service and develop ways to minimize adverse impacts of unforeseen circumstances.

- We will pursue a climate of excellence and intend to be a well-run, responsive, cost-effective company. We will measure our performance by regularly comparing it to the best that others achieve under similar conditions.

December, 1991
Extracted from "Vision, Values, Mission, Philosophy" booklet

447. Pepsico, Inc.

700 Anderson Hill Road; Purchase, NY 10577
(914) 253-3122
Industry: 20, 58—Food and beverage and restaurants

PepsiCo's Mission: To become the best consumer products company in the world by consistently generating the highest return to shareholders.

448. Perkin-Elmer Corporation

761 Main Avenue; Norwalk, CT 06859-0001
(203) 762-1000
Industry: 38—Analytical instruments and optics

VISION

We will all work together for the success of our company with mutual understanding, respect and trust. We will each take responsibility for our joint destiny, with knowledge of our company's status, goals and strategy. We will freely express and pursue diverse opinions, to gain the competitive advantage of a clear perspective.

We will be committed to teamwork, placing team effectiveness before personal gain. We will continuously improve through education, support and recognition, actively engaging in the problem solving process.

We will be sensitive to the needs of our customers, internal and external, and dedicated to satisfying those needs. We will provide strong financial growth opportunities for employees and shareholders. We will strive to be an asset to our community; leaders in quality and equality.

449. **Phelps Dodge Corporation**
     2600 North Central Avenue; Phoenix, AZ 85004-3014
     (602) 234-8100
     Industry: 10—Nonferrous metals mining

MISSION STATEMENT

We are an international mineral resource and industrial manufacturing company. We are committed to providing superior quality products, produced at internationally competitive costs, to customers around the globe. We seek to prosper by forging partnerships with our customers and suppliers.

Our mission in conducting business is to create and enhance long-term value for our shareholders and our employees, and to do so in an environmentally responsible manner as good citizens of the communities in which we live and work.

To accomplish our mission, we will:
- Invest the technological, financial and human resources necessary to assure world-class cost and quality levels for our products.
- Continue to grow our existing businesses that meet appropriate criteria, emphasizing mineral exploration and research and development.
- Diversify opportunistically into business areas we understand.
- Manage excellently and ethically, with emphasis on employee participation, health, safety, training and development.

450. **Philip Morris Companies, Inc.**
     120 Park Avenue; New York, NY 10017
     (212) 880-5000
     Industry: 20, 21—Food and tobacco

MISSION

Our Mission is to be the most successful consumer packaged goods company in the world, as demonstrated by our:
- Outstanding overall quality of people, products, and business plans and execution
- Superior understanding and service of customer and consumer wants and needs
- Excellent, growth-driven financial performance
- Honesty, integrity, and responsibility in all aspects of operations

The pursuit of this Mission is intended to benefit our shareholders, our customers and consumers, our employees, and the communities in which we operate.

People/Organization

We recognize that the quality, motivation, and performance of our people are the key factors in achievement of our Mission.

Accordingly, our human resources policies and practices are built on:
- A standard of excellence
- A dedication to assisting every employee in reaching his or her full potential in both performance and reward
- A total commitment to diversity, equal opportunity, and fair treatment
- Promotion based on merit, and from within whenever possible

We want our organization structure to promote maximum employee involvement and contribution, as well as communication and cooperation across all businesses.

Attitudes, Habits, and Practices

We want our way of doing business to show:
- Overarching commitment to quality
- Legal, moral, and ethical conduct
- Mutual trust and confidence
- Openness, honesty
- Initiative, imagination, and innovation
- Aggressiveness, competitiveness
- Risk acceptance
- Action orientation
- Teamwork

We want a constant sense of constructive dissatisfaction to drive a continuing search for improvement in everything we do.

We want to do the right things right.

Overall Business Strategies

We will pursue our Mission by:
- Maintaining the highest quality of people
- Protecting and building our brand franchises
- Growing profitable new business with:
  - line extensions
  - new products
  - geographic expansion
  - acquisitions
  - joint ventures and strategic alliances
- Maximizing productivity and synergy in all businesses at all times
- Making total quality management a reality in every aspect of our everyday operations
- Managing with a global perspective

451. **Phillips Petroleum Company**
Phillips Building; Bartlesville, OK 74004
(918) 661-6600
Industry: 13, 29—Integrated petroleum

OUR MISSION . . .

To be the top performer in each of our businesses.

OUR GOALS . . .

Through **continuous improvement**, we will:
Safety—Be the industry leader in safety.
Shareholder Value—Enhance the value of our shareholders' investment by providing them with total returns in the top 25 percent of the industry.
Customer Satisfaction—Provide quality products and services that meet customer requirements.
Technology—Enhance our competitive performance through technology.
Employee Satisfaction—Be one of the best companies to work for.
Corporate Citizenship—Be a leader in ethics and environmental stewardship and a valued partner in our communities.

OUR VALUES . . .

- Maintaining a safe work environment
- Communicating openly and honestly
- Improving continuously through teamwork, creativity and innovation
- Contributing to the quality of life wherever we operate
- Protecting the environment
- Treating one another with respect
- Giving equal opportunity to every employee
- Conducting ourselves ethically and responsibly

Physicians Health Plan of Minnesota
see Medica (368)

Pinto Valley Mining
see Magma Copper Company (350)

452. **Pioneer Hi-Bred International, Inc.**
6800 Pioneer Parkway; Johnston, IA 50131
(515) 245-3500
Industry: 28, 51—Agricultural chemicals and seed

MISSION STATEMENT

- Our mission is to provide products and services which increase the efficiency and profitability of the world's farmers.
- Our core business is the broad application of the science of genetics.
- We will ensure the growth of our core business and develop new opportunities which enhance the core business.

453. Pitney Bowes Inc.
World Headquarters; One Elm Croft Road; Stamford, CT 06926
(203) 356-5000
Industry: 26, 35—Business supplies

MISSION STATEMENT

Pitney Bowes is dedicated to achieving profitable growth through customer satisfaction. Pitney Bowes will fulfill this mission by using its technological expertise, its sales and service professionalism and its financial strength to deliver the innovative, quality products, systems and services that make Pitney Bowes the consistent choice of mailing, logistics and office systems customers worldwide.

454. Plourde Computer Services, Inc.
2333 Nissen Drive, Suite A; Livermore, CA 94550
(510) 606-0100
Industry: 73—Software

To provide quality system solutions and services to the retail, supermarket and related industries for the benefit of our customers, employees and shareholders.

455. Potlatch Corporation
P.O. Box 193591; San Francisco, CA 94119
(415) 576-8800
Industry: 24—Paper and forest products

Business Philosophy

Potlatch is a forest products company committed to increased earnings and a superior rate of return; achieved by talented, well-trained and highly motivated people; properly supported by a sound financial structure; and with a keen sense of responsibility for the environment and to all of the publics with whom the Company has contact.

Company Objectives

Within the framework of this business philosophy, the Company will strive to:

A. Achieve increased earnings and a superior rate of return, giving proper recognition to the inherent cycles in the economic climate.

B. Establish a balance between a disciplined drive for current earnings and a broad gauged program for long-term growth.

C. Manage a decentralized group of forest products businesses fully competitive within their own operating environments. Each business will be managed to capitalize upon its own strength as well as utilize the overall capabilities of the Company, while operating within the parameters established by total Company objectives and policies for planning, coordination and control.

D. Be sensitive to the needs and desires of employees.

E. Utilize efficiently all human, financial, physical and natural resources.

F. Maintain a sound financial structure, flexible enough to finance unique opportunities or unforeseen difficulties.

G. Provide quality products and services to our customers.

H. Fulfill our total commitment to environmental responsibility.

I. Maintain high ethical standards and open, forthright relationships with all publics.

J. Enhance and protect the natural life cycle of our renewable forests.

1972; revised April, 1992

Extracted from "The Company's Business Philosophy Objectives and Values" booklet

PP&L

see Pennsylvania Power & Light Company (446)

456. **PPG Industries, Inc.**
       One PPG Place; Pittsburgh, PA 15272
       (412) 434-3131
       Industry: 28, 32—Coatings and glass

OUR MISSION

PPG Industries is a commercial enterprise that is—
- Publicly held,
- Diversified,
- Global in operation.

PPG exists to serve customers in any market where, through the effective use of its resources, it can demonstrate excellence.

Binding us together in our mission are the values and beliefs that we hold in common:
- Dedication to the customer.
- The pursuit of excellence in everything we do.

- Respect for the dignity, rights and contributions of employees.
- Enhancement of the shareholder's investment.
- Commitment to integrity and high ethical standards in all relationships.
- Recognition of the concerns and needs of society.

OUR PRINCIPLES

In running our business, we will adhere to principles that recognize our responsibilities to customers, employees, shareholders and society.

Customers—As a customer-oriented company, we will provide our goods and services efficiently and effectively. We will do so to retain and build loyalty of our customers, and thus ensure that our businesses remain competitive and capable of growth.

Employees—At each location, we will maintain an environment that—
- Motivates employees to be productive, creative and innovative;
- Provides equal opportunities for all employees to develop their careers and find satisfaction in their jobs;
- Rewards performance.

Shareholders—Understanding our obligation to enhance PPG's value to shareholders, we will conduct our business intelligently, responsibly and capably, and mindful that risk-taking is an essential ingredient of a successful enterprise.

Society—We will manage our affairs in a way that supports the private enterprise system and identifies PPG as an outstanding corporate citizen in each country in which we do business.

OUR GOALS

In line with our mission, we have set high goals for ourselves for the decade ahead:

1. To be a leader in all areas of our business—human resources, technology, operations and marketing.

2. To be cost-effective in the use of all resources.

3. To meet customer requirements and expectations for quality products.

4. To rank among industry leaders in profitability and growth.

   (a) To achieve, under current conditions, an average return on equity (ROE) of 18% and an annual growth in real sales volume of 4%.

   (b) The corporate financial goal, above, is the sum total of all of our operations. We recognize that the individual profit center returns and growth will vary due to business characteristics and/or geographic location. But each profit center will have one thing in common—

financial goals set high enough to "stretch" each to achieve superior performance within their potential for profit and growth.

5. To increase the value added or output of each employee by at least 3% each year.

6. To operate in a manner to preserve safety, health and a sound environment. To support vigorously the reduction of waste disposal and toxic or noxious emissions, through recovery, recycling and/or reuse of raw materials and by-products.

7. To contribute to the development of sound public policy and, through internal programs, to encourage employees to be active in bettering the political process and quality of life in their communities.

OUR STRATEGY

A strategy has been developed to guide us toward achieving our goals and thus assuring that PPG grows profitably.
- We will strive to be the best in every business we pursue.
- We will participate only in businesses that contribute to excellence of performance, as measured by long-term benefits to shareholders.
- We will develop profitable growth through improvement in existing businesses, through new products and services generated internally, and through acquisitions and divestitures.
- We will have a global focus, with each line of business operating in regions of the world that are favorable to the achievement of our corporate goals.

Issued November 1, 1984
Extracted from "Blueprint for the Decade" brochure

457. **Premier Bank, N.A.**
P.O. Box 1511; Baton Rouge, LA 70821-1511
(504) 334-7021
Industry: 60—Banking

Our mission is to deliver a broad range of profitable financial services that satisfy our customers' needs and generate for our shareholders an above average return on invested capital. We will be the leading provider of high quality financial services to the citizens, businesses, and public bodies of the region in which we operate. We will conduct our efforts in such a manner that our image of integrity, leadership, and innovativeness will be enhanced.

Fall 1990

458. **Preston Trucking Company, Inc.**
151 Easton Boulevard; Preston, MD 21655
(301) 673-7151
Industry: 42—Trucking

THE MISSION OF PRESTON TRUCKING COMPANY, INC.,

A progressive transportation organization, is to provide its customers with superior services at a reasonable price through efficient operations and innovative thinking to the ultimate benefit of its associates and stockholders.

"Preston People Make the Difference."

[Acquired by Yellow Corporation in 1993]

459. **Price Waterhouse**
1251 Avenue of the Americas; New York, NY 10020
(212) 819-5000
Industry: 87—Accounting

THE CLIENT BILL OF RIGHTS

The Right to Professional Excellence

We will be technically proficient in all areas in which we provide advice. We will stay current on business and technical developments and seek counsel from appropriate firm professionals when in doubt about a course of action. We will keep abreast of all issues affecting our client so we can anticipate challenges and provide appropriate advice.

The Right to be Served by Professionals Who Understand Our Business

We will learn all we can about our client's industry and business. We will get to know people within the client organization and outside it who have in-depth knowledge of the client's business, its culture, and its strategic objectives, and we will listen to our client to understand its needs. Being in the thick of our client's business—not on the sidelines—will allow us to identify and anticipate issues of concern to our client. While others may learn on the job, we will strive to know as much as possible about the client and its industry before we ever begin working with a client.

The Right to Proactive Advice and Creative Business Ideas

We will take the initiative in proposing actions to enhance our client's success, striving always to offer the innovative recommendations our client expects from its business advisers. We will demonstrate to our client that we expect to be and are qualified to be among those who are consulted about significant client events at the planning stage. We will be thought of as the "idea people." When asked for creative ways to help our client achieve its objectives, we will be the firm that says "Yes, can do. . . ."

The Right to Independent Viewpoints and Perspectives

We will advise our client about actions that are in its best long-term interests. Although we will keep client objectives clearly in mind as we aid in decision-making, we will not be sycophants. We will have the independence of spirit, the courage, and the confidence to discourage the client from pursuing a course of action that we believe to be ill-advised.

The Right to Effective Communication

We will keep our client contacts informed about the progress of our work and any issues that require their attention. Our written communication will be literate and clear, and our oral communication equally articulate. We will treat our client contacts as professional equals, extending them and their staffs the same courtesy and respect we ourselves expect. In our communications with client executives and staff, we will demonstrate that we are well-rounded people they can relate to on levels other than the professional one; clients like to do business with people who are interesting and personable, just as we do.

The Right to a Wide Range of Professional Resources

We will tap the extensive resources of Price Waterhouse to provide our client with the most experienced and savvy business advice available. We will introduce our colleagues to our client contacts and, when relevant, involve them in client service planning and delivery. To promote well-coordinated services, we will ensure that all appropriate PW professionals are kept informed about services proposed and provided to a client.

The Right to Dependable Service

We will never miss a deadline or renege on a commitment. We will do it right the first time and complete the assignment better and faster than the client expects. We will avoid surprises about technical and reporting issues, fees, and staff turnover. When we are the best, we will let the client know; if we do not have the required depth in a particular area, we will have the confidence to direct the client elsewhere.

The Right to Service Anytime and Anyplace

We will always be available to our client, anytime and anyplace we are needed. That means spending more time in our client's office than in our own, being "on call" for our client at all times, and keeping in close touch with client contacts when we are not on the premises. And it means bringing the worldwide resources of the firm to bear on client issues, providing the services needed across town or across the globe.

The Right to State-of-the-Art Technology

We will take advantage of the vast technological resources the firm has created to benefit PW professionals and clients. We will use internal tools to enhance the efficiency and cost-effectiveness of our services. And we will implement PW proprietary software and customize other products that will help our client attain better management information and more effective operations.

The Right to Value-Added Service

We will always be thinking about how our client can be more successful and of ways we can help it achieve its business goals. We will make our client's concerns our concerns and put its needs ahead of our own. We will challenge ourselves and our client, asking the tough questions, not being afraid to be wrong. We will be ever vigilant in identifying additional ways we can strengthen our client's competitive edge, ways in which we can offer even more than the client expects.

460. **Prima Communications, Inc.**
      P.O. Box 1260; Rocklin, CA 95677
      (916) 786-0426
      Industry: 27—Publishing

Prima publishes books to educate, inform, and entertain. The books are written, edited, designed, and presented in ways that make their uniqueness, value, and originality clear to their intended readers.

461. **Procter & Gamble Company**
      P.O. Box 599; Cincinnati, OH 45201
      (513) 983-1100
      Industry: 20, 28—Toiletries and food products

STATEMENT OF PURPOSE

We will provide products of superior quality and value that best fill the needs of the world's consumers.

We will achieve that purpose through an organization and a working environment which attracts the finest people; fully develops and challenges our individual talents; encourages our free and spirited collaboration to drive the business ahead; and maintains the Company's historic principles of integrity and doing the right thing.

Through the successful pursuit of our commitment, we expect our brands to achieve leadership share and profit positions and that, as a result, our business, our people, our shareholders, and the communities in which we live and work, will prosper.

> Extracted from "Facts About Proctor & Gamble" brochure

462. **Progressive Corp.**
      6000 Parkland Boulevard; Mayfield Heights, OH 44124
      (216) 464-8000
      Industry: 63—Property and casualty insurance

We seek to be an excellent, innovative, growing and enduring business by reducing the human trauma and economic costs of auto accidents in cost-effective and profitable ways that delight customers.

463. **Promus Companies Incorporated**
        1023 Cherry Road; Memphis, TN 38117
        (901) 762-8600
        Industry: 70—Lodging and gaming
  Our vision is to provide the best experience to our gaming and hotel customers by having the best people trained, empowered and pledged to excellence, delivering the best service, quality and value to every customer, every time . . . guaranteed.

464. **PSI Energy, Inc.**
        1000 East Main Street; Plainfield, IN 46168
        (317) 838-1559
        Industry: 49—Electric utility
  We will be a leader in the emerging energy services industry by challenging conventional wisdom and creating superior value in a safe and environmentally responsible manner.

Adopted 1989–1990

  [At press time, PSI Energy, Inc. is involved in merger talks with Cincinnati Gas & Electric Co.]

465. **Public Broadcasting Service**
        1320 Braddock Place; Alexandria, VA 22314
        (703) 739-5000
        Industry: 48—Broadcasting
  Our vision for PBS is to enrich the human experience and build a better world.
  Our driving force is public service.
  Our mission is to educate, enlighten and inform viewers; provide leadership and support to member stations; and communicate the value of PBS and station services so as to merit financial support for public television.

  The PBS Agenda
  1. Provide PBS leadership and services that are ESSENTIAL to our society and to our licensees. Offer quality services that our licensees, the public, program producers, educational interests, Congress and the media consider to be ESSENTIAL to the well being of the American people.
  2. Constantly seek to make PBS the PREFERRED place to invest resources. Continue working to increase the satisfaction of those who support PBS (board members, licensees, viewers, funders) so that they'll see PBS as the PREFERRED place to invest their limited time and money.
  3. Continue to make PBS a GREAT place to work. Maintain an organizational structure and a management style that:

- Honors trust and trustworthiness as the basis for all interaction.
- Holds as its highest priority making PBS essential to its investors and the preferred place for continued investment of their time and money.
- Practices customer service that demonstrates the highest regard for all who use PBS services (board, staff, licensees, viewers, producers, funders, related organizations and the media).
- Secures adequate resources and wisely uses them to deliver essential services.
- Seeks "win-win" solutions to all challenges and problems, both internal and external.
- Is free from perceived bureaucracy and internal politics and fiefdoms.
- Demonstrates concern for organizational and personal success of all staff members.
- Encourages employees to achieve their highest professional goals by giving them opportunities to pursue their aspirations.

Adopted July 13, 1987; amended February 19, 1992

466. **Public Service Company of Colorado**
P.O. Box 840; Denver, CO 80201-0840
(303) 571-7511
Industry: 49—Electric utility

CORPORATE MISSION

PUBLIC SERVICE COMPANY OF COLORADO is an energy company that primarily provides gas, electricity and related services to present and potential markets.

1983

467. **Public Service Company of New Mexico**
Alvarado Square; Albuquerque, NM 87158
(505) 848-2700
Industry: 49—Public utility

WE BELIEVE

TOGETHER WE CREATE OPPORTUNITIES FOR GROWTH.

OUR MISSION is to be the energy supplier of choice in New Mexico and regional markets and to provide high-quality, competitive utility products and services.

WE BELIEVE that to achieve our mission, we must work together as a team unified by our commitment to excellence and high ethical standards.

CUSTOMERS

WE BELIEVE our first responsibility is to our customers. Customer satisfaction is the foundation for growth in a competitive energy environment. We are dedicated to serving our external customers' needs by providing safe, dependable, high-quality and competitively-priced electric, natural gas, and water services. We support each other, our internal customers, and believe each work force member serves a customer.

INVESTORS

WE BELIEVE that business must make a fair profit while dealing honestly and responsibly with our customers, work force members, our communities, and our environment. We are committed to generating profits that will provide a competitive return to those who invest in the company.

WORK FORCE

WE BELIEVE each of us is responsible for his or her performance and shares responsibility for the performance of the company. Acceptance of these responsibilities is critical to the success of the company. We respect the dignity of individual work force members. Our work environment shall provide an opportunity for personal growth and satisfaction, for working together as teams, for rewarding quality performance, and for recognizing the value of diversity in our work force.

COMMUNITY

WE BELIEVE we are responsible to the communities we serve. We accept our role in enhancing the quality of life by supporting civic pride, economic development, better health and education, and protection of the environment. We are dedicated to our communities through volunteer leadership and providing company resources where possible.

1991

468. **Public Service Company of Oklahoma**
     Subsidiary of Central and South West Company
     212 East Sixth Street; Tulsa, OK 74102-0201
     (918) 599-2000
     Industry: 49—Electric utility

Our mission is to understand and satisfy customer expectations for quality and energy and energy-related products and services and profitably serve Oklahoma markets.

1991

469. **Puget Sound Power & Light Company**
     411 108th Avenue, NE; Bellevue, WA 98004
     (206) 454-6363
     Industry: 49—Electric utility

OUR MISSION

Our mission at Puget Power is to:
- Provide competitive customer service
- Build shareholder value
- Enhance community quality

Plan and Innovate Together for Excellence"

OUR GOALS

CUSTOMER SERVICE

Set the standard for customer service excellence.

We want our customers to point to us as the example for meeting customer service expectations. This standard applies to all customers, whether we are serving the retail customer directly or another person or department within the company.

To accomplish this goal, we will determine what the expectations of our customers are, adapt our products and services to address those expectations in an efficient and cost-effective manner, implement in a way that we believe will meet or exceed those expectations, and monitor our customers' satisfaction with the service and products we provide.

FINANCIAL PERFORMANCE

Achieve financial performance that ranks in the upper third of our industry.

We have a financial responsibility to the shareholders who own Puget Power. We will meet their expectations by operating in ways that make the company an outstanding investment opportunity. We believe the best way to achieve this is to produce long-term, consistent improvement in total returns to the shareholder.

Our individual decisions affect the cost-effectiveness and efficiency of our work and ultimately the earnings the owners of this company receive.

COMMUNITY AND ENVIRONMENTAL PARTNERSHIPS

Be a leader in achieving progress on environmental, economic, educational and social needs of our communities.

We are an integral part of the communities we serve. We foster and encourage partnerships with our communities in addressing a wide range of community needs.

We will lead the way in protecting the environment through our daily activities and planning efforts. We will enhance the quality of life in our communities through leadership in volunteerism on environmental, educational, economic, and social issues.

TEAM BUILDING

Acknowledge and build upon the increasing diversity and skills of our team.

Puget Power's team is made up of individuals who bring to the workplace a valuable combination of skills, experiences, and perspectives. Each individual's contribution is important to the team's success. Together we make the difference through our commitment and creativity.

PWA Corp.

see Canadian Airlines International Limited (108)

470. **Quaker Oats Company**
       P.O. Box 9001; Chicago, IL 60604-9001
       (312) 222-7111
       Industry: 20—Food and beverages

OUR MISSION

Our mission is to maximize value for our shareholders over the long-term. This challenges us to employ our two key assets—our portfolio of brands and our people—to maximize their value creation potential. These two assets are vitally linked. Management is empowered to oversee the investment in and the maintenance of our brands. Its specific challenge is to maximize each brand's growth and profit contribution potential—to create economic value.

Annual Report, 1991

471. **Quaker State Corporation**
       P.O. Box 989; Oil City, PA 16301
       (814) 676-7676
       Industry: 29—Petroleum refining

Quaker State Corporation's mission is to be the quality leader in every area in which we do business. Quality leadership depends on delivering to every customer superior value, based equally on the quality of our service, and the integrity of our people.

Only by satisfying our customers' needs can all the members of Quaker State's community of common interest—shareholders, employees, and suppliers—achieve success, growth, and enhanced investment value. At Quaker State our major asset is the quality image projected by the Quaker State name.

The Big Q Stands for Quality—
Always Has. Always Will.

472. **QuikTrip Corporation**
       P.O. Box 3475; Tulsa, OK 74101-7017

(918) 836-7015

Industry: 54—Convenience stores

Vision Statement

To be clearly the best gasoline and convenience marketer in the eyes of the customer, the competition, and our employees.

Mission Statement

To seek maximum long-term profit growth as the primary means to ensure the prosperity and well-being of our employees, stockholders, and customers.

473. **Quintiles Transnational Corp.**
P.O. Box 13979; Research Triangle Park, NC 27709-3979
(919) 941-2888
Industry: 80—Health care services

Quintiles' Statement of Purpose

Mission

As an ethical, competitive, and profitable company, Quintiles' mission is to advance scientific knowledge for improved health care. To accomplish this mission, we provide strategic advice and implement the research required to develop products for pharmaceutical, medical device, and biotechnology clients as they evaluate the safety, efficacy, and benefit of new programs worldwide.

Quality

Founded on principles of scientific integrity, Quintiles takes pride in quality that is based on high ethical standards and which is consonant with the regulatory environment. We emphasize quality at every interface: with clients, between employees, across their various disciplines, and with the business community in which we work.

Leadership

Our approach has been and will continue to be one of scientific and technological leadership, pragmatism, and innovation. We believe success depends on the efforts of the talented and dedicated people at Quintiles who uphold the Company's proven standards.

Teamwork

Quintiles fosters global collegial relationships among employees and with clients to promote innovation and efficiency. We recognize the importance of a working environment that inspires creativity, challenges abilities, and rewards achievement. Through individual commitment and teamwork, we attain personal and corporate goals.

Value

Quintiles is committed to solid investments in global growth and service development to meet our clients' expanding business needs. With this commitment we create value for our stakeholders, that is, our employees, management, owners, and business affiliates, by performing in a manner that will benefit society and enhance the return on our investments.

Revised May 19, 1992

R

474. Raley's Inc.
500 West Capitol Avenue; West Sacramento, CA 95605-2696
(916) 373-3333
Industry: 54—Supermarkets

MISSION STATEMENT

RALEY'S BUSINESS PHILOSOPHY TODAY

Raley's is a retail business operating full service combination supermarket and drug center stores in the Northern and Central California and Nevada areas, with the following characteristics and relationships:

Our Customers view Raley's as a convenient, clean, well stocked, friendly place to shop with a good variety of quality products.

Our Employees regard Raley's as a growing family organization providing opportunities for the future and a good fair place to work.

Our Vendors regard Raley's as innovative, loyal, ethical, fair, partners in business.

Our Communities view Raley's as a good neighbor, responsible citizen and a good employer who is concerned about food safety, environmental and humanitarian issues.

Our Competition views Raley's as tough, fair, ethical, good merchants operating a progressive prototype store.

RALEY'S BUSINESS PHILOSOPHY FOR THE FUTURE

Raley's will be the leading retail business operating full service combination supermarket and drug center stores in the Northern and Central California and Nevada areas. We want:

Our Customers to view Raley's as the leader in customer service with clean, convenient stores and a wide selection of quality products at fair prices.

Our Employees to regard Raley's as a growing organization providing opportunities and training for the future; a good, fair place to work with competitive compensation; an employer who recognizes and rewards hard work and commitment and who strives to maintain a family orientation and a high level of trust.

Our Vendors to regard Raley's as innovative, loyal, ethical, reasonable partners in business who will expect and demand the same price and service given to our competitors.

Our Communities to view Raley's as a good neighbor, responsible citizen and a excellent employer who is concerned about food safety, environmental and humanitarian issues.

Our Competition to view Raley's as aggressive, tough, fair, ethical, first class merchants operating the dominant prototype store and able to respond quickly and effectively to any competitive challenge.

475. **RAND**
Formerly known as The Rand Corporation
1700 Main Street; Santa Monica, CA 90407
(310) 393-0411
Industry: 87—Consulting

To further and promote scientific, educational, and charitable purposes, all for the public welfare and security of the United States of America.

Extracted from "Articles of Incorporation and By-Laws," May 14, 1948; As amended through November 13, 1987

476. **Raychem Corporation**
300 Constitution Drive; Menlo Park, CA 94025-1164
(415) 361-3333
Industry: 36—Electronic components

Raychem Statement Of Corporate Values

Raychem is a global corporation dedicated to creating and manufacturing unique products based on leadership in materials science.

We aim:
- to delight our customers with excellent service and products;
- to be proud of our performance, our people, our practices, and our products;
- to generate superior returns for our shareholders.

At Raychem, we:

Perform according to the highest principles of integrity and honesty.

Employ outstanding people, with a diverse blend of skills and backgrounds.

Create superior products that anticipate and fulfill real customer needs.

Encourage innovation in technology and prudent risk taking.

Commit to total quality management, continuously improving everything we do throughout the organization.

Expect and enable our managers to provide leadership and vision.

Communicate openly, sensitively, and realistically with each other.

Develop the talents of all our people through training and coaching, while respecting individual aspirations.

Recognize and reward both individual and team performance and share in the success of the corporation.

Insist on the highest level of concern for our people, our communities, and our environment.

Copyright © 1990 Raychem Corporation

Red Cross
see American Red Cross (36)

477. Redken Laboratories, Inc.
P.O. Box 7935; Canoga Park, CA 91309-7935
(818) 992-2700
Industry: 28—Health and beauty products

REDKEN MISSION

Through full service distributors, fulfill stylist and client needs for the highest quality hair care, hair fashion, skin care beauty products and services based on the application of science and education on a worldwide basis to improve salon, stylist, and Redken income and profitability.

Drafted February, 1992

478. Rhode Island Hospital
593 Eddy Street; Providence, RI 02903
(401) 444-5123
Industry: 80—Hospital

RHODE ISLAND HOSPITAL MISSION

The mission of Rhode Island Hospital, as a leading Academic Medical Center, is to improve the health status of the people of Rhode Island and southeastern New England. This mission will be accomplished by:

- Providing a full range of patient care services, ranging from preventative to complex tertiary care, in setting spanning hospital and home, with access ensured for all members of the communities served;

- Educating and training physicians, nurses, and allied health care professionals, believing that education programs are the best assurance that the highest quality clinical care will be provided;

- Supporting biomedical and healthcare delivery research which advances medical and healthcare knowledge and heightens the intellectual aspirations of healthcare providers;

- Working with government, business leaders, and other providers to develop an equitable and fiscally responsible health policy;

- Providing opportunities for employees to develop and apply their skills and abilities in a work environment which is safe and fosters a healthful lifestyle.

479. **Rhône-Poulenc Rorer, Inc.**
500 Arcola Road; Collegeville, PA 19426
(215) 454-6800
Industry: 28—Pharmaceuticals

THE RHÔNE-POULENC MISSION

Our mission is to become the BEST pharmaceutical company in the world by dedicating our resources, our talents and our energies to help improve human health and the quality of life of people throughout the world.

BEING THE BEST MEANS:

- Being the BEST at satisfying the needs of everyone we serve: patients, healthcare professionals, employees, communities, governments and shareholders;
- Being BETTER AND FASTER than our competitors at discovering and bringing to market important new medicines in selected therapeutic areas;
- Operating with the HIGHEST professional and ethical standards in all our activities, building on the Rhône-Poulenc and Rorer heritage of integrity;
- Being seen as the BEST place to work, attracting and retaining talented people at all levels by creating an environment that encourages them to develop their potential to the full;
- Generating consistently BETTER results than our competitors, through innovation and a total commitment to quality in everything we do.

THE RHÔNE-POULENC RORER PRINCIPLES

Satisfying the needs of our customers
We will strive for the highest quality and continuous improvement in our products and services for all our customers, external and internal, maintaining the highest standards of integrity in all our relationships.

Global communication and collaboration
We will be a global company, fostering open communication, receptivity to new ideas and worldwide collaboration on strategies that support the growth and success of the company.

Being entrepreneurial and acting quickly

We will be entrepreneurial, working with a great sense of urgency, encouraging teamwork and quick decision-making, rewarding innovation and results at every level of the organization.

Treating each other fairly and valuing diversity

We will treat each other fairly, with trust and respect, valuing cultural and individual differences so that our company is strengthened by our diversity.

Caring for our communities and the environment

We will be good neighbors, working to improve the safety of the environment and the vitality of our communities and our workplace.

When we operate according to these principles, Rhône-Poulenc Rorer will grow and prosper as a company and so will we as individuals.

480. **Rich Products Corporation**
1150 Niagara Street; Buffalo, NY 14213
(716) 878-8034
Industry: 20—Food products

Our Philosophy Statement

Our Mission

Rich Products Corporation is a dynamic, growth-oriented company on a World Class Mission to set new standards of excellence in customer satisfaction and achieve new levels of competitive success in every category of business in which we operate.

Our Strategy

We will achieve our World Class Mission by working together as a team in a total quality effort to:

Impress Our Customers

Provide exceptional service to our external and internal customers the first time and every time.

Improve, Improve, Improve!

Continuously improve the quality and value of the goods we produce and services we provide.

Empower People

Unleash the talents of all our Associates by creating an environment that is safe, that recognizes and rewards their achievements, and encourages their participation and growth.

Work Smarter

Drive out all waste of time, effort, and material—all the barriers and extra steps that keep us from doing our jobs right.

Do the Right Thing!

Maintain the highest standards of integrity and ethical conduct and behave as good citizens in our communities.

481. **Ritz-Carlton® Hotel Company**
      3414 Peachtree Road, NE, Suite 300; Atlanta, GA 30326
      (404) 237-5500
      Industry: 58, 70—Restaurants and hotels

MISSION STATEMENT

The Ritz-Carlton Hotel Company will be recognized by frequent traveling executives and meeting planners, as well as the travel and hotel industry, as a dynamic, fast growing and highly professional company operating the finest and most successful hotels in each of their locations.

The Ritz-Carlton will be known for consistency in providing the very highest quality in facilities and product; and for friendly, personal and efficient comfortable service.

Guests will enjoy the natural warm welcome and relaxed, comfortable ambience of The Ritz-Carlton Hotels.

Creative, entrepreneurial food and beverage operations will be a hallmark of The Ritz-Carlton, providing a strong personality for each hotel and attracting significant local patronage.

Considered the social center in each community, The Ritz-Carlton will be the first choice for important events. Through careful attention to detail and creativity, banquets and conferences will be remembered as special occasions. All those factors will contribute to an unusually high level of customer loyalty and repeat business.

The Ritz-Carlton will be regarded as an industry leader for its innovation in each discipline of the business, blending effectively the finest traditions of our profession with progressive management philosophy.

The Ritz-Carlton will be known as the easiest company in the industry to do business with. The Ritz-Carlton's Marketing and Sales team will be seen by their peers as highly aggressive and competitive and regarded by their clients as reliable, helpful and resourceful.

The Ritz-Carlton will have earned a reputation for achieving a positive share of each market it serves.

The Ritz-Carlton will be known as the best company in the industry to work for.

Because the team approach to management and philosophy of promotion from within, employees will have a strong sense of proprietorship and pride. This will result in high morale, low turnover and exceptional company loyalty.

Through open, two-way communication, employees will share the company's objectives and strive toward achievement of the highest industry awards such as the Mobil 5-Star and AAA 5-Diamond recognition. Throughout The Ritz-Carlton there will be a thoughtful awareness that the guest is always right.

The company's partners and owners will view The Ritz-Carlton as successful because of its unparalleled reputation for quality, and because of its achievement of operating results and profits in excess of industry norms.

Copyright © 1983 The Ritz-Carlton Hotel Company

RITZ-CARLTON is a federally registered trademark of The Ritz-Carlton Hotel Company.

482. RJR Nabisco Inc.

1301 Avenue of the Americas; New York, NY 10019
(212) 258-5600
Industry: 20, 21—Food and tobacco products

RJR NABISCO PRINCIPLES

- The marketplace is the driving force behind everything we do.
- We will operate in an entrepreneurial, decentralized organization with a minimum of bureaucracy.
- We will think and act with a sense of urgency.
- We will see quality as a way of life.
- We will have a sense of ownership that demands resources be used wisely and prudently.
- We will cherish teamwork.
- We will act in an ethical manner with each other, our customers and the general public.
- We will be sensitive to the needs of all employees.

483. Roadway Services, Inc.

1077 Gorge Boulevard; P.O. Box 88; Akron, OH 44309-0088
(216) 384-8184
Industry: 42—Trucking

Roadway Services, Inc.

MISSION STATEMENT

Roadway Services, Inc. through its operating companies, is in the business of satisfying customers by meeting their requirements for value added transportation and logistics services, thereby creating value for our shareholders.

- We will be quality driven and customer focused in pursuit of this mission. We will be the best there is at the art and science of satisfying the customer.
- We will be efficient in the use of human and other resources.
- We will provide our people with a challenging and satisfying work experience.
- We will conduct our affairs with integrity as a responsible corporate citizen.

February, 1990

Roadway Express, Inc.

OUR MISSION

We will provide the highest quality freight transportation and related products and services in both domestic and international markets. Our principal focus is longhaul motor carrier based services. We will achieve an unsurpassed level of customer satisfaction by providing flexible and efficient service to our customers.

OUR VISION

By dedicating ourselves to both customer and employee satisfaction, we will accomplish our mission.

Our customers will view us as partners who work with them to meet their changing needs and expectations. They will be confident doing business with Roadway and will be an "extension of our sales force" in the marketplace.

We will work together to make Roadway the type of company where people would rather work than in any other place; where everyone enthusiastically participates in the company's success. We will achieve this goal by emphasizing that everyone:

- Is a valued and respected member of the Roadway team.
- Is empowered to make decisions to achieve our mission.

We will conduct our business in a lawful and socially responsible manner and support the communities in which we do business.

By being the best at meeting or exceeding customer expectations, we will be the industry leader in quality and profits.

October, 1989

484. Robbins & Myers, Inc.
1400 Kettering Tower; Dayton, OH 45423
(513) 222-2610

Industry: 35—Pumps

Robbins & Myers, Inc. is an international company committed to leadership in the design, manufacture and marketing of superior quality, high value products primarily for the fluids handling and motion control markets. Our objective is to grow through the development of new products, the expansion of existing markets and the search for new, related markets on a worldwide basis. This mission is best accomplished by providing the highest level of customer satisfaction through motivated employees dedicated to quality and service.

Robbins & Myers is committed to these basic values:

We believe CUSTOMER SATISFACTION is essential to our success. Their needs must be understood and satisfied with the highest quality products and service.

We recognize our EMPLOYEES as essential to the success of our company. All will be treated with dignity and fairness. We will promote an environment which encourages, recognizes and rewards innovation and productivity.

We are committed to fulfilling our SHAREHOLDER RETURN expectations over the long-term through sustained value-creating performance.

We will conduct our business activities with INTEGRITY, complying with all legal requirements and ethical standards.

We are committed to being GOOD CORPORATE CITIZENS, participating in the economic, educational and social well-being of the communities in which we operate.

We view our SUPPLIERS, DISTRIBUTORS, and REPRE-SENTATIVES as partners and recognize that their success is critical to our goals of superior quality and service.

485. The Robert R. McCormick Tribune Foundation

435 North Michigan Avenue, Suite 770; Chicago, IL 60611
(312) 222-3510
Industry: 67—Charitable foundation

The Robert R. McCormick Tribune Foundation is dedicated to a democratic society and its quality of life.

Mission:

- To improve the social and economic environment.
- To encourage a free and responsible discussion of issues affecting the nation.
- To enhance the effectiveness of American education.
- To stimulate responsible citizenship.

486. **Robert Wood Johnson Foundation**
      P.O. Box 2316; Princeton, NJ 08543
      (609) 452-8701
      Industry: 67—Charitable foundation

We have framed our program goals as societal objectives in order to make explicit our vision of the changes needed to improve America's health and health care. They are:
- to assure that Americans of all ages have access to basic health care
- to promote health and prevent disease by reducing harm caused by substance abuse
- to improve the way services are organized and provided to people with chronic health conditions
- to seek opportunities to help the nation address, effectively and fairly, the overarching problem of escalating health care expenditures.

                    Extracted from "Guidelines for Grant Applicants," 1992

487. **Rochester Gas and Electric Corporation**
      89 East Avenue; Rochester, NY 14649
      (716) 546-2700
      Industry: 49—Electric utility

Our mission is to deliver energy and energy-related services with 100% Customer Satisfaction 100% of the time.

                                                        November, 1991

488. **Rochester Telephone Corp.**
      180 South Clinton Avenue; Rochester, NY 14646-0700
      (716) 777-1000
      Industry: 48—Telecommunications

ROCHESTER TEL

OUR VISION

WE WILL BE THE PREMIER COMPANY IN THE TELE-COMMUNICATIONS INDUSTRY

By providing products, services and applications that delight our **customers**

By being a team of qualified **employees** committed and accountable to this vision

By delivering exceptional returns to our **owners**

                                                        November, 1992

489. **Rockwell International Corporation**
      2201 Seal Beach Boulevard; Seal Beach, CA 90740
      (310) 797-3311

Industry: 34, 35, 37—Aerospace and defense products

WHAT ROCKWELL BELIEVES

We believe maximizing the satisfaction of our customers is our most important concern as a means of warranting their continued loyalty.

We believe in providing superior value to customers through high-quality, technologically-advanced, fairly-priced products and customer service, designed to meet customer needs better than all alternatives.

We believe Rockwell people are our most important assets, making the critical difference in how well Rockwell performs; and, through their work and effort, separating Rockwell from all competitors.

We believe we have an obligation for the well-being of the communities in which we live and work.

We believe excellence is the standard for all we do, achieved by encouraging and nourishing:
- Respect for the individual
- Honest, open communication
- Individual development and satisfaction
- A sense of ownership and responsibility for Rockwell's success
- Participation, cooperation and teamwork
- Creativity, innovation and initiative
- Prudent risk-taking
- Recognition and rewards for achievement

We believe success is realized by:
- Achieving leadership in the markets we serve
- Focusing our resources and energy on global markets where our technology, knowledge, capabilities and understanding of customers combine to provide the opportunity for leadership
- Maintaining the highest standards of ethics and integrity in every action we take, in everything we do.

We believe the ultimate measure of our success is the ability to provide a superior value to our shareholders, balancing near-term and long-term objectives to achieve both a competitive return on investment, and consistent increased market value.

490. **Rohm and Haas Company**
Independence Mall West; Philadelphia, PA 19105
(215) 592-3000
Industry: 28—Chemicals

COMPANY VISION

Rohm and Haas is a highly innovative, growing global specialty polymer and chemical company building on an ever-broadening technical base.

Our customers regard us as indispensable to their success. We are their best and most consistent supplier of products and services. The general public views the Company as a valued corporate citizen and a good neighbor.

Our employees behave as owners and feel accountable for their performance and success of the Company.

Ethical behavior, teamwork, fast action and a passion for constant improvement are the hallmarks of our culture.

491. **Rollins, Inc.**
     2170 Piedmont Road; Atlanta, GA 30324
     (404) 888-2000
     Industry: 07, 73—Pest control and security services

Our mission is to be the Nation's Best Service Company. We will accomplish this goal by delivering the finest quality services and value to our customers, while being environmentally responsible. This will provide opportunities and security for employees, as well as maximize long-term financial performance for stockholders.

492. **Royal LePage Limited**
     33 Yonge Street, Suite 1000; Toronto, Ontario; Canada M5E 1S9
     (416) 359-2405
     Industry: 65—Real estate development

Our mission is to be Canada's finest, most professional real estate services organization.

In fulfilling our mission, we make these commitments:

To clients who are served by Royal LePage, we commit to delivering high quality, industry leading and innovative real estate products and services on a complete cost-efficient basis. Our business relationships will be characterized in the highest degree by honesty, credibility and fair dealing. We are committed to setting the pace in service excellence.

To our fellow sales representatives, management and support staff of Royal LePage, we commit to providing a work environment, industry leading support and service systems, along with compensation and recognition programs that encourage the highest level of personal contribution and achievement, while maximizing opportunities for personal development and fulfillment.

To the common shareholders of Royal LePage, we commit to consistently increasing your total return as measured by earnings, asset values and share price.

To those who share the business community with Royal LePage, we commit to delivering a level of real estate professionalism that contributes to the overall well being of the community.

Setting the pace in service excellence

493. **RR Donnelley & Sons Company**
      77 West Wacker Drive; Chicago, IL 60601
      (312) 326-8020
      Industry: 27—Printing and publishing

RR DONNELLEY & SONS COMPANY

R. R. Donnelley & Sons Company is an enduring company. We have been successful because of the quality and the integrity of the people we have employed; because we have committed to and honored certain basic values; and because we have maintained a proper balance among the long-term interests of customers, shareholders, employees, suppliers and the public at large. We will continue to be successful because we have the resources—*human, financial* and *material*—and the will to be forward-looking and forward-acting and to continue to honor our basic commitments.

OUR MISSION

It is the mission of R. R. Donnelley & Sons Company to be a preeminent worldwide provider of printing and related information and value-added services and products for owners, publishers and users of information.

OUR BASIC COMMITMENTS

To Our Customers

- We will provide services of superior quality and value.
- Customer satisfaction will be the paramount consideration in the performance of every aspect of our work.

To Each Other

- Each of us is entitled to and will be treated with dignity and respect.
- We will deal fairly and openly with each other as individuals and provide fair and equal employment opportunities to all.
- Each of us must act with integrity and adhere to the highest standards of business ethics.

To Our Shareholders

- We will strive to provide our shareholders with a consistently superior financial performance measured against other medium-to-large publicly held companies of any kind.
- Lawful conduct will be present in every aspect of our business.

To Quality and Excellence

- Quality must permeate everything about our company.
- Quality of our services and products must be preeminent.
- We will lead in the research, development and implementation of new technology as it applies to the growth and betterment of our business.

To Profit and Growth

- We will consistently increase our earnings and maintain a superior return on shareholders' equity.
- We will grow profitably in order to meet our responsibilities to employees, shareholders and others with whom we deal.

To Others

- We will deal fairly and honorably with our suppliers.
- We will be a responsible corporate citizen in the communities in which we have facilities and in society in general.

Our company is "The House that Quality Built." As we grow, as we put additions on that house, each of us must exercise great care so as not to give less attention to the foundation of quality than did our predecessors.

494.   **Rubbermaid Incorporated**
       1147 Akron Road; Wooster, OH 44691
       (216) 264-6464
       Industry: 30—Plastic products

MISSION

Our mission is to be the leading world-class producer of best value, brand-name, primarily plastic products for the consumer, commercial, agricultural and industrial markets which are responsive to significant trends.

We will achieve this mission by having each Rubbermaid business earn a leading marketshare position. We will think, plan, experiment and manage strategically and globally. We will monitor, interpret and respond to changing trends to pursue the following avenues of growth:

- Continuous Value Improvement—Make our products a better value
- Market Penetration—Sell more of our current products
- Product Enhancement—Revitalize our current products

- Product Line Extensions—Expand our current products
- New Product Lines—Add lines to strengthen current market positions
- New Markets—Enter where strengths can be leveraged
- New Technology—Leverage new materials and processes
- Global Expansion—Think and compete internationally
- Service—Combine complementary product and service offerings
- Franchising—Create businesses with partners
- Licensing—Leverage our and our partners' brand names
- Acquisitions—Add complementary businesses
- Joint Ventures and Alliances—Leverage partners' expertise
- Rubbermaid Resources—Utilize the full resources of Rubbermaid

We will be a learning organization.

FUNDAMENTAL PRINCIPLES

We believe that by eliminating boundaries between partners, we can continuously improve the total value we create for our consumers and end users.

We believe that our associates, consumers, customers, suppliers, shareholders and communities are entitled to share in the economic benefit derived from our efforts to create, develop, produce, source and market products worldwide.

To this end,

FOR OUR CONSUMERS we will strive to

- understand their needs and delight them with our products and service
- give them ever-improved value
- help protect and improve the environment

FOR OUR CUSTOMERS we will strive to

- work as partners with integrity and principled negotiations
- understand and innovatively respond to their changing requirements
- invest aggressively in research, new products and technology
- offer on-trend products of exceptional quality, design and utility
- provide customization, variety and creative programs

FOR OUR SUPPLIERS we will strive to

- foster mutually beneficial long-term business partnerships
- work together to reduce or eliminate non-value activities
- be objective and ethical in all transactions

FOR OUR ASSOCIATES we will strive to
- recognize and develop the potential of each associate and the power of teams
- provide an environment which is motivational and reinforces initiative
- invest wisely and consistently in building associates' skills
- nurture diversity and variety of thought
- create focused decentralized operating units
- reinforce experimentation, listening and risk taking
- create operating hubs of skills and capabilities
- offer equal opportunity for career growth and advancement
- provide rewards and opportunity consistent with their contribution

FOR OUR COMMUNITIES
- be a good corporate citizen
- conduct business in an ethical and responsible manner
- support the economy and general welfare of the community
- encourage our associates to participate actively in community affairs
- communicate the benefits of the free enterprise system

FOR OUR SHAREHOLDERS we will strive to
- provide an attractive and consistent return on investment
- provide leadership which is proactive and demands excellence
- utilize both incremental and leap growth avenues
- optimize the full resources of the organization
- provide superior management with depth and continuity
- communicate effectively the Company's performance on a timely basis

FOR EVERYONE we will strive to
- Ensure that every Rubbermaid associate acts with the highest ethical standards

Extracted from "The Best Getting Better Together, Philosophy Management Principles Mission Objectives" brochure

Copyright © 1992 Rubbermaid Incorporated

495. Rush-Presbyterian-St. Luke's Medical Center
1633 West Congress Parkway; Chicago, IL 60612
(312) 942-6844
Industry: 80—Hospital

Mission Statement

The primary mission of Rush-Presbyterian-St. Luke's Medical Center is to improve the health status of a defined population through the development and operation of a voluntary health care system. This system is a multi-faceted corporate entity that provides a full range of health care services, alternative financing arrangements and organizational elements that are integrated through a single governance structure and through contractual relationships with other health care and educational entities. High quality, compassionate, comprehensive health care services will be provided within the system to a representative regional population and selected specialty services to a national population. New knowledge will be fostered and disseminated and a broad spectrum of health manpower educated and trained through the system's academic component, Rush University. The full integration of the academic function will be developed to reinforce the positive aspects of one on the other. Rush-Presbyterian-St. Luke's Medical Center will strive to achieve a position of national and international leadership in setting standards of excellence in patient care, education, research and management. Rush-Presbyterian-St. Luke's Medical Center will maintain financial strength, effectively and efficiently manage resources and be adaptive to the changing environment.

November 13, 1985

Russell, H.J. & Company
see H.J. Russell & Company (284)

496. Ryder System, Inc.
3600 NW 82nd Avenue; Miami, FL 33166
(305) 593-3726
Industry: 42, 47, 75—Leasing and transportation

Direction for the 90s

Ryder's mission is to be the preeminent transportation services company. In pursuing our mission, we will have:
- A carefully selected array of market-leading, high-quality products and services which consistently meet or exceed our customers' needs and expectations.
- Costs for our service offerings which are consistent with marketplace requirements and, supported by strong suppliers and systems, create competitive advantage.
- Highly motivated people who are well trained, fairly compensated and working in a safe environment.
- A corporate culture which fosters leadership, high ethical standards and awareness of market dynamics, enabling our strategies and tactics to be on the leading edge in our markets.

The successful pursuit of this mission will allow us to consistently be the supplier of choice in our markets and to generate a premium return on our shareholders' investment.

Annual Report 1991
Copyright © 1992 Ryder System, Inc.

497. **Ryland Group, Inc.**
     P.O. Box 4000; Columbia, MD 21044
     (410) 715-7000
     Industry: 15, 61—Residential builder and finance

THE RYLAND MISSION

Our goal is to achieve the highest satisfaction rating from customers, shareholders, employees and business partners. We will accomplish this by providing continuously improved products and services while being socially responsible.

THE RYLAND OPERATING POLICY

The quality process is the fundamental business practice of the Ryland Group, leading to increased shareholder value and opportunities for employees' personal and professional growth. Quality means providing our external and internal customers with continuously improved products and services that fully conform to mutually agreed upon, customer-driven requirements. Ongoing progress toward the goal of error-free work, completed on time, is the job of every Ryland employee. Assuring that employees have the tools to accomplish defect-free performance is the task of every manager. By living quality, the people of Ryland will guarantee the company's success as well as their own.

Annual Report 1991

S

498. Safety-Kleen Corp.
777 Big Timber Road; Elgin, IL 60123
(708) 468-2002
Industry: 49, 73—Waste disposal services

Corporate Mission

To maximize the value of the Company's unique marketing, distribution, and recycling capabilities by becoming the world's leading specialty reclaimer of hazardous and quasi-hazardous automotive and industrial fluids, with primary emphasis placed on serving the needs of the small quantity generator of these fluids.

499. Safeway Inc.
4th & Jackson Streets; Oakland, CA 94660
(510) 891-3000
Industry: 54—Supermarkets

SAFEWAY'S MISSION is to grow and prosper by being the best food retailer in terms of customer appeal, operating philosophy and financial results.

CUSTOMER APPEAL

We want to be known for providing superior quality, selection and service at competitive prices in attractive facilities.

OPERATING PHILOSOPHY

We want our operations to be as efficient and cost-effective as any of our competitors', while maintaining a true concern for and sense of partnership with all our employees.

FINANCIAL RESULTS

We expect each of our operations to produce targeted returns on current investment while generating opportunities for future growth and investment.

Developed 1985; revised 1987

Copyright © 1987 Safeway Stores, Incorporated

500. **St. John Medical Center**
      1923 South Utica Avenue; Tulsa, OK 74104
      (918) 744-2180
      Industry: 80—Hospital

MISSION

St. John Medical Center is a not-for-profit Catholic healthcare corporation sponsored by the Sisters of the Sorrowful Mother since 1926 in Tulsa, Oklahoma. It operates in conformance with "The Ethical and Religious Directives for Catholic Health Facilities."

The Medical Center carries on the mission of the Sisters of the Sorrowful Mother, that of continuing the healing ministry of Jesus Christ. Faithful to the sponsorship mission, philosophy, and values, the Medical Center's mission is to: provide high quality healthcare, contribute to the continuing improvement of the overall health status, and promote the well-being of people in Tulsa and the surrounding communities we serve, being especially sensitive to the dignity and needs of the sick, the poor, and the powerless.

In collaboration with others, the Medical Center ascertains community needs and provides a broad array of services along the healthcare continuum including preventative, diagnostic, therapeutic, and rehabilitative programs, with emphasis on health promotion and disease prevention.

The Medical Center takes an active part in advocating public policies which will advance a healthy and a just society. It plans and works with local, state, and national leaders and organizations to bring about a new healthcare delivery system which will provide dignified access to and affordable healthcare for all persons.

We are committed to continue this mission of service, and in our day-to-day interactions with those who serve and are served, we are guided by the **Core Values** of Service, Presence, Human Dignity, and Wisdom.

VALUES

Service

We value the opportunity to serve the sick, one another, the community, and society through the utilization of our skills and giftedness. We strive for excellence and continuous improvement in our service, making the human touch (compassion), a vital component in the healing process.

- We respond to the needs of each person by taking into consideration the whole person: body, mind, and spirit.

- We continuously improve the quality of our service through the encouragement of self-directed work teams and employee empowerment.

- We promote wellness within the community we serve through health education, health screening, and health promotion.

- We advocate for a new health delivery system which provides dignified access to an adequate level of health services.

- We assume our obligation to share our unique gifts and skills to improve the living conditions of humanity.

Human Dignity

We reverence all human life, promote the dignity of each human being, and share in one another's gifts in ways that preserve a sense of self-worth and equality. We foster responsive, value-driven cultures, structures, and processes that promote basic human rights, individual growth, effective use of talents, and development of maximum potential.

- We respect the unique personhood of every individual with whom we come in contact in the provision of our services.

- We encourage open, honest, and timely communication between all levels of the organization.

- We value the talents and giftedness of each person and appropriately recognize individual contributions to organizational goals and success.

- We create an atmosphere that fosters mutual respect, recognizes one another's worth, and enhances self-esteem.

- We provide a compensation system that is internally equitable and externally competitive.

Presence

We enrich interactions and encounters with those we serve, with those to whom we minister, and with those with whom we collaborate through our total attentiveness to each individual person and to each individual situation.

- We provide compassionate care to our patients by entering into their pain and suffering.

- We give to every person with whom we interact our undivided attention.

- We create a welcoming space into which others feel free to enter.

- We receive every person we serve as a guest.

Wisdom

We exercise responsible stewardship, using available resources to maintain the critical balance of addressing individual and community health needs while sustaining the institution's long-term financial strength. We use processes which enable us to discover what is true and right in making decisions which call us to just actions.

- We act ethically and with integrity, honesty, and confidentiality in all our dealings.

- We carefully balance the needs of charity with the demands of justice.

- We carefully balance the need for continually improving quality with the need to control healthcare costs.

- We foster free exchange of ideas, innovation, and teamwork and seek guidance and input prior to decision-making.

- We collaborate with physicians and other healthcare providers to assure effective and efficient use of all types of resources.

- We use resources wisely and strive for reasonable financial returns to enable us to continue our mission.

Extracted from "Philosophy Mission Values Vision" brochure

501. **St. Jude Children's Research Hospital**
      332 North Lauderdale; P.O. Box 318; Memphis, TN 38101-0318
      (901) 522-0300
      Industry: 80—Hospital

SCOPE AND MISSION

St. Jude Children's Research Hospital is a nonprofit, nonsectarian institution. Its mission, simply stated, is to advance the health of children through biomedical research.

Laboratory research at St. Jude is directed toward understanding the molecular, genetic, and biochemical bases of childhood cancer and other catastrophic diseases, and elucidating the fundamental processes of normal cellular function.

Clinical research efforts are aimed at understanding the mechanisms of disease, developing better diagnostic and therapeutic tools, and providing a bridge from the laboratory to the bedside.

Education of new investigators and health care providers and dissemination of research findings to the international biomedical community are crucial to the hospital's mission. These efforts reach far beyond the confines of the hospital, with outreach/consultation programs designed to share the knowledge and skills gained at St. Jude with health care providers and researchers working in less advantaged settings. We too have much to learn from these collaborative efforts.

Annual Report 1991

502. **St. Paul Companies, Inc.**
      385 Washington Street; St. Paul, MN 55102-1396
      (612) 221-7911
      Industry: 63—Property and casualty insurance

THE ST. PAUL COMPANIES MISSION

To operate in all facets of the worldwide property-liability insurance business where exceptional expertise and quality service will provide a competitive edge.

Extracted from *Spectrum*, vol. 35, no. 4, August/September/October, 1992.

Sallie Mae
see Student Loan Marketing Association (547)

503. **Salvation Army**
P.O. Box 269; Alexandria, VA 22313
(703) 684-5500
Industry: 83—Social services

MISSION STATEMENT

The Salvation Army, an international movement, is an evangelical part of the universal Christian Church.

Its message is based on the Bible. Its ministry is motivated by the love of God. Its mission is to preach the gospel of Jesus Christ and to meet human need in His name without discrimination

Annual Report 1991

504. **San Francisco Foundation**
685 Market Street, Suite 910; San Francisco, CA 94105
(415) 495-3100
Industry: 67—Charitable foundation

PURPOSE

The San Francisco Foundation's purpose is to improve the quality of life, promote greater equality of opportunity and assist those in need or at risk in the San Francisco Bay Area.

PHILOSOPHY

- We strive to protect and enhance the unique resources of the Bay Area—its diversity of race and culture, its richness of artistic creation and appreciation, and the beauty and quality of its land, air and water—so that these resources may be enjoyed now and in the future.

- We are committed to equality of opportunity for all and the elimination of any injustice, prejudice or indifference that denies or delays its attainment.

- We seek to enhance human dignity by providing support for community members to exercise personal responsibility and participate actively in determining the course of their own lives and the life of the community.

- We seek to establish mutual trust, respect and communication among the Foundation, its grantees and the communities within which they operate. We will respond to the creative impulses of organizations and individuals as they seek to address the opportunities and dilemmas of changing community needs and interests.

- We are committed to using the resources entrusted to us for funding the highest quality projects from throughout the Bay Area, recognizing that issues are often complex, interdependent and changing. We will seek out new and creative approaches to solving problems as well as methods that are tried and effective.

- We recognize that the process of change and enhancement often involves a partnership of individuals, groups and institutions. We will be an active partner in that process as a member of the philanthropic community.

- The San Francisco Foundation is a steward through which private assets entrusted to us by generations of donors are invested to meet the challenges of contemporary life. We are committed to respecting the trust and intent of our donors, while maintaining the integrity of our philanthropic tradition as a community foundation.

Annual Report 1992

San Manuel Mining

see Magma Copper Company (350)

505.   Sara Lee Corporation

Three First National Plaza; Chicago, IL 60602-4260
(312) 726-2600
Industry: 20, 23—Food and clothing products

Mission

Sara Lee Corporation's mission is to be a premier, global branded consumer packaged goods company. We shall aspire to have the leading position in each product category and in each world marketplace in which we choose to participate.

Strategies

To achieve our mission and to maximize long-term stockholder value, Sara Lee Corporation applies two corporate strategies:

Margin Improvement—increase corporate returns by emphasizing profitable growth. We will enhance profitability by capitalizing on low-cost producer programs in major markets, by leveraging strong brand names across businesses, by developing cross-channel distribution opportunities and by introducing value-added products.

Global Expansion—accelerate growth by extending major brands and product positions worldwide. We will invest in global expansion of our strong U.S. and European businesses, and we will make strategic acquisitions to gain competitive leadership in key markets.

Goals

Sara Lee Corporation strives to achieve three key financial goals: real (inflation-adjusted) growth in earnings per share of 8% per year over time; a return on equity of at least 20%; and a total-debt-to-total-capital ratio of no more than 40%.

Annual Report 1992

506. Saskatchewan Oil and Gas Corporation

1777 Victoria Avenue; P.O. Box 1550; Regina, Saskatchewan;
Canada S4P 3C4
(306) 781-8200
Industry: 13—Oil and gas

STATEMENT OF SASKOIL VALUES

Saskoil's success in meeting the challenges of our industry is built upon the capabilities and dedication of our people, and the key values which guide our activities in conducting our company's business. We will strive to have these values reflected in all we do.

Profitability

We conduct our business to ensure that Saskoil has the profits to continue to meet its obligations to its employees, investors, host communities, customers, suppliers and other stakeholders.

Integrity

We conduct our activities with integrity, displaying the highest ethical standards.

Teamwork

We encourage and place a high value on teamwork.

Confidence

We approach our work confident in our abilities, individually and collectively.

High Standards

We strive for high standards in technology, business and personal lives.

Respect

We exercise care, attention, consideration and respect for our stakeholders and strive to earn the same in return.

Innovation

We promote creative and entrepreneurial skills to foster the environment in concepts, methods, opportunities and solutions.

Job Satisfaction

We approach work with enthusiasm, dedication and good humor and take enjoyment from our daily activities.

Written June, 1992

507. Saskatchewan Wheat Pool

2625 Victoria Avenue; Regina, Saskatchewan; Canada S4T 7T9
(306) 569-4228
Industry: 20, 51—Grain marketing and distribution

MISSION

A diversified agricultural co-operative dedicated to improving the well-being of members through leadership and excellence in meeting customer needs.

Objectives

- To provide efficient, competitive, viable commercial services, and to initiate flexible and aggressive marketing practices, for the benefit of members.
- To encourage effective communication throughout the organization and with external agencies.
- To promote and ensure democratic control and participation by members.
- To initiate and advance public and commercial policies in the interests of farmers.
- To provide fair and equitable treatment to members and customers.
- To provide a workplace environment and human resource policies which attract, motivate and reward employees for excellence in performance.
- To practice prudent financial management to achieve the earnings necessary for continuing growth, financial strength, and the revolvement of member equity.
- To promote, and where appropriate, to participate in agricultural research, value-added processing, and other activities that will benefit members.

- To promote awareness of the importance of agriculture, family farm operations and Saskatchewan Wheat Pool.

- To promote and demonstrate the benefits of co-operation, and to work with other co-operatives.

- To support and encourage the orderly marketing of agricultural products.

- To encourage the conservation of soil and water, and protection of the environment.

Approved April, 1990

Saskoil

see Saskatchewan Oil and Gas Corporation (506)

508. **Save the Children**
    54 Wilton Road; Westport, CT 06880
    (203) 226-7271
    Industry: 83—Social services

Save the Children helps to make lasting, positive differences in the lives of disadvantaged children.

Extracted from "On Behalf of Children: Strategic Directions for Save the Children in the 1990s" booklet, December, 1990.

509. **SCEcorp**
    Southern California Edison
    P.O. Box 99; Rosemead, CA 91770
    (818) 302-1212
    Industry: 49—Electric utility

OUR VISION

We will be a great company that provides business and regional leadership.

Business Leadership

We will set the national standard of performance among utilities. We will provide our customers cost-competitive, reliable electricity; energy-saving services; and creative solutions to their energy needs.

Regional Leadership

We will anticipate and address the challenges of economic competitiveness and environmental quality facing our customers and communities. As a public utility, we are committed to helping Southern California prosper as an excellent place to live and do business.

OUR VALUES

Challenge

We will challenge ourselves to continuously improve our performance and constantly renew our understanding of our changing business.

Candor

We will conduct ourselves with honesty, openness and integrity in all our relationships.

Commitment

We will achieve:
- Value for our customers
- Leadership for our community and environment
- Excellence as a team
- Shared purpose with regulators and
- Value for our shareholders

510. **Schneider National, Inc.**
     P.O. Box 2545; Green Bay, WI 54306
     (414) 592-2000
     Industry: 42—Trucking

"THE ORANGE ON-TIME MACHINE"

Safe, Courteous, Hustling Associates Creating Solutions That Excite Our Customers

MISSION STATEMENT

Mission:

To provide measurably superior transportation and communications services incorporating value added features such that we exceed agreed upon service commitments which result in a competitive advantage for our customers.

Strategy:

Customers

Be recognized as their most responsive, innovative, cost effective and best value added supplier.

Associates

Be treated with dignity and respect and work in an environment which facilitates teamwork, initiative, creativity, hustle and trust.

Suppliers

Play a critical role in our long-term success. Therefore, we will establish partnerships and expect our suppliers to provide us a competitive advantage.

Community

Conduct our business in a fair, ethical, and legal manner and pursue programs to enhance the quality of life within our community.

Technology

Use to align ourselves closer and closer to our customers and to eliminate routine and redundant work; thereby allowing our associates more time and space to work on continuous improvement.

Investors

Provide our shareholders a competitive return.

Vision:

We are committed to the never ending improvement of quality. We will strive to surpass all customer expectations thereby becoming the supplier, customer, and employer of choice in the industries we serve.

Schwab, Charles

see Charles Schwab Corporation (127)

Scripps Howard Broadcasting

see E.W. Scripps Company (219)

511. Seagram Company Limited

1430 Rue Peel; Montreal, Quebec; Canada H3A 1S9
(514) 849-5271
Industry: 20—Beverages

THE MISSION OF THE SEAGRAM COMPANY LTD. is to be the best-managed beverage company in the world. To accomplish this goal, we will improve our financial performance and competitive position, build an organization that encourages individuals to contribute to our success, and create an environment in which all employees are valued and motivated.

We will achieve a long-term pattern of earnings growth and enhanced returns on our assets and sales in order to continue to provide superior returns to our shareholders.

We will strengthen our portfolio of premium brands and focus on improving their profitability and competitive position. We will build on our other sources of strength: our worldwide beverage distribution network; our family tradition; and the knowledge, skill and dedication of our employees.

We will place authority and accountability as close to the customer as possible. We will encourage innovation and prudent risk taking. We will ensure that recognition and rewards are based on performance.

Integrity and the highest ethical standards will guide all our actions. We will foster a spirit of teamwork throughout the organization, and we remain committed to equality of opportunity and to the development of the full potential of all our employees.

512. **Sematech**
   2706 Montopolis Drive; Austin, TX 78741
   (512) 356-3500
   Industry: 87—Research consortium
   The SEMATECH mission statement is:

Create fundamental change in manufacturing technology and the domestic infrastructure to provide U.S. semiconductor companies the continuing capability to be world-class suppliers.

The SEMATECH vision statement:

SEMATECH is a quality driven team of America's best, establishing a new model for national cooperation in high technology.

513. **Sentara Health System**
   6015 Poplar Hall Drive, Suite 300; Norfolk, VA 23502
   (804) 455-7020
   Industry: 80—Hospital

MISSION

Our mission is to be a leader in meeting the present and future health care needs of the people of our communities through a network of high quality services, teaching and research programs which share common goals and values.

VALUES

SERVICE

We are committed to help the sick and needy by providing superior service to our patients and our community with skill, concern and compassion.

QUALITY

Because our patients are our primary concern, we will strive to achieve excellence in everything we do.

PEOPLE

The men and women who work as employees, volunteers, physicians and students are the source of our strength. They create our success and determine our reputation. We will treat all of them with respect, dignity and courtesy. We will endeavor to create an environment in which all of us can work and learn together.

STEWARDSHIP

Fulfilling our mission requires that we use our resources wisely and with accountability to our publics.

INTEGRITY

We will be honest and fair in our relationships with all those who are associated with us, and other health care providers as well.

514. **ServiceMaster Company Limited Partnership**
One ServiceMaster Way; Downers Grove, IL 60515
(708) 964-1300
Industry: 73—Cleaning services

Our Vision

To be an ever expanding and vital market vehicle for use by God to work in the lives of people as they serve and contribute to others.

The Objectives of ServiceMaster

To honor God in all we do.
To help people develop.
To pursue excellence.
To grow profitably.

Annual Report, 1990

515. **SERVISTAR Corporation**
P.O. Box 1510; Butler, PA 16003
(412) 283-4567
Industry: 50—Distribution
The Mission of **SERVISTAR Corporation** is:
  I. To ideally provide our owners with merchandise and services that are complete, low in cost, reliable, supportive and enduring.
  II. To sell and create consumer demand for the business of our owners.
  III. To identify, research and develop niche opportunities for our owners.
  IV. To be an ideal employer emphasizing a caring and supportive atmosphere, opportunities for personal growth, recognition of accomplishment, security and a general philosophy of building through the strengths of our people.

516. **Shaw Industries, Inc.**
P.O. Drawer 2128; Dalton, GA 30722
(706) 278-3812
Industry: 22—Floorcoverings

VISION

Shaw Industries will position itself as the pre-eminent marketing entity in the worldwide floorcoverings business. This will be founded in the corporate vision of being a World Class company **as determined by our customers.**

Our emphasis will be to better understand the structure and requirements of our markets, design quality products to meet these market requirements, communicate effectively our company's commitment of service and support to our customers and end-users, and develop the company infrastructure, support and marketing programs to take full responsibility for our own destiny and success. We will establish a set of marketing principles that will form the philosophy and set the agenda for how we conduct ourselves in achieving this goal.

MARKETING PRINCIPLES

1. Shaw Industries will strive to provide total customer satisfaction by exceeding the expectations of our customers in all of their interactions with our company.

2. Shaw Industries will establish industry leadership in all markets and businesses we choose to participate in.

3. Shaw Industries will be a market and customer driven company. Every Shaw employee is part of our marketing effort in producing quality products, servicing, and supporting our customers. Marketing is everybody's job!

4. We will define market requirements for our products and businesses and fully understand our customers' business and long-term needs.

5. Shaw Industries assumes responsibility for the stated uses and performance expectations of all of our products. To fulfill our obligations, we must maintain as much control as possible over manufacturing, marketing, and distribution of our product.

6. Shaw Industries will market and represent our products and services with the utmost truth and integrity. This will include the specifications, quality, performance expectations and intended end-uses of our product.

7. Shaw Industries will provide a level of product, services, and support to our customers that will enable them to succeed and prosper. Our success will be measured by their success.

8. Shaw Industries will effectively communicate to all markets, customers, and consumers our leadership position and commitments we have stated above.

March 23, 1992

517. **Shell Oil Company**
P.O. Box 2467; Houston, TX 77252
(713) 241-6161
Industry: 13, 29—Oil and gas production and marketing

MISSION

Our mission is to excel in our three principal businesses—exploration and production, refining and marketing, and chemical. To accomplish our mission, we will be guided by three fundamental objectives: leadership in health, safety and environmental performance; return on net investment of at least 12 percent; and highly competitive earnings.

Annual Report 1991

518. **Shoney's Inc.**
P.O. Box 1260; 1727 Elm Hill Pike; Nashville, TN 37210
(615) 391-5201
Industry: 58—Restaurants

MISSION STATEMENT

Shoney's Inc. is a progressive, national diversified hospitality company committed to growth and maximizing return to shareholders through understanding service and value to our customers and franchisees, and investment in our people.

CREDO

We believe our initial responsibility is to our customers who buy our products and services. In satisfying their needs, everything we do must be of high quality.

It is imperative that we constantly strive to control costs, and improve the value of our products and services for our customers.

We will maintain our leadership position in the industry by customer driven innovation, and by outstanding operations and customer service.

We are also responsible to our employees, the men and women who are the real assets of our company. Everyone must be appreciated as an individual. We must respect their dignity and recognize their merit. They must have a sense of security in their jobs. Compensation must be fair and adequate, and working conditions clean, orderly and safe. Employees must feel free to make suggestions and complaints. There must be equal opportunity for employment, development and advancement for all qualified.

We must respect our franchisees as independent business people and make them feel part of the Shoney's Inc. family. Their participation and input is important to the long term health of the Shoney's Inc. family.

We are responsible to the communities in which we live and work. We intend to be good citizens, supporting good works and charities. We must encourage civic improvements and better health and education. We must maintain, in good order, the property we are privileged to use, protecting the environment and natural resources.

Our ultimate responsibility is to our shareholders. We must make a sound profit. We must experiment with new ideas. Research must be carried on, innovative programs developed, and mistakes paid for. New equipment must be purchased, new facilities provided, and new products launched.

It it through all the foregoing principles that we intend to maximize the returns to our shareholders.

Formulated 1990

519. **Sierra Club**
      730 Polk Street; San Francisco, CA 94109
      (415) 776-2211
      Industry: 86—Membership organization

Statement of Purpose:

To explore, enjoy, and protect the wild places of the earth; to practice and promote the responsible use of the earth's ecosystems and resources; to educate and enlist humanity to protect and restore the quality of the natural and human environment; and to use all lawful means to carry out these objectives.

520. **Sisters of Providence**
      520 Pike Street; Seattle, WA 98101
      (206) 464-3355
      Industry: 80—Hospitals and social services

SISTERS OF PROVIDENCE RELIGIOUS COMMUNITY:
IDENTITY AND PURPOSE

The Sisters of Providence, a religious community of women within the Catholic Church, are inspired by trust in Divine Providence. They are guided by the charism of compassionate love for the poor, manifested by Mother Emilie Gamelin, foundress of the community in Montreal in 1843. Mother Gamelin dedicated her resources and ultimately her life to serving the needy in a spirit of humility, simplicity, and charity. Impelled by the love of Christ and trust in Divine Providence that inspired Mother Gamelin, Mother Joseph of the Sacred Heart came west in 1856 and founded hospitals, orphanages, schools, and homes for the aged.

Building upon this heritage, the Sisters of Providence continue to reach out to those in need. They live out their mission through individual and institutional ministries which serve the health, education, and social needs of others. In the name of the Catholic Church, the Sisters of Providence invite men and women to work with them in continuing Christ's work of caring, healing, and teaching. The Sisters bear witness to these Christian truths: human life is sacred, suffering and death have meaning, and Christ loves the poor. They value people as Christ did in the Gospels and dedicate themselves to loving and serving those in need, especially the poor. The responsibility for the commitments of the Sisters of Providence Religious Congregation and its ministries lies with the Provincial Superior and the Provincial Council.

One manner in which the Sisters of Providence carry out their mission is to sponsor health, education, and social services incorporated as the Sisters of Providence in Washington, Oregon, and California. These non-profit corporations function as an integrated Catholic system to meet the needs of people in a manner consistent with the values and philosophy of the Sisters of Providence. Responsibility for the actions of the Corporations lies with the Board of Directors, with delegated authority of the President. The President and the administrators assure that the purposes and commitments of the organization are fulfilled.

CORPORATIONS OF THE SISTERS OF PROVIDENCE: IDENTITY AND PURPOSE

We, the people who share the mission of the Sisters of Providence Corporations, dedicate ourselves to furthering quality of life through the provision of health, educational, and social services. We are faithful to the central Gospel value of love. This calls for recognition of the dignity of the individual, identification with the poor, solidarity with the voiceless and powerless in society, compassionate concern for the healing of the total person, and respect for the sacredness of the human being throughout life, from conception through death to resurrection.

Through the health care ministry, we strive to meet the health care needs of the communities we serve. We provide compassionate care for the sick, injured, dying and grieving. We believe in providing quality health services which reflect standards of excellence and are sensitive and appropriate to individual needs. We have evolved into a comprehensive Catholic health care system which provides a full continuum of services including preventative care, home care, outpatient services, acute care, long-term care, mental health treatment, and hospice. Clinical training programs are also available at several of our institutions. We have accepted a leadership role in designing quality health care delivery and financing systems that promote access to needed care in a cost effective manner. In caring and comforting others, we seek always to meet the needs of the total person within an environment of Christian faith and love.

Through the education ministry, we seek to continue in the world today the liberating action of Jesus Christ, Teacher. We work to create an experience of living in a just and faith-filled community and strive to provide persons with opportunities to develop self-awareness for ongoing personal growth. We teach students skills for understanding and judging society's systems and institutions and we foster the ability to direct change for the betterment of our world. Because the family is a source of support for the whole of society, we work to strengthen the family structure through education.

We have a special concern for the homeless and are helping to meet their needs through our endeavors in low-income housing. We strive against isolating ourselves from the socially and economically poor, either in lifestyle or in service. We seek creative ways to empower the powerless and to serve those whose growth is limited by social and economic circumstances.

Today, the Sisters of Providence Corporations operate acute care hospitals, long-term care facilities, primary care clinics, educational facilities, housing units, and managed care plans in the states of Alaska, California, Oregon, and Washington.

CARITAS CHRISTI URGET NOS

Extracted from "Mission and Philosphy Statement" brochure
Revised November, 1989

521. Skillman Foundation
333 West Fort Street, Suite 1350; Detroit, MI 48226
(313) 961-8850
Industry: 67—Charitable foundation

Statement of Purpose

The purpose of The Skillman Foundation is to improve the well-being of residents of Southeastern Michigan and, in particular, the Detroit metropolitan area. Developing children and youth to their maximum potential is the Foundation's primary goal. A central concern is meeting the needs of the disadvantaged. The Foundation functions both as a resource for the nonprofit community and as a catalyst for positive change. In functioning as a resource for the community, the Foundation responds to grant proposals directed to its current areas of interest. As a catalyst for positive change the Foundation not only responds to proposals, but also identifies and meets community needs through foundation initiated grant programs.

Annual Report 1991

Smith, A. O. Corporation
see A. O. Smith Corporation (46)

522. **Smith International, Inc.**
16740 Hardy Street; Houston, TX 77032
(713) 233-5211
Industry: 13, 76—Oilfield and repair services

MISSION

Our people and technology make us a world leader in drilling tools and services. We work together to constantly improve customer satisfaction, employee opportunity and shareholder value.

PHILOSOPHY

Committing ourselves to integrity, we will:
- Earn the respect, confidence and loyalty of OUR CUSTOMERS by serving them so well that they profit from their association with us.
- Provide OUR PEOPLE the highest degree of challenge and opportunity so they can realize their ambitions in terms of career, rewards and family security.
- Fulfill our obligations to OUR INVESTORS to such an extent that they are both proud and eager to share in our enterprise.
- Be fair to OUR SUPPLIERS and encourage their contributions to our success.
- Not malign OUR COMPETITORS and gain their respect through our ethical practices.
- Be good citizens of OUR COMMUNITIES and OUR COUNTRIES.

523. **Smithsonian Institution**
1000 Jefferson Drive, SW; Washington, DC 20560
(202) 357-1300
Industry: 84—Museum and research organization

GOALS OF THE INSTITUTION

Thus the Institution seeks to achieve its basic mission for the "increase and diffusion of knowledge" among its many publics in the following ways:

- By pursuing original research, exhibitions, collections management, public programs, publications, and other activities devoted to explaining the present state of understanding of the diverse fields of the arts, humanities, and sciences and related issues of contemporary importance.

- By giving special emphasis to exhibitions and other educational programs that will increase participation by the broadest possible audience, including culturally and socio-economically diverse communities, the disabled, and senior citizens.

- By devoting careful attention to the acquisition, care and preservation of collections and institutional facilities that house them.

- By dedicating research and educational efforts to the long-term need for conservation and improvement of our natural and human resources, and by drawing attention to the special responsibility each generation has to its successors.

- By striving for professional leadership and staff excellence, with particular emphasis on expertise from diverse cultural backgrounds, access to solid technical support systems, and vigorous fellowship programs.

- By promoting collegial exchange with and services to other research, museum and educational institutions worldwide.

- By maintaining management, administrative, and other services to meet program needs, by assuring strong internal financial and other management systems, by periodically assessing the effectiveness and efficiency of programs and support activities, and by orderly planning for new and renovated facilities.

Extracted from "Choosing the Future," Smithsonian Institution, Five-Year Prospectus, fiscal years 1993–1997

524. **Snap-on Tools Corporation**
      2801-80th Street; Kenosha, WI 53140
      (414) 656-5382
      Industry: 34—Tools

OUR VISION FOR SNAP-ON

This is our vision for Snap-on in the years ahead.

- Snap-on will be the *global leader* in professional tool and equipment markets by retaining, developing or acquiring a meaningful market share in selected regions of the world.

- Our major *customers* are those who service transportation equipment, maintain industrial plants or manufacture products.

- Our *products* will consist of those tools and equipment required by our customers.

- We will utilize *any distribution channel* to serve our customers.

- We will be the *highest quality and most cost-efficient manufacturer* utilizing the best technologies, methods and systems.

- We will achieve a superior *return on investment* for Snap-on's shareholders.

- We will always adhere to the highest *ethical standards*.

THE VALUES WE SHARE

Success in reaching our vision requires that we share certain beliefs. As Snap-on employees, we recognize the value of:

- Utilizing brand recognition to achieve a *leadership position* in the professional tool and equipment markets.
- *Long-term relationships* with dealers, distributors, customers, employees and suppliers.
- Being committed to and guided by the process of *continuous improvement* through Snap-on Tools' Total Quality System.
- Being a *responsible Corporate citizen.*
- Abiding by a Corporate *code of ethics.*

CRITICAL AREAS OF PERFORMANCE

To achieve this vision, we must conduct business in a leadership role. Those areas of performance critical to the vision are:

- *Respond to customer needs with quality products and services.*

The value of product quality will be measured by customers in terms of innovation, performance, selection and reliability; and the value of quality service as it pertains to delivery, salesmanship, dependability, training, repairs, parts, financing and warranties.

- *Deliver value to customers.*

Value in the form of product and service differentiation is critical in making Snap-on the quality and performance choice. Consistency of high quality and proficient delivery of customer service is essential. These components of perceived value must be continually earned and improved.

- *Use new technologies.*

Snap-on shall be a leader in the application of new technologies for competitive advantage in products, manufacturing processes and services.

- *Improve earning power of dealers, distributors and internal sales force.*

Snap-on's sales representatives' success and their ability to increase their individual earnings are essential to Snap-on's financial success and future growth.

- *Achieve economic effectiveness of assets employed.*

Assets employed in the business will be directed toward productivity and efficiency improvements which will yield long-term financial returns.

- *Achieve effectiveness of workforce.*

It is critical to match the skills and talents of our people to customer requirements for product and service. Snap-on will develop the necessary partnership with its employees in meeting their needs and will provide an environment for their growth and development.

-   *Create financial returns for shareholders.*

Earnings per share growth of at least 10 percent per year on a five-year moving average will be the primary financial goal of the Company. Combined with responsible financial management, this will provide Snap-on's shareholders with economic gains from their investment.

-   *Develop and execute business plans.*

Snap-on will create challenging, measurable and realistic business plans which, when implemented, will attain the objectives of the strategic plan.

525. Software Spectrum Inc.
2140 Merritt Drive; Garland, TX 75041
(214) 840-6600
Industry: 73—Software

Software Spectrum mission statement:

Software Spectrum is committed to providing superior customer service and value through the timely delivery of products and quality technical information and services.

Various department mission statements:

Human Resources recruits and develops—while Payroll calculates and pays—the company's most important asset: its employees, so Software Spectrum can provide the highest level of customer service.

The Purchasing department is committed to providing quality customer service including product information, through accurate and timely placement of purchase orders, while maintaining the most cost effective service level of inventory.

The Administration department is committed to sustaining effective communication with our customers and to providing necessary information and services to our employees, while maintaining a safe and pleasant working environment.

The Outside Sales department drives revenues by effectively communicating the corporate mission statement to the marketplace, growing the business in existing accounts, and aggressively engaging the competition at every opportunity.

The Inside Sales department is committed to providing the highest level of customer service in the industry by quick response to the customer's needs and relentless follow-up to ensure timely delivery of products and accurate information.

The Technical Information Center is dedicated to offering technical assistance to customers by providing accurate answers, effective solutions, and responsible recommendations in a prompt and friendly manner.

The Marketing department is committed to providing the most progressive seminar program, high-quality technical publications and sales promotion and materials, and memorable and exciting employee events.

526. Sonoco Products Company
North Second Street; Hartsville, SC 29550
(803) 383-7000
Industry: 24, 26—Paper and packaging

MISSION STATEMENT

Sonoco will be a customer-focused, global packaging leader, recognized for superior quality and high-performance results. Integrity and a commitment to excellence will be the hallmark of our culture.

STRATEGY STATEMENT

We will achieve this mission by satisfying customers, creating value through the consistent delivery of products and services which clearly meet the present and future needs of our customers worldwide.

PRIMARY GOALS

Safety: We will maintain a safe, injury-free work place.

Customer Satisfaction: We will understand the present and future requirements and expectations of our customers and provide value that meets or exceeds these expectations.

Shareholder Value: We will improve shareholder value by growing after-tax earnings 10%–15% or more annually, and increase dividends as the Company grows.

Market Leadership: We will be a leading supplier in all markets served.

Technology Leadership: We will be recognized for technology leadership in the markets we serve and use our technology to consistently maintain competitive advantage.

Integrity: We will be characterized by the trust and confidence we share with our customers, our employees, our shareholders, our communities and our suppliers.

Organizational Effectiveness: We will be well managed and maintain a highly motivated, qualified workforce, providing all employees with continuous training and the guidance, resources, support, recognition and rewards to accomplish continuous improvement.

Environmental Stewardship: We will take seriously our responsibility to protect the environment in which we work and live, and will conduct our business in accordance with all legal requirements and ethical responsibilities, using scientific knowledge, technical innovation and sound environmental management practices.

Cost Effectiveness: We will always be committed to cost effectiveness and to continuous cost reduction in all areas of our business.

SUPPORTING PRINCIPLES

Participation: We will nurture an atmosphere of teamwork, built around loyal, dedicated employees who are given the opportunity to participate in the decision-making process related to their jobs, and who are equipped with the training, resources and authority to act.

Creativity: We will foster an environment of creativity, innovation and personal ownership, taking well-calculated risks to continuously improve existing businesses and to generate new products and services.

Continuous Improvement: Every employee will be involved in the never-ending improvement of our products, services and processes.

Fact-Based Decision-Making: We will base our decisions on facts and not opinions.

Cross-Functional Linkage: We will allocate, align and monitor staff resources and line operating personnel, based on customer-driven priorities, to work as a team towards solving problems and improving processes, products and services.

Process Management: We will view our jobs as value-adding processes and adopt the approach of process improvement, using analytical measurement and statistical techniques.

Internal/External Customers: We will focus on meeting the needs of our internal and external customers; both are essential and inseparable.

Annual Report 1991
Copyright © 1992 Sonoco Products Company

Southern California Edison Company
    see SCEcorp. (509)

527. **Southern Company**
        64 Perimeter Center East; Atlanta, GA   30346
        (404) 393-0650
        Industry: 49—Electric utility

    VISION

    CORE VALUES

    The Southern Company is committed to the highest ethical standards. We pledge integrity, trust, and candor in our business relationships. Through our actions, we will be worthy of public confidence—both as individuals and as a company.

CUSTOMER COMMITMENT

Our commitment to our customers will be marked by quality, value, dependability, and technical excellence. We intend to guarantee the highest level of customer satisfaction with world-class service that makes our company the competitive choice. Through research and listening, we will thoroughly understand our customers' needs, and we will meet their expectations.

EMPLOYEE ACHIEVEMENT

We will encourage employees to be innovative, aggressive team players—taking personal responsibility to better satisfy customers, solve problems, and improve business results. For their initiative and accomplishments, employees will earn recognition, professional satisfaction, and financial reward.

The Southern Company respects the dignity of each employee and emphasizes strongly the importance of a safe work place. The company is committed to providing opportunities for individual fulfillment and professional development.

BUSINESS DIMENSIONS

The Southern Company will continue to be a leading supplier of energy and energy services. We will be market-driven—the needs of our customers will be the driving force in all our decisions. Our business units will maximize the efficiencies and economies available to them as part of The Southern Company. We will prudently expand electric sales in traditional markets and compete in the independent power business. We will make sound acquisitions related to our energy businesses.

We will provide for the future energy needs of our customers by building and owning power supply facilities, supplemented by purchases from others as appropriate. We will build and maintain our electric system to the highest practical standards of quality.

As a company that takes action based on the needs of its markets, we will expand our sales "beyond the meter"—offering a range of energy products and related services. We will explore all avenues to profitably increase our revenues.

As the regulation of our business changes, we will work to balance and protect the interests of our customers and shareholders. Where competition is permitted, we will aggressively pursue sustainable, profitable market share. We will succeed in a more competitive environment by developing the necessary cost structures, product quality, skills, and culture.

We will build relationships with our regulators that are based on mutual trust and respect and that permit innovative approaches to the pricing and marketing of our products.

We will establish partnerships with other businesses that will allow us to offer our customers technologies to improve energy efficiency.

INVESTOR VALUE

The Southern Company will seek to provide investors with long-term appreciation and dividend growth—consistently delivering returns on investment that are in the upper range as compared with similar companies. Growth in earnings will come by achieving our allowed rates of return and by profitably participating in free-market activities. We will become a premier investment through gains derived from new activities and by sharing with customers and stockholders the productivity improvements in our traditional business.

BUSINESS EXCELLENCE

Throughout The Southern Company, we will encourage innovation, reward initiative, build teamwork, and focus on business results. We will minimize the number of management layers between the top and the front lines, creating broader spans of control and improved communication. Decision making will be pushed downward, and employees will be given greater individual responsibility, authority, and accountability. They will be expected to make decisions as if the business were their own.

Employees will be appropriately informed and trained in vital aspects of the business so that they fully understand the consequences of their actions and decisions. We will develop leaders from within our ranks and provide career opportunities throughout the company.

Our communications will be honest, open, timely, and widely shared.

COMMUNITY ENHANCEMENT

The Southern Company will enhance the standard of living, the quality of life, and the economic success of the communities we serve. As a corporate citizen, we will improve the welfare of our communities and encourage broad community involvement by our employees.

ENVIRONMENTAL COMMITMENT

We affirm the importance of protecting the environment and making wise use of our natural resources. We will set and achieve environmental goals that are in concert with other goals needed to further the well-being of society.

528. **Southern Indiana Gas and Electric Company**
20 NW Fourth Street; Evansville, IN 47741
(812) 464-4469
Industry: 49—Electric utility

SIGECO'S QUALITY VISION STATEMENT

Working together, will create an environment in which all employees will be able to use their unique capabilities to achieve excellence in meeting or exceeding the expectations of both internal and external customers.

SIGECO News, September 1992

529. **Southern National Corp.**
P.O. Box 1489; Lumberton, NC 28359
(919) 671-2000
Industry: 60—Bank

SOUTHERN NATIONAL MISSION

We exist to serve customers and, while doing so, to maximize the long-term return to our Shareholders. We will accomplish this by, and within this framework:

Providing top quality products and services fairly priced to our customers.

Employing and developing high achieving People, and

Providing them with the training and supervision they need to realize their full potential.

Recognizing and rewarding high performance.

Encouraging teamwork.

Expecting loyalty and commitment.

Achieving quality and consistently increasing earnings.

Maintaining a strong balance sheet with very carefully managed credit and interest rate risk.

Being a good corporate citizen in the communities we serve by encouraging our people to be involved in community development, providing financial support to quality community needs, and providing loan programs consistent with sound lending practices. We will make every effort to obtain the highest rating on our Community Reinvestment Act efforts.

Participating in mergers that are beneficial to long-range shareholder wealth.

Building market share and increasing volumes per capital and operating funds deployed.

Conducting all aspects of our business within the highest ethical standards.

530. **The Southland Corporation**
2711 North Haskell Avenue; Dallas, TX 75221
(214) 841-6711
Industry: 54—Convenience stores

CORPORATE MISSION

The Southland Corporation exists to maximize the long-term market value of shareholder equity.

Our heritage is 7-Eleven. Its profitable growth and increasing dominance in convenience retailing will remain the core of our existence. We will be successful to the degree that we fulfill the needs of our customers—what they want, when and where they want it—in a manner that provides added value, engenders loyalty and promotes a lasting relationship. To ensure Southland's continued excellence, we must retain the flexibility to anticipate opportunities and to master all forms of competitive challenge.

Our most important resource is people. Southland excels because of the quality, motivation and loyalty of every member of the Southland family. We are committed to innovation through participative involvement, and to fostering an environment of trust, respect and shared values.

As a responsible corporate citizen, Southland will conduct its business in an ethical manner with the highest integrity, while contributing to the quality of life in the communities it serves.

The ultimate measure of Southland's success is the optimal utilization of our collective resources and the perpetuation of a culture that is distinguished for its clarity of purpose, emphasis on individual responsibility and standards of excellence.

531. **Southwest Airlines Co.**
Love Field; P.O. Box 36611; Dallas, TX 75235
(214) 904-4000
Industry: 45—Airline

The Mission of Southwest Airlines

The mission of Southwest Airlines is dedication to the highest quality of Customer Service delivered with a sense of warmth, friendliness, individual pride, and Company Spirit.

To Our Employees

We are committed to provide our employees a stable work environment with equal opportunity for learning and personal growth. Creativity and innovation are encouraged for improving the effectiveness of Southwest Airlines. Above all, employees will be provided with the same concern, respect, and caring attitude within the organization that they are expected to share externally with every Southwest Customer.

January, 1988

532. **Southwest Gas Corporation**
P.O. Box 98510; Las Vegas, NV 89193
(702) 876-7173
Industry: 49—Gas distribution

MISSION STATEMENT

The mission of Southwest Gas Corporation is to conduct its business in a manner that fosters integrity, social responsibility, and best balances the divergent interests of the four constituencies—shareholders, customers, employees and the communities it serves.

CORPORATE VISION

Southwest Gas Corporation will continue to be a premier energy and financial services company. Building on core businesses of the energy company and banking, the corporation will strive for the long-term optimization of shareholder value.

As a premier corporation, the company will be recognized for:
- Excellence in customer services and products.
- Excellence in management and leadership as seen by its employees, its peer groups, the financial community and within the communities it serves.
- Enthusiastic, results-oriented employees who work together to accomplish the corporation's strategies and business plans.
- Being an excellent investment opportunity by shareholders and by the financial and investor communities.

533. **Special Libraries Association**
1700 18th Street, NW; Washington, DC 20009
(202) 234-4700
Industry: 86—Library membership organization

Strategic Plan

The Special Libraries Association (SLA) is an international association of information professionals and special librarians in business, media, finance, science, research, government, academic institutions, museums, trade associations, nonprofit organizations, and institutions that use or produce specialized information.

Mission

- to advance the leadership role of its members in putting knowledge to work for the benefit of the general public and decision-makers in industry, government, the profession; and
- to shape the destiny of our information society.

The Board of Directors recognizes strategic planning as a high priority, essential for the Association to carry out its mission in an environment of risk and uncertainty.

From "A Visionary Framework for the Future: SLA's Strategic Plan 1990–2005"

1989

534. The Spencer Foundation
900 North Michigan Avenue, Suite 2800; Chicago, IL 60611
(312) 337-7000
Industry: 67—Charitable foundation

The Spencer Foundation is committed by its mandate to the improvement of education. We pursue that commitment by supporting research whose outcome shows promise of contributing new knowledge, insight, or understanding to the ongoing venture of education. The work we support falls into a broad range of disciplinary and interdisciplinary categories, chiefly, though not exclusively, in the social and behavioral sciences. Education we define broadly, to include all the situations and institutions in which learning takes place, throughout the life span of the individual, both in the United States and elsewhere in the world.

From The Spencer Foundation Annual Report, 1992

535. Sprint Corp.
2330 Shawnee Mission Parkway; Shawnee Mission, KS 66205
(913) 624-3000
Industry: 48—Telecommunications

Our Vision:

To be a world-class telecommunications company—the standard by which others are measured.

Sprint Value

Customer First

We anticipate, understand, meet and exceed our customers' needs and expectations to achieve Total Customer Satisfaction.

Excellence Through Quality

We will individually and collectively use Sprint Quality in our daily activities to achieve excellence as a company.

Integrity In All We Do

Our actions and decisions reflect the highest ethical, legal and professional standards.

Respect For Each Other

We care about our company, our work, our customers and each other. This caring is a unique source of our company's energy, strength and excellence.

Growth Through Change

We will grow as a company, as individuals and as professionals by creating, anticipating and responding to change.

Community Commitment

We willingly serve the charitable and civic needs of our communities.

Shareholder Value

We will increase shareholder value, build the financial strength of our company and, therefore, prosper as individuals.

Extracted from Sprint 1992 corporate brochure
Copyright © 1992 Sprint

536. SPX Corporation
700 Terrace Point Drive; Muskegon, MI 49443
(616) 724-5011
Industry: 33, 34, 35—Filters, pumps, fasteners, and forgings

Statement of Mission and Driving Forces

SPX Corporation's mission is to build stakeholder value through leadership in specialty service tools and equipment, vehicle replacement and original equipment components, and building and industrial products.

In the global specialty service tool and equipment market, SPX is the world leader. The driving force behind this worldwide market leadership is the Company's close partnership with its original equipment and aftermarket customers, and its unique ability to anticipate and meet customer needs.

In North American replacement components, SPX is a leader in engine parts, and an emerging force in under vehicle parts. The driving force for SPX in this market is its reputation for providing quality parts and service of superior value to aftermarket distributors and professional engine rebuilders.

In proprietary original equipment components and high pressure hydraulics, SPX is a global leader, while in window and door hardware, it is the North American leader. The driving force behind the Company's leadership in these markets is its production capabilities, market position, and value added quality products and services.

SPX intends to be the leader in each of the markets it serves and will provide business units with the resources required for building value when:

- There is an acceptable contribution to building long-term value.

- The unit has a high probability of sustained earnings growth.
- There is a clear synergy or match between the investment and the Company's strategic domestic and international markets.
- The unit has a strategic commitment to total quality, people empowerment, teamwork and continuous improvement.

The priority for new business opportunities for SPX units serving the specialty service tool and equipment and vehicle replacement parts markets shall be to focus on identifying and meeting new and emerging needs of key customer groups. For those units serving the original equipment, building and industrial markets, their priority for new business opportunities shall be to focus on developing new markets, including customers and geographic regions.

Moving forward, SPX will consider value building opportunities that complement existing businesses and build on the management team's experience and strengths. SPX will also provide guidance and resources to assist its business units to identify their future strategies, providing human, material and informational resources as appropriate.

Philosophy, Values and Beliefs

SPX people are the single most important element behind successful implementation of our mission and strategies. We therefore will provide an environment which:

- Attracts and retains action oriented, creative, high achieving people;
- Presents opportunities for personal development, satisfaction and teamwork, in an atmosphere characterized by free and open communication;
- Provides recognition for excellence through innovation and prudent risk taking, and;
- Is founded upon teamwork, mutual respect, trust and strict standards of legal and ethical conduct.

We are committed to total quality in everything we do as evidenced by:

- External and internal customer satisfaction;
- Focus on quality training, planning, and elimination of waste in all processes, products and services;
- Continuous improvement targets and monitoring for all processes, products and services;
- Teamwork within and across all functional areas of the Company, and;
- Long-term customer and supplier cooperative partnerships.

Value building results from excellent customer service and continuous improvement. Ultimately, value is measured by:

- Exceptional customer satisfaction;

- Returns to the shareholders in excess of the Company's cost of capital;
- The teamwork, motivation and commitment of SPX people;
- Quality commitment and long-term partnerships with key suppliers; and,
- The Company's reputation as a fair and responsible corporate citizen.

Revised 1992

537. **SRI International**
333 Ravenswood Avenue; Menlo Park, CA 94025
(415) 326-6200
Industry: 87—Research and development

SRI International Mission Statement

SRI International is dedicated to world leadership in the development and application of research and consulting services for both the public and private sectors.

SRI will accomplish its mission by achieving the following strategic objectives:

Leadership

To be recognized as a world leader in advancing scientific investigation and resolving technological, economic, sociological, business, and policy challenges in a manner that results in exceptional client satisfaction.

Quality

To be recognized by its clients and peers as an organization that provides exceptional value, continuously strives for perfection, and delivers on its promises.

Products and Services

To conduct basic and applied research, advanced development, prototype production, and technology transfer in the engineering, biological, physical, information, and social sciences. To benefit a broad range of clients worldwide with technology and business consulting services.

Marketing

To adopt a global orientation and focus only on businesses in which it will excel and for which an adequate market has been defined.

Growth

To grow in size and expand financial resources through a variety of means including income from operations, capitalizing on intellectual properties, establishing endowments, dividends from subsidiaries, and use of other financial instruments in order to sustain leadership, enhance financial well-being, and expand the client base.

Environment

To create an internal environment that encourages and generates innovative and creative work and collaboration among individuals and organizations to serve our clients better.

Employee Commitment

To hold employees in the highest regard and strive to provide a satisfying and challenging work environment with opportunity for personal achievement and growth, equitable compensation, honest and timely communications, recognition of accomplishments, and reward for excellence. To gain, in return, employees who are committed to the goals of the company, are diligent in the execution of their responsibilities, and exhibit a positive attitude.

Citizenship

To be a responsible corporate citizen and to cultivate an attitude of commitment to public service on the part of all employees.

Ethics

To adhere to the highest ethical standards in the pursuit of these objectives.

538. **Standard Federal Bank**
     2600 West Big Beaver Road; P.O. Box 3703; Troy, MI 48007-3703
     (313) 643-9600
     Industry: 60—Federal savings bank

MISSION STATEMENT

The mission of Standard Federal Bank is to create value for its customers, employees, stockholders and the various communities it serves by continuing to develop as a major Midwest banking institution. The Bank strives to conduct its business with the utmost integrity and to cultivate its relationships with each of its constituent groups.

Customers

Providing the best banking products and delivering them with the highest level of professionalism and courtesy to customers is the responsibility of each and every Standard Federal employee.

Employees

The Bank is dedicated to developing a team of motivated, knowledgeable employees and to creating an environment which stimulates, recognizes and rewards creativity and productivity.

Stockholders

Standard Federal's Board of Directors, officers and employees are committed to using all of the means at their disposal in order to maximize stockholder value.

Communities

The directors and officers will endeavor to ensure that the Bank contributes to the strength and stability of every community in which it operates.

539. **Stanford University Hospital**
2680 Hanover Street; Palo Alto, CA 94304
(415) 723-7951
Industry: 80—Hospital

MISSION STATEMENT

The mission of Stanford University Hospital is to deliver patient-centered, scientifically advanced care, as the primary teaching and research hospital for a distinguished university medical school. It aspires to leadership in this and the next generation in both the art and science of health care.

Stanford University Hospital responds to community health care needs, coordinates a regionally integrated delivery system, and is committed to operate a sound financial organization.

1988

540. **The Stanley Works**
1000 Stanley Drive; New Britain, CT 06053
(203) 225-5111
Industry: 34, 35—Tools, hardware and industrial equipment

MISSION STATEMENT

To be the World's Most Effective Producer and Marketer of Tools, Hardware and Specialty Hardware for Home Improvement, Consumer, Professional, and Industrial Use.

March, 1993

541. **Staples, Inc.**
100 Pennsylvania Avenue; P.O. Box 9328; Framingham, MA 01701
(508) 370-8500

Industry: 51, 59—Wholesale and retail office supplies

WHAT STAPLES STANDS FOR

Our Corporate Goals

We will satisfy the needs of our customers

We strive to offer customers an unbeatable combination of service, savings, selection, and quality—every single day. In particular, we work to build long-term customer loyalty by providing:

- The lowest possible prices
- Outstanding, proactive service
- 100% satisfaction guarantees
- The convenience of one-stop shopping
- Quality products and services

We will provide a challenging, rewarding workplace for our Associates

Our success depends upon the talent and performance of every Staples Associate. Therefore:

- We hire the best-qualified people.
- We trust in the maturity and judgment of our Associates and give them the authority to do whatever it takes to serve the customer better.
- We encourage and reward teamwork, initiative, personal responsibility, enthusiasm, caring, and commitment.
- We maintain a build-and-share philosophy toward compensation and Associate stock ownership.
- We encourage the personal growth and professional development of every Staples Associate.

We deliver a quality return to our shareholders by building market-leading businesses in our target markets

We are committed to creating real business growth based on sustainable competitive advantages. In each market we serve, we strive to build high-quality, market-leading businesses.

We will act as a good corporate citizen in the communities we serve

- We create job opportunities in the communities where we operate.
- We invest in the community through the buildings and equipment the stores require.
- We support manufacturing across the country through the growth of our business.
- We contribute to the vitality of the communities we work in through focused corporate support in the field of education, helping to provide rewarding educational experiences for the less fortunate.

Our Working Priorities

Will it help serve the customer better?

- By helping us offer the lowest possible prices every day
- By allowing us to offer the right products and services to match the needs of our customers, supporting our reputation for one-stop shopping
- By securing the best possible prices from our suppliers
- By being the best in the industry at keeping product in stock
- By making our supply chain as efficient as possible
- By being the first in the industry to offer new or innovative products

Will it help keep the company strong, lean, and adaptable?

- By giving all Associates the means and authority to satisfy the customer, every time
- By continually challenging our accepted ways of doing business and helping surpass our customers' expectations
- By increasing productivity, allowing us to offer lower prices and generate higher revenues
- By fostering teamwork and candid two-way communication throughout the organization
- By sharing the fruits of the business with all Staples Associates through pay-for-performance and Associate ownership plans
- By investing in training and developing our Associates, to foster their personal and professional growth and build a strong organization at every level

Will it help us meet our financial goals?

- By achieving revenue and earnings growth among leading growth retailers
- By improving our return on capital
- By winning strong market positions with leading market shares
- By supporting the lowest cost structure
- By investing the resources to reach the best customers in each of our markets, increasing our long-term value as a company

Will it improve our competitive position?

- By creating clear value for the customer—ahead of the competition
- By building revenues to enhance our business and our competitive advantages
- By supporting our commitment to database marketing, helping us understand what our customers need and improve our cost-effectiveness

At Staples, our working priorities guide every decision we make. Before we choose a new course of action, we ask four key questions.

542. **State Street Bank and Trust Company**
      225 Franklin Street; Boston, MA 02110
      (617) 786-3000
      Industry: 60—Banking

STATE STREET PLAN

State Street's goal is to be a quality institution, for our customers, our employees, our stockholders, and the society in which we live.

We serve a growing number of customers worldwide by emphasizing quality. We place a high priority on innovation. In each of our businesses, we aim to be a recognized leader in the reliability and value of our services.

By demonstrating concern for individuals, we continually strive to make State Street a quality organization in which to work. We want all State Street employees to share their pride in their institution and dedication to its goals. We recognize and reward the contributions of individuals throughout the organization.

Our stockholders expect to realize a competitive return on their investment. We plan to meet this need by competing successfully in regional, national, and international markets, achieving sustainable real growth in earnings per share.

As a corporate citizen, we take an active role in helping our society develop with efficiency and fairness to all. We participate in the governmental process, and we contribute our efforts and resources to serving the common good.

State Street was founded in 1792. In our third century, we are working to widen our reputation as a quality institution.

543. **Steelcase Inc.**
      P.O. Box 1967; Grand Rapids, MI 49501-1967
      (616) 246-9464
      Industry: 25—Office furniture

Primary Objective

Be the best office environment company in the world. Provide customers with worldwide office environment products, services and information that fully satisfy their requirements.

Values

- The customer comes first at Steelcase and satisfying customer requirements is the driving force.

- All employees are important team participants in serving customers and are treated with integrity and respect.

- A diverse work force is essential in terms of nationality, race, sex, creed, color, age, and physical abilities.

- Relationships with customers, employees, dealers, suppliers, and shareholders are conducted in a spirit of partnership that recognizes the need for mutual benefit.

- The company and its employees actively support the communities in which they work and live.

- Business decisions are made considering the needs of the environment.

- The company is known for doing what it says it will do. Through its employees, the company keeps the commitments it makes.

- Integrity is inherent in all activities.

Goals

- Consistent with "World Class Performance," by July 1, 1996:
  - Reduce customer complaints to fewer than four per one million opportunities;
  - Reduce customer cycle time to two weeks;
  - Reduce product development time to 10 months;
  - Reduce costs by 30% (in real terms);
  - Reduce safety incidents by 90%;
  - Reduce everything thrown away by 75%; and
  - Reduce quality audits by 80%.

- Achieve sales growth equal to or greater than the markets served to reach desired market share objectives.

- Earn a return on invested capital that comfortably exceeds its cost and meets shareholder requirements.

- Establish and maintain strong Steelcase identities in worldwide markets.

- Achieve recognized design leadership.

- Develop an organization that serves the needs of multinational customers worldwide and facilitates the exchange of ideas and information among the Steelcase, Inc. family of companies.

Broad Statement of Strategy

Serve office environment markets worldwide by providing:

- Innovative and well designed office environments, systems and furniture;
- Information about knowledge workers and their working environment needs;
- Services that help customers plan, specify, acquire, and install office environment products and address working environment needs.

- Perform at "world class" levels in all areas of the business.
- Recognize opportunities where the company's resources and capabilities may be profitably applied.

Principles of Performance

- The customer comes first.
- All employees serve external and internal customers and are accountable to successfully serve their customers, both individually and in teams, thereby contributing to the success of the company.
- A working environment is maintained that encourages, rewards, and recognizes active involvement by all employees because
    - The energies and ideas of all employees are required to perform at "world class" levels;
    - Decisions made closest to the customer are the best decisions; and
    - Employees are most effective when they are included in the decisions that affect their jobs and performance.
- Learning and the exchange of knowledge are essential to the success of the business.
- The company strives to develop the potential inherent in every employee.
    - The company fosters an entrepreneurial attitude:
    - Employees are expected to take calculated risks in their decision making.
    - Mistakes are viewed as learning opportunities.
    - Performance is evaluated by measuring progress toward established goals.
- Continuous improvement is a way of life.

Mid-1991

544. **Stelco Inc.**
      Stelco Tower; P.O. Box 2030; Hamilton, Ontario; Canada L8N 3T1
      (416) 528-2511
      Industry: 33—Steel

Stelco is a market-driven, technologically-advanced Canadian steel-maker dedicated to maintaining a leadership role as a materials supplier and fabricator and to meeting the requirements of its customers as well as providing an appropriate return for its shareholders. Stelco people will achieve these objectives in a safe and healthy environment through maximum development of their skills; by the creation and application of innovative process and product technology; through identification and pursuit of new growth opportunities and by providing superior levels of quality and service.

Annual Report 1988

545. **Storage Technology Corporation**
    2270 South 88th Street; Louisville, CO 80028-0001
    (303) 673-5151
    Industry: 35—Computer equipment

    STORAGETEK MISSION

    To be the preferred provider of information storage and retrieval solutions to mainframe, midrange and large network marketplaces worldwide.

    StorageTek—Innovation in Storage

546. **Stride Rite Corporation**
    Five Cambridge Center; Cambridge, MA 02142
    (617) 491-8880
    Industry: 31—Shoes

    The Stride Rite Mission

    We will provide to our worldwide customers and consumers branded, quality, high-value footwear and do this better than any other footwear company in the world. By doing so, we will provide shareholders with superior financial returns, our employees with excellent rewards and opportunities and society with innovative programs that we see as our obligation and essential to our long-term interest.

547. **Student Loan Marketing Association**
    1050 Thomas Jefferson Street, NW; Washington, DC 20007-3871
    (202) 298-3010
    Industry: 61—Student loan finance

    Sallie Mae is the major financial intermediary to the nation's education credit market. Primarily a wholesale provider of credit, its clients are financial institutions, educational institutions, and certain state agencies.

    Sallie Mae's main financial products for originators of federally guaranteed student loans—its core market—are loan purchases and secured funding. It also offers operational support, including automated loan management systems. In pursuing its business, Sallie Mae has always adhered to a consistent set of management principles to maximize shareholders' value and best serve its market.

    Attainment of Service Leadership

    Sallie Mae strives to provide the highest quality service to all segments of the education finance market—lenders, schools, guarantors, and, ultimately, students and their parents.

Maximization of Return on Equity

Sallie Mae strives to provide investors with the greatest possible return on their investment over the long term primarily by achieving consistently strong growth of quality earnings and maintaining balance sheet quality.

Management of Interest Rate Risk

Sallie Mae avoids exposure to interest rate risk by matching the interest rate sensitivities of virtually all of its assets and liabilities.

Attainment of Low Cost Funding

Sallie Mae seeks to achieve the lowest possible cost of funds by tapping domestic and international capital markets, consistent with credit and rate risk policies.

Containment of Servicing Costs

Sallie Mae continuously seeks to increase the efficiency and quality of student loan servicing, while containing the cost of servicing, its largest operational expense.

Control of Operating Expenses

Sallie Mae controls operating expenses by minimizing the size of infrastructure used to manage its operations.

548. Sun Company, Inc.
1801 Market Street; Philadelphia, PA 19103
(215) 293-6000
Industry: 13, 29—Integrated petroleum

OUR PURPOSE

To be a rewarding investment for our shareholders; to be a reliable source of products and service to our customers; to be a stimulating professional experience for our employees; to be a respected citizen of community and country—this is the purpose of the Sun Company.

Strengthened by a century of experience and motivated by our determination to continue the traditions of excellence established by the founders, we are vigorously committed to:

- Being a profitable, growth-oriented competitor in the petroleum and petrochemical industry, pledged to produce quality products at competitive prices.

- Creating value for our customers, employees and shareholders through the integrity of our purpose and the quality of our performance.

- Insuring that health, safety and the environment always command the high priority attention they deserve.

- Conducting all phases of this enterprise with the highest ethical standards.

- Offering employees equal opportunity, a challenging career, a good place to work and pay for performance.

- Encouraging teamwork throughout this unique alliance of employees, shareholders, customers and communities by being responsive to issues, open in our communications, positive in our attitude and decisive in our actions.

549. Sundstrand Corporation

4949 Harrison Avenue; P.O. Box 7003; Rockford, IL 61125-7003
(815) 226-6000
Industry: 34, 35—Aerospace and defense products

SUNDSTRAND CORPORATION COMMITMENTS

Mission

- To satisfy the needs of selected worldwide aerospace and industrial markets by developing and manufacturing high quality, proprietary, technology-based components and subsystems and by achieving customer satisfaction.

- To serve market segments where we can either be a market leader or have a strategy to become one while achieving returns that reward shareholders and employees and permit the business to grow and prosper.

Goals

- To provide superior rewards to investors by achieving returns on equity among the top quartile of Fortune 500 manufacturing companies.

- To anticipate and fully satisfy customer needs by providing superior products utilizing appropriate advanced technology and customer service.

- To recognize that every member of the Sundstrand team is a valued individual and important contributor.

- To be a responsible Corporate citizen by being an active participant and a positive contributor both in the local community and at the national level.

- To team with strong business partners with similar philosophies and objectives.

Beliefs

- Continuously improving the way we do our jobs, managing our businesses and serving our customers.

- Having a genuine concern for cost while fulfilling all commitments and providing total value to our customers.

- Maintaining the highest level of integrity and trust in all our relationships, reflecting respect and fairness in all our actions.

- Adhering strictly to our Code of Business Conduct and Ethics.
- Managing our businesses aggressively yet prudently.
- Encouraging the personal and professional growth of each member of the Sundstrand team.
- Developing a sense of ownership and belonging in each team member through effective two-way communications.
- Fostering innovation in all business and technical activity by recognizing and rewarding superior contribution.
- Developing and maintaining relationships rather than just executing transactions.
- Providing superior quality in all things. This is our most important belief.

January 11, 1990

Superior Mining
see Magma Copper Company (350)

550. Supervalu Inc.
P.O. Box 990; Minneapolis, MN 55440
(612) 828-4000
Industry: 51—Food wholesale

Statement of Philosophy

The philosophy of SUPERVALU companies will always be a "total commitment to serving customers more effectively than anyone else could serve them." We believe the pursuit of this meaningful goal is the continuing and overriding responsibility from which every corporate activity must evolve. We value today's success as merely the beginning of a constantly expanding level of achievement.

We believe that customers are most knowledgeable, skilled and capable buyers who will always seek out and do business with that supplier or store which most effectively serves their wants and needs.

Therefore, by serving our customers more effectively than anyone else could serve them, and by efficiently managing our business with highly skilled and dedicated people, we are confident that we shall continue to increase SUPERVALU's sales and share of market. We believe that this philosophy and practice will result in continuing profitable growth for SUPERVALU and provide security and opportunity for our many thousands of loyal employees.

January, 1974

551. Sutter Health Inc.
2800 L Street; Sacramento, CA 95816
(916) 733-8800

Industry: 80—Health care

Vision For The 1990's

Epilogue

Time 1995:

Sutter Health is an integrated healthcare organization serving the communities of Northern California by providing high quality services along a continuum of care. The continuum is characterized by the coordination of quality, cost-effectiveness and continuity of care. Access to care is facilitated through a geographic distribution of facilities and multiple healthcare financing mechanisms, including cooperative arrangements and formal linkages with physicians, other hospitals, insurers and other partners with similar values. Pluralistic physician relationships range from support of solo fee-for-service practice to facilitation of group practice. Sutter Health has a strong, assured philanthropic base undergirding a research effort of growing national notice. A unique healthcare organization has been created!

552. **Symmetrix Inc.**
One Cranberry Hill; Lexington, MA 02173
(617) 862-3200
Industry: 87—Consulting services

We seek to be a truly learning enterprise, composed of exceptional, upbeat professionals with varied backgrounds and expertise, bound together by a highly supportive internal culture and sense of integrity, focusing on "adding value" for our clients.

553. **Synergen, Inc.**
1885 33rd Street; Boulder, CO 80301
(303) 938-6200
Industry: 80, 87—Pharmaceutical research and development

Synergen Vision Statement

Synergen will be a profitable, protein-based pharmaceutical company selling products in North America and Europe. World class drug research will be applied to discover and develop innovative drugs for patients with serious diseases. Synergen will grow while maintaining its existing corporate culture and standards of excellence.

554. **Syntex Corporation**
3401 Hillview Avenue; Palo Alto, CA 94304
(415) 855-5050
Industry: 28—Pharmaceuticals

SYNTEX COMMITMENTS

As a multi-national health care company, we are committed to utilizing our scientific capabilities to provide significant, cost-effective products that enhance the quality of life of people throughout the world. We will market products only if they are safe and effective, and offer genuine advantages to our customers.

We are committed to maintaining an environment within Syntex that encourages productivity and creativity, and contributes to the satisfaction and growth of all employees. We will maintain policies and encourage practices that promote the fair treatment of employees and a respect for their dignity and self-esteem. Compensation and opportunities for growth and development will be available to all based on merit. Employees will be provided safe and healthy conditions, and we will never willfully mislead them.

We are committed to producing a fair return to those who invest in our company and entrust their resources to us. We will strive to improve all company practices in the service of efficiency and profitability.

We are committed to achieving our corporate goals while strictly adhering to the law and the highest standards of ethics. We will honor our responsibilities as stewards to the physical environment and make every effort to utilize resources effectively. Honesty and integrity will govern our interactions and communication with customers, suppliers, regulatory agencies, fellow employees, and communities in which we operate.

T

555. Tambrands® Inc.
777 Westchester Avenue; White Plains, NY 10604
(914) 696-6000
Industry: 26—Personal care products

MISSION STATEMENT

Our core business is the manufacture and sale of tampons. Our objective is to be leading supplier of all types of tampons in each market we serve on a worldwide basis. We will exert great effort to expand the tampon category worldwide.

We will accomplish our share and market growth objectives through continuous improvement to our products and through product line extensions, utilizing innovative techniques of manufacturing, marketing, distribution, and education that are appropriate to local conditions.

We will be the low-cost producers in every market in which we compete, while maintaining our traditional high product quality. We will conduct all aspects of our business at a level that makes us burst with pride.

Diversification opportunities must build on our existing strengths and/or hold the potential for near-term profitability. Profit—not volume—will be our creed. Unless we can see a measurable benefit to our shareholders, we will not diversify. Rather, we operate our basic business profitably for the shareholders.

Copyright © 1990 Tambrands Inc.

556. Team Bankshares, Inc.
3300 Oak Lawn; P.O. Box 190667; Dallas, TX 75219-0667
(214) 559-7326
Industry: 60—Banking

MISSION STATEMENT

Team Bank is a Texas based banking organization committed to offering high quality services to our customers, excellent career opportunities for our employees and a superior return to our shareholders.

OBJECTIVES

1. Team Bank will be a sales oriented organization, focusing all employees and operational activities on selling quality banking services to the customer.

2. Team Bank will be targeted in its marketing, not attempting to be all things to all people, but providing services that 80% of the market desires from a bank.

3. Team Bank will be a low-cost provider of banking services.

4. Team Bank will provide employees opportunities for professional growth and emphasize good communication and teamwork.

5. Team Bank will maintain a financially strong balance sheet by closely monitoring asset risk, mix and liquidity.

6. Team Bank will consistently generate higher than average returns within its peer group.

557. **Tektronix Inc.**
      26600 SW Parkway; Wilsonville, OR 97070
      (503) 682-3411
      Industry: 35, 38—Computer and laboratory equipment

— **Our Values**

At Tektronix, we share six core values that should guide our relationships with all those with whom we are mutually dependent: customers, employees, suppliers, shareholders and our communities. These basic values do not change, but all of us must seek continuous improvement in the ways we apply them.

A Strong Sense of Ethics

We conduct our business according to the highest ethical standards. This underlies all that we do as a company and all that we do as individual employees working together.

A Passion for Innovation

We push for continuous growth, improvement and innovation. Each of us has a leadership role to play within our own areas of responsibility. That role calls on us to grow, improve and innovate both as individuals and as team members for the benefit of our customers, our shareholders, our suppliers, our communities and ourselves.

A Commitment to Customers and Suppliers

We constantly strive to provide our customers with products and services of the highest value and quality. Our goal is 100 percent satisfaction. The central purpose of our business is to satisfy customers' needs and constantly exceed their expectations. We also view our suppliers as key members of the Tektronix/customer partnership—an essential link for improved quality and value.

A Commitment to Our Shareholders

The company as a whole and each of our businesses have the same goal: to operate in a manner which will maximize the return on our shareholders' investment. Our primary financial objective is to continuously achieve top level return for our shareholders from overall company performance.

A Commitment to Ourselves

We are committed to fostering teamwork, respect, open communication and trust in our working relationships with each other. We believe each employee makes a difference as an individual. At the same time, teamwork is a critical priority; it is the way we achieve our common objectives. We also strive to give ourselves maximum opportunity to exceed our own expectations in the work we do today, as well as where we want to be tomorrow.

A Commitment to Our Communities

We contribute positively to our communities. We are a company with facilities in large and small communities throughout the world. We recognize the benefits we gain from and give to them. We will be responsible citizens by striving to be an economic, intellectual, social and environmental asset in each country and community where we are located.

Our Strategic Goals

In addition to our customer satisfaction and financial goals, we judge ourselves against other equally vital standards to determine our success. These are Tektronix' long-range goals to reach and sustain over time.

A Company with a Worldwide Focus

Because we compete in the worldwide marketplace, we will manage our business with a global perspective. This means thinking of ourselves in a worldwide context in all that we do. We are working together across the company to develop joint marketing strategies, while maintaining local market sensitivity and customer responsiveness. We will find more effective ways to develop, maintain and leverage our engineering, manufacturing and distribution capabilities worldwide.

Test and Measurement Leadership

We will maintain dominant market share in oscilloscopes and expand our position for other Test and Measurement products. We will move further ahead through solid, steady growth with innovative new products and systems for selected vertical markets.

Television Systems Leadership

We will continue to capitalize on our leadership position in television measurement, production and distribution. We will grow by leveraging our expertise in television to lead the merging of digital video, computer and telecommunications technology.

Computer Graphics Leadership

We will advance and expand the computer graphics industry. We are earning a leadership position and growing market share through our efficient, practical and innovative application of color printing and imaging technologies.

By achieving these goals, we will deliver long-term value to our customers, shareholders and employees. We will aggressively apply the Tektronix traditions of innovation, technical leadership and customer satisfaction as the means to achieve growth.

Our Responsibilities

We are Tektronix. Collectively, we encourage shareholders to invest in our company's future, customers to buy our products and services, suppliers to help us meet our customers' needs, people to come and work alongside us. Our collective character—the attitudes, behaviors, values and goals we share—has a major impact on Tektronix' success.

Our core values and goals, when built upon by each of us, will result in growth and success for all of us.

Extracted from "Our Company" brochure

558. **Telesat Canada**
     1601 Telesat Court; Gloucester, Ontario; Canada K1B 5P4
     (613) 748-0123
     Industry: 48—Telecommunications

Vision Statement

Building on our expertise in satellite communications, we are committed to being a world leader in communications, information services and space systems services.

We stand for value for money, excellence in service, business integrity and long term commitment to our customers.

We further stand for outstanding profitability and growth for our shareholders and employees.

559. **TELUS Corp.**
     32A, 10020–100 Street; Edmonton, Alberta; Canada T5J 0N5
     (403) 498-7310
     Industry: 48—Telecommunications

TELUS Corporation Mission

The Mission Statement clearly conveys the present and future purpose of the TELUS Group of companies.

Core Statement We are a leader at enriching people's lives at home, work or leisure, through reliable information and telecommunications services that are accessible wherever, whenever, and however our customers want. The key works in the core statement are defined as follows:

Leader We will be positioned in the forefront of telecommunications and its niches.

Enriching People's Lives Our products/services will add to the quality of life by enabling people and organizations to maximize success and well being.

We will provide products and services where our customers require them, in every aspect of life.

Reliable Information and Telecommunications Services We will provide the highest quality and most reliable information and telecommunications products/services.

Accessibility We will provide access to our products and services for our customers without time or space constraints.

Customers' Needs Our products and services will be congruent with our customers' needs; we will know our customers' needs as well as they do.

AGT Cellular Mission

This mission statement conveys the present and future purpose of AGT Cellular: We are the preferred provider of quality communications services to "people on the move."

The key works in this statement are defined as follows:

Preferred First choice of the customer

Provider Build, operate and deliver

Quality The right product or service in the right place, at the right time, in the right package which exceeds customer expectations.

Communications Services Sending and receiving information utilizing wireless networks, products, processes and systems.

People on the Move Individuals who need to be "in touch" no matter when or where they are, and who want their telecommunications device(s) to be untethered (i.e. not physically linked to location).

Subsidiary of TELUS Corp.

560. Tembec Inc.

Temiscaming, Quebec; Canada J0Z 3R0
(819) 627-9244

Industry: 26—Forest products

CORPORATE MISSION

Tembec's mission is to develop into a profitable integrated forestry company, capable of converting forest resources into competitive and innovative quality products while protecting the environment and creating positive long term social, cultural and economic benefit for the region and its people, our employees and shareholders.

Our mission will be accomplished while respecting the following principles and guidelines.

FINANCIAL

- Provide shareholders with an above average five-year return on shareholders' equity, as measured by net profit after tax over average shareholders' equity when compared to our competitors.

- Earn a five year after-tax return on capital employed of 3% above prime as measured by net earnings after tax plus interest divided by the average of the total assets less current liabilities.

- Maintain a strong liquidity ratio as measured by a working capital ratio above 2:1.

- Operate with a long term debt to equity ratio below 1:1 and exceeding this only in periods when major capital projects are undertaken.

HUMAN RESOURCES

- Maintain high standards of performance of all employees by providing effective training and encouraging all employees to maximize their potential and participate in building their own future.

- Provide our employees with a safe and healthy work environment at competitive wage scales.

- Maintain open lines of communication at and between all levels of the corporate organization.

- Provide our employees with the opportunity to share in the growth and financial success of the company through share ownership and participation in profits.

PRODUCTS

- Dedicate ourselves to leadership in excellence, innovation and competitiveness of our products through sound capital investments, emphasis on research, creativity and continuous improvement of our products and operations.

CUSTOMERS

- Meet our customers' expectations with competitive quality products and superior service on a consistent basis.

- Treat our customers as long term partners in our growth and development.

SOCIAL RESPONSIBILITY

- Dedicate a minimum of 1% of our pre-tax profits to promote health, educational, cultural and recreational endeavors that contribute to improving the individual and collective quality of life. Encourage individual involvement in the community and professional group activities.

ENVIRONMENT

- Establish policies and guidelines in all phases of our operations which provide for the responsible stewardship and sustained development of our resources while protecting the health and safety of our employees, customers and the public.

- Develop and provide new technologies which are aimed at conserving and renewing the resources we utilize in our operations.

ETHICS

- Conduct our business and our relationships with respect, openness, integrity and in an exemplary fashion.

CREATIVITY

- Stimulate and create an atmosphere promoting new ideas and creativity at all levels in the company.

Revised 1992

561. **Texaco Inc.**
2000 Westchester Avenue; White Plains, NY 10650
(914) 253-4000
Industry: 13, 29—Integrated petroleum

OUR VISION

To be one of the most admired, profitable, and competitive companies, and to make Texaco the leader in its industry.

Texaco's Guiding Principles And Objectives

The principles and objectives which guide Texaco in doing the best possible job of finding and producing increasing quantities of oil and natural gas, refining superior products, transporting and marketing products efficiently and economically, and further improving its operations and products through continuing research, are:

To deliver to customers only products of proven high quality at fair prices and to serve them in such a manner as to earn their continuing respect, confidence, and loyalty, both before and after sale.

To be financially sound and responsible; pay a fair return to shareholders for the use of their capital; maintain a record of productivity and profits which will enable the company to attract new capital, and continue to grow and expand its earning power; and, through inspired leadership and effective teamwork, strive to be the most highly respected company in industry.

To maintain a high level of employee morale through fostering, by example, an atmosphere of hard work; recognize dignity of the individual by treating every person in the company with respect and courtesy; provide opportunities for employees to develop and advance to the utmost of their capabilities; encourage and carefully consider all suggestions from employees and, if not acceptable, explain reasons why to employees; pay compensation which compares favorably with others in the industry; and provide safe and efficient places in which to work.

To obey all laws, be a good corporate citizen, and willingly assume our share of the responsibilities in communities where we operate both at home and abroad; conduct our affairs in a capable and friendly manner so that everyone who comes in contact with us will find it pleasant to do business with us; observe the highest moral and ethical standards in carrying on our business; and keep our organization a fine example of the American system of freedom and opportunity.

To maintain free and open channels for the mutual exchange of information between management, stockholders, employees, retailers, customers, and others having a proper interest in the affairs of the company; work constructively toward securing public understanding and acceptance of the company's policies and performance; defend the company against unwarranted and unjustified criticism and attack; support industry efforts to resolve mutual problems in the areas of public affairs; cooperate in other activities undertaken for the benefit of the industry as a whole, where these activities do not involve competitive or operating matters or infringe upon the company's right to independent action.

Extracted from "Texaco Our Vision and Values" brochure
Copyright © Texaco 1989

562. Texas Industries, Inc.
7610 Stemmons Freeway; Dallas, TX 75247
(214) 647-6740
Industry: 32, 33—Cement, sand, gravel, and steel

OUR MISSION:

We will be the most efficient, high value supplier of cement and aggregate products and will provide superior service in the markets we serve. We will continue to grow in our industry through innovation and geographic diversification.

Annual Report, 1992
Copyright © 1992 Texas Industries, Inc.

563. **Texas Instruments**
13500 North Central Expressway; P.O. Box 655474; Dallas, TX 75265
(214) 995-2011
Industry: 35, 36—Computer peripherals

THE TI COMMITMENT

Mission

Texas Instruments exists to create, make, and market useful products and services that satisfy the needs of customers throughout the world.

Principles

We will accomplish this with "Excellence in everything we do"
- Perform with unquestionable ethics and integrity
- Achieve customer satisfaction through total quality
- Be a world-class technology/manufacturing leader
- Provide profitable growth/fair return on assets
- Achieve continuous improvement with measurable progress
- Be a good corporate citizen

Values

We expect the highest performance and integrity from our people. We will create an environment where people are valued as individuals and treated with respect and dignity, fairness and equality. We will strive to create opportunities for them to develop and reach their full potential and to achieve their professional and personal goals.

November 14, 1989

564. **Thiokol Corporation**
2475 Washington Boulevard; Ogden, UT 84401-2398
(801) 629-2270
Industry: 28, 34, 37—Specialty chemicals and propulsion systems

MISSION STATEMENT

We are a company of high integrity and excellence. We will continually enhance our commitment to safety and quality. We have highly competent, dedicated employees. We have engineering expertise that puts us in an industry leadership position. We have specialized facilities for efficient manufacturing. We have the desire to achieve, excel, and win.

We will promote continuous improvement in our production and administrative processes.

We Owe Stockholders: A fair return for their investment.

We Owe Customers: A reliable, safe, quality product, on time, at a competitive cost. Highest standards of business conduct. Increased communication and understanding.

We Owe Employees: A safe working environment. Open lines of communication. Competitive compensation and benefits. Potential for growth and achievement.

We Owe the Communities in Which We Live and Work: Attention to our responsibilities as a corporate citizen.

We, Thiokol Corporation, are cognizant of our abilities and commitments, and are dedicated to exceeding our challenges. Our mission is to thrive through continual increase in market share of our business and continual increases in stockholder value.

565. **Tiffany & Co.**
     727 Fifth Avenue; New York, NY 10022
     (212) 755-8000
     Industry: 39, 59—Jewelry manufacture and sales

THE MISSION OF TIFFANY & CO.

Tiffany & Co. will be the world's most respected source of fine jewels, timepieces, sterling silverware, leather goods and the arts of the table. We will be distinguished by our quality, exclusivity and service.

The products offered to Tiffany customers will include jewelry, silver, watches, clocks, leather goods, fragrance, stationery, china and crystal. We will consider additions to our product line if they complement the basic line and enhance the Tiffany image. Our products will be superior to our competition in quality of design, materials and craftsmanship.

Tiffany & Co. is a retailer. We operate retail stores in major market areas in the United States and selected International markets. Retail expansion will be a priority for the future.

The Corporate Division markets a line of recognition and service awards, trophies and gifts to business organizations. The products offered are principally drawn from the retail line and may be custom designed or developed exclusively for the corporate market. All products offered meet the same standard of excellence in design, materials and craftsmanship.

The Direct Mail Division complements and supports the Retail Division by marketing a selection of Tiffany products to customers and prospective customers through prestigious direct mail catalogs.

The Trade Division offers a collection of Tiffany products through other prestigious retail stores in the United States and selected International markets.

Tiffany products will be offered at prices that represent recognizable value for the customer and a proper profit margin for the company, recognizing that our superior quality, exclusivity and service may be reflected in pricing.

The excellence of customer service will distinguish Tiffany from our competition. We will be recognized for the courtesy, efficiency, and professionalism of our service, for prompt merchandise availability and delivery, and for the immediate resolution of any service issue.

Tiffany will manufacture fine jewelry, silver and watches. Outside sources of production will also be utilized for these and other product categories, selected on the basis of quality, service and cost. Tiffany will also maintain internal repair, engraving, estate and appraisal services.

The objective of Tiffany will be to build shareholder value through consistent growth in sales and profits. We will expand our business aggressively, but within capital and cash flow requirements that can be generated internally and within a scope that maintains Tiffany's image and exclusivity.

Tiffany recognizes that the success of its mission is dependent on the quality and dedication of its people. We will recruit, train and develop highly capable people, provide superior levels of compensation and benefits, and maintain a working atmosphere that encourages success and satisfaction. We will instill in our people a commitment to unquestioned integrity in all our relationships, both internal and external.

566. **Times Mirror Company**
Times Mirror Square; Los Angeles, CA 90053
(213) 237-3700
Industry: 27, 48—Publishing and broadcasting

MISSION STATEMENT

The Times Mirror Company is committed to gathering and disseminating the information people need to live, work and govern themselves in a free society. We will strive to do so with the highest standards of accuracy, fairness, quality and timeliness.

In pursuing this mission, we will constantly strive to strike an appropriate balance among the following objectives:

Continue to grow in size and stature so as to ensure a preeminent national scope, reach and voice.

Preserve corporate independence and stability provided by substantial Chandler family and employee stock ownership.

Provide above-average total financial return—share-price appreciation plus dividends—for shareholders over the long term.

Maintain conservative risk posture, and hence, financial flexibility.

Enhance our position as a leading force among American newspaper groups.

Balance newspaper holdings with significant positions in related communications and information fields, including magazines, broadcast television, cable television and professional information and book publishing.

Attract, motivate and retain a high-quality workforce that reflects the diversity of our society, and provide a positive work environment that allows employees' talents to be developed to the fullest.

Provide independent editorial voices.

Contribute to the economic and social well-being of the communities we serve.

Extracted from "About Times Mirror" booklet

567. **Timken Company**
      1835 Dueber Avenue, SW; Canton, OH 44706-2798
      (216) 438-3000
      Industry: 33, 36—Industrial equipment

OUR MISSION

We are an independent organization with a leadership position in high-quality anti-friction bearing and alloy steel products. To maximize shareholder value and sustain our competitive position, we will capitalize on the relationships between our businesses, emphasize the application of technology to products and processes, and combine these with unmatched customer service. Through the strength of our people, we will strive to become the best manufacturing company in the world.

OBJECTIVES TO ACHIEVE OUR MISSION

- Achieve customer recognition as a company offering higher value in products and services than our competitors.

- Attract and retain superior people and provide for them an opportunity for the full development of their skills and abilities in an environment of open communication, mutual trust and respect. The success of the Company depends upon the achievements of the people who make up the Company.

- Increase penetration in markets providing long-term profit opportunities.

- Achieve an inflation-adjusted return on assets of approximately thirteen percent. This will provide our shareholders with growth in their investment and dividends. It will also provide the funds necessary for reinvestment in our businesses to maintain and advance our leadership position.

- Maintain excellence through investment in technology with a continuing commitment to timely implementation of the results.

HOW WE WILL ATTAIN OUR OBJECTIVES

- We will take a long-term view in our decision making by strategically managing our business.

- We will gain competitive advantage through continuous improvement obtained by each employee's superior individual performance of responsibilities in a spirit of team effort.

- We will adopt an organizational style that encourages bigger changes at a faster pace to capitalize on opportunities in our ever-changing environment.

- We will be dedicated to the highest degree of ethics and integrity in the conduct of our business.

- We will meet or exceed customer expectations through each employee's active participation in and dedication to customer service.

- We will achieve excellence by emphasizing the fundamental operating principles of quality, cost, investment usage, and timeliness.

568. **Toro Company**
     8111 Lyndale Avenue South; Bloomington, MN 55420
     (612) 888-8801
     Industry: 35—Lawn and garden equipment

Our mission is to beautify and preserve the outdoor environment— make the landscapes green, healthy and safe—with superior quality, innovative and environmentally-sound products, services and systems. We believe the environment to our customers is as much about the grass under foot and the trees outside the front door as it is about acid rain and global warming. Simply put, to Toro the environment is about green grass, clean water and fresh air.

Annual Report July 31, 1992

569. **Toromont Industries Ltd.**
     65 Villiers Street; Toronto, Ontario; Canada M5A 3S1
     (416) 465-3518
     Industry: 33, 35—Refrigeration equipment

MISSION STATEMENT

Our mission is to produce attractive financial returns for our shareholders through above average growth in earnings and steadily increasing dividends.

We will develop business units in North America that will achieve leading positions in the markets they serve.

Our current focus is in the low temperature refrigeration and gas compression industries. Our emphasis is on service and parts distribution, supported by sales of fabricated equipment and construction services.

Annual Report 1991

570. **Toronto Hydro-Electric System**
Operated by Toronto Electric Commissioners
14 Carlton Street ; Toronto, Ontario; Canada M5B 1K5
(416) 599-0400
Industry: 49—Hydroelectric power

GOALS & OBJECTIVES

MISSION: To meet the requirements of the City of Toronto for electrical service so as to result in the greatest overall benefit to the community.

Goal #1: To provide electricity to our customers at reasonable rates and on a sound financial basis.

Goal #2: To provide high quality service in all of our business processes.

Goal #3: To maintain a safe, positive, productive and equitable working environment for our employees in a manner that is consistent with our Management Principles.

Goal #4: To continue to modernize and refurbish our aging physical plant in order that we may ensure reliability of supply.

Goal #5: To implement and maintain environmentally responsible programmes.

Goal #6: To build cooperative relationships with other municipal bodies, governments and community organizations.

MANAGEMENT PRINCIPLES

CUSTOMER FOCUS is the continuous identification and meeting of all internal and external customer service needs and expectations.

EMPLOYEE SUPPORT is the caring attitude and genuine interest in supporting employees' efforts to reach their full potential.

ACCOUNTABILITY is being responsible for our own actions and empowered to meet commitments. These commitments are accepted and understood.

ETHICAL STANDARDS are acting in good faith and with mutual respect, characterized by honesty, integrity and sensitivity to the dignity and cultural background of others. Embodied in these standards is a commitment to ensure that safety takes precedence in the workplace.

PRIDE is the satisfaction and self-esteem resulting from positive recognition for contributions to organizational and individual quality and achievements.

TEAM APPROACH is working with others toward a common goal with visible and effective leadership.

TRUST is the relying on open communications developed through positive relationships.

Strategic Plan 1992–93

571. **Tracor, Inc.**
6500 Tracor Lane; Austin, TX 78725-2000
(512) 926-2800
Industry: 35, 36, 37, 38—Defense electronics

MISSION

At Tracor, we believe that mutual dedication to excellence in performing every task we undertake, large or small, is the key to our future. We accomplish excellence by carrying out our responsibilities to:
- achieve profitable growth consistent with the best in our industry;
- provide high quality, innovative technological products, systems, and services which give the best value to our customers;
- ensure the highest standards of integrity in all activities;
- create a safe, pleasant, and motivating work environment providing both job fulfillment and career growth opportunities for employees; and
- support the communities in which we have operations to develop a better environment for all citizens to enjoy.

Growth at Tracor is through excellence.

Drafted January, 1992

572. **TransAlta Utilities Corporation**
110–12th Avenue, SW; P.O. Box 1900; Calgary, Alberta; Canada
T2P 2M1
(403) 267-7110
Industry: 49—Electric utility

Corporate mission

To satisfy customers with competitive electric and thermal energy services in a safe, reliable and environmentally responsible manner.

Annual Report 1991

573. **TransCanada Pipelines**
TransCanada Pipelines Tower
111-Fifth Avenue SW; P.O. Box 1000, Station M; Calgary, Alberta;
    Canada T2P 4K5
(403) 267-6100
Industry: 49—Gas pipelines

TransCanada Pipelines—Mission Statement

We are committed to achieving profitable growth by providing the highest quality services to our customers with our primary focus on achieving preeminence in the transportation and marketing of natural gas in North America. We will fulfill this mission by building on the strong foundation of our existing business and through the pursuit of business excellence.

October, 1990

Western Gas Marketing Limited—Mission Statement

To be the natural gas marketer of choice in North America by being the best at everything we do.

Spring 1991

Cancarb Limited—Mission Statement

Cancarb is committed to profitable growth and maintenance of its position as the world's preeminent supplier of thermal carbon black.

Spring 1991

574. **Tribune Company**
435 North Michigan Avenue; Chicago, IL 60611
(312) 222-3394
Industry: 27, 48—Publishing, broadcasting, and entertainment

TRIBUNE'S MISSION, VALUES, AND STRATEGIES

What we do

Our mission is to develop leading sources of information and entertainment. We will continue to grow in major metropolitan markets, as well as through related businesses of national and international scope.

How we do it

Four strategies form the foundation of our actions:

- Emphasize local market growth
- Emphasize content creation and control
- Add targeting to efficient mass media
- Foster a development orientation

How we act

We are guided by a strong set of values:

- Integrity
- Customer Satisfaction
- Innovation
- Employee Involvement
- Financial Strength
- Citizenship
- Diversity
- Teamwork

Annual Report 1992

575. **TRW Inc.**
1900 Richmond Road; Cleveland, OH 44124
(216) 291-7000
Industry: 37, 73—Transportation equipment and business credit
services

Mission

TRW is a global company focused on providing superior products and services to customers in the space and defense, automotive, and information systems markets. Our mission is to achieve leadership positions in these markets by serving the needs of our customers in innovative ways—by being the best in everything we do. We will create value for our shareholders by balancing short-term performance and long-term financial strength.

Values

Customers

Customer satisfaction is essential. We will deliver superior value to our customers through quality, reliability and technology. We grow and prosper by serving the needs of our customers better than our competitors, while effectively controlling costs.

People

The men and women of TRW make our success possible. We encourage the involvement and reward the contribution of each employee. We value open and honest communications. We create a workplace where every employee can share a sense of ownership for TRW's success. We provide equal opportunity in our employment and promotion practices.

Quality

Quality is important in everything we do. Quality is everyone's responsibility, and is achieved through continuous improvement. We routinely seek ways to do things better.

Integrity

We pursue our business interests worldwide in a socially responsible manner. We conduct our businesses in accordance with the highest standards of legal and ethical conduct. We encourage every TRW employee to participate in and support community activities.

U

UAL
see United Airlines Inc. (579)

576. **Unifax Inc.**
Cross Creek Pointe; 1065 Highway 315, Suite 203;
Wilkes-Barre, PA 18702-6980
(717) 822-0902
Industry: 51—Food wholesale
Buy low—Sell high!

UniGroup, Inc.
see United Van Lines, Inc. (587)

577. **Unilever United States, Inc.**
390 Park Avenue; New York, NY 10022-4698
(212) 888-1260
Industry: 20, 28—Food and toiletries

Lever Brothers Company—Mission Statement
THE MISSION OF OUR COMPANY
AS WILLIAM HESKETH LEVER SAW IT
IS TO MAKE CLEANLINESS COMMONPLACE
TO LESSEN WORK FOR WOMEN
TO FOSTER HEALTH AND
CONTRIBUTE TO PERSONAL ATTRACTIVENESS
THAT LIFE MAY BE MORE ENJOYABLE
AND REWARDING FOR THE PEOPLE
WHO USE OUR PRODUCTS
This inscription appears on the plaque at Lever House, home of Lever Brothers Company, 390 Park Avenue, New York 22, NY.

578. **Union Carbide Corp.**
39 Old Ridgebury Road; Danbury, CT 06817-0001
(203) 794-2000
Industry: 28—Chemicals

493

MISSION

The mission for Union Carbide and its businesses:

Union Carbide exists to provide its shareholders with maximum value in the long term from all of the resources available to it.

Each Carbide business must strive to be among the best in its field.

The principle role of the corporate entity is to create an enabling environment in which each of its businesses can be more successful than it could be independently.

As we achieve this mission, we will comply with the laws of the countries in which we do business, and, we will adhere to the highest standards of business integrity and ethics.

In fulfilling this mission, we will emphasize quality in all that we do. This will require the best efforts of all Carbide people. Union Carbide will provide services and value for our customers and challenging and rewarding careers for employees; and we carry out our social responsibility by making significant contribution to the well being of the communities in which we live and work.

VALUES

The following values underlie our mission:

Safety and Environmental Excellence

We are dedicated to safety and environmental protection. We must be responsible to our people and our plant communities. We will not compromise safety or environmental protection for profit or production. We will be second to none in the industries in which we compete.

Customer Focus

We are deeply committed to serving customers. We must be a quality supplier they can count on to provide exactly what they need, when they need it, at a competitive price. To achieve and maintain a competitive edge, we must serve customers with unsurpassed efficiency and attention to detail.

Technology Leadership

Union Carbide has been built on distinguished technology. Technological imagination, vision, and creativity must continue to provide value to our customers and future growth for our businesses. We must protect and advance our technologies, test their limits, and lead change. We must use the latest technology to improve the productivity of our people, the cost effectiveness of our operations, and the quality of our products.

People Excellence

Our people should believe in themselves, their work and their company. Union Carbide must be a place where each individual will be given equal opportunity; a place where all can achieve recognition and reward based on their performance. It must be a place where employees can perform with excellence and achieve personal growth, whatever their jobs. We will measure everything we do against the very best, and then reach for even higher quality and better performance.

Simplicity and Focus

The environment of Union Carbide will foster timely decisions, encourage taking reasonable risk, and stimulate new thinking and new approaches. We must be able to change rapidly to meet challenges and opportunities of a fast changing world. We will all challenge the complex, the bureaucratic, and the status quo in the interest of doing better.

ACTIONS

The actions necessary to establish an enabling environment follow:

Simplify and streamline the organization at every level. Eliminate unnecessary work.

Adhere to the corporate standards for health, safety and environment, and thereby reestablish the corporate reputation for excellence in these areas.

Delegate to the businesses the functional activities that will help them be self-sufficient and independent, reserving only those functions that must be retained at the corporate level.

Communicate in a timely, forthright, and credible manner to people in and out of the Corporation.

Promote an atmosphere of cooperation among the businesses that takes advantage of skills, knowledge and experience across organizational lines.

GOALS

With these values and actions, we must meet the following performance goals:

Short Term:

Generate sufficient cash to meet the interest on our debt and our dividend commitment.

Provide financial support for continuing businesses.

Reduce the amount of our debt.

Long Term:

Achieve return on equity that is greater than its cost.

Achieve equity growth.

Provide challenging and rewarding careers and commensurate compensation for our people.

579. **United Airlines Inc.**
     Subsidiary of UAL Corp.
     P.O. Box 66100; Chicago, IL 60666-0100
     (708) 952-4000
     Industry: 45—Airline

UNITED AIRLINES' MISSION

The people of United are dedicated to being the world's best airline.

Ever pursuing a passion for innovation, we will never be satisfied with the performance of today.

We strive to serve you with style and sophistication, building upon our unparalleled legacy of professionalism and technical leadership.

Uniting a broad mosaic of cultures and traditions, we hope to foster economic prosperity and inspire human understanding.

That's why we fly.

580. **United Farm Workers of America AFL-CIO**
     P.O. Box 62; Keene, CA 93570
     (805) 822-5571
     Industry: 86—Labor union

Mission

A safe and just food supply

Adopted 1985

581. **United Food and Commercial Workers International Union,**
     AFL-CIO
     1775 K Street, NW; Washington, DC 20006-1598
     (202) 223-3111
     Industry: 86—Labor union

Constitution of the United Food and Commercial Workers
International Union

PREAMBLE

Because the history of workers has been but the record of constant struggle against oppression by the wealthy and powerful;

And because wealth, with its accompanying power, is becoming more and more concentrated in the hands of the few;

And because the organization of workers into trade unions is essential to the economic, social, and political freedom of society and to the successful functioning of a democracy;

And because in union there is strength and workers are better able collectively to secure their fair share of the profits accruing from their toil;

This International Union is created in order to elevate the social and economic status of workers and, further, to advance the principles and practice of freedom and democracy for all.

ARTICLE 2

Objectives and Principles

The object of this International Union shall be the elevation of the position of its members and further: to conduct an International Union of persons engaged in the performance of work within its jurisdictions; to organize, establish, and charter bodies in all states, provinces, and territories of North America; to organize, unite, and assist persons, without regard to race, creed, color, sex, religion, age, or national origin, engaged in the performance of work within its jurisdiction for the purpose of improving wages, hours, benefits, and working conditions on local, national, or international levels; to obtain the status of exclusive bargaining representative of persons employed within the jurisdiction of the International Union and to process and resolve grievances and enforce all other rights arising out of such collective bargaining relationships; to encourage members and all workers to register and vote; to support research in our industries for the benefit of its members; to advance and safeguard the full employment, economic security, and social welfare of its members and of workers generally; to protect and extend democratic institutions, civil rights and liberties, and the traditions of social and economic justice of the United States and Canada; to function as an autonomous International Union affiliated with other International Unions in national and international federations; to print and disseminate publications; to protect and preserve the International Union as an institution and to perform its legal and contractual obligations; to protect the International Union and all of its chartered bodies from any and all corrupt influences and from the undermining efforts of all who are opposed to the basic principles of democracy and democratic unionism; to acquire, receive, hold, manage, lease, convey, invest, expend, or otherwise use the funds and property of this organization to carry out the duties and to achieve the objectives set forth in this International Constitution; to take all steps and actions, which are reasonable and proper, to promote the welfare and interests of its members, of workers within its jurisdiction, and of workers generally and to afford mutual protection to members against unwarranted rules, unlawful discharge, or other forms of injustice or oppression; to sponsor, encourage, engage in, and support financially through contributions and otherwise any educational, legislative, political, civic, social, health, welfare, community, or charitable projects or activities; and to support and encourage such other objectives for which working people may lawfully combine for their mutual protection and benefit.

582. **United Grain Growers Limited**
     433 Main Street; Winnipeg, Manitoba; Canada R3C 3A7
     (204) 944-5411
     Industry: 51—Food wholesale

Mission Statement

UGG's strategy is to seek out and satisfy the production, handling and marketing needs of commercially viable Western Canadian farmers.

We will respond with innovative, high-quality services, products and programs that enhance value to farmers and users, and improve the competitive position of Western Canadian farmers and UGG.

OUR BELIEFS

CUSTOMERS ARE OUR FIRST COMMITMENT

We persevere in meeting customer needs.

PEOPLE CREATE SUCCESS

We foster trust, competence, commitment and job satisfaction.

QUALITY IS ACHIEVED THROUGH PERSONAL EXCELLENCE

We pursue quality in everything we do.

SOUND BUSINESS PRACTICES ARE VITAL

We are committed to responsible fiscal management, productivity and profit.

OUR COMPANY PLEDGES INTEGRITY

We conduct business truthfully. We do what we say.

CHANGE CREATES OPPORTUNITY

We encourage innovation and creativity.

Annual Report July 31, 1992

583. **United Parcel Service**
     400 Perimeter Center—Terraces North; Atlanta, GA 30346
     (404) 913-6000
     Industry: 42—Package delivery

UPS CORPORATE STRATEGY STATEMENT

UPS will achieve worldwide leadership in package distribution by developing and delivering solutions that best meet our customers' distribution needs at competitive rates. To do so, we will build upon our extensive and efficient distribution network, the legacy and dedication of our people to operational and service excellence and our commitment to anticipate and respond rapidly to changing market conditions and requirements.

UPS CORPORATE MISSION STATEMENT

CUSTOMERS

Serve the ongoing package distribution needs of our customers worldwide and provide other services that enhance customer relationships and complement our position as the foremost provider of package distribution services, offering high quality and excellent value in every service.

PEOPLE

Be a well-regarded employer that is mindful of the well-being of our people allowing them to develop their individual capabilities in an impartial, challenging, rewarding, and cooperative environment and offers the opportunity for career advancement.

SHAREOWNERS

Maintain a financially strong, manager-owned company earning a reasonable profit providing long-term competitive returns to our shareowners.

COMMUNITIES

Build on the legacy of our company's reputation as a responsible corporate citizen whose well-being is in the public interest and whose people are respected for their performance and integrity.

Announced Spring 1991

584. **United States Air Force**
The Pentagon; Washington, DC 20330-1000
(703) 697-7376
Industry: 97—Air force

MISSION STATEMENT

To defend the United States through control and exploitation of air and space.

June, 1992

VISION STATEMENT

Air Force people building the world's most respected air and space force . . . global power and reach for America.

November, 1991

585. **United States Central Intelligence Agency**
Washington, DC 20505

(703) 351-2053

Industry: 97—Government agency

CIA Credo

We are the Central Intelligence Agency.

We produce timely and high quality intelligence for the President and Government of the United States.

We provide objective and unbiased evaluations and are always open to new perceptions and ready to challenge conventional wisdom.

We perform special intelligence tasks at the request of the President.

We conduct our activities and ourselves according to the highest standards of integrity, morality and honor and according to the spirit and letter of our law and Constitution.

We measure our success by our contribution to the protection and enhancement of American values, security and national interest.

We believe our people are the Agency's most important resource. We seek the best and work to make them better. We subordinate our desire for public recognition to the need for confidentiality. We strive for continuing professional improvement. We give unfailing loyalty to each other and to our common purpose.

We seek through our leaders to stimulate initiative, a commitment to excellence and a propensity for action; to protect and reward Agency personnel for their special responsibilities, contributions, and sacrifices; to promote a sense of mutual trust and shared responsibility.

We get our inspiration and commitment to excellence from the inscription in our foyer: "And ye shall know the truth and the truth shall make you free."

586. **United States Junior Chamber of Commerce**
     P.O. Box 7; Tulsa, OK 74121-0007
     (918) 584-2481
     Industry: 86—Membership organization

THE UNITED STATES JAYCEES HEADQUARTERS MISSION

To further the growth of The United States Jaycees by promoting the creation, growth and development of chapters through cost-effective development and distribution of services and resources to be utilized by state organizations, chapters and young people for the development of personal skills and leadership skills opportunities.

MISSION STATEMENT

To provide young people the opportunity to develop personal and leadership skills through local community service and organizational involvement while expanding the Jaycee movement.

VISION

To Become . . .

The organization of choice for young people, providing direction and leadership to our communities and nation.

587. **United Van Lines, Inc.**
Subsidiary of UniGroup, Inc.
One United Drive; Fenton, MO 63026
(314) 326-3100
Industry: 42—Moving services

UNITED VAN LINES' SERVICE PLEDGE

Our goal is to develop and maintain permanent relationships with our customers by providing outstanding service, move after move, with no exceptions. We pledge to find a way to get the job done to the customer's satisfaction, no matter how great the challenge; to stand behind every service commitment; and to employ friendly, skilled, knowledgeable people who, in the event of a problem, will do whatever is necessary to make things right . . . right away. In short, we are dedicated to proving, through our performance, that United is the very best professional mover in the world, in the eyes of our most demanding critics—our customers.

588. **Universal Foods Corporation**
433 East Michigan Street; Milwaukee, WI 53201
(414) 271-6755
Industry: 20—Food

CORPORATE CREED

Universal Foods Corporation is committed to conducting a business enterprise which is of real and continuing value to society. This requires bringing together, in an optimal manner, shareholders, employees, suppliers, and civic resources so that customers are well served, profits are fairly earned in the competitive marketplace, investors are rewarded, employees grow in their careers, and the needs of communities are recognized by appropriate commitment of corporate time and wealth.

VISION STATEMENT

Universal Foods Corporation, will grow as an international manufacturer and marketer of value added food products. Through dedication to our customers and employees, and commitment to continuous improvement and innovation, we will achieve superior quality, service and operating performance.

589. **Upjohn Company**
7000 Portage Road; Kalamazoo, MI 49001-0199
(616) 323-4000
Industry: 28—Pharmaceuticals

Mission Statement

Bring high-quality, innovative health and nutritional products to our customers worldwide through the meaningful commercial application of science and medicine, while consistently returning value to our shareholders.

Strategic Vision

Be a leader and innovator in the industries in which we compete and retain the independence to pursue our mission. Upjohn is committed to quality improvement—in service to our customers, our products, and our performance in the work place—and dedicated to conducting our business in an environmentally and socially responsible manner.

UPS
see United Parcel Service (583)

U.S. . . .
see United States . . .

590. **USAir Group, Inc.**
2345 Crystal Drive; Arlington, VA 22227
(703) 418-7000
Industry: 45—Airline

Mission Statement

USAir begins with you . . . its shareholders.

This is our commitment to return to profitability, strengthen our balance sheet, and produce a return on equity.

USAir begins with you . . . its customers.

This is our commitment to provide safe and reliable air transportation, offer excellent service, and provide added value for our customers.

USAir begins with you . . . its employees.

This is our commitment to value employees and their ideas, provide a work place that offers a secure future, promote professional and personal growth, and foster a spirit of teamwork.

USAir begins with you . . . its neighbors.

This is our commitment to meet or exceed federally-mandated aircraft noise standards, follow environmentally responsible procedures, and be an active member of our communities.

Annual Report 1991

591. **U.S. Bancorp**
111 SW Fifth Avenue; P.O. Box 8837; Portland, OR 97208-8837
(503) 225-6111
Industry: 60—Banking

MISSION

To maximize the long-term value of our shareholders' investment by being widely recognized as a premier provider of financial services in the western United States and other selected markets.

592. **U.S. Bioscience**
One Tower Bridge; 100 Front Street; West Conshohocken,
PA 19428
(215) 832-0570
Industry: 28, 87—Health care research and development

U.S. Bioscience

A pharmaceutical company focused on cancer and allied diseases
- Discovery, development and commercialization of cytotoxic, hormonal and biological therapies
- Increasing patient survival and improving their quality of life

Business Strategy

- Acquire exclusive marketing rights to unique anticancer therapies
- Establish U.S. Bioscience as an important participant in the worldwide Oncology Market—focus on North America and Europe
- Leverage product assets in other markets by out-licensing, joint ventures and corporate alliances

March 13, 1992

593. **U.S. Chamber of Commerce**
1615 H Street, NW; Washington, DC 20062
(202) 463-5427
Industry: 86—Trade organization

Mission Statement

To achieve human progress through an economic, political and social system based on individual freedom, incentive, initiative, opportunity and responsibility.

Drafted and adopted in 1975

594. **U.S. Shoe Corp.**
      One Eastwood Drive; Cincinnati, OH 45227-1197
      (513) 527-7000
      Industry: 31, 56—Shoes and retail stores

THE U.S. SHOE FOCUS

OUR MISSION

The U.S. Shoe Corporation exists to create and grow exceptional value for customers, associates, and shareholders by building leadership businesses in well-defined retail niches.

OUR STRATEGY

U.S. Shoe's business growth will be grounded on fundamental integrity and a constant effort to create superior products, concepts, and services that uniquely meet our customers' needs. The company will carefully balance short-term requirements with the long-term desire for associate growth and brand dominance. We will create exceptional value through:

- Dominant brands
- Legendary customer satisfaction
- Empowered associates
- Uncompromising integrity

HOW WE WILL IMPLEMENT

- Aggressively develop leaders
- Reward associates well for their contributions
- Invest in associate training and development
- Develop and leverage Corporate strengths and synergies
- Base decisions on superior understanding of consumer needs
- Creatively mix fun, challenge, and mutual respect
- Foster aggressive business growth
- Nurture teams and teamwork
- Improve measurably and continuously
- Develop breakthrough thinking and initiatives

595. **U S West, Inc.**
      7800 East Orchard Road; Englewood, CO 80111
      (303) 793-6559
      Industry: 48—Telecommunications

Our mission is to provide quality products and services to customers in responsive and innovative ways in order to create the highest possible value for our investors, through long-term growth and profitability.

596.   **UtiliCorp United Inc.**
911 Main Street, Suite 3000; Kansas City, MO 64105
(816) 421-6600
Industry: 49—Gas distribution

VISION

To meet the challenges of providing energy and services for society's changing needs throughout selected countries in the world.

BUSINESS DEFINITION

A growth-oriented multi-national energy and services corporation that builds upon its core strengths.

V

597. Vanguard Cellular Systems, Inc.®

2002 Pisgah Church Road, Suite 300; Greensboro, NC 27408
(919) 282-3690
Industry: 48—Cellular telephone

OUR VISION

To build one of the nation's leading telecommunications companies by providing products and services of such premium quality, convenience and value that we *delight* our customers beyond their expectations, while at all times, living up to the highest standards of professionalism, integrity, humility and community service.

OUR GOALS AND VALUES

PEOPLE Hire, train and empower only the most qualified, team-oriented people.

INTEGRITY Preach, never breach, our Code of Conduct.

PROFESSIONALISM Treat our internal and external customers with respect, responsiveness, cooperation and open communication.

QUALITY Relentlessly pursue perfection in our systems, services and in performing our jobs.

SERVICE *Delight* our internal and external customers by accommodating them beyond their expectations.

VALUE Constantly add value to our internal and external customers' investments in us.

PROFITABILITY Take action only after proving it can be done profitably and efficiently.

VISION Keep an open mind and embrace change if it will benefit our company and customers.

SIMPLICITY Find solutions that will make things more understandable, convenient and efficient for our customers and company.

COMMUNITY Establish us as a respected, responsible corporate citizen in every community we serve.

1990

598. **Varian Associates**
3100 Hansen Way; Palo Alto, CA 94303
(415) 493-4000
Industry: 36, 38—Semiconductors and electronic components

VARIAN'S BASIC BELIEFS . . .

- Satisfying customers is our primary responsibility; we must deliver quality products and services that meet specific customer needs, on time, every time.

- Our success is tied to achieving a balance between innovative technology, creative marketing, superior quality, quick-response manufacturing, and outstanding customer service; that balance is the means by which we gain competitive advantage.

- The talents of our employees are the key to our future; we are committed to continuous development to expand those talents and enhance leadership.

- We can succeed only as a team; we are committed to maintaining a quality-oriented organization and respectful work environment that will encourage teamwork, creativity, and an entrepreneurial spirit.

- High ethical standards are mandatory; we will conduct our business in a way that meets both the spirit and the letter of the law.

- Our employees deserve a safe workplace and our plant communities a clean environment; we will manage our operations accordingly.

- Good corporate citizenship is essential; we will respect the rights of our neighbors and communities, and will share in resolving matters of mutual concern.

- Satisfactory profits are required to meet these goals; we must operate in a way that builds long-term shareholder value by generating consistent profits and cash flow.

April, 1990

The Varian Associates Vision

We will maximize value for our customers, shareholders, employees, and the communities in which we operate as we pursue worldwide growth.

We will gain competitive advantage by achieving excellence in innovative technology, creative marketing, superior quality, quick-response manufacturing, and outstanding customer service.

We will focus on opportunities with significant market potential and gain market share leadership in analytical instrumentation, electron devices, medical therapy equipment, and semiconductor process equipment.

We will seek breakthrough technologies from internal and external sources that lead us to attractive markets.

Spring, 1990

599. VIA Rail Canada, Inc.

P.O. Box 8116, Station A; Montreal, Quebec; Canada H3C 3N3
(514) 871-6000
Industry: 41—Passenger rail service

Corporate Mission

VIA's mission is to serve travellers in Canada by providing a safe, efficient intercity and tourist passenger rail service responsive to market needs.

In pursuing this mission, VIA applies corporate strategies to achieve the following long-term goals:
- to offer passengers safe train travel, with high standards of operating performance;
- to provide a competitive level of service to every customer in a cost-effective manner;
- to acquire the powers and resources necessary to operate as a successful business; and
- to continue to reduce dependency on government operating funding.

600. The Vons Companies, Inc.

618 Michillanda Avenue; Arcadia, CA 91007-6300
(818) 821-7000
Industry: 54—Supermarkets

MISSION STATEMENT

Our mission is to be a premier retailer of foods and related categories including those products and services normally associated with drug stores. To do so we respond to needs and preferences of a wide spectrum of customer segments with a dense store network employing several names and store types. This network grows via new stores including acquisitions. All stores are merchandised, staffed and operated with highest integrity and provide quality shopping experiences that are designed to create and keep customers. We provide a rewarding work environment which attracts, develops and retains quality people. In this manner, we grow our business in volume, share and profits so that shareholder value is maximized.

W–Z

601. Wachovia Corporation
P.O. Box 3099; Winston-Salem, NC 27150
(919) 770-5000
Industry: 60—Banking

Mission and Objectives

Wachovia Corporation and Subsidiary Companies

Basic Mission

To serve in an exceptional manner the interests of shareholders, customers, employees and the public, by pursuing progressive business strategies, by practicing sound financial principles, by providing superior service and by being an exemplary corporate citizen.

Basic Objectives

To protect the shareholder investment, customer deposits and other resources entrusted to the organization by maintaining sound assets, comfortable funding, healthy reserves, strong capital and an overall financial condition which inspires confidence, provides stability and permits growth.

To recruit, develop, motivate, reward and retain personnel of exceptional ability, character and dedication by providing good working conditions, superior leadership, merit-based compensation, competitive employee benefits, personal growth opportunities and employment security.

To provide the company's customers and markets the fullest feasible variety of quality deposit, loan, operational, investment, and other permissible financial services at the lowest possible prices, consistent with the philosophies, strategies and capabilities of the organization.

To earn dependable and diverse profits which increase sufficiently over time to afford exceptional growth in shareholder value, to provide meritorious employee compensation, to give quality customer service, to meet public responsibilities, to maintain a strong equity base and to finance modernization and expansion.

To fulfill responsibilities to communities, states and the nation by promoting and contributing to economic and social progress, by giving to worthy charitable causes, by participating in public interest activities, by complying with applicable laws and by practicing impeccable ethics.

602. **Wallace Computer Services, Inc.**
      4600 West Roosevelt Road; Hillside, IL 60162-2079
      (708) 449-8600
      Industry: 27, 35—Computer forms and computer equipment

THE WALLACE PHILOSOPHY

Market Driven

The customer needs and requires proper attention from all job functions of a company. Any weak area in the chain of processing orders for customers, and we can lose business. We must make our customers aware that Wallace is Market Driven.

Quality Products and Services

We need to improve our quality of product, we need to constantly be aware of the quality of our service. Again this factor of quality plays a most important part of our future success and relates to job security, expansion and opportunity.

Innovations

Ideas are the basis for moving ahead of the competition. New products, new methods and new ways to solve problems will make Wallace more successful and allow for greater growth. Innovation is related to good employee attitudes and concerns to do things better, to do things smarter, and to eliminate competition.

Cost Control

We must remember that cost control is a key to growth in profits. Reduction in costs is the responsibility of all employees. Cost control can be defined as coming to work on time, getting more production for time spent on the job, reduction of wasted time, reduction of the use of supplies and caring for conservation in this area. Cost control is a lot of little actions that results in big savings.

Standards of Performance

Each employee must have a high standard of performance. This relates to an inward successful approach to the work that the employee is doing. It means that no matter what the task, we do it at our best performance. It means we do not settle for less than our best. A high standard of performance is an indication of the strength of a company.

Sans Tache calls for honesty and fairness with our customers, employees, communities, and shareholders.

Revised November, 1992

606. **Weirton Steel Corporation**
400 Three Springs Drive; Weirton, WV 26062-4989
(304) 797-2000
Industry: 33—Steel

VISION FOR SUCCESS

Weirton Steel Corporation will lead the industry in satisfying customers with high quality products and services. We are committed to accomplishing this through highly trained and informed employee owners who participate fully in the continuous process of improving performance, achieving the highest possible level of personal development.

WE ARE BOUND TOGETHER IN THESE COMMON BELIEFS AND VALUES

WE MUST . . .

FOR THE CUSTOMER

- Have a total quality commitment to consistently meet the product, delivery and service expectations of all customers.
- Give customers increased value through processes that eliminate waste, minimize costs and enhance production efficiency.

FOR THE EMPLOYEE

- Reward teamwork, trust, honesty, openness and candor.
- Ensure a safe workplace.
- Recognize that people are the corporation and provide them with training and information that allows for continuous improvement.
- As employee owners, obligate ourselves to provide a high level of performance and be accountable for our own actions.
- Respect the dignity, rights and contributions of others.

FOR THE COMPANY

- Continuously invest in new technology and equipment to ensure competitiveness and enhance stockholder value.
- Manage our financial and human resources for long-term profitability.

FOR THE COMMUNITY

- Commit to environmental responsibility.
- Fulfill our responsibility to enhance the quality of community life.

607. **Wendy's International, Inc.**
     P.O. Box 256; 4288 West Dublin Granville Road; Dublin, OH 43017
     (614) 764-3100
     Industry: 58—Fast food restaurants

Mission Statement

Deliver Total Quality

Vision Statement

To be the customer's **Restaurant of Choice** and the **Employer of Choice**

Western Gas Marketing Limited
     see TransCanada Pipelines (573)

608. **Western Publishing Group, Inc.**
     444 Madison Avenue; New York, NY 10022
     (212) 688-4500
     Industry: 27—Publishing

Meeting The Challenge

A few words about Western Publishing Group, Inc.: committed to the long-term success of our enterprise while providing security and opportunity for our employees; wholesome quality products for our consumers; capital appreciation for our shareholders and a strong foundation for our future. We seek to accomplish these goals while providing above average profit opportunities for our customers and service to the communities in which we live.

Our philosophy is a simple one: "Delight the Customer" by being in the right place at the right time with the right product and the right people for the long term.

Annual Report February 1, 1992

609. **Western Resources, Inc.**
     818 Kansas Avenue; P.O. Box 889; Topeka, KS 66601
     (913) 296-6300
     Industry: 49—Natural gas distribution

Mission Statement

We are dedicated to providing the highest quality energy services to our customers. We are committed to being a good place to work, maintaining the public trust, and building financial strength.

Adopted October, 1992

610. **Weyerhaeuser Co.**
Weyerhaeuser Building; Tacoma, WA 98477
(206) 924-2017
Industry: 24, 26—Paper and lumber products

OUR VISION

The best forest products company in the world

STRATEGIES

We shall achieve our vision by:
- Making Total Quality the Weyerhaeuser Way of doing business.
- Relentless pursuit of full customer satisfaction.
- Empowering Weyerhaeuser people.
- Leading the industry in forest management and manufacturing excellence.
- Producing superior returns for our shareholders.

OUR VALUES

CUSTOMERS

We listen to our customers and improve our products and services to meet their present and future needs.

PEOPLE

Our success depends upon high-performing people working together in a safe and healthy workplace where diversity, development and teamwork are valued and recognized.

ACCOUNTABILITY

We expect superior performance and are accountable for our actions and results. Our leaders set clear goals and expectations, are supportive, and provide and seek frequent feedback.

CITIZENSHIP

We support the communities where we do business, hold ourselves to the highest standards of ethical conduct and environmental responsibility, and communicate openly with Weyerhaeuser people and the public.

FINANCIAL RESPONSIBILITY

We are prudent and effective in the use of the resources entrusted to us.

611. **WGBH Educational Foundation**
125 Western Avenue; Boston, MA 02134
(617) 492-2777
Industry: 48—Broadcasting

WGBH Mission Statement

The preamble of the WGBH Educational Foundation states:

The purpose of the corporation is to promote, through broadcasting or other means, the general education of the public by offering programs that inform, stimulate and entertain, so that persons of all ages, origins and beliefs may be encouraged, in an atmosphere of artistic freedom, to learn and appreciate the history, the sciences, the humanities, the fine arts, the practical arts, the music, the politics, the economics, and other significant aspects of the world they live in, and thereby to enrich and improve their own lives.

Program Commitments:

1. A commitment to use our facilities to foster an informed active citizenry;
2. A commitment to make knowledge and the creative life of the arts, sciences and humanities available to the widest possible public;
3. A commitment to help different community groups, especially minorities, find a positive reflection of their own identities and come to know each other's strengths as well as problems;
4. A commitment to serve the individual not just as a spectator but as a participant, able and willing to learn new skills through our programs.

612. **Wheeling-Pittsburgh Steel Corporation**
      1134 Market Street; Wheeling, WV 26003
      (304) 234-2400
      Industry: 33, 34—Steel

MISSION STATEMENT

The mission of Wheeling-Pittsburgh Steel Corporation is to strive for excellence and prosperity for the mutual benefit of our customers, stockholders, employees, and communities. We are dedicated to being a progressive, integrated manufacturer of selected flat rolled, tin mill, and fabricated products and are committed to satisfying our customers' requirements through quality, service, and low-cost production.

PRINCIPLES

In the pursuit of our mission, Wheeling-Pittsburgh Steel Corporation espouses twelve principles which should guide the actions of all employees in all circumstances.

I. **Quality.** We are dedicated to customer-driven quality. We constantly strive to improve our processes, products, and services, guided by understanding and satisfying changing customer needs.

II. **Low-Cost/High Quality Production.** We recognize a direct and positive connection between high-quality products and services and low-cost production. Maintaining this connection is the best way to serve our customers.

III. **Ethics.** We are guided by ethical business practices and demand ethical conduct from all employees.

IV. **Safety and Health.** We are committed to providing a safe and healthy working environment. We emphasize the importance of safety through regular communication with all employees regarding their and the company's responsibilities for the safety of themselves and others.

V. **Employees' Opportunity to Contribute.** We strive to maintain an environment that fosters every employee's opportunity to make a positive contribution to the company. Our goals are fair treatment, mutual respect among all employees, acceptance of individual responsibility, and educational growth.

VI. **Drugs and Alcohol.** We are committed to high standards of employee health, including support for a drug and alcohol abuse free working environment and employee wellness programs.

VII. **Capital Investment.** We understand that our long-term success depends upon making substantial capital investments in new equipment and adequately maintaining existing equipment and structures.

VIII. **Processes Improvements.** We recognize the need to improve our processes as customer demand requires and as economical technologies become available.

IX. **Compliance with Laws.** We act within the spirit and letter of all applicable laws of the United States and any other countries in which we do business.

X. **Fiduciary Duty.** We will carry out our fiduciary duty by seeking fully to protect the rights and entitlements of all legitimate interests.

XI. **Dividends.** We seek to preserve and enhance the value of stockholders' investments and believe that all stockholders are entitled to a fair return by payment of appropriate dividends.

XII. **Community Involvement.** We fully recognize our responsibilities to the communities in which we reside. Therefore, we adopt a principle of community involvement.

613. **Whirlpool Corporation**
     Administrative Center; Benton Harbor, MI 49022-2692
     (616) 926-5000
     Industry: 35, 36—Appliances

VISION

One World. One Vision.

WHIRLPOOL . . . REACHING WORLDWIDE TO BRING EXCELLENCE HOME

Whirlpool, in its chosen lines of business, will grow with new opportunities and be the leader in an ever-changing global market. We will be driven by our commitment to continuous quality improvement and to exceeding all of our customers' expectations. We will gain competitive advantage through this, and by building on our existing strengths and developing new competencies. We will be market-driven, efficient and profitable. Our success will make Whirlpool a company that worldwide customers, employees and other stakeholders can depend on.

GOALS

Whirlpool Corporation is dedicated to achieving global leadership and to delivering shareholder value. Our objective is to drive high total shareholder returns by performing consistently in the top 25 percent of large publicly held corporations, and by achieving and sustaining return-on-equity levels of 18 percent or more. To assure this, our global business goals (Value Creating Objectives) are as follows:

CUSTOMER SATISFACTION

Through the intense customer focus of all Whirlpool people, we will measure and deliver the highest levels of customer satisfaction in all of our markets and with all of our products and services, assuring that we are the company of preference with our customers.

GROWTH & INNOVATION

Our accomplishments and management system will assure innovation in all areas of global business conduct and create consistent internal growth in our revenues of at least six percent per year.

PEOPLE COMMITMENT

A High Performance Partnership with all of our people will encourage and enable contribution and commitment from each individual and team, and will provide a dynamic and diverse workplace environment which is valued by all.

TOTAL QUALITY

Our Worldwide Excellence System will deliver products and services that by measurement exceed customer expectations and outperform all of our competitors. We will achieve at least a 30 percent annual improvement in Worldwide Excellence implementation through 1994. This will also improve our corporate total cost productivity to a sustainable five percent per year improvement level as we assure that we are always doing the right things, the right way, the first time.

VALUES

We, the people of Whirlpool, aren't "in" the company, we "are" the company. As such, we recognize our individual responsibility to assure our collective success by practicing and promoting the following values.

These values reflect a shared view of how we seek to operate and to be seen by others. Further, they serve as a standard for creating a climate in which we can embrace continual change and challenge worldwide.

BUSINESS WITH INTEGRITY

We will pursue our business with honour, fairness and respect for both the individual and the public at large . . . ever mindful that there is no right way to do a wrong thing.

QUALITY AS A QUEST

Success depends on our ability to deliver a level of excellence respected by all who rely on us. We will lift the quality and values of our products and services above the expectations of those who receive them . . . always recognizing that our best today can be bettered tomorrow.

CUSTOMER AS A FOCUS

We will dedicate ourselves to anticipate the changing needs of consumers, customers and colleagues and to create innovative and superior products and services, faster and more effectively than can our competitors.

COMMITMENT TO THE COMMON GOOD

We will serve responsibly as members of all communities in which we live and work, respecting cultural distinctions throughout the world. We will preserve the environment, prudently utilize natural resources and maintain all property we are privileged to use.

POWER OF TRUST

A mutual and inspiring trust, nurtured by honest and open communication and equal opportunity, should unite our actions and relationships with one another . . . providing a foundation for teamwork, confidence and loyalty.

LEARNING TO LEAD

Our competitive edge in the marketplace ultimately depends on how our skills and expertise measure against the world's best. To lead the best, we must cultivate our talents through continuous training . . . confident that we'll be provided every opportunity to widen our horizons.

SPIRIT OF WINNING

At the heart of company values lies company spirit. It encompasses the determination, resourcefulness, boldness and vigour by which we work. Collectively, we believe this urgent and relentless drive will enable us to shape the future of our industry . . . and deliver the performance that earns us success in the marketplace.

Extracted from Whirlpool Corporation's "Vision, Goals, and Values" brochure

614. William and Flora Hewlett Foundation

525 Middlefield Road; Menlo Park, CA 94025-3495
(415) 329-1070
Industry: 67—Charitable foundation

The Hewlett Foundation, incorporated as a private foundation in the State of California in 1966, was established by the Palo Alto industrialist William R. Hewlett, his late wife, Flora Lamson Hewlett, and their eldest son, Walter B. Hewlett. The Foundation's broad purpose, as stated in the articles of incorporation, is to promote the well-being of mankind by supporting selected activities of a charitable, religious, scientific, literary, or educational nature, as well as organizations or institutions engaged in such activities.

The Foundation concentrates its resources on activities in the performing arts; education, particularly at the university and college level; population issues; environmental issues; conflict resolution; and children, youth, and families. Some subareas of interest to the Foundation are listed in the program descriptions that follow. Special projects outside these broad areas may from time to time be approved by the Board of Directors. Although the Hewlett Foundation is a national foundation, with no geographic limit stipulated in its charter, a proportion of disbursable funds has been earmarked for projects in the San Francisco Bay Area.

The Foundation has a strong commitment to the voluntary, nonprofit sector. It will therefore assist efforts to improve the financial base and efficiency of organizations and institutions in this category. Proposals that show promise of stimulating private philanthropy are particularly welcome.

In its grantmaking decisions as well as in its interests and activities, the Hewlett Foundation is wholly independent of the Hewlett-Packard Company and the Hewlett-Packard Company Foundation.

Annual Report 1991

615. William Penn Foundation

1630 Locust Street; Philadelphia, PA 19103-6305
(215) 732-5114

Industry: 67—Charitable foundation

The William Penn Foundation is a private grantmaking organization created in 1945 by Otto Haas and his wife, Phoebe. The principal mission of the Foundation is to help improve the quality of life in the Delaware Valley.

Extracted from "Foundation Priorities and Grant Application Procedures" brochure

Williamsburg Foundation
see Colonial Williamsburg Foundation (148)

616. Wisconsin Electric Power Company
Subsidiary of Wisconsin Energy Corporation
231 West Michigan; P.O. Box 2046; Milwaukee, WI 53201
(414) 221-2345
Industry: 49—Electric utility

WISCONSIN ELECTRIC POWER COMPANY MISSION STATEMENT

Wisconsin Electric Power Company (WE) is an electric utility whose principal mission is being the energy supplier of choice in the region it serves while providing earnings to support its financial goals. WE's core business is generating, transmitting and distributing electric and steam energy to meet the needs and wants of its customers and to assure the economic vitality of the region. WE is committed to improving the quality of life in the area it serves, to maintaining employee excellence and to providing a working environment that encourages each employee to achieve superior results and satisfaction.

Drafted 1988; published 1989

Wisconsin Power & Light Company
see WPL Holdings, Inc. (622)

617. W.K. Kellogg Foundation
One Michigan Avenue E; Battle Creek, MI 49017-4058
(616) 968-1611
ndustry: 67—Charitable foundation

W.K. Kellogg Foundation Mission

The W.K. Foundation is concerned with the application of knowledge to solving the problems of people. It pursues this objective by making grants for charitable purposes and activities.

Such problems are numerous and complex, and Foundation financial resources are limited. Therefore, the Foundation establishes programming priorities that focus its efforts to achieve maximum effect. Attention is centered on agriculture, education, health, leadership, and youth. All of the Foundation's work also in some fashion reflects Mr. Kellogg's belief that the advancement of learning provides "the greatest opportunity for really improving one generation over another." In making grants, emphasis is placed on individual and group initiative.

The Foundation believes there is particular need to test and apply existing knowledge that has been incompletely or unevenly used for human advancement. In doing so, innovative ideas and ways of work often are discovered. If they are effective, new insights are gained about the application of knowledge, and become available for use in other settings.

The Foundation continuously assesses the effectiveness of its projects in achieving its mission. It is committed to public accountability and open access to information for the wise allocation of funds through its philanthropic role in society.

Annual Report 1992

618. W.L. Gore & Associates, Inc.
551 Paper Mill Road; P.O. Box 9206; Newark, DE 19714-9329
(302) 738-4880
Industry: 22, 33, 38—Fabrics, electronics, and medical products

OBJECTIVE OF THE ENTERPRISE by W.L. Gore

The objective of the Enterprise is to make money and to have fun doing so.

It is necessary for any business to make money in order to buy the facilities and tools required to produce goods and services, to pay the operating expenses, and to provide a satisfactory living for the people working in the business. We associates sell our products in the free market places of the world. If our products have high value and we can produce them at a low cost, we are rewarded by making a lot of money. We invest such money in needed tools and facilities and share the rest among us.

Any of our business teams that are making a lot of money seem to be enjoying it, having a lot of fun. Any team working on a developing product or business that they anticipate **will** make a lot of money appear to be having still more fun.

Fun includes the pleasure of working with friends on teams, the enjoyment of parties and celebrations, but also the knowledge and conviction that what we are doing is important and of high value to people throughout the world. Fun also derives from the satisfaction that each of us have in the recognition that we have learned new skills, gained new knowledge in the course of our work. Also, we expect new challenges and opportunities ahead that will continue to require us to grow in our capability. Fun of these kinds is an integral part of our objective of making money.

We all recognize that in our Lattice Organization certain principles and policies are necessary to success in achieving our personal and organizational objectives. I'd like to review why I think each of our four basic principles are necessary:

Fairness

It is necessary for each of us to try to be fair in order to maintain and preserve the good feelings among us. Deliberate or thoughtless unfairness generates resentment and anger, destroying the cooperation and communication required for good teamwork.

Freedom

Freedom is the source of inventions, innovations, and creativity. Trying new ideas involves risk as well as requiring unusual effort, thought, and imagination. The risk factor can lead to mistakes. All of us need freedom to make mistakes.

Commitment

Consistency of principles require that we organize projects and functions by free commitment rather than by systems of authoritarian command. Associates dedicated to the objectives of the Enterprise are willing to commit whatever is needed to insure success. These individual commitments allow us to carry out complex projects and businesses throughout the world.

Waterline

Security and success of the Enterprise require that we be discreet in the exercise of our freedom if the reputation, financial security, or future opportunities of the Enterprise are at risk. Consultation with appropriate associates is necessary before actions are taken that may involve these risks.

The Gore Associates Enterprise faces a future of opportunity and challenge. In spite of the inevitable continued growth in the number of associates, we must maintain a universal dedication to our principles, policies, and objectives if we are to continue our successes in the future. This is a leadership challenge to each of us.

February, 1984

WNET

see Educational Broadcasting Corporation (209)

619. Woods Hole Oceanographic Institution
9 Maury Lane; Woods Hole, MA 02543

(508) 548-1400
Industry: 84—Research Organization

Mission Statement

The Woods Hole Oceanographic Institution (WHOI) is a private, independent, non-profit corporation dedicated to working and learning at the frontier of ocean science and attaining maximum return on intellectual and material investments in oceanographic research.

WHOI strives to provide the climate and resources to facilitate the scientific endeavors not only of its staff and students, but of the entire oceanographic community. WHOI serves society directly through the process and products of its research and educational programs, by defining approaches to addressing ocean science issues relevant to sustaining and improving life on earth, and by helping governments, industry and the public understand the oceanic system in both its natural state and as it is influenced by human activity.

WHOI achieves its unique international leadership position in ocean science by:
- staffing for world class expertise and providing education in all the fundamental disciplines of ocean science;
- stressing a flexible, multidisciplinary and collaborative approach to postulating and testing hypotheses about ocean characteristics, structure, and processes;
- promoting the development and use at sea of tools to extract information from the entire global ocean; and
- maintaining an entrepreneurial and innovative spirit, and an internal organization dedicated to equity, support of its people and the science, and a stimulating and pleasant working environment.

May, 1990

620. **Woolworth Corporation**
233 Broadway; New York, NY 10279
(212) 553-2000
Industry: 53, 56—Discount and drug stores

The mission of Woolworth Corporation is to provide value to the consumers it serves through its distinctly individual retailing businesses around the world. Under the general guidance of corporate management, these businesses seek to generate levels of profit that not only satisfy investors and sustain long-term growth, but also provide competitive financial rewards for associates and benefit the communities in which those associates live and work.

621. **World Vision International**
919 West Huntington Drive; Monrovia, CA 91016
(818) 357-7979
Industry: 86—Religious service organization

WORLD VISION'S MISSION STATEMENT

The Umbrella Under Which The Partnership Operates

WORLD VISION is an international partnership of Christians whose mission is to follow our Lord and Savior Jesus Christ in working with the poor and oppressed to promote human transformation, seek justice and bear witness to the good news of the Kingdom of God.

WORLD VISION UNITED STATES VISION STATEMENT

Our Vision For Our Role In The Partnership

As a member of a Christ-centered community, I am; bringing the Good News to the poor, relieving suffering and providing hope. I do this by partnering with people and institutions in transforming our worlds.

622. **WPL Holdings, Inc.**
P.O. Box 192; 222 West Washington Avenue; Madison, WI
53701-0192
(608) 252-3311
Industry: 49—Electric utility

OUR MISSION

To become a profitable and growing regional supplier of energy products and services

Profitable—Achieve a competitive rate of return on our shareowners' investment while ensuring that the prices we charge our customers are consistent with the realities of our marketplaces.

Growing—Increase our market share in the market segments we serve. Expand our product offerings, particularly in non-regulated and conservation areas.

Regional—Offer our energy products and services in selected markets throughout the Upper Midwest.

OUR STRATEGY TO ACHIEVE OUR MISSION

Wisconsin Power and Light Company will provide high-quality products and services at the lowest-possible cost, meeting our customers' expectations at all times, and striving to exceed them whenever possible.

Annual Report, 1989

623. **W.W. Grainger, Inc.**
5500 West Howard Street; Skokie, IL 60077

(708) 982-9000

Industry: 50—Wholesale

COMPANY OPERATING PRINCIPLES

The Company has been managed successfully since its founding in 1927. This success has been due in large part to a philosophy of management expressed in the following principles:

Operate with the highest moral and legal standards.

Be committed to:

- Superior service and satisfaction for all customers.
- Mutually fair and responsible arrangements with suppliers.
- Fairness, dignity, and opportunity for all employees.
- Competitive compensation and benefits.
- Professionalism in all aspects of business operations.

Operate for prudent growth while sustaining:

- Historic or improved operating ratios.
- Sound and conservative financial policies.
- An attractive rate of return for the shareholders.

Employ persons who:

- Are qualified to discharge their assigned responsibilities.
- Are dependable and loyal.
- Have high standards and integrity.
- Have empathy and concern for others.

Be a good corporate citizen in the communities in which we operate.

VISION

Business

- To be the preeminent broad line distributor of equipment, components, and supplies to the commercial, industrial, contractor, and institutional markets in the United States.

- To attain leadership positions as a specialty distributor in selected markets.

Recognition

- As a source for excellent value and service by our customers.
- As an outstanding place to work by our employees.
- As an efficient, reliable marketer of their products by our suppliers.
- As a superior financial investment by our shareholders and the financial community.
- As a good corporate citizen in the communities in which we operate.
- As one of America's best-managed companies.

Financial Performance

- Achieve sales growth significantly above historical levels.
- Achieve operating earnings growth as high as, or higher than, the sales growth.
- Achieve an operating return on net working assets above our historical average.

The Company's Operating Principles have provided the foundation for its record of success.

Similarly, its Vision statement provides the framework to assist our employees in achieving future growth.

Annual Report 1991

624. XCAN Grain Pool Limited

1200-201 Portage Avenue; Winnipeg, Manitoba; Canada R3B 3K6
(204) 949-4500
Industry: 51—Wholesale grain

XCAN's mission is to be the leading Canadian agricultural marketing company, providing quality agri-food products and services to satisfy the needs of customers and for the benefit of farmer owners.

Drafted September, 1990

Owned by Alberta Wheat Pool (7), Saskatchewan Wheat Pool (507), and Manitoba Pool Elevators.

Geographical Index

This is an index to organizations by geographic location. Entries are arranged first by state or province and then by city. United States entries come first, followed by Canadian entries. Numbers following organizational names refer to entry numbers, not to page numbers.

Industry Index

This is an index to organizations by line-of-business. The index is based on the 1987 revision of the *Standard Industrial Classification Manual* from the U.S. Commerce Department. Entries are indexed at the broad, two-digit level. S.I.C. codes for each entry were derived from standard business directories, such as the Dun and Bradstreet *Million Dollar Directory*. The purpose is to convey one or two broad types of business or activity in which an organization is involved, rather than an attempt to list all possible products or services offered by each organization. S.I.C. codes are excluded if no listed organization has them as a chief line-of-business.

Standard Industrial Classification Structure:

01–09—Agriculture, forestry, and fishing
10–14—Mining
15–17—Construction
20–39—Manufacturing
40–49—Transportation, communications, electric, gas, and sanitary services
50–51—Wholesale trade
52–59—Retail trade
60–67—Finance, insurance, and real estate
70–89—Services
90—Governmental agencies

01–09—Agriculture, forestry, and fishing

07—Pest control and agricultural services

Rollins, Inc. (491)

09—Fishing

Fishery Products International Limited (232)

10–14—Mining

10—Metal mining

Amax Gold Inc. (14); Battle Mountain Gold Company (69); Cambior, Inc. (107); Magma Copper Company (350); Noranda Inc. (418); Phelps Dodge Corporation (449)